37TH ANNUAL EDITION

2014

SONGWRITER'S MARKET

James Duncan, Editor

WD

WRITER'S DIGEST
BOOKS

WritersDigest.com
Cincinnati, Ohio

Writer's Market website: www.writersmarket.com
Writer's Digest website: www.writersdigest.com
Writer's Digest Bookstore: www.writersdigestshop.com

SONGWRITER'S MARKET. Copyright © 2014 by F+W Media, Inc. Published by Writer's Digest Books, an imprint of F+W Media, Inc, 10151 Carver Road, Suite # 200, Blue Ash, OH 45242. Printed and bound in the United States of America. All rights reserved. No other part of this book may be reproduced in any form or by any electronic or mechanical means including information storage and retrieval systems without permission in writing from the publisher, except by a reviewer, who may quote brief passages in a review.

Publisher: Phil Sexton

Distributed in Canada by Fraser Direct
100 Armstrong Avenue
Georgetown, Ontario, Canada L7G 5S4
Tel: (905) 877-4411

Distributed in the UK and Europe by F&W Media International
Brunel House, Newton Abbot, Devon, TQ12 4PU, England
Tel: (+44) 1626-323200, Fax: (+44) 1626-323319
E-mail: postmaster@davidandcharles.co.uk

Distributed in Australia by Capricorn Link
P.O. Box 704, Windsor, NSW 2756 Australia
Tel: (02) 4577-3555

ISSN: 1-59963-731-6
ISBN 13: 978-1-59963-731-0

Attention Booksellers: This is an annual directory of F+W Media, Inc.
Return deadline for this edition is December 31, 2014.

Edited by James Duncan
Editorial assistance by Marielle Murphy
Cover designed by Claudean Wheeler
Interior designed by Claudean Wheeler
Page layout by Geoff Raker
Production coordinated by Greg Nock

CONTENTS

FROM THE EDITOR

Being a poet, I find I share many creative methods, aspirations, and stumbling blocks with songwriters, but despite what poets and writers may tell you, the life and career of a songwriter is much more complex. Collaborations are more common among songwriters (just you *try* to suggest a change in a poet's third stanza and see if you don't lose a hand), and there are far more organizations and individuals a songwriter must work with (or suffer with) in order to get a song on the airwaves—everyone from music publishers and record producers to band managers and venue owners, and of course, the musicians who will perform the song.

Of all of those people, I believe the most important person in the process is *you*, the songwriter. Without you there would be no song to perform, and thus no record, no record company, and no venue or radio summer hit, and in the grand scheme of life, far less happiness in the world. You've got a tough job. A lot is riding on you. Are you ready for it? The aim of the 2014 edition of *Songwriter's Market* is to make that job—that work of passion and joy—a little easier. We've included a new series of articles that discuss the paths of Grammy-winning artists as well as musicans who are just starting out and are utilizing the most current fundraising and networking trends. And you're in there too, trying to break in and find the right manager, publisher, collaborator, agent, and A&R kingmaker who will help lift your career to heights unimaginable.

It's a big dream, an important one, and I hope this guide helps you along the way. Good luck out there, and keep writing!

James Duncan
Content Editor, Writer's Digest Community
http://blog.writersdigest.com/therearenorules

Follow us on Twitter @WritersDigest

HOW TO USE *SONGWRITER'S MARKET*

Before you dive into the *Songwriter's Market* listings and start submitting songs willy-nilly, it's a good idea to take the time to read the following information. By educating yourself on how to best use this book, you'll be better prepared when you actually do send off your CD.

Let's take a look at what is inside *Songwriter's Market*, why these articles were put into the book in the first place, and how they can help your career.

THE LISTINGS

Beyond the articles, there are eight market sections in this book, from Music Publishers and Record Companies to Contests & Awards. Each section begins with an introduction detailing how the different types of companies function—what part of the music industry they work in, how they make money, and what you need to think about when approaching them with your music.

These listings are the heart of *Songwriter's Market*. They are the names, addresses, and contact information of music biz companies looking for songs and artists, as well as descriptions of the types of music they are looking for.

So how do I use *Songwriter's Market*?

The quick answer is that you should use the indexes to find companies that are interested in your type of music; then read the listings for details on how they want the music submitted. For support and help, join a songwriting or other music industry association (see the Organizations section of this book). Read everything you can about songwriting (see the

Publications of Interest section at the back of this book). Talk to other songwriters. That's a good start!

How does *Songwriter's Market* work?

The listings in *Songwriter's Market* are packed with information. It can be intimidating at first, but they are structured to make them easy to work with. Take a few minutes to get used to how the listings are organized, and you'll save time in the long run. For more detailed information about how the listings are put together, skip ahead to the Where Should I Send My Songs? section.

The following are general guidelines about to how to use the listings:

1. **READ THE ENTIRE LISTING** to decide whether to submit your music. Please do not use this book as a mass mailing list. If you blindly mail out demos by the hundreds, you'll waste a lot of money on postage and annoy a lot of people, and your demos will likely end up in the trash.

2. **PAY CLOSE ATTENTION TO THE "MUSIC" SECTION IN EACH LISTING.** This will tell you what kind of music the company is looking for. If they want rockabilly only and you write heavy metal, don't submit to that company. That's just common sense.

3. **PAY CLOSE ATTENTION TO SUBMISSION INSTRUCTIONS** shown under How to Contact. A lot of listings are particular about how they want submissions packaged. If you don't follow their instructions, your submission will probably be discarded. If you are confused about a listing's instructions, contact the company for clarification.

4. **IF IN DOUBT, CONTACT THE COMPANY FOR PERMISSION TO SUBMIT.** This is a good general rule. Many companies don't mind if you send an unsolicited submission, but some require you to get special permission prior to submitting. Contacting a company first is also a good way to determine their latest music needs, and it's an opportunity to briefly make contact on a personal level.

5. **BE COURTEOUS, BE EFFICIENT, AND ALWAYS HAVE A PURPOSE** to be in touch with your personal contact. Don't waste a contact's time. If you call, always have a legitimate reason: permission to submit, checking on guidelines, following up on a demo, etc. Once you have their attention, don't wear out your welcome. Always be polite.

6. **CHECK FOR A PREFERRED CONTACT.** A lot of listings have a designated contact person shown after a bolded Contact in the heading. This is the person you should contact with questions or to whom you should address your submission.

7. **READ THE "TIPS" SECTION.** This part of the listing provides extra information about how to submit or what it might be like to work with the company. This is just the

beginning. For more detailed information about the listings, see the next section—Where Should I Send My Songs?—and check out the heading "A Sample Listing Decoded."

FREQUENTLY ASKED QUESTIONS

How do these companies get listed in the book anyway?

No company pays to be included—all listings are free. The listings come from a combination of research the editor does on the music industry and questionnaires requested by companies who want to be listed (many of them contact us to be included). All questionnaires are screened for known sharks and to make sure they meet our requirements.

Why aren't other companies I know about listed in the book?

There are many possible reasons. We may have sent them a questionnaire, but they did not return it, were removed due to reader complaints, went out of business, specifically asked not to be listed, could not be contacted for an update, space restrictions, etc.

What's the deal with companies that don't take unsolicited submissions?

In the interest of completeness, the editor will sometimes include listings of crucial music companies and major labels he thinks you should be aware of. We want you to at least have some idea of what their policies are.

In one listing, a company claimed to accept that they take unsolicited submissions. But my demo came back unopened. What happened?

Some companies' needs change rapidly and may have changed since we contacted them for this edition of the book. That's why it's often a good idea to contact a company before submitting.

So that's it. You now have the power at your fingertips to become the professional songwriter you've always wanted to be. Let us know how you're doing. Drop us a line at marketbooks@fwmedia.com and tell us about any successes you have had because you used the materials found in this book.

WHERE SHOULD I SEND MY SONGS?

It depends a lot on whether you write mainly for yourself as a performer, or if you only write and want someone else to pick up your song for his or her recording (often the case in country music, for example). Are you mainly a performing songwriter or a nonperforming songwriter? This is important for figuring out what kind of companies to contact, as well as how you contact them. (For more detail, skip to the Submission Strategies section.)

What if I'm a nonperforming songwriter?

Many well-known songwriters are not performers in their own right. Some are not skilled instrumentalists or singers, but they understand melody, lyrics, and harmony and how those things go together. They can write great songs, but they need someone else to bring their music to life through skilled musicianship. A nonperforming songwriter will usually approach music publishers first for access to artists looking for songs, as well as artists' managers, their producers, and their record companies. On the flip side, many incredibly talented musicians can't write to save their lives and need someone else to provide them with good songs to perform. (For more details on the different types of companies and the roles they play for nonperforming and performing songwriters, see the section introductions for Music Publishers, Record Companies, Record Producers, and Managers & Booking Agents.)

What if I am a performing songwriter?

Many famous songwriters are also famous performers. They are skilled interpreters of their own material, and they also know how to write to suit their own particular talents as musicians. In this case, their intention is also usually to sell themselves as a performer in hopes of recording and releasing an album, or they have an album and want to find gigs and people who can help guide

TYPES OF MUSIC COMPANIES

- **MUSIC PUBLISHERS**—evaluate songs for commercial potential, find artists to record them, find other uses for the songs such as film or TV, collect income from songs, protect copyrights from infringement

- **RECORD COMPANIES**—sign artists to their labels, finance recordings, promotion and touring, release songs/albums to radio and TV

- **RECORD PRODUCERS**—work in the studio and record songs (independently or for a record company), may be affiliated with a particular artist, sometimes develop artists for record labels, locate or co-write songs if an artist does not write their own

- **MANAGERS & BOOKING AGENTS**—work with artists to manage their careers, find gigs, locate songs to record if the artist does not write their own

their careers. They will usually approach record companies or record producers first, on the basis of recording an album. For gigs and career guidance, they talk to booking agents and managers.

A smaller number also approach publishers in the hope of getting others to perform their songs, much like nonperforming songwriters. Some music publishers in recent years have also taken on the role of developing artists as both songwriters and performers, or are connected to a major record label, so performing songwriters might go to them for these reasons.

How do I use *Songwriter's Market* to narrow my search?

Once you've identified whether you are primarily interested in getting others to perform your songs (nonperforming songwriter) or you perform your own songs and want a record deal, etc., there are several steps you can take:

1. **IDENTIFY WHAT KIND OF MUSIC COMPANY YOU WISH TO APPROACH.** Based on whether you're a performing or nonperforming songwriter, do you want to approach a music publisher for a publishing deal? Do you want to approach a record producer because you need someone to help you record an album in the studio? Maybe you want to approach a producer in hopes that an act he's performing needs songs to complete his album.

2. **CHECK FOR COMPANIES BASED ON LOCATION.** Maybe you need a manager located close by. Maybe you need to find as many Nashville-based companies as you can because you write country music and most country publishers are in Nashville. In this case, start with the Geographic Index. You can also recognize Canadian and foreign listings by the icons in the listing (see "A Sample Listing Decoded" on the next page).

3. **LOOK FOR COMPANIES BASED ON THE TYPE OF MUSIC THEY WANT.** Some companies want country. Some record labels want only punk. Read the listings carefully to make

sure you're maximizing your time and sending your work to the appropriate markets.

4. **LOOK FOR COMPANIES BASED ON HOW OPEN THEY ARE TO BEGINNERS.** Some companies are more open than others to beginning artists and songwriters. If you are a beginner and it would help to approach these companies first. Some music publishers are hoping to find that wild card hit song and don't care if it comes from an unknown writer. Maybe you are just starting out looking for gigs or record deals, and you need a manager willing to help build your band's career from the ground up.

A SAMPLE LISTING DECODED

What do the little symbols at the beginning of the listing mean?

Those are called "icons," and they give you quick information about a listing with one glance. Here is a list of the icons and what they mean:

Openness to Submissions

○ means the company is open to beginners' submissions, regardless of past success

◑ means the company is mostly interested in previously published songwriters/well-established acts, but will consider beginners

● these companies do not want submissions from beginners, only from previously published songwriters/well-established acts

⊘ companies with this icon only accept material referred by a reputable industry source

TYPES OF MUSIC COMPANIES

- **MUSIC PUBLISHERS**—evaluate songs for commercial potential; find artists to record them; find other uses for the songs, such as film or TV; collect income from songs; protect copyrights from infringement
- **RECORD COMPANIES**—sign artists to their labels, finance recordings, manage promotion and touring, release songs/albums to radio and TV
- **RECORD PRODUCERS**—work in the studio and record songs (independently or for a record company)—may be affiliated with a particular artist, sometimes develop artists for record labels, locate or co-write songs if an artist does not write his or her own
- **MANAGERS & BOOKING AGENTS**—work with artists to manage their careers, find gigs, locate songs to record if the artist does not write his or her own

Other icons

○ means the listing is Canadian

● means the market is located outside of the U.S. and Canada

⊕ means the market is new to this edition

⊗ means the market places music in film/TV

EASY-TO-USE REFERENCE ICONS

E-MAIL AND WEBSITE INFORMATION

TERMS OF AGREEMENT

DETAILED SUBMISSION GUIDELINES

WHAT THEY'RE LOOKING FOR

INSIDER ADVICE

○ RUSTIC RECORDS

6337 Murray Lane, Brentwood, TN 37027. (615)371-8397. Fax: (615)370-0353. E-mail: rusticrecordsam@aol.com. Website: www.rusticrecordsinc.com. President: Jack Schneider. Executive VP & Operations Manager: Nell Schneider. VP Publishing and Catalog Manager: Amanda Mark. VP Marketing and Promotions: Ross Schneider. Videography, Photography, and Graphic Design: Wayne Hall. Image consultant: Jo Ann Rossi. Independent traditional country music label and music publisher (Iron Skillet Music/ ASCAP, Covered Bridge/ BMI, Old Town Square/ SESAC). Estab. 1979. Staff size: 6. Releases 2-3/year. Pays negotiable royalty to artists on contracts; statutory royalty to publisher per song on record.

DISTRIBUTED BY CD Baby.com and available on iTunes, MSN Music, Rhapsody, and more.

HOW TO CONTACT Submit professional demo package by mail. Unsolicited submissions are OK. CD only; no mp3s or e-mails. Include no more than 4 songs with corresponding lyric sheets and cover letter. Include appropriately sized SASE. Responds in 4 weeks.

MUSIC Good combination of traditional and modern country. 2008-09 releases: *Ready to Ride*—debut album from Nikki Britt, featuring "C-O-W-B-O-Y," "Do I Look Like Him," "Long Gone Mama," and "I'm So Lonesome I Could Cry."

TIPS "Professional demo preferred."

DEMO RECORDINGS

What is a "demo"?

The demo, shorthand for *demonstration recording*, is the most important part of your submission package. Demos are meant to give music industry professionals a way to hear all the elements of your song as clearly as possible so they can decide if it has commercial potential.

Should I send a cassette or a CD?

Most music industry people want CDs or DVDs, although cassettes may still be accepted. A few companies want demos sent on CD only. It's cheap and easy to burn recordings, so it is worth the investment to buy a burner or borrow one. Other formats, such as DAT (Digital Audio Tape) or MP3, may also be requested.

What should I send if I'm seeking management?

Some companies want a video of an act performing their songs. Check with the companies for specific requirements.

How many songs should I send, and in what order and length?

Most music industry people agree that three songs is enough. Most music professionals are short on time, and if you can't catch their attention in three songs, your songs probably don't have hit potential. Also, put three *complete songs* on your demo, not just snippets. Make sure to put your best, most commercial song first. An up-tempo number is usually best. If you send a cassette, *put all the songs on one side of the cassette and cue the tape to the beginning of the first song so no time is wasted fast-forwarding or rewinding.*

Should I sing my own songs on my demo?

If you can't sing well, you may want to hire someone who can. There are many resources for locating singers and musicians, including songwriter organizations, music stores, and songwriting magazines. Some aspiring professional singers will sing on demos in exchange for a copy they can use as a demo to showcase their talent.

Should I use a professional demo service?

Many songwriters find professional demo services convenient if they don't have the time or resources to hire musicians on their own. For a fee, a demo service will produce your songs in their studio using in-house singers and musicians (this is fairly common in Nashville). Many of these services advertise in music magazines, songwriting newsletters and bulletin boards at music stores. Make sure to listen to samples of work they've done in the past. Some are mail-order businesses—you send a rough recording of your song or the sheet music, and they produce and record a demo within a couple of months. Be sure to find a service that will allow some control over how the demo is produced, and tell them exactly how you want your song to sound. As with studios, look for a service that fits your needs and budget. (Some will charge as low as $300 for three songs, while others may go as high as $3,000 and boast a high-quality sound—*shop around and use your best judgment!*)

Should I buy equipment and record demos myself?

If you have the drive and focus to learn good recording techniques, yes. Digital multitrack recorders are readily available and affordable. If not, it might be easier to have someone else do it. For performing songwriters in search of record deals, the actual sound of their recordings can often be an important part of their artistic concept. Having the "means of production" within their grasp can be crucial to artists pursuing the independent route. But, if you don't know how to use the equipment, it may be better to utilize a professional studio.

How elaborate and full should the demo production be if I'm a nonperforming songwriter?

Many companies listed in *Songwriter's Market* tell you what types of demos they're looking for. If in doubt, contact them and ask. In general, country songs and pop ballads can often be recorded with just a vocal plus a guitar or piano, although many songwriters in those genres still prefer a more complete recording with drums, guitars, and other backing instruments. Up-tempo pop, rock, and dance demos usually require a full production.

What kind of production do I need if I'm a performing songwriter?

If you are a band or artist looking for a record deal, you will need a demo that is as fully produced as possible. Many singer/songwriters record their demos as if they were going to be released as an album. That way, if they don't get a deal, they can still release it on their own. Professionally pressed CDs are also now easily within reach of performing songwriters, and many companies offer graphic design services for a professional-looking product.

HOW DO I SUBMIT MY DEMO?

You have three basic options for submitting your songs: submitting by mail, submitting in person, and submitting over the Internet (the newest and least widely accepted option at this time).

SUBMITTING BY MAIL

Should I call, write, or e-mail first to ask for permission or submission requirements?

This is always a good idea, and many companies require you to contact them first. If you call, be polite, brief, and specific. If you send a letter, make sure it is typed and to the point. Include a typed SASE (self-addressed stamped envelope) for reply. If you send an e-mail, again, be professional and to the point. Proofread your message before you send it, and then be patient. Give them some time to reply. Do not send out mass e-mails or otherwise overload their e-mail account with repeated requests.

What do I send with my demo?

Most companies have specific requirements, but here are some general pointers:

- Read the listing carefully and submit *exactly* what they ask for, in the exact way they describe. It's also a good idea to call first, just in case they've changed their submission policies.
- Listen to each demo to make sure it sounds right and is in the right order (see the previous section—Demo Recordings).
- Enclose a *brief*, typed cover letter to introduce yourself. Indicate what songs you are sending and why you are sending them. If you are pitching your songs to a particular artist, say so in the letter. If you are an artist/songwriter looking for a record deal, you should say so. Be specific.

SUBMISSION MAILING POINTERS

Send your package with bubble wrap or a padded envelope to protect pieces.

Laser print all text on a computer for a professional look.

Include lyric sheets with your demo, and label each song selection (verse, chorus, etc.).

Keep cover letter brief, and let the song speak for itself.

Be sure to enclose sufficient return postage for all your materials.

Be sure to obtain permission before submitting songs over the Internet.

Include contact information on each piece.

W&T Music Publishing
1234 Note St.
Cincinnati, OH 45236
513/555-3253

I LOVE A GOOD LYRIC
by Willie Words and Tania Tunes

VERSE:
Capitalize the first word in each line
Start off your lyric flush with the left margin
Each line corresponds with a melodic phrase
Skip a line between sections

CHORUS:
I LOVE A GOOD LYRIC
And I want to show it
I LOVE A GOOD LYRIC
And I'll let your know it
By keeping it simple
And keeping it clean
I LOVE A GOOD LYRIC – sheet, I mean

VERSE:

W&T Music Publishing
1234 Note St.
Cincinnati, OH 45236
513/555-3253

August 23, 2013

Peter Publisher
Everyone's Music (ASCAP)
4321 Music Ave.
Nashville, TN 37207

Dear Mr. Publisher,

I am responding to your listing
three of my
"Radio Blue
are country,
Americana
partner, Tan

Thanks for li

Best,

Willie Word

Willie Wordsn
Enclosure

Put Postage Here

Willie Wordsmith
1234 Note St.
Cincinnati, Ohio 45236

I LOVE A
GOOD LYRIC
by Willie Wordsmith

Willie Wordsmith
1234 Note St.
Cincinnati, Ohio 45236
513/555-3253

- Include *typed* lyrics sheets or lead sheets, if requested. Make sure your name, address and phone number are on each sheet.
- Neatly label each tape or CD with your name, address, e-mail and phone number, along with the names of the songs in the order they appear on the recording.
- Include a SASE with sufficient postage and make sure it's large enough to return all your materials. Warning: Many companies do not return materials, so read each listing carefully.
- If you submit to companies in other countries, include a self-addressed envelope (SAE) and International Reply Coupon (IRC), available at most post offices. Make sure the envelope is large enough to return all of your materials.
- Pack everything neatly. Neatly type or write the company's address and your return address so they are clearly visible. Your package is the first impression a company has of you and your songs, so neatness counts!
- Mail first class: Stamp or write "First Class Mail" on the package and the SASE you enclose.
- Do not use registered or certified mail unless requested. Most companies will not accept or open demos sent by registered or certified mail for fear of lawsuits.
- Keep records of the dates, songs, and companies you submit to.

Is it OK to send demos to more than one person or company at a time?

It is usually acceptable to make simultaneous submissions. One exception is when a publisher, artist, or other industry professional asks you to put your song "on hold."

What does it mean when a song is "on hold"?

This means they intend to record the song and don't want you to give the song to anyone else. This is not a guarantee, though. Your song may eventually be returned to you, even if it's been on hold for months. Or it may be recorded and included on the album. If either of these happens, you are free to pitch your song to other people.

How can I protect myself from my song being put "on hold" indefinitely?

One approach is to establish a deadline for the person who asks for the hold, e.g., "You can put my song on hold for [number of] months." Or you can modify the hold to specify that you will still pitch the song to others but won't sign another deal without allowing the person with the song on hold to make you an offer. Once you sign a contract with a publisher, they have exclusive rights to your song and you cannot pitch it to other would-be publishers.

SUBMITTING IN PERSON

Is a visit to New York, Nashville, or Los Angeles to submit in person a good idea?

A trip to one of the major music hubs can be valuable if you are organized and prepared to make the most of it. You should have specific goals and set up appointments before you go. Some industry professionals are difficult to see and may not consider meeting out-of-town writers a high priority. Others are more open and even encourage face-to-face meetings. By taking the time to travel, organize, and schedule meetings, you can appear more professional than songwriters who submit blindly through the mail.

What should I take?

Take several copies of your demo and typed lyric sheets of each of your songs. More than one company you visit may ask you to leave a copy for them to review. You can expect occasionally to find a person has canceled an appointment, but wants you to leave a copy of your songs so they can listen and contact you later. (Never give someone the only (or last) copy of your demo if you absolutely want it returned, though.)

Where should I network while visiting?

Coordinate your trip with a music conference or make plans to visit ASCAP, BMI, or SESAC offices while you are there. For example, the South by Southwest Music Conference in Austin and NSAI Spring Symposium in Nashville often feature demo listening sessions, where industry professionals listen to demos submitted by songwriters attending the seminar. ASCAP, BMI, and SESAC also sometimes sponsor seminars or allow aspiring songwriters to make appointments with counselors who can give them solid advice.

How do I deal with rejection?

Many good songs have been rejected simply because they were not what the publisher or record company was looking for at that particular point. Do not take it personally. If few people like your songs, it does not mean they are not good. On the other hand, if you have a clear vision for what your particular songs are trying to convey, specific comments can also teach you a lot about whether your concept is coming across as you intended. If you hear the same criticisms of your songs over and over—for instance, the feel of the melody isn't right or the lyrics need work—give the advice serious thought. Listen carefully and use what the reviewers say constructively to improve your songs.

SUBMITTING OVER THE INTERNET

Is it OK to submit over the Internet?

It can be done, but it's not yet standard practice. There can still be problems with audio file formats. Although e-mail is widely used now, if you look through the listings in *Songwriter's Market*, you'll notice that not all music companies are necessarily equipped to make the process easy. But it shows a lot of promise for the future. Web-based companies like Tonos.com or TAXI, among many others, are making an effort to connect songwriters and industry professionals over the Internet. The Internet is proving important for networking. Garageband.com has extensive bulletin boards and allows members to post audio files of songs for critique.

If I want to try submitting over the Internet, what should I do?

First, send an e-mail to confirm whether a music company is equipped to stream or download audio files properly (whether MP3 or real audio, etc). If they do accept demos online, one strategy is to build a website with audio files that can be streamed or downloaded. Then, when you have permission, send an e-mail with links to that website or to particular songs. All they have to do is click on the link and it launches their Web browser to the appropriate page. Do not try to send MP3s or other files as attachments. They are often too large for the free online e-mail accounts people commonly use, and they may be mistakenly erased as potential viruses.

HOW DO I AVOID THE RIP-OFFS?

The music industry has its share of dishonest, greedy people who will try to rip you off by appealing to your ambition, by stroking your ego, or by claiming special powers to make you successful—for a price, of course. Most of them use similar methods, and you can prevent a lot of heartbreak by learning to spot them and stay away.

What is a "song shark"?

"Song sharks," as they're called, prey on beginners—songwriters unfamiliar with how the music industry works and what the ethical standards are. Two general signs of a song shark are:

- song sharks will take *any* songs—quality doesn't count.
- they're not concerned with future royalties, since they get their money up front from songwriters who think they're getting a great deal.

What are some of the most blatant rip-offs?

A request for money up front is the most common element. Song sharks may ask for money in the form of submission fees, an outright offer to publish your song for a fee or an offer to re-record your demo for a sometimes hefty price (with the implication that they will make your song wildly successful if you only pay to have it re-demoed in *their studio*). There are many variations on this theme.

Here is a list of rules that can help you avoid a lot of scams:

- **DO NOT SELL YOUR SONGS OUTRIGHT!** It's unethical for anyone to offer such a proposition. If your song becomes successful after you've sold it outright, you will never get royalties for it.

- **NEVER PAY "SUBMISSION FEES," "REVIEW FEES," "SERVICE FEES," "FILING FEES," ETC.** Reputable companies review material free of charge. If you encounter a company in this book that charges to submit, report them to the editor. If a company charges "only" $15 to submit your song, consider this: *If "only" 100 songwriters pay the $15, this company has made an extra $1,500 just for opening the mail!*

- **NEVER PAY TO HAVE YOUR SONGS PUBLISHED.** A reputable company interested in your songs assumes the responsibility and cost of promoting them, in hopes of realizing a profit once the songs are recorded and released. If they truly believe in your song, they will accept the costs involved.

- **DO NOT PAY A COMPANY TO PAIR YOU WITH A COLLABORATOR.** It's much better to contact a songwriting organization that offers collaboration services to their members.

- **NEVER PAY TO HAVE YOUR LYRICS OR POEMS SET TO MUSIC.** This is a classic rip-off. "Music mills"—for a price—may use the same melody for hundreds of lyrics and poems, whether it sounds good or not. Publishers recognize one of these melodies as soon as they hear it.

- **AVOID "PAY-TO-PLAY" CD COMPILATION DEALS.** It's totally unrealistic to expect this will open doors for you. These are mainly a moneymaker for the music company. CDs are cheap to manufacture, so a company that charges $100 to include your recording on a CD is making a killing. They claim they send these CDs to radio stations, producers, etc., but they usually end up in the trash or as drink coasters. Music industry professionals have no incentive to listen to them. Everybody on the CD paid to be included, so it's not as if they were carefully screened for quality.

- **AVOID "SONGPLUGGERS" WHO OFFER TO "SHOP" YOUR SONG FOR AN UP-FRONT FEE OR RETAINER.** This practice is not appropriate for *Songwriter's Market* readers, many of whom are beginners and live away from major music centers like Nashville. Professional, established songwriters in Nashville are sometimes known to work on a fee basis with songpluggers they have gotten to know over many years, *but the practice is controversial even for professionals.* Also, the songpluggers used by established professionals are very selective about their clients and have their own reputation to uphold. Companies who offer you these services but barely know you or your work are to be avoided. Also, contracting a songplugger long distance offers little or no accountability—you have no direct way of knowing what they're doing on your behalf.

- **AVOID PAYING A FEE UP FRONT TO HAVE A PUBLISHER MAKE A DEMO OF YOUR SONG.** Some publishers may take demo expenses out of your future royalties (a negotiable contract point usually meant to avoid endless demo sessions), but avoid paying up front for demo costs. Avoid situations where it is implied or expressed that a company will publish your song in return for you paying up front to use their demo services.

- **NO RECORD COMPANY SHOULD ASK YOU TO PAY THEM OR AN ASSOCIATED COMPANY TO MAKE A DEMO.** The job of a record company is to make records and decide which artists to sign *after* listening to demo submissions.
- **READ ALL CONTRACTS CAREFULLY BEFORE SIGNING.** And don't sign any contract you're unsure about or that you don't fully understand. It is well worth paying an attorney for the time it takes her to review a contract if you can avoid a bad situation that may cost you thousands of dollars.
- **BEFORE ENTERING A SONGWRITING CONTEST, READ THE RULES CAREFULLY.** Be sure that what you're giving up in the way of entry fees, etc., is not more than what you stand to gain by winning the contest (see the Contests & Awards section).
- **VERIFY ANY SITUATION ABOUT AN INDIVIDUAL OR COMPANY IF YOU HAVE ANY DOUBTS.** Contact the company's Performing Rights Society—ASCAP, BMI, SESAC, or SOCAN (in Canada). Check with the Better Business Bureau in the company's town, or contact the state attorney general's office. Contact professional organizations of which you're a member and inquire about the reputation of the company.

IF YOU WRITE LYRICS, BUT NOT MUSIC

- You must find a collaborator. The music business is looking for the complete package: music plus lyrics. If you don't write music, find a collaborator who does. The best way to find a collaborator is through songwriting organizations. Check the Organizations section for songwriting groups near you.
- Don't get ripped off. "Music mills" advertise in the back of magazines or solicit you through the mail. For a fee they will set your lyrics or poems to music. The rip-off is that they may use the same melody for hundreds of lyrics and poems, whether it sounds good or not. Publishers recognize one of these melodies as soon as they hear it.

- **IF A RECORD COMPANY OR OTHER COMPANY ASKS YOU TO PAY EXPENSES UP FRONT, BE CAREFUL.** Record producers commonly charge up front to produce an artist's album. Small indie labels sometimes ask a band to help with recording costs (but seek less control than a major label might). It's up to you to decide whether or not it is a good idea. Talk to other artists who have signed similar contracts before you sign one yourself. Research companies to find out if they can deliver on their claims, and what kind of distribution they have. Visit their website, if they have one. Beware of any company that won't let you know what it has done in the past. If a company has had successes and good working relationships with artists, it should be happy to brag about them.

I noticed record producers charge to produce albums. Is this bad?

Not automatically. Just remember what your goals are. If you write songs, but do not sing or perform, you are looking for publishing opportunities with the producer instead of someone who can help you record an album or CD. If you are a performing artist or band, then you might be in the market to hire a producer, in which case you will most likely pay them up front (and possibly give them a share in royalties or publishing, depending on the specific deal you negotiate). For more information see the Record Producers section introduction and the Royalties section.

Will it help me avoid rip-offs if I join a songwriting organization?

Yes. You will have access to a lot of good advice from a lot of experienced people. You will be able to research and compare notes, which will help you avoid pitfalls.

What should I know about contracts?

Negotiating a fair contract is important. You must protect yourself, and there are specific things you should look for in a contract. See the Contracts section for more information.

Are companies that offer demo services automatically bad?

No, but you are not obligated to make use of their services. Many music companies have their own or related recording studios, and with good recording equipment becoming so cheap and easy to use in recent years, a lot of them are struggling to stay afloat. This doesn't mean a company is necessarily trying to rip you off, but use your best judgment. In some cases, a company will submit a listing to *Songwriter's Market* for the wrong reasons—to pitch their demo services instead of finding songs to sign—in which case you should report them to the *Songwriter's Market* editor.

SUBMISSION STRATEGIES

NONPERFORMING SONGWRITERS

Here's a short list of avenues nonperforming songwriters can pursue when submitting songs:

1. **SUBMIT TO A MUSIC PUBLISHER.** This is the obvious one. Look at the information under Music in the listing to see examples of a publisher's songs and the artists they've found cuts with. Do you recognize the songs? Have you heard of the artists? Who are the writers? Do they have cuts with artists you would like to get a song to?

2. **SUBMIT TO A RECORD COMPANY.** Are the bands and artists on the record company's roster familiar? Do they tend to use outside songs on their albums? When pursuing this angle, it often helps to contact the record company first. Ask if they have a group or artist in development who needs material.

3. **SUBMIT TO A RECORD PRODUCER.** Do the producer's credits in the listings show songs written by songwriters other than the artist? Does he produce name artists known for using outside material? Be aware that producers themselves often write with the artists, so your song might also be competing against the producer's songwriting.

4. **SUBMIT TO AN ARTIST'S MANAGER.** If an artist needs songs, his or her manager is a prime gateway for your song. Contact the manager and ask if he has an act in need of material.

5. **JOIN A SONGWRITING ORGANIZATION.** Songwriting organizations are a good way to make contacts. Through the contacts you make you'll discover opportunities that others might not hear about. Some organizations can put you in direct contact with publishers for song critique sessions. You can increase your chances of a

hit by co-writing with other songwriters. Your songs will get better because of the feedback from other members.

6. **APPROACH PERFORMING RIGHTS ORGANIZATIONS (PROS).** PROs like ASCAP and BMI have writer relation representatives who can sometimes (if they think you're ready) give you a reference to a music company. This is one of the favored routes to success in the Nashville music scene.

PERFORMING SONGWRITERS

This is a bit more complicated, because there are a lot of different avenues available.

Finding a record deal

This is often a performing songwriter's primary goal—to get a record deal and release an album. Here are some possible ways to approach it:

1. **APPROACH A RECORD COMPANY FOR A RECORD DEAL.** This is an obvious one. Independent labels will be a lot more approachable than major labels, which are usually deluged with demos. Independent labels give you more artistic freedom, while major labels will demand more compromise, especially if you do not have a previous track record. A compromise between the two is to approach one of the "fake indie" labels owned by a major. You'll get more of the benefits of an indie, but with more of the resources and connections of a major label.

2. **APPROACH A RECORD PRODUCER FOR A DEVELOPMENT DEAL.** Some producers sign artists, produce their albums and develop them like a record company, and then approach major labels for distribution deals. This has advantages and drawbacks. For example, the producer gives you guidance and connections, but it can also be harder to get paid because you are signed to the producer and not the label.

3. **GET A MANAGER WITH CONNECTIONS.** The right manager with the right connections can make all the difference in getting a record deal.

4. **ASK A MUSIC PUBLISHER.** Publishers are taking on more of the role of developing performing songwriters as artists. Many major publishers are sister companies to record labels and can shop you for a deal when they think you're ready. They do this in the hope of participating in the mechanical royalties from an album release, and these monies can be substantial when it's a major label release.

5. **APPROACH AN ENTERTAINMENT ATTORNEY.** Entertainment attorneys are a must when it comes to negotiating record contracts, and some moonlight by helping artists make connections for record deals (they will get their cut, of course).

6. **APPROACH PROS.** ASCAP and BMI can counsel you on your career and possibly make a referral. They also commonly put on performance showcases where A&R ("artist and repertoire') people from record labels attend to check out the new artists.

Finding a producer to help with your album

Independently minded performing songwriters often find they need help navigating the studio when it comes time to produce their own album. In this case, the producer often works for an up-front fee from the artist, for a percentage of the royalty when the album is released and sold (referred to as "points," as in "percentage points"), or a combination of both.

Things to keep in mind when submitting a demo to a producer on this basis:

1. **IS THE PRODUCER KNOWN FOR A PARTICULAR GENRE OR "SOUND"?** Many producers have a signature sound to their studio productions and are often connected to specific genres. Phil Spector had the "Wall of Sound." Bob Rock pioneered a glossy metal sound for Metallica and the Cult. Daniel Lanois and Brian Eno are famous for the atmospheres they created on albums by U2. Look at your favorite CDs to see who produced them. Use these as touchstones when approaching producers to see if they are on your wavelength.

2. **WHAT ROLE DOES A PARTICULAR PRODUCER LIKE TO TAKE IN THE STUDIO?** The Tips information found at the end of many of the Record Producers listings often have notes from the producer about how they like to work with performing songwriters in the studio. Some work closely as a partner with the artist on developing arrangements and coaching performances. Some prefer final authority on creative decisions. Think carefully about what kind of working relationship you want.

Finding a manager

Many performing songwriters eventually find it necessary to locate a manager to help with developing their careers and finding gigs. Some things to keep in mind when looking:

1. **DOES THE MANAGER WORK WITH ARTISTS IN MY GENRE OF MUSIC?** A manager who typically works with punk rock bands may not have as many connections useful to an aspiring country singer-songwriter. A manager who mainly works with gospel artists might not know what to do with a hedonistic rock band.

2. **HOW BIG IS THE MANAGER'S AGENCY?** If a manager is working with multiple acts but has a small (or no) staff, you might not get the attention you want to read. Some of the listings include information about the agency's staff size.

3. **DOES THE MANAGER WORK WITH ACTS FROM MY REGION?** Many of the listings have information in their headings provided by the companies describing whether they work with regional acts only or artists from any region.

4. **DOES THE MANAGER WORK WITH NAME ACTS?** A manager with famous clients could work wonders for your career. Or you could get lost in the shuffle. Use your best judgment when sizing up a potential manager, and be clear with yourself about the

kind of relationship you would like to have and the level of attention you want for your career.

5. **IF I'M A BEGINNER, WILL THE MANAGER WORK FOR ME?** Check the listings for the Openness to Submissions icons ⊘ ○ ◑ ● to find companies open to beginners. Some may suggest extensive changes to your music or image. On the other hand, you may have a strong vision of what you want to do and need a manager who will work with you to achieve that vision instead of changing you around. Decide for yourself how much you are willing to compromise in good faith.

REMEMBER THAT A RELATIONSHIP BETWEEN YOU AND A MANAGER IS A TWO-WAY STREET. You will have to earn each other's trust and be clear about your goals for mutual success.

ROYALTIES

NON-PERFORMING SONGWRITERS

How do songwriters make money?

The quick answer is that songwriters make money from rights available to them through copyright law. For more details, keep reading and see the upcoming Copyright section.

What specific rights make money for songwriters?

There are two primary ways songwriters earn money on their songs: performance royalties and mechanical royalties.

What is a performance royalty?

When you hear a song on the radio, on television, in the elevator, in a restaurant, etc., the songwriter receives royalties, called performance royalties. Performing Rights Organizations (ASCAP, BMI and SESAC in the U.S.A.) collect payment from radio stations, television, etc., and distribute those payments to songwriters (see below).

What is a mechanical royalty?

When a record company puts a song onto a CD or online and distributes copies for sale, they owe a royalty payment to the songwriter for each copy they press of the album. It is called a mechanical royalty because of the mechanical process used to mass-produce a copy of a CD or sheet music. The payment is small per song (see the "Royalty Provisions" subhead of the Basic Song Contract Pointers sidebar in the Contracts section), but the earnings can add up

MUSIC PUBLISHING ROYALTIES

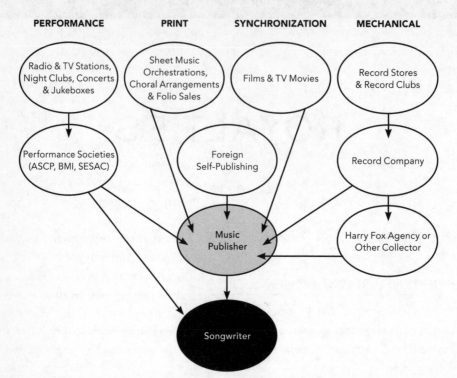

and reach massive proportions for songs appearing on successful label albums. Note: This royalty is totally different from the artist royalty on the retail price of the album.

Who collects the money for performance and mechanical royalties?

Performing Rights Organizations collect performance royalties. There are three organizations that collect performance royalties: ASCAP, BMI, and SESAC. These organizations arose many years ago when songwriters and music publishers gathered together to press for their rights and improve their ability to collect fees for the use of their songs. ASCAP, BMI, and SESAC collect fees for the use of songs and then pass along the money to their member songwriters and music publishers.

MECHANICAL RIGHTS ORGANIZATIONS COLLECT MECHANICAL ROYALTIES. There are three organizations that collect mechanical royalties: the Harry Fox Agency (HFA), the American Mechanical Rights Organization (AMRA) and the Songwriters Guild of America (SGA). These three organizations collect mechanical royalties from record companies of all sizes—major labels, midsize, and independents—and pass the royalties along to member music publishers and songwriters.

How do songwriters hook up with this system to earn royalties?

For performance royalties, individual songwriters affiliate with a Performing Rights Organization of their choice, and register their songs in the PRO database. Each PRO has a slightly different method of calculating payment, a different ownership, and a different membership structure, so choosing a PRO is an individual choice. Once a songwriter is affiliated and has registered his or her songs, the PROs then collect fees as described above and issue a check to the songwriter.

For mechanical royalties, three different things can happen:

1. The songwriter is signed to a publisher that is affiliated with the Harry Fox Agency. The Harry Fox Agency collects the mechanical royalties and passes them along to the publisher. The publisher then passes these along to the songwriter within thirty days. This case usually happens when a songwriter is signed to a major publisher and has a song on a major label album release.

2. The songwriter is not signed to a publisher and owns exclusive rights to his songs, and so works with AMRA or the Songwriters Guild of America, who cuts a check directly to the songwriter instead of passing him or her to the publisher first.

3. They are signed to a publisher, but the songs are being released on albums by independent labels. In this case, the songwriter often works with AMRA since they have a focus on the independent music publishing market.

PERFORMING SONGWRITERS / ARTISTS

How do performing songwriters make money?

Performing songwriters and artists (if they write their own songs) make money the same way non-performing songwriters do, but they also make money through royalties made on the retail price of an album when it is sold online, in a store, etc.

What about all the stories of performing songwriters who get into bad deals?

The stories are generally true, but if they're smart, performing songwriters will try to hold on to performing and mechanical royalties. But when it comes to retail sale royalties, all they will usually see is an "advance"—essentially a loan—which must then be paid off from record sales. You will not see a royalty check on retail sales until your advance is paid off. If you are given a $600,000 advance, for example, you will have to pay back the record company $600,000 out of your sales royalties before you see any more money.

Do performing songwriters and artists get to keep the advance?

Not really. If you have a manager who has gotten you a record deal, he or she will take a cut. You will probably be required in the contract to pay for the producer and studio time to make the album. Often the producer will take a percentage of subsequent royalties from album sales, which comes out of your pocket. There are also music video costs, promotion to radio stations, tour support, paying sidemen, etc. Just about anything you can think of is eventually paid for out of your advance or out of sales royalties. Deductions to royalties that make it harder to earn out an advance are usually built into record company contracts.

What should a performing songwriter wanting to sign with a major label do?

Songwriters' best option is to negotiate a fair contract, get as large an advance as possible, and then manage that advance money the best they can. A good contract will keep the songwriting royalties described above separate from the flow of sales royalties, and will also cut down on the number of royalty deductions the record company builds into the contract. And because of the difficulty in earning out any size advance or auditing the record company, it makes sense to get as much cash up front as you can. You will need a good lawyer.

RECORD COMPANIES, PRODUCERS , MANAGERS, & BOOKING AGENTS

How do music publishers make money?

A publisher works as a songwriter's agent, looks for profitable commercial uses for the songs he or she represents, and then takes a percentage of the profits. This is typically 50 percent of all earnings from a particular song—often referred to as the *publisher's share*. A successful publisher stays in contact with several A&R reps, in order to fine out what upcoming projects are in need of new material and whether any songs he or she represents will be appropriate.

How do record companies make money?

Record companies primarily make their money from profits made selling CDs, DVDs, downloads, etc. Record companies keep most of the profit after subtracting manufacturing costs, royalties to recording artists, distribution fees and the costs of promoting songs to radio (for major labels this can reach up to $300,000 per song). Record companies also usually have music publishing divisions that make money performing all the functions of publishers.

How do record producers make money?

Producers make most of their money by charging a flat fee up front to helm a recording project, by sharing in the royalties from album sales, or both. A small independent producer might charge $10,000 (sometimes less) up front to produce a small indie band, while a "name" producer such as Bob Rock, who regularly works with major label bands, might charge $300,000. Either of these might also take a share in sales royalties, referred to as "points"—as in "percentage points." A producer might say, "I'll produce you for $10,000 and

2 points." If an artist is getting a 15 percent royalty on album sales, then two of those percentage points will go to the producer instead. Producers also make money by cowriting with the artists to get publishing royalties, or they may ask for part of the publishing from songs written by outside songwriters.

How do managers make money?

Most managers make money by taking a percentage commission of their clients' income, usually 10–25 percent. If a touring band finishes a show and makes a $2,000 profit, a manager on 15 percent commission would get $300. If an artist gets a $40,000 advance from a midsize label, the manager would get $6,000. Whether an artist's songwriting income is included in the manager's commission comes down to negotiation. The commission should give the manager incentive to make things happen for your career, so avoid paying flat fees up front.

COPYRIGHT

How am I protected by copyright law?

Copyright protection applies to your songs the instant you put them down in fixed form—a recording, sheet music, lead sheet, etc. This protection lasts for your lifetime plus 70 years (or the lifetime of the last surviving writer, if you co-wrote the song with somebody else). When you prepare demos, place notification of copyright on all copies of your song—the lyric sheets, lead sheets, and labels for CDs, etc. The notice is simply the word "copyright" or the symbol © followed by the year the song was created (or published) and your name (Example: © 2013 by John Q. Songwriter).

What parts of a song are protected by copyright?

Traditionally, only the melody line and the lyrics are eligible for copyright. Period. Chords and rhythm are virtually never protected. An incredibly original arrangement can sometimes qualify. Sound recordings can also be copyrighted, but this applies strictly to the actual sounds on the recording, not the song itself (this copyright is usually owned by record companies).

What songs are not protected?

Song titles or mere ideas for music and lyrics cannot be copyrighted. Very old songs in the "public domain" are not protected. You could quote a melody from a Bach piece, but you could not then stop someone else from quoting the same melody in his song.

When would I lose or have to share the copyright?

If you collaborate with other writers, they are assumed to have equal interests unless you state some other arrangement, in writing. If you write under a work-for-hire arrangement, the company or person who hired you to write the song then owns the copyright. Sometimes your spouse may automatically be granted an interest in your copyright as part of his or her spousal rights, which might then become important if you get divorced.

Should I register my copyright?

Registering your copyright with the Library of Congress gives the best possible protection. Registration establishes a public record of your copyright—even though a song is legally protected whether or not it is registered—and could prove useful in any future court cases involving the song. Registration also entitles you to a potentially greater settlement in a copyright infringement lawsuit.

How do I register my song?

To register your song, request government form PA from the Copyright Office. Call the 24-hour hotline at (202)707-9100 and leave your name and address on the messaging system. Once you receive the PA form, you must return it, along with a registration fee and a CD (or tape) and lead sheet of your song. Send them to the Register of Copyrights, Copyright Office, Library of Congress, Washington DC 20559. It may take several months to receive your certificate of registration from the Copyright Office, but your songs are protected from the date of creation (the date of registration will reflect the date you applied). For more information, call the Copyright Office's Public Information Office at (202)707-3000 or visit their website at www.copyright.gov.

How likely is it that someone will try to steal my song?

Copyright infringement is very rare. But if you ever feel that one of your songs has been stolen—that someone has unlawfully infringed on your copyright—you must prove that you created the work and that the person you are suing had access to your song. Copyright registration is the best proof of a date of creation. You must have your copyright registered in order to file a lawsuit. Also, it's helpful if you keep your rough drafts and revisions of songs, either on page, CD, or digitally.

Why did song sharks begin soliciting me after I registered my song?

This is one potential, unintended consequence of registering your song with the Library of Congress. The copyright indexes are a public record of your songwriting, and song sharks often search the copyright indexes and mail solicitations to songwriters who live out of the range of major music centers such as Nashville. They figure these songwriters don't know any better and are easy prey. *Do not allow this possibility to stop you from registering your songs!* Just be aware, educate yourself, and then throw the song sharks' mailings in the trash.

What if I mail a CD to myself to get a postmark date on a sealed envelope?

The "poor man's copyright" has not stood up in court, and is not an acceptable substitute for registering your song. If you feel it's important to shore up your copyright, register it with the Library of Congress.

CAREER SONGWRITING

///

What career options are open to songwriters who do not perform?

The possibilities range from a beginning songwriter living away from a music center like Nashville who lands an occasional single-song publishing deal, to a staff songwriter signed to a major publishing company. And there are songwriters who operate independently, have developed a lot of connections, work with numerous artists, and have set up their own independent publishing operations.

What is "single-song" songwriting about?

In this case, a songwriter submits songs to many different companies. One or two songs gain interest from different publishers, and the songwriter signs separate contracts for each song with each publisher. The songwriter can then pitch other songs to other publishers. In Nashville, for instance, a single-song contract is usually the first taste of success for an aspiring songwriter on his or her way up the ladder. Success of this sort can induce a songwriter to move to a music center like Nashville (if he or she hasn't already) and is a big boost for a struggling songwriter already living there. A series of single-song contracts often signals a songwriter's maturing skill and marketability.

What is a "staff songwriter"?

A staff songwriter usually works for a major publisher and receives a monthly stipend as an advance against the royalties he or she is likely to earn for the publisher. The music publisher has exclusive rights to everything the songwriter writes while signed to the company. The publisher also works actively on the writer's behalf to hook him or her up with co-writers and other opportunities. A staff songwriting position is highly treasured by many because it offers a steady income. In Nashville, landing such a position is a sign the song-writer "has arrived."

What comes after the staff songwriting position?

Songwriters who go to the next level have a significant reputation for their ability to write hit songs. Famous artists seek them out, and they often write actively in several markets at once. They also write on assignment for film and television, and commonly keep their own publishing companies to maximize their income.

As my career grows, what should I do about keeping track of expenses, etc.?

You should keep a ledger or notebook with records on all financial transactions related to your songwriting—royalty checks, demo costs, office supplies, postage, travel expenses, dues to organizations, class and workshop fees, plus any publications you purchase pertaining to songwriting. You may also want a separate checking account devoted to your songwrit-ing activities. This will make record keeping easier and help to establish your identity as a business for tax purposes.

What should I know about taxes related to songwriting income?

Any royalties you receive will not reflect taxes or any other mandatory deductions. It is your responsibility to keep track of income and file the correct tax forms. For specific informa-tion, contact the IRS or talk to an accountant who serves music industry clients.

CONTRACTS

CO-WRITING

What kind of agreements do I need with co-writers?

You may need to sign a legal agreement between you and a co-writer to establish percentages you will each receive of the writer's royalties. You will also have to iron out what you will do if another person, such as an artist, wants to change your song and receive credit as a cowriter. For example, in the event a major artist wants to cut your song for his or her album—but also wants to rewrite some lyrics and take a share of the publishing—you and your co-writer need to agree whether it is better to get a song on an album that might sell millions (and make a lot of money) or pass on it because you don't want to give up credit. The situation could be uncomfortable if you are not in sync on the issue.

When do I need a lawyer to look over agreements?

When it comes to doing business with a publisher, producer, or record company, you should always have the contract reviewed by a knowledgeable entertainment attorney. As long as the issues at stake are simple, the co-writers respect each other, and they discuss their business philosophies before writing a song together, they can probably write an agreement without the aid of a lawyer.

SINGLE-SONG CONTRACTS

What is a single-song contract?

A music publisher offers a single-song contract when he or she wants to sign one or more of your songs, but doesn't want to hire you as a staff songwriter. You assign your rights to a particular song to the publisher for an agreed-upon number of years, so that he or she may represent the song and find uses profitable for both of you. This is a common contract and quite possibly will be the first you encounter in your songwriting career.

What basic elements should every single-song contract contain?

Every contract should have the publisher's name, the writer's name, the song's title, the date, and the purpose of the agreement. The songwriter also declares that the song is an original work and that he is creator of the work. The contract *must* specify the royalties the songwriter will earn from various uses of the song, including performance, mechanical, print, and synchronization royalties.

How should the royalties usually be divided in the contract?

The songwriter should receive no less than 50 percent of the income his or her song generates. That means the songwriter and publisher split the total royalties 50/50. The songwriter's half is called the "writer's share" and the publisher's half is called the "publisher's share." If there is more than one songwriter, the songwriters split the writer's share. Sometimes successful songwriters will bargain for a percentage of the publisher's share, negotiating what is basically a co-publishing agreement. For a visual explanation of how royalties are collected and flow to the songwriter, see the chart called Music Publishing Royalties in the Royalties section.

What should the contract say about a "reversion clause"?

Songwriters should always negotiate for a "reversion clause," which returns all rights to the songwriter if some provision of the contract is not met. Most reversion clauses give a publisher a set amount of time (usually one or two years) to work the song and make money with it. If the publisher can't get the song recorded and released during the agreed-upon time period, the songwriter can then take his song to another publisher. The danger of not getting some sort of reversion clause is that you could wind up with a publisher sitting on your song for the entire life-plus-70-years term of the copyright—which may as well be forever.

Is a reversion clause difficult to get?

Some publishers agree to it and figure if they can't get any action with the song in the first year or two, they're not likely to ever have much luck with it. Other publishers may be reluctant to agree to a reversion clause. They may invest a lot of time and money in producing the demo and pitching it to artists and may want to keep working at it for a longer period of time. Or, for example, a producer might put a song on hold for a while and then go into a lengthy recording project. A year can easily go by before the artist or producer decides which songs to release as singles. This means you may have to agree to a longer time period, be flexible, and trust that the publisher has your best mutual interests in mind. Use your judgment.

BASIC SONG CONTRACT POINTERS

The following list, taken from a Songwriters Guild of America publication, enumerates the basic features of an acceptable songwriting contract:

1) **WORK FOR HIRE.** When you receive a contract covering just one composition, you should make sure the phrases "employment for hire" and "exclusive writer agreement" are not included. Also, there should be no options for future songs.

2) **PERFORMING RIGHTS AFFILIATION.** If you previously signed publishing contracts, you should be affiliated with ASCAP, BMI, or SESAC. You must receive all performance royalties directly from your performing rights organization, and this should be written into your contract.

3) **REVERSION CLAUSE.** The contract should include a provision that if the publisher does not secure a release of a commercial sound recording within a specified time (one year, two years, etc.), you may terminated the contract.

4) **CHANGES IN THE COMPOSITION.** If the contract includes a provision that the publisher can change the title, lyrics, or music, this should be amended so that only with your consent can such charges be made.

5) **ROYALTY PROVISIONS.** You should receive 50 percent of all publisher's income on all licenses issued. If the publisher prints and sells his own sheet music, your royalty should be 10 percent of the wholesale selling price. The royalty should not be stated in the contract as a flat rate ($.05, $.07, etc.).

6) **NEGOTIABLE DEDUCTIONS.** Ideally, demos and all other expenses of publication should be paid 100 percent by the publisher. The only allowable fee is for the Harry Fox Agency collection fee, whereby the writer pays one-half of the amount charged to the publisher for mechanical rights. The current mechanical royalty collected by the Harry Fox Agency is $.091 cents per cut for songs under 5 minutes; and $.0175 cents per minute for songs over 5 minutes.

7) **ROYALTY STATEMENTS AND AUDIT PROVISION.** Once the song is recorded, you are entitled to receive royalty statements at least once every six months. In addition, an audit provision with no time restriction should be included in every contract.

8) **WRITER'S CREDIT.** The publisher should make sure that you receive proper credit on all uses of the composition.

9) **ARBITRATION.** In order to avoid large legal fees in case of a dispute with your publisher, the contract should include an arbitration clause.

10) **FUTURE USES.** Any use not specifically covered by the contract should be retained by the writer to be negotiated as it comes up.

What other basic issues should a single-song contract cover?

The contract should also address these issues:

- Will an advance be paid, and if so, how much will the advance be?
- When will royalties be paid (annually or semiannually)?
- Who will pay for demos—the publisher, songwriter or both?
- How will lawsuits against copyright infringement be handled, including the cost of lawsuits?
- Will the publisher have the right to sell its interest in the song to another publisher without the songwriter's consent?
- Does the publisher have the right to make changes in a song, or approve changes by someone else, without the songwriter's consent?
- The songwriter should have the right to audit the publisher's books, if he feels it is necessary and gives the publisher reasonable notice.

WHEN DOES 50% EQUAL 100%?

NOTE: The publisher's and songwriter's share of the income are sometimes referred to as each being 100%—for 200% total! You might hear someone say, "I'll take 100% of the publisher's share." Do not be needlessly confused! If the numbers confuse you, ask for the terms to be clarified.

Where else can I go for advice on contracts?

The Songwriters Guild of America has drawn up a Popular Songwriter's Contract, which it believes to be the best minimum songwriter contract available (see the Basic Song Contract Pointers sidebar). The Guild will send a copy of the contract at no charge to any interested songwriter upon request (see the Songwriters Guild of America listing in the Organizations section). SGA will also review—free of charge—any contract offered to its members, and will check it for fairness and completeness. Also check out these two books published by Writer's Digest Books: *The Craft and Business of Songwriting*, 3rd edition, by John Braheny; and *The New Songwriter's Guide to Music Publishing*, 3rd edition, by Randy Poe.

HARVEY MASON, JR.

First-Class Success Is a Full-Time Commitment

....

by Vanessa Herron

Harvey Mason, Jr. is a six-time Grammy award-winning songwriter who grew up in Los Angeles, California. The son of professional musicians. he played every sport imaginable, even attending the University of Arizona on a basketball scholarship, but music was always his passion. By continuing to write songs and to network with producers, he became a co-founder of The Underdogs, a production team that worked with the likes of Tyrese, Stacie Orrico, and Jordin Sparks, and he eventually wrote and produced music for dozens of chart toppers, such as Britney Spears, Whitney Houston, Justin Timberlake, Aretha Franklin, and Mary J. Blige. He now oversees Harvey Mason Media, his film and music production company which has also expanded into music publishing and website ventures. In 2009, he was elected to the Board of Trustees for NARAS (National Academy of Recording Arts and Sciences).

He took time out of his busy schedule to tell us how he attained his status in the industry, and how others songwriters can get their feet in the door.

What is your musical background?

I took piano lessons as a kid for about seven years. Growing up, I was always writing and playing songs. My mom and dad were both musicians, so I was just kind of expected to be interested in music. It was great, being exposed to so much good music and so many other musicians at such a young age. Just seeing other people being creative, I was able to appreciate a lot of different genres of music and draw from that when I started writing my own songs.

How old were you when you wrote your first song?

Shoot, I was probably five years old. Grover Washington, Jr. recorded my first song when I was about 10 or 11 years old, so that's how I got started.

As an adult, how did you get your first commercial song placed and who was it for?

It was an overseas artist, someone in the U.K. After that, a Motown A&R guy named Guy Abraham hired me to do remixes. Eventually, he gave me a shot to produce a group called Impromptu for them. My first "big" placement was with Brandy for her "Never Say Never" record. After that, I met more L.A. executives, songwriters, and producers and went from there.

How did you start doing the remixes for Guy Abraham? Did you just submit a demo to him or was he someone you knew from your earlier connections?

I was always in L.A. hustling my demos to people and, you know, shopping and sending people my cassettes. Eventually he heard some of my music and offered to pay me two thousand dollars to do a remix. We didn't really know each other; I just connected with him through my stalking ways.

So how did you know who to send your demos and cassettes to, since we didn't have the Internet back in those days?

I just studied the backs of record covers and credits, and reading which person did what. I realized that it was the A&R people whose job it was to pick the songs. So I started focusing on A&R people and record label executives, vice presidents and even presidents. I was following guys around to their houses and in their parking garages, throwing cassettes at them.

How did you hone your songwriting skills to the point where you could sell your songs?

I started out listening to a lot of other producers and songwriters, emulating what they did and reproducing songs that I really loved, figuring out how they made the sounds that they did. That taught me a lot, and at that time, it was Babyface, Devante, Teddy Riley, Al B. Sure, Jimmy Jam & Terry Lewis, L.A. Reid. Those were the guys that I looked up to, because they were really the first producers that got a lot of visibility.

Did you ever consider being a performer yourself?

No, not really. I didn't really have an interest in that. I just really wanted to make the music. I mean, I've sung on demos and things like that. My real passion was in creating the songs.

What comes first for you when you're creating songs—the tracks or the lyrics?

Either one. Sometimes a track will inspire a lyric. You'll hear a track and it will make you think of something. Another time, I'll just be driving around and I'll jot down some notes on a lyric and then access them later. Sometimes an experience that either I or someone I know may be going through will inspire a concept to a song or some lyrics.

If you had to pick one element of a song—the lyrics, the hook, the track—what is the most important component of a song that makes it "good"?

I don't think there's an answer to that question. The most important component to a successful song is a mixture and the blend of all of those components. You can have a great track, and not say anything in the hook and it's not going to be a great record. You can have a great lyric, but the track is horrible and you won't have a hit song. It's really a combination of how it all fits and works together. There are plenty of songs on the radio that don't have great lyrics or they have a boring track. I won't name them, but there are a ton of them.

Do you ever get writer's block? And if you do, what do you do about it?

I've never really experienced writer's block. I'm not the type of writer that gets in the booth and writes the song from top to bottom off the top of my head.

Someone like that would tend to have writer's block more than me. I have to sit and think and craft, and really study and work for the lyrics. It doesn't just flow from me naturally. It's always been a very cerebral process for me. Doing it instinctively all at once like that calls for a level of talent that I don't have.

Did you have a mentor?

I had a few. My dad was a big part of my development. He was a writer before me, so I definitely looked to him as a producer. This is kind of out of left field, but my basketball coach in college, Lute Olson, was also an amazing mentor. He taught me how to create something of quality and to always do things in a first-class manner, not to compromise or cut corners. I use that in my music and production every day.

Ultimately, my mentor over the last 12 years has been Clive Davis. From a songwriting and production standpoint, he has been very instrumental in my pushing the bar, raising the bar, and expecting more from myself. He was a lot like Coach Olson in that regard.

Has your music career crossed over to other industries?

Yes, we do a lot of film stuff, from doing music for the movies to producing the film itself. I think music is the starting point, and I'll always do that, but it can also lead to lots of other cool things.

Where do you see your career going in the next five to 10 years?

I'll always want to continue making music. Hearing people say that they love one of my songs or heard one of my songs that made them think about this or that, that's what really motivates me. I want to sign other artists, producers, and songwriters and make sure that people are still making great records and writing good songs.

How do you find new talent? Where do you look?

I get a lot of submissions through the Internet, emails, my website, Twitter, and my Blazetrak.com account. I get submissions from all over the place. I listen to a lot of them—I try to work with as many new people as I can and help them the way that others helped me.

So, I take it that you are open to new submissions from songwriters?

Always.

What advice would you give to songwriters who are just starting out, trying to establish themselves?

I would say that you have to write songs every day. You can't do it as a part-time thing. You have to be dedicated and persistent. Study and listen to what's on the radio. Right now, your music has to be relevant and accessible for a promotions staff and A&R staff to be able to really get behind it. Study history and know other great songs. Study songwriters that came before you and know what it took to make a good hit song in the 70s, 80s, 90s, and so forth.

Another way to create success is to collaborate with other people. Work with a lot of other great writers and get to as many producers and studios as you can. Get as many co-write sessions as you can, too. Everybody's trying to find new talent, and most people are open to co-writing with new writers.

It's a great way to network, to learn, and to get your music out.

Vanessa Herron is an optioned screenwriter, who has over 10 years of experience as an award-winning freelance writer and lyricist. She is currently completing her first novel, and was a 2012 Fellow of the Guy Hanks and Marvin Miller Fellowship (aka the "Cosby Writing Program"). She is also a public speaker and works as an executive producer for Clear Channel Media and Entertainment in Burbank, California. She can be reached at vanessaherron@gmail.com.

OBJECT WRITING: PRACTICE YOUR CRAFT

by Pat Pattison

Turn down the lights, turn down the bed, turn down these voices inside my head.

"I Can't Make You Love Me" - Reid/Shamblin

Where do these words take you? Do they make you see something? What kind of bed? Single? Double? What color is the bedspread? The pillows? Where is the light coming from? A table lamp? Above the headboard?

When a lyric stimulates and provokes your senses, you draw the images from your own experiences. You fill Mike Reid's and Alan Shamblin's words with your stuff. They involve you, so the song becomes *about you*. That's the power of sense-bound writing. It pulls the listener into the song by using his own memories as the song's material.

Sense-bound writing turns observers into participants. It is one of the most powerful tools a writer has.

The best way I know to exercise the sense-bound writing muscle is to use a technique called "object writing." Object writing is timed, sense-bound writing usually done first thing in the morning.

You pick an object—a real object, like a paper clip, a coffee cup, a Corvette—and treat it as a diving board to launch you inward to the vaults of your seven senses: **Sight, Sound, Taste, Touch, Smell, Body, Motion**.

Although you're familiar with five of your senses, you could probably stand a few exercises to sharpen them, especially the four you don't normally tap into when you write. If I asked you to describe the room you're in, your answer would be primarily, if not completely, visual. Even if it is only visual, remember that the visual sense has at least three aspects—color, shape, and texture. Try isolating each and noticing, for example, only shapes. Look for similar shapes. Then look for texture "rhymes." How many colors does the tree really have?

Try spending a little time alone with each sense. How big does the room sound? (If it were twice as big? Half as big?) How would the table taste if you licked it? (No, it's not silly. You just lick more selectively because Mom warned you all about germs.) How would the rug feel if you rubbed your bare back on it? How does the kitchen table smell? Remember this, it is important: The more senses you incorporate into your writing, the better it breathes and dances. Take your time and practice.

Object Writing

Two additional senses need greater explanation.

Organic sense (body) is your awareness of inner bodily functions, for example, heartbeat, pulse, muscle tension, stomachaches, cramps, breathing. Athletes are most keenly focused on this sense, but you use it constantly, especially in responsive situations. I've been sitting here writing too long. I need a back rub.

Kinesthetic sense (motion) is, roughly, your sense of relation to the world around you. When you get seasick or drunk, the world around you blurs—like blurred vision. When the train you're on is standing still and the one next to it moves, your kinesthetic sense goes crazy. Children spin, roll down hills, or ride on tilt-a-whirls to stimulate this sense. Dancers and divers develop it most fully—they look onto a stage or down to the water and see spatial possibilities for their bodies. It makes me dizzy just thinking about it.

Timed Writing

It's important that you time your object writing. Make it a manageable task, one that you feel good about doing every day. And do it first thing in the morning.

Guarantee yourself only the time allotted for each prompt. Set a timer, and stop the second it goes off. I mean the second, as you'll see from some of the examples in this challenge. Be sure you always stop right at the buzzer. Don't finish the sentence. Don't even finish the word you're in the middle of. You're much more likely to sit down to a clearly limited commitment than if you get on a roll some morning and let yourself write for thirty minutes. Then, guess what you'll say the next morning:

"Ugh, I don't have the energy to do it this morning (remembering how much energy you spent yesterday), and besides,

"I've already written enough for the next two days. I'll start again Thursday."

Songwriting Without Boundaries

Breaking the timed commitment is how most people stop morning writing altogether. Any good coach will tell you that more is gained practicing a short time each day than doing it all at once. Living with it day by day keeps writing on your mind and in your muscles.

Two beings inhabit your body: you, who stumbles groggily to the coffeepot to start another day, and the writer in you, who could remain blissfully asleep and unaware for days, months, even years as you go about your business. If your writer is anything like mine, lazy, or even sluggish, is too kind a word. Always wake up your writer early so you can spend the day together. It's amazing the fun the two of you can have watching the world go by. Your writer will be active beside you, sniffing and tasting, snooping for metaphors. It's like writing all day without moving your fingers.

Soon, during your timed writing, something like this will happen: Your writing will start to roll, diving, plunging, heading directly for the soft pink and blue glow below when, beep! The timer goes off. Just stop. Wherever you are. Stop. Writus Interruptus. All day your frustrated writer will grumble, "Boy, what I might have said if you hadn't stopped me."

Guaranteed, when you sit down the next morning, you will dive deeper faster. You'll reach the bottom in three minutes flat. Next time, one minute. Finally, instantly. That is your goal: immediate access—speed and depth. So much information and experience tumbles by every minute of your life, the faster you can explore each bit, the faster you can sample the next. But, of course, speed doesn't count without depth. The ten-minute absolute limit is the key to building both. And it guarantees a manageable task. Look at this example:

OBJECT: ELEVATOR - TIME LIMIT: 10 MINUTES

Cathy Brettell: Breath sucks back into my throat—stomach ball jellies to my toes like an anchor hoisted over a ship—dull brass dragging thick fingers of midnight, current's chain unspools—like roller skates gliding freely—wind sassing back against stubborn waves, black fallen angels bow and thrash in the darkness—thunder twists between sweaty muscled clouds—silver daggers spear the sky horizon, lashing down at the warm sleeping distant halls—sandy upper lip catching foam of a root beer float—eyes widen—thirst deepens, a throat of parched earth guzzles a torpedo stream of charcoal water—stars mirror in the salty crystals—reeds bristle against oncoming Northern winds—smooth moonlit feathers hug against one bony leg for support—a white beam sweeps the coastal blanket—lighthouse calling a lone love—darkness capes around her tall slender body—urchins clinging, bottle bristles against her feet—sunrise begins to touch her—threads of melon flesh across cradled lids—shades of light lift the dreamy nightmare up—rolling it back into heaven's closet—soft crystal knob pulls shut ... (time!)

Sense-Bound Free Association

Think of object writing as sense-bound free association. As you can see from the prior example "breath sucks back into my throat—stomach ball jellies to my toes like an anchor hoisted over ship" took Cathy from an elevator ride to an ocean storm, no permission asked.

There's no reason to stay loyal to the subject that sets you on your path. Your senses are driving the bus—you can go wherever they take you. The object you begin with might only be your starting point. Full right turns or leaps to other places are not only allowed but encouraged.

If you try to stay focused on the object you start with, you may get bored with object writing after a few weeks. Let your hot morning shower with its rolling steam take you to thick clouds hanging overhead to the taste of rain to stomping through a puddle, splashing water up so it sprays like fireworks, to the boom in your chest and the smell of gunpowder and the taste of cotton candy.

Always stay with your senses, all seven of them. All within ten minutes. Don't worry about story lines or "how it really happened." No rhyme or rhythm. Not even full sentences. No one needs to understand where you are or how you got there. Save more focused writing for when you need to be focused.

SONGWRITING TIPS

Fanning the Flames of Inspiration

....

by Mark Bacino

Whether or not we care to admit it, all songwriters can, from time to time, make use of a little extra kindling to help fuel the flames of inspiration. From new and interesting ways to jumpstart our own creativity to fending off the dreaded effects of writer's block, here are some songwriting tips and ideas I hope you'll try and incorporate into your own work.

DON'T WORRY BE HAPPY

As writers, we all settle into our own individual writing processes—sitting at that piano late at night or strumming that guitar with the TV on mute, and so on. Every process is as unique and personal as the musical results they yield. Yet the one thing these songwriting exercises hold in common is that they all usually center around an instrument. What if, just to change things up, we took that instrument out of the equation?

A CAPPELLA SONGWRITING

Next time you decide to write, if only for experiment's sake, leave the guitar in the case and attempt to create something fresh, solely a cappella. Don't worry, be happy; try to embrace the fun and the freedom that humming a melody or singing nonsensical words can provide.

If you think about it, a cappella composing (arguably the first form of songwriting) makes a lot of sense. When writing with your given instrument(s), you're basically confined by the physical limits of that instrument and your skill level. In reality, our voices and our brains are actually the most powerful/versatile instruments we possess. Think; if someone sang a melody line and asked you to repeat it, you could almost instantaneous sing it right back, even if you don't consider yourself "a singer". Conversely, if you were asked to repeat the same melody using your guitar, I'd bet most of us non-virtuoso types would take more than a beat or two to transcribe said melody. When it's head vs. shred, the noggins trump every time. Why not harness some of that amazing primordial brain power for songwriting?

REVERSE ENGINEERING

Once you've created some a cappella jams, take them back to your respective instruments. See where your scat singing journeys have taken you. Maybe you'll find they've pushed you down some musical roads less traveled; an angular melody your fingers would never have played here or a cool change that feels foreign to your hands there. Hopefully a cappella writing will help you cultivate some interesting and surprising results.

IT'S STILL ROCK AND ROLL TO ME

When I first began writing songs, I pretty much felt new musical ideas could only be discovered with guitar in hand, sitting at the piano or, if lucky, via a melody I might have found myself absentmindedly humming. As time went on, I started to realize that little bits of sonic inspiration were actually everywhere, waiting for me to scoop them up, if I just kept my mind open to the prospect. I found by implementing that small mental adjustment, I could make a sizable increase in the amount of source material available to me as a songwriter.

Now the rhythmic clicking of my car's turn signal was no longer background noise but a makeshift percussion loop I could vocally riff over while waiting at a light. Suddenly the beeping tones generated by that delivery truck as it backed up my street weren't merely part of the urban cacophony but repeating musical figures waiting to be harmonized and expand upon.

Harry Nilsson, the great singer/songwriter of '60s-'70s fame, once confided that his hit song "One," with it's opening repetitive electric piano chord, was inspired by, none other than (and sorry if this reference is lost on the children of smartphones), a landline telephone's busy signal. Pretty cool, right?

As mentioned earlier and illustrated above, song ideas or the seeds of such are indeed all around us, if we choose to acknowledge and absorb them. By simply cleansing ourselves of preconceived notions and redefining what we categorize as legitimate musical inspiration, we allow ourselves access to a veritable treasure trove of new and interesting audible opportunities.

SLAVE TO THE RHYTHM

From it's earliest uses as a primitive means of communication to the party-down, rave-ups of the modern dance club, it seems rhythm is as instinctual and natural to human beings as the pounding of arguably the world's first beat box; our hearts.

Harnessing that innate power of rhythm/beat as catalyst for inspiration can be very useful to us as writers (and a lot of fun, too). Here are a few ideas for using rhythm as a tool to help get your songwriting groove on:

• As band rehearsal winds down for the evening, ask your drummer if he/she can hang a bit longer. Have him lay down a beat, any pattern of his choosing. Without thinking too much about it, let your instrument of choice follow rhythm's lead and play whatever the beat inspires your hands to play. Do that for half an hour and you might just walk away with the bones of a song you probably never would have written strumming a guitar at home alone.

• If you own a Digital Audio Workstation (DAW), fire it up and search within your recording software for its stock, virtual drum machine. Most DAW programs such as Pro Tools and the like include a virtual instrument (VI) that offers the capability of sequencing single-hit drum samples or prerecorded drum loops via MIDI. Using your particular drum VI, set up a simple, repeating pattern that strikes your fancy (if you're unsure how to do this there are plenty of tutorials on the Web), grab your instrument and play along; play anything. Again, as mentioned earlier, don't think too much about it. Let the rhythm and your hands lead you toward a new and unexpected song idea.

• Beat challenged and stuck for a drum pattern to program? Pull up a song in iTunes that features one of your all-time favorite grooves. Try to recreate the basic pattern of said groove with your drum VI, then play your own chord changes over the top to render a jam that's totally unique to you.

• If you're feeling adventurous, scan eBay or Craigslist for an affordable, vintage drum machine. Tons were mass-produced in the '80s and onward so they're usually easy to find. Given the technological limitations of many early models, a lot of these machines have their own wonderfully quirky sounds and personalities. Pick one up if you dare, plug it in and see what kind of inspiration its cheesy muse may provide.

I'VE GOT YOU UNDER MY SKIN

As songwriters, our musical influences play a big part in molding our sensibilities and ultimately our own personal creative output. It's probably safe to say that our sonic wellsprings are the sums of all we've heard throughout our lifetimes; from the cartoon music we listened to as kids, to that favorite album we obsessed over in college and everything else in between. All of it, collectively, makes us who we are—musically speaking—today. Riffing on that premise, here's an exercise to try that will hopefully get under your skin and help strengthen those songwriting muscles.

INFUSED SONGWRITING

Courtesy of Mirriam-Webster, I share this definition: "Infuse: To cause to be permeated with something (as a principle or quality) that alters usually for the better."

1. Pick a favorite band or artist whose music you love, any genre, even if different from the musical style you work in.

2. Cue up an album or playlist of said artist's work, grab a pair of earbuds and listen, without interruption, for 20 minutes. Let the music flow over you and really take it all in. Don't make a sandwich while doing so either; give the tracks your full attention.

3. After listening for 20, kill the music, immediately pick up your instrument of choice, let your fingers do the walking and write something. Anything. Don't censor yourself and, for now, don't worry about being derivative. Explore what that short blast of concentrated inspiration has done to stoke your creative furnace.

Now of course, your mileage may vary. Maybe after a half hour of woodshedding you'll discover you've just rewritten, in part, one of the tunes you soaked up during your listening session. That said, perhaps, conversely, you'll find you've stumbled upon something interesting and fresh; a unique melody inspired by the music you love, yet a melody that's clearly and undeniably your own.

LET'S WORK

In my musical travels, I've found there to be generally two types of songwriters; those who create solely when inspiration calls and those who write via a structured work schedule. If, like me, you fall into the former, waiting-for-that-lightning-to-strike category of writers, this section is for you.

In the spirit of expanding our creative horizons, what if we temporarily set aside our ethereal, inspired ways and wandered over to the dark side? What if we decided, if only for the sake of experimentation, to approach our writing with more of a workmanlike ethic, reported for the (gasp) job and gave this structured, disciplined songwriting thing a try?

If you're up for the gig, here are some ideas to help us slackers get down to business:

- Save the date. Even if it goes against every fiber of your creative being, pencil in writing sessions for specific days and times. Afterward, adamantly stick to the schedule. Accept that a few of your sessions will most likely begin with a silent instrument and a blank piece of paper.

- Assignment desk. Try giving yourself a specific songwriting assignment and see if you can pull it off; compose a tune in 3/4 time or write a Dylan-esque story song that carries a narrative, etc.

- Take it to the limit. Set some limitations for yourself and your writing, and exercise your creative powers within the confines of that framework. Indie-singer/songwriter, WFMU DJ, and friend Michael Shelley once told me he challenged himself to write an entire song utilizing only two chords. The result? His catchy, "Listening to the Band," a tune that proves limitations can sometimes, surprisingly, help rather than hinder the creative process.

Even if, ultimately, the exercises above do very little aside from reaffirming your aversion to structured writing methods at the moment, maybe one or two will be worth revisiting down the road the next time that flighty muse of yours decides to blow off work for a couple of weeks.

STOP! IN THE NAME OF LOVE…AND DO THE LAUNDRY

"A writer writes" as the old saying goes, but I'm here, right now, to tell you to stop. Odd thing to say, I know, since this is a songwriting article but I mean it.

If you're one of many disciplined writers who keeps to a daily schedule, great, hold to it but if you find yourself hitting a wall, rather than trying to muscle through for schedule's sake, forget it. Go do the laundry.

Now you may ask, why the laundry? It kind of smells bad. Can I do my bills instead? The answer is no. Your bills will make you think too much. Never underestimate the head-cleansing power of performing mundane household tasks, such as doing the wash. After you've fluffed and folded, go back to the piano and see if that wall you hit earlier got whisked away in the spin cycle.

GO TO BED

Just as you should never underestimate the mind-clearing power of performing menial tasks, never dismiss the power of the nap.

When little kids get cranky what do they do? They take a nap. When they wake, they're usually refreshed, happy, and raring to go knock down that table lamp. As adults we tend to devalue the concept of sleep. Next time your writing session comes to an impasse, stop and lie down for 15 minutes. Even if you're too wired to drift off, closing your eyes and lying in silence for a few might just be enough to clear the cobwebs and get you back to knocking down that creative barricade (table lamp optional).

So, of course, I don't really want you to stop writing—quite the opposite actually—but I do hope you'll incorporate the above rejuvenation techniques into your writing process and see if they help stop "the block". Hopefully they'll make a positive difference in the quality of your output as well.

Mark Bacino is a singer-songwriter based in New York City with three album releases to his credit as an artist. When not crafting his own melodic brand of retro-pop, Mark can be found producing fellow artists or composing for television/advertising via his Queens English Recording Co. Mark is also a contributing writer for *Guitar World* as well as the founder-curator of intro.verse.chorus, a website dedicated to exploring the art of songwriting. Visit him at www.markbacino.com

THE COLLABORATIVE JOY OF DIY

Using Kickstarter, Taking Risks, and Saying "Yes."

....

by James Duncan

We live in a DIY world. Writers are publishing books through print-on-demand and e-Book platforms; painters are hosting shows in their own rented spaces; and even comedians and actors are posting viral webisodes and short films online, making names for themselves in ways unimagined by gatekeepers a generation ago.

Musicians are no different. Through constant networking, a persistent focus on craft, and the desire to swap an immediate financial windfall for quantifiable happiness, musicians now have the ability to carve out a piece of the pie for themselves, and better yet, to plan their own futures.

That isn't to say DIY ventures are a guaranteed success. The major record companies are still kingmakers—for good or ill—but the things they provide can now be found elsewhere in varying degrees. Some savvy social networking on Twitter and Facebook can provide marketing and PR; utilizing sources such as CD Baby and iTunes takes care of distribution; and financial backing? The major record companies no longer have an iron grip on the purse strings. It has never been easier for bands and songwriters to raise money through services like Kickstarter, and thus, it has never been a better time for up-and-coming artists to find their own path.

Kendra McKinley, a young singer-songwriter based in California, is one such DIY artist making strides into the music business. To paraphrase Frank Sinatra's classic line, she's doing it her way, and like all dedicated artists striving for creative fulfillment, it starts with the music.

"Music has always been an integral part of my life," McKinley says. "I was introduced to music at a very early age and became infatuated with the music of the 1960s and 1970s—The Beatles, The Beach Boys, Joni Mitchell, etc. But it wasn't until age 9 that I received my first guitar. My older brother A.J. [of the band Battlehooch] gave me my first lessons, teaching me basic open chord shapes and how to use them to play my favorite songs."

Like many young artists, McKinley's early attempts at music existed solely in her bedroom, but she experienced a sea change in her attitude when she brought her talents before an audience of her peers. "I was very shy about performing in front of people, but I played the song 'Tiger Mountain Peasant Song' by Robin Pecknold of the band Fleet Foxes in a high school play, and that experience was a game changer for me. At that point, I decided to pursue music in college. "

It was around that time that McKinley began experimenting with her own songs. "From the beginning, I'd create songs using some strange chord voicing that I'd find (or make up) on the guitar. By discovering different chord shapes without necessarily being aware of what chords were ensured the most organic songwriting process." This method steered McKinley towards experimenting with alternate tunings. "Joni Mitchell and Nick Drake, two of my biggest influences, are known for their alternate guitar tunings," she adds. "I was able to find the sounds that fit the exact sentiment I was attempting to express rather than using whatever musical devices or vocabulary I had been exposed to."

McKinley's process evolved over time, and she began recording herself improvising to capture any spontaneous moment of creation worth building upon later. "I'll often record the improvisation and then wait until the next day to listen to it. I've found that approaching that recording with fresh ears makes it really clear as to how I want to expand the idea." And regardless of whether or not the lyrics comes naturally or after a long period of tinkering, McKinley says she has to "be very, very clear about what the song is about as I work on it. If that clarity is there, then the song will eventually write itself."

Armed with a growing songbook and a sense of confidence in her music, McKinley continued to perform in local venues and at open mics, and she never said no to an opportunity to meet other musicians and professionals. This is how she fell into the working with the North Pacific Company, a local collective of musicians in Santa Cruz who share a passion for folk music. It was during her first week of college when she overheard them jamming, and she summoned the courage to ask to join in. From that moment on, a natural sense of collaboration took hold.

As McKinley explains, "I had never even considered launching an album myself using Kickstarter until my friend Steven Stubblefield (a member of the North Pacific Company) suggested it. His band, North Pacific String Band, had used Kickstarter to fund their album Steak and Eggs a few months earlier. I really lucked out having a friend that could share his campaign experiences." Other members of the collective knew someone with access to a studio, and another member had a passion for mixing, and everything McKinley needed to create an album began to fall into place—simply by saying 'yes' to new opportunities to network, jam, and collaborate.

"I was fortunate enough to have found a large network of support, but there was no way I'd be able to fund the project myself without Kickstarter," McKinley says. Through Kickstarter, she was able to raise over $2,600 in a matter of weeks. Some of the prizes she included in the Kickstarter campaign were signed copies of the album, customized handmade lyric songbooks, an offer to record a donator's favorite song just for them, and an opportunity to have McKinley perform at a private concert. "The fact that there is an outlet for people of all disciplines to bring their wonderful projects to life is absolutely incredible. There are so many meaningful projects that would have otherwise gone uncreated."

But recording an album can be an entirely more daunting prospect, even after the money has been raised. "I was very unaware of how much went into making an album," she says. "One of the other fellows at North Pacific Company, Alex Bice, is an aspiring audio engineer with a passion for analog recording. Because he owned a tape machine and was seeking to gain more recording experience, we were able to utilize his talents while keeping the entire project extremely affordable."

CROWD FUNDING

Kickstarter is a form of "crowd funding," in which an artist posts about an impending project that hinges on the financial support of the wider community. Artists offer special prizes and incentives at specific donation amounts, enticing fans to donate money for unique, one-of-a-kind rewards. The perks for both artist and audience are compelling, but there are risks, too. Not meeting fundraising goals can be embarrassing, and might affect future projects. Those donating must be savvy enough to spot a scam and should only donate to projects that they have vetted through online research.

While Kickstarter has become the most notable source for crowd funding (with some projects raising millions of dollars), there are many others sites that cater specifically to funding creative projects, including Indiegogo, ArtistShare, and PledgeMusic—a direct-to-fan platform that has helped fund projects by the likes of The Lumineers, The Damnwells, Rhett Miller, and Matthew Mayfield.

McKinley tried to keep a hand in as much of the process as possible. "The fact that I was able to be there to observe and voice my thoughts made the entire experience so much more educational. Also, being able to record to tape was a gift in itself; the sound was so much richer and more reminiscent of all of my favorite."

To save money, they rented a space on the University of California, Santa Cruz campus for three days. "We worked each day from ten to five in the afternoon, so we had a total of about 21 hours to lock down all of the recordings," McKinley explains. "With this in mind, I chose eight of the songs that I had been performing regularly for the last few months; some on acoustic guitar, others making vocal arrangements with my looping pedal. It was definitely intense nailing down that many songs considering the amount of time we had, but we did it."

The album, *Chestnut Street*, was released in December 2012. McKinley was able to sell a number of CDs at a handful of performances, but she found that selling her album over the Internet has been more successful. "Outlets like Bandcamp.com, CD Baby, and iTunes have been very effective," she says. Each offered a way for her fans to purchase her music after hearing it online or after watching a Vimeo.com music video of her first single "Ivory Town" (with filmmaker Marina Fini).

Every opportunity to network with local professionals helped her create buzz for her work, but she understands that it's all about the slow, gradual process toward building something bigger. "I'd definitely encourage others to begin with the DIY route," she says. "I think it is beneficial for everyone to be open to collaboration and to gain as much experience as possible for future endeavors. Connecting with the North Pacific Company was a fantastic jumping off point for me. Making art, music, whatever, is fun to do collectively. That needs to be remembered and celebrated. But when it comes to the business aspect, being as clear as possible with your personal creative vision is extremely important. So long as you are honest with your work, others will catch on and want to work with you."

For more information about Kendra McKinley's story, her music, and her album *Chestnut Street*, visit her website at www.kendramckinley.com.

....

James Duncan is a content editor for the Writer's Digest Writing Community, editing such titles as *You've Got a Book in You*, *The Kick-Ass Writer*, *Writing Fantasy & Science Fiction*, and *Write Your Novel in a Month*. He is also a contributor to the Writer's Digest blog, "There Are No Rules." He is the founding editor of *Hobo Camp Review*: Poetry & Prose from the Road, a literary magazine celebrating the traveling word. He released his debut collection of short fiction, *The Cards We Keep*, in 2013, and his seventh collection of poetry, *The Darkest Bomb of All*, is due out from Dog On a Chain Press. For more, visit www.jameshduncan.blogspot.com.

....

MARKET YOUR WORK LIKE A PR PRO

Tips for the Independent Musician

....

by Jennifer Billock

///

Independent online music promotion is no small undertaking. Most of the websites dedicated to promotions sound great but in the long run they never get an artist anywhere. The good news? Some of them can. And with the right website choices and determination in your arsenal, your music can go far.

SELF-PROMOTION

"It's very difficult to sell music these days, period," says Jimmy Ether, musician and chief engineer at Jimmy Ether Mastering and Recording. "No service, online or off, is going to sell your music simply by your use of them. You have to do all the hard work of building a following and exciting your base of listeners. What services can do is provide you a simple, inexpensive and usable place to point your following for various purposes."

Bandcamp.com is the best place to start. It's free for an artist to create a profile, and flexible graphics allow musicians to practically mirror their website. Bandcamp will also provide you with a digital storefront to sell your music. And once you've uploaded your album, coded players make it easy to share your songs on many social networking sites. **NoiseTrade.com** works on the same principles as Bandcamp, and the two of them together can prove invaluable for marketing and discovery.

"I've gained quite a lot of new fans through these sites," says Milwaukee-based musician Kyle Gray Young. "I've found that there are a lot of people out there who routinely look for new indie artists on these sites and will download any new albums that spark their interest."

Once you've got your band set up with a profile, hit the marketing angle. Starting a **Facebook** fan page is PR 101 nowadays, and it is vital for promoting yourself with interactive status updates and **YouTube** videos.

"Any musician that doesn't have a YouTube channel is not promoting themselves properly," says Los Angeles-based musician Circe Link. "Even if they don't have video content, they could do a lyric video, which is a static image with lyrics scrolling by on the screen. [YouTube is] the number one music discovery source that I know of today. If you're not taking the time to develop a YouTube presence, then you're missing a huge part of marketing."

A good website and newsletter are also essential tools for developing and promoting your music and brand. **WordPress.com**, although typically known as a blogging platform, offers comprehensive website hosting services complete with customizable design templates and built-in site traffic analytics, which detail user information down to gender and location for each page view. You can use that information to tailor your newsletter to a particular audience.

MailChimp.com allows users to customize email campaigns with photo, video, and text integration while still maintaining a streamlined image that matches your website brand. Email newsletters come out looking professional and high quality.

"When you're sending something out, I think the difference between someone's materials looking amateur and someone's materials looking professional is the amount of clutter and the color selection," Link says. "You can tell when someone sends you something with a bunch of yellow highlighting all over it that you're going to throw it away because it looks like spam."

Email campaigns through MailChimp can be separated into profiles as well, so fans at a gig that sign up for your newsletter can receive a custom mailing specific to their location—or any other profile you'd like to target.

ALBUM PROMOTION

Still, just getting your band name out there isn't enough. People need to hear your music and should have every opportunity to listen. Luckily, the days of hawking CDs on the sidewalk are over. It's easier than ever to distribute your album to the vast public—and you don't even have to take the reins yourself.

Link, Young, and Ether all use **CDBaby** and **Tunecore** to handle digital distribution of their music. The services send songs on your behalf to iTunes, Amazon, Spotify, and many other major online retailers. CDBaby also provides distribution services for physical CDs when necessary—but try to avoid having CDs made unless it's absolutely critical. Ether uses the website **Kunaki.com** to produce quality CD short runs, about 10 discs at a time, and the company will ship the CDs to CDBaby or Amazon so you don't have to.

"CD sales are awful these days," Ether says. "Unless you are on a national tour opening for a well-known band, do not under any circumstances do large-run traditional compact disc replication. They will end up in a closet."

APP-LY YOURSELF

Opportunities to further your career as a musician flood the digital marketplace. Here are the top five apps to simplify recording, distributing, and selling your music.

GarageBand—This is the ultimate one-stop app for any musician, aspiring or experienced. Create music with any of the included instruments, or plug your own into the device and record what you play. Get together with your band and have a jam session on multiple devices. Then use the eight-track recording studio to perfect your music. Upload it to iTunes, email the file, or even make your own ringtone. Platform: Apple.

iMovie—The movie making tools in iMovie allow you to record and design complex music videos and upload them for your Facebook and YouTube followers. And you can record with anyone, anywhere. Device sharing allows long-distance virtual collaborations with musicians across the world. Platform: Apple.

Propellerhead Figure—Create digital music tracks with a synth and a drum machine. Then upload right to your SoundCloud page from the app. Platform: Apple.

MailChimp—Forget easy-to-lose email sign-up sheets and add fans to your mailing list right from your gigs with the MailChimp app. You can also check your campaign stats and demographics. Platform: Android, Apple.

WordPress—Manage your website from anywhere with the companion app to the popular blogging and website platform. Add videos, add photos, and make updates to your site or your blog, all from your phone. Platform: Android, Apple.

BUYER BEWARE

Today's digital world can certainly provide an exhausting amount of opportunities for musicians to promote their craft, but with the good comes the bad. The amount of scams has skyrocketed past the legitimate sites as people scramble to capitalize on the music industry's size and presence. Websites and companies asking for money up front should generally be avoided. Always be sure to thoroughly research every website before signing up—although that still may not disclose hidden costs.

For example, Young once spent four hours investigating a supposedly free new music promotion and film placement company that followed him on Twitter, and he even went through the extensive application process, only to get smacked with a $400 membership fee on the final page. The company not only established itself as a liar—every webpage said the service was free—but also jeopardized its credibility.

"Back in the day, someone who demanded money in exchange for listening to your music was considered a shark," Young says. "These days, it seems to be an almost legitimate business. Be cautious of any sites that promise you success for a fee. There's no such thing as guaranteed success. No amount of money you can spend will make anything certain in this business."

Thinking of your music career as a business will go a long way in protecting you from money-pit sites and scams. Protect your money and keep track of your income and expenses. Legitimate services for musicians will work on sales and licensing commissions. If a service costs more than you expect to make from using it, look elsewhere.

"Musicians should build their career just as someone would build a small niche business," Ether says. "Always ask yourself what you realistically have to gain and lose from any service with a focus on the financial outcome. If the sales income doesn't at least balance the cost, there is probably a better place you could focus that money."

Jennifer Billock is a writer, editor, and layout designer based in the Chicago/Milwaukee area. Her work has appeared in publications including *World Travel Buzz, Tea Magazine, Taste of Home Magazine, Broughton Quarterly, Healthy Cooking Magazine, The Ambler,* and *The Real Chicago Magazine.* Her book, *Images of America: Keweenaw County* will be released in March 2014.

THE ART OF GETTING NOTICED

How To Use Electronic Press Kits and One Sheets

by Charlene Oldham

To quote writer Shel Silverstein, every artist dreams of having their "picture on the cover of the *Rolling Stone*," but most novice musicians would settle for seeing their photo featured on the pages of their city's free weekly. Despite what most musicians might think, getting press coverage and the radio airplay and higher-profile gigs that come with it is indeed possible when artists are willing to put in the time, effort, and research it takes to produce a polished electronic press kit (EPK) and one sheet that effectively promotes their latest work. And the plethora of free and low-cost tools available make publicizing projects easier than ever for musicians without a lot of money to spend.

That doesn't mean musicians can throw together an electronic press kit or send out a hastily written one sheet and expect interview requests to come rolling in overnight. The process starts with thorough research into what works—and what doesn't—when it comes to packaging promotional material for specific markets.

Combing the Internet for advice and examples of press material from admired artists can help musicians avoid common pitfalls and identify the best online tools for their band. While it's tempting to start a Facebook page and Twitter account, launch a Wordpress blog and design your own website using tools like Joomla all at once, it's important to decide first how much time and effort band members are willing to devote to online promotion, and investigate and identify the best options before jumping in.

"Do your research. Don't start a personal profile on Facebook named after your band," says Charlie Hogland, a St. Louis web developer and musician who has designed online promotional material for his band, 8UZ, and others. "Do an artist page instead. I'm still learning more [things like this] every day because things are constantly changing."

Indeed, manila envelopes and jewel cases were once the standard for sending press kits and promotional discs. Those made way for MySpace and other outlets, including Bandcamp and ReVerbNation. All are useful, but one thing that hasn't changed is the need for a primary website that serves as a hub for all a musician's media outreach. By including an electronic press kit on your own website, you also make your website a one-stop shop for reporters, talent buyers and radio station music managers who may all be looking for different information.

When they use their own website, artists have flexibility to hook readers with a short biography that links to enticing quotes from published reviews and full write-ups elsewhere online. They can also include songs, videos, tour dates, links to their other social media sites, or anything else they want since the main site is accessible to everyone from fans to record label executives who type their band name into a search engine.

"It's nice to be on Twitter, Facebook, and Wordpress, but I think having your own website and own domain name is essential," says Hogland. "That's your professional display."

Given that, it's critical musicians' sites and the press materials are professional and free of grammatical errors, punctuation mistakes and copyright infringement concerns that may land them in legal trouble or make them look like amateurs to business contacts interested in offering them a gig, songwriting opportunity or record label contract. While there are ways to balance professionalism with personality, writing a one sheet or press release as if it were a text message to a friend isn't one of them.

"Just make sure everything is clean and professional," says Jake Snyder, venue manager and talent buyer at The Demo in St. Louis. "I don't mind fun at all, but nothing makes bands look less credible that poor spelling, grammar, or punctuation."

The same goes for poorly designed album covers, obviously hand-drawn logos or websites that feature free clip art better suited to a high school yearbook than a professional online calling card. As music director for 88.1 KDHX in St. Louis, Nick Acquisto receives 100 or more CDs each week from artists hoping to get airplay on the community radio station. Some of those CDs come with one sheets and other promotional material, while others arrive without even a track listing. And while a disc might be a perfect fit for one or more of the station's eclectic mix of shows, it's hard to sift through CDs that offer few clues to the music etched on them.

"I think just spending some money to have an artist do your album artwork can go a long way to get the attention of a music director," says Acquisto. "Not to mention giving a good vibe about what the album is going to sound like."

Things to include in a well-designed one sheet:

- a track listings that note any FCC violations that could get a DJ in trouble

- a picture of the eye-catching album cover

- a photo that features musicians with their instruments,

- a brief biography that indicates their artistic influences

- song suggestions that give DJs an idea of the tracks the band likes best

Creating those one sheets and EPKs can be economical if musicians find fans with video, copyediting, or graphic design skills who are willing to trade tickets and T-shirts for professional-looking promotional materials. There are also sites like Virb.com that offer attractive, ready-made themes that let people build and customize their own websites for free or for small monthly fees, says designer Katie Canada.

"I always believe that good design does matter. It makes you look professional," says Canada, partner and creative director for Departika, a Springfield, Mo., firm that specializes in web development and digital marketing. "But you can get a long way without paying for stuff."

Musicians looking to save money need to spend time, though. Putting together professional press materials and distributing them without help from a full-time publicist requires advance planning and a willingness to do legwork months before a planned tour or album release party. Musicians hoping to get good reviews to include in press kits should send out promotional copies of their album as soon as they are ready. And artists looking to earn press coverage for an album release or tour should start sending materials months in advance since some publications have surprisingly early deadlines or might require musicians to enter information about their own gigs using an online calendar listing.

"Set aside a few hours a week. It's kind of like working out. You can't just work out once a year and expect any results," says Canada. At the same time, she insists that promotions shouldn't take precedence over the product. "You can't just have fancy artwork. You have to have the practice and the gigs under your belt."

QUICK TIPS ON ONE SHEETS AND EPKS

Start a one sheet by answering the five W's and one H—who, what, when, where, why, and how (or how much). "The thing to remember is a one sheet is a one sheet—and it's usually just one side of one sheet," says publicist Cash Edwards, who often uses the other side for a more-detailed press release. "So that one sheet has to be short and sweet and have all the information."

Include both vertical and horizontal photos (at least 300 dots per inch, but no larger than 2 megabytes) in your EPK to make layout easier for newspaper designers working on deadline.

Keep the biography very brief and pull the best quotes from reviews and other press coverage. Use hyperlinks to jump to a more-detailed bio and full versions of previous press coverage. "People aren't really interested in the background details until you've caught their attention," says Edwards.

Ask venue managers for advice on creating a local media list before a show and send press kits to reporters and DJs in the area. Most managers are happy to share their contacts. "The worse they can do is say no, but I don't know why they would do that," says Jake Snyder, of The Demo in St. Louis. "It's just nice to see when bands are willing to do some work."

Include current contact information and quotes from the band in any press releases that feature a new project. Interviews are always preferable, but you include compelling quotes could encourage time-pressed reporters to write about an album or event even if they can't reach the musician by phone.

Update your website and press materials as often as you can to reflect recent news and upcoming events. "You've got to be able to manage it," says musician and web developer Charlie Hogland. "When you can't keep up—that's when you need a professional."

Avoid sending press materials or booking requests in blanket emails that list hundreds of addresses. "Take the time to mask it, or actually do the homework to see who the buyer is for that room," says Snyder.

And most of all, make sure you are promoting a quality product. "I never work with an artist I haven't seen," says Edwards. "There's only one thing that really counts, and it's the music."

Charlene Oldham is a Saint Louis–based freelance writer and professor of journalism and business communications at Lindenwood University. She blogs about writing and life at www.charleneoldham.com.

THE LUMINEERS

Finding a Balance

....

by Marielle Murphy

Performing what they call "rustic, heart-on-the-sleeve music," The Lumineers have worked their way from humble beginnings in small clubs in New York and Denver to the forefront of the roots-rock revival. Their debut self-titled album has been certified gold in the US, UK, Australia, and Canada, and platinum in Ireland. Founded by Wesley Keith Schultz and Jeremiah Caleb Fraites in 2005, with Neyla Pekarek, Stelth Ulvang, and Ben Wahamaki joining them along the way, The Lumineers have energized a growing fanbase with their infectious and heartfelt music.

Vocalist and guitarist Wesley Schultz recently agreed to take time from the band's busy schedule to answer some questions from *Songwriter's Market*.

The biography on your website says you and Jeremiah started writing together in the spring of 2005. How did you decide to collaborate? What was your writing process together?

We were brought together accidentally by a mutual friend that I was playing music with. This mutual friend connected us, against both of our wills at the time for a casual musical meeting. It took a while to get going and trust each other, but we ended up being able to share musical ideas very easily and work on music together incessantly. The writing process is basically this: I write the lyrics. Jer and I work on everything else (melody, chord progression, song structure, other parts) together. We always begin small, as if we were going to present it that week at an open mic—one guitar, one voice, and basic percussive elements like stomps and claps.

Do you enjoy co-writing or do you prefer to write songs alone?

It's a bit of a hybrid—most of the crux of what we do, we do alone. But then the collaborative efforts lie in the arrangements—the demolition and construction of these songs over and over until a lot of the fat is gone.

In your opinion, what makes a good co-writer?

A good co-writer, for me, is someone who is willing to go down whatever road the person with the vision for the song wishes to go down, full steam ahead. Regardless of the outcome, a good co-writer trusts the process. After all, it takes a lot of wrong turns and circles for us to get where we end up. Another important element is the ability to never be nostalgic about an idea, never be overly attracted to new ideas (because new ones always sound better and less tired), and never become attached to an idea simply because it took a lot of time to work out.

What comes first: the words or the music?

The music. The melody. It's musical hangman.

How often is a personal experience involved in your songwriting?

It's usually based on something imagined or lived, or both. Something is not believable, or even entertaining or engaging, if it doesn't contain within it some beautiful contradictions. The worst thing you can do as a writer is create a caricature.

Do you know a "hit" song when you write it? "Ho Hey" has been huge. Did you know it would be so big?

Not at all! We knew it worked well live. But I also figured, because live and on record are such different animals, that it would annoy the listener and would fail miserably with all those shouts in it.

How important is the rewriting process and how long does it usually take?

That's what we do best. So for us, it's an integral part of it all. It varies, as to how long it takes. "Morning Song" took the longest—about 3 and a half years.

What is more important in songwriting: being artistic or being accessible?

I heard a quote that I liked recently—it went something like, "Just because people don't get it, doesn't mean it's artistic." I think you need some sugar with the medicine. I used to place all my efforts on the lyrics, and none on the music and melody. Once I found more of a balance, I noticed that a good melody provided a loudspeaker for what were, otherwise, unheard lyrics. So a good hook can provide a writer with an important element—people's undivided attention.

How do you deal with the balancing act between being successful and avoiding becoming too "commercial" or "trendy"?

I'd say a lot of that work, of dealing with it somehow, is about the years prior to it happening. I spent 8 or 10 years failing at something and figuring out who I was (which I'm still learning, and will probably never stop). It's important to decide who you are, and not let the accolades or the criticism define you (in your own head). But let's not forget, there are people who play music their whole lives and never get an ounce of recognition and continue to work side jobs to make it happen. We have a lot to be thankful for.

What made you decide to move from NYC to Denver?

Money! It made no sense to live in a city where you could never possibly make enough to go out and do what you need to do on early tours, lose money every time, and because of the cost of living, you could never have enough free time after the side jobs were done, to work on your craft. If you've got parents and they're paying your rent, I get how you afford it. I didn't have that. And I'm lucky for that. I think.

Can you explain the process of getting signed, recording an album, touring, etc. Basically what got you from playing at the Meadowlark to touring all over the world?

That is far too long an answer. [Laughs]. I will sum it up like this—the DIY mentality has always been a part of this band—I wrote a song 7 years ago, and the line was "You're waiting and waiting for your break. You're waiting and waiting, there's your first mistake." What got us playing the Meadowlark is luck and hard work, and doing it ourselves until we basically outgrew our resources. People, i.e., management and labels, recognized that and invested in us.

Considering your future not just as performers, but also just as songwriters, what are some goals you have?

I hope to understand how to write on the road in a more consistent way. Touring, promotions, and a lack of privacy has changed my normal regimen—I'm hoping to learn how to adjust and write on the road.

What is the best piece of advice you've ever received?

The best musicians know when to shut up (musically speaking).

What advice do you have for songwriters trying to make it in the music business?

There's no success like failure, and that failure's no success at all.

Marielle Murphy is a travel and fashion writer who has written for *Cincinnati Magazine, AlliQDesign,* and the fashion social network, StyledOn.com.

PERFORMANCE RIGHTS ORGANIZATIONS

Taking the Mystery Out of PROs

....

by Mark Bacino

///

One sometimes overlooked subject for songwriters and performers is performance rights organizations (PROs), and I'd like to briefly explain what they do and why they're important to us as songwriters.

(I realize this topic might be a bit old hat for the seasoned songwriters among us but stick around fogies, there's something for you at article's end.)

PROS: THE WHAT AND WHY

Basically, PROs collect monies/royalties due songwriters and publishers earned from the "public performance" of a writer's music. If one of your tunes is played (live or recorded) on radio, or Internet, or used in a TV show or even performed in a live venue, as a writer you're entitled to a royalty for that use. It's the job of the PRO that you're personally affiliated with to discover that performance, collect the royalty on your behalf and pass it on to you the writer and your publisher if you have one. Most new writers don't have publishers so in that case the writer is considered the publisher as well and all royalties earned are paid to the songwriter in total.

Now, if you're a songwriter starting out and your music has yet to be played on radio, TV, etc., you don't really need to affiliate yourself with a PRO just yet, but it couldn't hurt. With most, sign-up is free (some charge a nominal fee) and they usually offer tons of resources for writers. And hey, why not be ready when the next Jersey Shore spin-off wants to use one of your tunes behind that pivotal bar fight scene?

WHICH ONE?

Deciding which PRO to affiliate yourself with is usually (but not exclusively) dependent upon where you live. Almost every country has at least one PRO. Some have several. In the United States there's ASCAP, BMI, and SESAC. In Canada there's SOCAN; in Japan there's JASRAC and so on. Google "Performance Rights Organizations" and you'll find more resources readily available.

Ultimately, whatever PRO you decide to join is up to you. They all basically do the same thing but are different in what they offer, their approach, etc. Best to do a little research to see what PRO best fits your needs as a writer before you leap.

Now, as promised, here's one for all you experienced writers who've stuck it out thus far: Did you know in addition to whatever PRO you're already affiliated with, there's a relatively new, additional one (in the United States) with which you should register as well? It's called SoundExchange, and what it does is collect royalties on behalf of sound recording copyright owners and artists for non-interactive digital transmissions, like internet and satellite radio. So if you're a writer/recording artist, seasoned or beginner, remember to check out SoundExchange.

I hope this article helps in demystifying PROs and why, as songwriters, we need them. And new writers, don't forget to copyright your tunes too!

Mark Bacino is a singer-songwriter based in New York City with three album releases to his credit as an artist. When not crafting his own melodic brand of retro-pop, Mark can be found producing fellow artists or composing for television/advertising via his Queens English Recording Co. Mark is also a contributing writer for *Guitar World* as well as the founder-curator of intro.verse.chorus, a website dedicated to exploring the art of songwriting. For more, visit www.markbacino.com

SONGWRITING GRANTS

Funding Your Way to Success

....

by David McPherson

//

Northern Ireland is a very strange place for musicians and songwriters alike. As Christmas bids goodbye and the New Year's bills roll in, every musician asks themselves the same question: "How will I get the job done?"

Mike Donaghy – whom I met at the 2013 Folk Alliance International conference (FAI) in Toronto – shared that sentiment with me. The songwriter from Northern Ireland was attending FAI with the goal of turning more people on to his music and landing more jobs at North American folk festivals and clubs.

"With Northern Ireland being such a small country, the easiest way for us musicians to have an outlet is to travel to mainland UK, Europe, or North America," Donaghy explains. "Unfortunately, no matter where we wish to head, money is the key."

Looking to find the necessary dough to finance his travel, Donaghy's search for help eventually took him to various UK grants organizations.

"As a songwriter, from a small town on the east coast of Ireland, I was determined to do everything I could to get my music out there," he comments. "I had a back catalog of songs, a band that was also eager to succeed, and a plan that did not sit well with my bank balance."

Donaghy's plan was to travel to the countries and towns where his music was most appreciated and where he sold the most records. First, he assembled a team that included a promoter, a publicist and a manager to help him achieve these goals. Second, he calculated how much money he would need. Finally, he searched for the most important piece of the plan: funding.

"We are lucky in Northern Ireland to have a very involved Arts Council," the songwriter reveals. "The Arts Council is the lead development agency for the arts in Northern Ireland.

They are the main support for artists and arts organizations, offering a broad range of funding opportunities through our Exchequer and National Lottery funds."

While promoting his first album, *I Wish You Well*, Donaghy applied for an Arts Council SIAP Travel Fund to pay for his expenses.

"Our whole promotion campaign was hanging on which way the funding application went," he recalls. "So I approached a few artists who had successful applications and asked them for advice."

When filling out a funding application, the main question is always: What is the funding for? "I've heard many stories of artists filling in grant applications assuming it is about how good you are, the better you are the more chance you have of funding, but this is not the case," Donaghy explains. "You need to be clear about exactly what the grant is for. Anyone willing to give you money needs to know what it is being used for, no matter how good you are."

A CANADIAN PERSPECTIVE

While the life of a touring musician and/or songwriter in Canada is no less rigorous than it is for artists in other countries, musicians who live above the 49th parallel are lucky to have many grants – large and small – available.

From $100 touring grants to larger handouts to help songwriters finance a record or make a video, the options are plentiful. But in Canada, just like overseas, Donaghy's sage advice on planning ahead still applies. And for Canadians, the time to start thinking about applying for grants is the month T.S. Eliot once penned "the cruellest month."

"If you are going to apply for a project, April is a good time because everyone has a lot of money," says Catharine Bird, a past executive director of the Songwriters Association of Canada, and owner of Catbird.ca – a home-based business that helps artists write grants. "If you leave your application to the end of the year, some of the programs, especially the arts councils, have run low on money, making the competition greater."

Bird equates the grant-writing process to preparing an annual business plan. Musicians, she says, need to think long-term, and plan accordingly. Write a year's calendar of all the grants for every organization (Bird offers a great link on her website), and seek help from a professional grant writer, if you can afford it.

"One of the mistakes artists make is they think short-term," Bird comments. "If the deadline is tomorrow, they think, 'what can I throw together to make it happen?' as compared to thinking about the full project from the beginning to the end. When April comes around, think about what you want to do for the next year. Know the deadlines and the parameters, so you can apply early."

Bird's services include walking the artist though the whole process of writing a grant: from preparing the materials to advising, writing, and editing the finished application. "We often advise on everything from accounting to choosing a studio, licensing and small business issues just because we've amassed a lot of experience and knowledge from our years in the music business."

If you cannot afford to pay a professional grant writer such as Bird, turn to your own community of songwriters to mentor you and look over your application. Often, once you get to know your community, the sky's the limit as far as the amount of help people are willing to offer.

Before applying for any grant, keep in mind that artists need to know what grants are appropriate for their particular genre and whether they are even eligible. In Canada, if you are in the pop or rock genre, then FACTOR is the place to go, while singer-songwriters, folk, jazz, or blues artists, should apply for grants from Canada Council or the provincial arts organizations. FACTOR gets some money from the department of Canadian Heritage and some money from the actual radio stations to fund more music that radio can play. If your stuff is going to be on the radio, then FACTOR is the one.

GET OUT AND PLAY: GROUNDBREAKER GRANT PROGRAM

One hundred dollars goes a long way—especially if you're a Canadian artist toiling the ever-tough musical road, trying to eke out a living.

That's the objective of the Groundbreaker Grant Program, which turned two in 2013. Run by the Canadian Independent Recording Artists' Association (CIRAA), these micro-grants provide small sums of money to musicians without requiring a lengthy application process.

"Who can't use another $100 to pay for the band's meals, gas, or equipment rentals," says Gaby Harvey, CIRAA Member Services. "There are so many large grants out there, which are great, but to receive a large grant is time-consuming for artists to apply for and few people receive them."

CIRAA created the Groundbreaker Grant to make it easy for up-and-coming artists to get extra funding. "We want them to play shows," Harvey explains. "One of the most important things an artist can do is to build his audience by doing live shows; we like to encourage that."

THE UNITED STATES: BIG COUNTRY, FEWER GRANTS, BUT THERE'S STILL HELP IF YOU LOOK HARD

Many of the music industry veterans from the United States that I interviewed for this article lamented the fact that the funds available for songwriters these days are not plentiful.

That said, ARTINFO (www.artiinfo.com) offers a good overview of some of the top artist grants available to U.S.-based musicians in these fiscally challenging times. The website stresses there are tiers to all fellowships and grants, and not all are created equal. And, when it comes to grant money attainable by open application, "the pool is wide but the eligibility requirements also vary greatly." The list covers all of "the arts," but it does reference some opportunities specific to musicians.

For example, musicians might be eligible for one of the annual fellowships awarded by The New York Foundation for the Arts. First launched in 1985, NYFA's Artist Fellowship Program has provided more than $27 million in unrestricted cash grants to artists in 15 disciplines at critical stages in their careers. To be eligible for a NYFA Fellowship, applicants must be a resident of New York State for at least two years prior to the application deadline and cannot be enrolled in a degree program of any kind. In 2012, a total of 94 Fellowships of $7,000 each were awarded in the following disciplines: Fiction; Film/Video; Folk/Traditional Arts; Interdisciplinary Work, and Painting. The Folk/Traditional Arts category is a brand-new addition and a good potential grant for songwriters.

When asked about her selection as one of the inaugural group of Folk/Traditional Art Fellows, fifth-generation ballad singer Colleen Cleveland of Warren County said, "I am absolutely thrilled. For many of us who practice a folk art of any kind, we make a living doing other work and our art is relegated to spare time and spare finances. A program like this allows us to accomplish things that we would not be able to produce without this kind of support." Visit www.nyfa.org for more information about this grant program.

The American Center for Artists also offers a good overview of the various forms of U.S. agencies that give grants to the arts. See www.americanartists.org for more information.

Check the following for more information on various grants:

UNITED STATES
Government granting agencies
The U.S Federal Government support for the arts funnels through the National Endowment for the Arts. An appropriate grant category for individual artists is "Art Works" grants (www.nea.gov/grants/apply/GAP14/MusicAW.html).

A majority of states have state government-funded arts councils or commissions, many of whom make grants to individual artists. Learn more here: www.nasaa-arts.org.

There are also various music funds in the United States such as the Frank Huntington Beebe Fund for Musicians (http://www.beebefund.org).

CANADA
http://www.catbird.ca/Full_Grant_List.html
http://treefortartists.com/
www.factor.ca
http://www.ciraa.ca/grant.php
http://www.socan.ca/jsp/en/pub/music_creators/REFundList.jsp
http://www.canadacouncil.ca/grants/

UNITED KINGDOM
www.helpmusicians.org.uk
www.artscouncil-ni.org/
www.princes-trust.org.uk/
www.artswales.org.uk/

TEN TIPS FOR GRANT APPLICATION SUCCESS

1. Make a list of how the money will be used; this is not a necessity but may help in the final stages.
2. Think about the long-term plan. How will the funding be of assistance in your present and future career?
3. Be precise. If you want to use a grant to promote an album, explain what part of promotion the money will pay for.
4. Don't drag out paragraphs and paragraphs of explanations: nice and simple does it.
5. Be realistic with your grant application. Don't ask for more than you need.
6. Know the deadlines and apply early. For example, in the UK, grant applications usually run from February to March, while in Canada grant season for most funding organizations begins April 1. The sooner you apply the more funds that are available.
7. Get help either from a fellow musician or hire a professional grant writer.
8. Do your homework first: i.e. research the grants for which you are eligible.
9. Read the guidelines over and over and over again before submitting.
10. If you don't succeed, don't take it personally. Thousands of musicians are in need of grants and the competition is tough. Just try again, and again.

David is president and chief creative officer of McPherson Communications (www.mcpherson-communications.com)—a Toronto-based writing and public relations consulting business. Ever since attending his first rock concert in 1989 (The Who) and buying his first LP (The J. Geils Band), music has become the "elixir" of his life. With more than 17,177 songs on his iPod, and an ever growing vinyl collection, it's a joy for him to discover new music; he loves sharing these discoveries with his wife and two children. Before starting his business, David spent 12 years as a senior communications consultant, specializing in employee communications. Contact him at david_mcpherson2002@yahoo.ca and follow him on Twitter @aspen73.

LEARNING TO SAY *NO*

How Being Selective Can Improve Your Lyrics

by Pat Pattison

Writing a lyric is like getting a gig: If you're grateful for any idea that comes along, you're probably not getting the best stuff. But if you have lots of legitimate choices, you won't end up playing six hours in Bangor, Maine, for twenty bucks. Look at it this way: The more often you can say no, the better your gigs get. That's why I suggest that you learn to build a worksheet—a specialized tool for brainstorming that produces bathtubs full of ideas and, at the same time, tailors the ideas specifically for a lyric.

Simply, a worksheet contains two things: a list of key ideas and a list of rhymes for each one. There are three stages to building a worksheet.

I. FOCUS YOUR LYRIC IDEA AS CLEARLY AS YOU CAN

Let's say you want to write about homelessness. Sometimes, you'll start the lyric from an emotion: "That old homeless woman with everything she owns in a shopping cart really touches me. I want to write a song about her." Sometimes you'll write from a cold, calculated idea: "I'm tired of writing love songs. I want to do one on a serious subject, maybe homelessness." Or, you may write from a title you like, maybe "Risky Business." Then the trick is to find an interesting angle on it, perhaps: "What do you do for a living?" "I survive on the streets." "That's pretty risky business."

In each case, it's up to you to find the angle, brainstorm the idea, and create the world the idea will live in. Since you always bring your unique perspective to each experience, you will have something interesting to offer. But you'll have to look at enough ideas to find the best perspective.

Object writing is the key to developing choices. You must dive into your vaults of sense material—those unique and secret places—to find out what images you've stored away, in the present example, around the idea of homelessness.

EXERCISE ///

Stop reading, get out a pen, and dive into homelessness for ten minutes. Stay sense-bound and very specific. How do you connect to the idea? Did you ever get lost in the woods as a child? Run away from home? Sleep in a car in New York?

Now, did you find an expressive image, like a broken wheel on a homeless woman's shopping cart, that can serve as a metaphor—a vehicle to carry your feelings? Did you see some situation, like your parents fighting, that seems to connect you with her situation? These expressive objects or situations are what T.S. Eliot calls "objective correlatives"—objects anyone can touch, smell, and see that correlate with the emotion you want to express. Broken wheels or parents fighting work nicely as objective correlatives.

Even if you find ideas that work well, keep looking a while longer. When you find a good idea, there is usually a bunch more behind it. (The gig opening for Aerosmith could be the next offer.) Jot down your good ideas on a separate sheet of paper.

---

2. MAKE A LIST OF WORDS THAT EXPRESS YOUR IDEA

You'll need to look further than the hot ideas from your object writing. Get out a thesaurus, one set up according to Roget's original plan according to the flow of ideas—a setup perfect for brainstorming. Dictionary-style versions (set up alphabetically) are useful only for finding synonyms and antonyms. They make brainstorming a cumbersome exercise in cross-referencing.

Your thesaurus is better than a good booking agent. It can churn up images and ideas you wouldn't ever get to by yourself, stimulating your diver to greater and greater depths until a wealth of choices litter the beaches.

Let's adopt the working title "Risky Business" and continue brainstorming the idea of homelessness. In the index (the last half of your thesaurus), locate a word that expresses the general idea, for example, *risk*. From the list below it, select the word most related to the lyric idea. My thesaurus lists these options for *risk*: *gambling 618n*; *possibility 469n*; *danger 661n*; *speculate 791vb*. The first notation should be read as follows: "You will find the word *risk* in the noun group of section 618 under the key word *gambling*."

Key words are always in italics. They set a general meaning for the section, like a key signature sets the tone center in a piece of music.

Probably the closest meaning for our purposes with "Risky Business" is *danger 661n*. Look in the text (front half) of the thesaurus for section 661 (or whatever number your thesaurus lists; numbers will appear at the tops of the pages). If you peruse the general area around danger for a minute, you will find several pages of related material. Here are the surrounding section headings in my thesaurus:

Ill health, disease	Insalubrity	Deterioration
Relapse	Bane	Danger
Pitfall	Danger signal	Escape
Salubrity (well-being)	Improvement	Restoration
Remedy	Safety	Refuge. Safeguard
Warning	Preservation	Deliverance

This related material runs for sixteen pages in double-column entries. Risk is totally surrounded by its relatives, so if you look around the neighborhood, you'll find a plethora of possibilities. Start building your list.

Look at these first few entries under danger: *N. danger, peril; . . . shadow of death, jaws of d., dragon's mouth, dangerous situation, unhealthy s., desperate s., forlorn hope 700n. predicament; emergency 137n. crisis; insecurity, jeopardy, risk, hazard, ticklishness . . .*

Look actively. If you take each entry for a quick drive through your sense memories, you should have a host of new ideas within minutes. (Frequent object writing pays big dividends here. The more familiar you are with the process, the quicker these quick dives get. If you are slow at first, don't give up—you'll get faster. Just vow to do more object writing.) Jot down the best words on your list and keep at it until you're into serious overload.

Now the fun begins. Start saying no to words in your list until you've trimmed it to about ten or twelve words with different vowel sounds in their stressed syllables. Put these survivors in the middle of a blank sheet of paper, number them, and enclose them in a box for easy reference later on. Keep these guidelines in mind:

1. If you are working with a title, be sure to put its key vowel sounds in the list.
2. Most of your words should end in a stressed syllable, since they work best in rhyming position.
3. Put any interesting words that duplicate a vowel sound in parentheses.

Your goal is to create a list of words to look up in your rhyming dictionary. Here's what I got banging around in the thesaurus, looking through the lens of homelessness:

1. risk
2. business
3. left out
4. freeze (wheel, shield)
5. storm
6. dull (numb)

7. night (child)
8. change
9. defense
10. home (hope, broken, coat)

This is not a final list. Don't be afraid to switch, add, or take out words as the process continues.

3. LOOK UP EACH WORD IN YOUR RHYMING DICTIONARY

Be sure to extend your search to imperfect rhyme types, and to select only words that connect with your ideas. Above all, don't bother with cliché rhymes or other typical rhymes. First, a quick survey of rhyme types.

Perfect Rhyme

Don't let yourself be seduced by the word "perfect." It doesn't mean "better," it only means:

1. The syllables' vowel sounds are the same.
2. The consonant sounds after the vowels (if any) are the same.
3. The sounds before the vowels are different.

Remember, lyrics are sung, not read or spoken. When you sing, you exaggerate vowels. And since rhyme is a vowel connection, lyricists can make sonic connections in ways other than perfect rhyme.

Family Rhyme

1. The syllables' vowel sounds are the same.
2. The consonant sounds after the vowels belong to the same phonetic families.
3. The sounds before the vowels are different.

Here's a chart of the three important consonant families:

		PLOSIVES	FRICATIVES	NASALS	
VOICED	t	b d g	v TH z zh j	m n ng	← companions
UNVOICED	n	p t k	f th s sh ch	← companions	

Each of the three boxes—plosives, fricatives, and nasals—form a phonetic family. When a word ends in a consonant on one of the boxes, you can use the other members of the family to find perfect rhyme substitutions.

Rub/up/thud/putt/bug/stuck are members of the same family—plosives—so they are family rhymes.

Love/buzz/judge/fluff/fuss/hush/touch are members of the fricative family, so they also are family rhymes.

Strum/run/sung rhyme as members of the nasal family.

Say you want to rhyme this line:

I'm stuck in a rut

First, look up perfect rhymes for *rut*: *cut, glut, gut, hut, shut.*

The trick to saying something you mean is to expand your alternatives. Look at the table of family rhymes below and introduce yourself to t's relatives:

ud	uk	ub	up	ug
blood	buck	club	hard up	bug
flood	duck	hub	makeup	jug
mud	luck	pub	cup	unplug
stud	muck	scrub		plug
thud	stuck	tub		shrug
	truck			snug
				tug

That's much better. Now we find that we have a lot of interesting stuff to say no to.

What if you want to rhyme this:

There's nowhere I can feel safe

First, look up perfect rhymes for *safe* in your rhyming dictionary. All we get is *waif.* Not much.

Now look for family rhymes under f's family, the fricatives. We add these possibilities:

as	av	az	aj
case	behave	blaze	age
ace	brave	craze	cage
breathing-space	cave	daze	page
chase	grave	haze	rage
face	shave	phrase	stage
disgrace	slave	paraphrase	
embrace	wave	praise	
grace			
lace			
resting-place		ath	aTH
space		faith	bathe

Finally, nasals. The word "nasals" means what you think it means: All the sound comes out of your nose. Rhyme this line:

> *My head is pounding like a drum*

Look up perfect rhymes for *drum: hum, pendulum, numb, slum, strum.*

Go to the table of family rhymes and look at m's relatives:

un	ung
fun	hung
gun	flung
overrun	wrung
won	sung
jettison	
skeleton	

Finding family rhyme isn't difficult, so there's no reason to tie yourself in knots using only perfect rhyme. Family rhyme sounds so close that when sung, the ear won't know the difference.

Additive Rhyme

1. The syllables' vowel sounds are the same.
2. One of the syllables add extra consonants after the vowel.
3. The sounds before the vowels are different.

When the syllable you want to rhyme ends in a vowel (e.g., play, free, fly), the only way to generate alternatives is to add consonants after the vowel. The guideline is simple: The less sound you add, the closer you stay to perfect rhyme.

Look again at the table of family rhymes. Voiced plosives—b, d, g—put out the least sound. Use them first, rhyming, for example, *ricochet* with *paid*; then the unvoiced plosives, rhyming *free* with *treat*. Next, voiced fricatives, rhyming *fly* and *alive*. Then on to unvoiced fricatives, followed by the most noticeable consonants (aside from l and r), the nasals. You'd end up with a list moving from closest to perfect rhyme to furthest away from perfect rhyme. For example, for *free*, we find: *speed, cheap, sweet, grieve, belief, dream, clean, deal.*

You can also add consonants even if there are already consonants after the vowel, for example: street/sweets, alive/drives, dream/screamed, trick/risk.

You can even combine this technique with family rhymes, such as dream/cleaned, club/floods/shove/stuffed. This gives you even more options, making it easier to say what you mean.

Subtractive Rhyme

1. The syllables' vowel sounds are the same.

2. One of the syllables adds an extra consonant after the vowel.
3. The sounds before the vowels are different.

Subtractive rhyme is basically the same as additive rhyme. The difference is practical. If you start with *fast*, *class* is subtractive. If you start with *class*, *fast* is additive.

> Help me please, I'm sinking fast
> Girl, you're in a different class

For *fast*, you could also try: *glass*, *flat*, *mashed* (family), *laughed* (family), *crash* (fam. subt.).

> *The possibilities grow.*

Assonance Rhyme

1. The syllables' vowel sounds are the same.
2. The consonant sounds after the vowels are unrelated.
3. The sounds before the vowels are different.

Assonance rhyme is the furthest you can get from perfect rhyme without changing vowel sounds. Consonants after the vowels have nothing in common. Try rhyming:

> *I hope you're satisfied*

For *satisfied*, we come up with: *life, trial, crime, sign, rise, survive, surprise.*

Use these rhyming techniques: You'll have much more leeway saying what you mean, and your rhymes will be fresh and useful. Again, look actively at each word. Use them to dive through your senses, as though you were object writing.

You'll find more on these rhyme types, including helpful exercises, in my book *Songwriting: Essential Guide to Rhyming.*

Rhymes and Chords

You can think about rhyme in the same way you think about chords. Go to the piano and play three chords: an F chord with an F as the bass note in the left hand, then G7 with G as the bass note, then, finally, C. Play the C chord with the notes C, E, and G in the right hand, and a C as a bass note in the left hand. Sing a C, too. It really feels like you've arrived home, doesn't it?

Next, do the same thing again with your right hand, singing a C when you get to the C chord, but this time, put a G in the left hand. It still feels like you're home, though not quite as solidly as when you played C in the bass. Still, it's difficult to notice the difference.

Do it all again, this time playing the third in the bass, an E. It still feels like a version of home, but less stable. It seems to have some discomfort at home—a very expressive chord.

Do it again, keeping the E in the bass, but this time take the C out of the chord in your right hand. Sing the C. This feels even less comfortable.

Last time, add a B to the right hand, still leaving the C out. Now, you're actually playing an E minor chord, the three minor in the key of C, still singing the C. Now we have only a suggestion of home, rather than sitting down to the supper table.

All of these voicings are useful, and all of these voicings are tonic (home) functions. Some land solidly and bring motion to a complete halt. Others express a desire to keep moving somewhere else—a kind of wanderlust. Each has its own identity and emotion.

Rhymes work the same way. Some are stronger than others and express a desire to stay put; they are stable. Others may have a foot at home, but their minds are looking for the next place to go. They feel less stable.

Here are the rhyme types, listed like the chords you played, in a scale from most stable to least stable:

RHYME TYPES: SCALE OF RESOLUTION STRENGTHS

Most Resolved				Least Resolved
		Family Rhyme		Assonance Rhyme
Perfect Rhyme		Additive/Sub-tractive Rhyme		Consonance Rhyme

Look at the simple example below—a stable, four-stress couplet. With perfect rhyme, it feels very solid and resolved.

> A lovely day to have some fun
> Hit the beach, get some sun

As we move through the rhyme types, things feel less and less stable, even though the structure remains the same:

Family rhyme:

> A lovely day to have some fun
> Hit the beach, bring the rum (a lot like C with G in the bass)

Additive rhyme:

> A lovely day to have some fun
> Hit the beach, get some lunch (a lot like C with E in the bass)

Subtractive rhyme:

> Hit the beach and get some lunch
> A lovely day, have some fun (a lot like C with E in the bass)

Assonance rhyme:

> A lovely day to have some fun
> Hit the beach, bring it on (a lot like the E minor in the key of C)

Consonance rhyme:

> A lovely day to have some fun
> Hit the beach, bring it on (a lot like the E minor in the key of C)

Expanding your rhyming possibilities accomplishes three things:

1. It multiplies the possibility of saying what you mean (and still rhyming) exponentially.
2. It guarantees the rhymes will not be predictable or cliché.
3. Most important, it allows you to control, like chords do, how stable or unstable the rhyme feels, allowing you to support or even create emotion with your rhymes.

Together, these offer a pretty good argument against the proponents of "perfect rhyme only."

> Baby baby take my hand
> Let me know you _____

Ah yes, understand. Telegraphed and locked down. Mostly, I find it disappointing when I know what's coming. When it's already telegraphed and waltzing in your brain, why say it? If you instead said something different, you'd have both messages at the same time:

> Baby baby take my hand
> Let me know you'll take a stand (*understand*, the expected cliché, is still present)

I like the perfect rhyme here. The full resolution seems to support the idea. Now, how about:

> Baby baby take my hand
> Let me know you'd like to dance

I love the surprise here. It also uses the telegraphing of *understand* as a second message. It's not a cliché rhyme. Pretty close, though, with n in common but d against c. That little bit of difference introduces something that perfect rhyme can't: a tinge of longing created by the difference at the end. The lack of perfect rhyme creates the same kind of instability as, say, the C major triad with a G in the bass. Almost, but not fully resolved. Just as a chord can create an emotional response, so can a less-perfect rhyme:

> Baby baby take my hand
> Let me know you're making plans

The same tinge of instability.

> Baby baby take my hand
> Let me know you want to laugh

What do you think the chances of hooking up are now? They seem about as remote as the assonance rhyme. Yup, the rhyme type really can affect and color the idea.

It's still a "tonic" function, but now it seems more like a C major triad with an E in the bass. Finally:

> Baby baby take my hand
> Let me know I'm on your mind

Now there's curiosity and uncertainty, expressed completely and only by the consonance rhyme. Pretty neat, huh?

WORKSHEET: RISKY BUSINESS

1. risk	2. business	3. left out	4. freeze	5. storm
cliff	collisions	proud	grieve	reform
fist	visions	bound	leave	(re)born
kissed	frigid	count	peace	court
stiff	forgiveness	vowed	appeased	cord
itch	submissive	aloud	street	scorn
pitch	delicious	renowned	debris	divorce
drift	riches	aroused	diseased	reward
switch	suspicious	crowned	guarantee(s)	warm
shift	kisses		wheel	torn
pinched	finish		shield	ignored
chips	wind			

6. dull	7. night	8. change	9. defense	10. home
sulk	flight	cage	expense	disowned
annulled	spite	slave	bench	blown
cult	bride	grave	trench	bone

pale	strike	safe	drenched	unknown
brawl	prize	faith	friend	stoned
numb	despised	castaway	revenge	dethroned
opium	deprived	ricochet	content	zone
martyrdom	child	haste	condemned	hope
crumbs	fault		contempt	coat
gun	crawl			throat
young				remote
				ghost
				Job
				load
				broken

Brainstorming

Brainstorming with a rhyming dictionary prepares you to write a lyric. At the same time you are brainstorming your ideas, you are also finding sounds you can use later. With solid rhyming techniques that include family rhymes, additive and subtractive rhymes, assonance and even consonance rhymes (especially for l and r), using a rhyming dictionary can be as relaxed and easy as brainstorming with a friend, except it's more efficient than a friend, and it won't whine for a piece of the song if you get a hit.

A worksheet externalized the inward process of lyric writing. It slows your writing process down so you can get to know it better, like slowing down when you play a scale to help get it under your fingers. The more you do it, the faster and more efficient you'll get.

The sample worksheet on the previous pages includes both perfect and imperfect rhymes. Reading this worksheet should be stimulating. But doing your own worksheet will set you on fire. Decide now that you will do a complete worksheet for each of your next ten lyrics, then stick to it. The first one will be slow and painful, but full of new and interesting options. By the third one, ideas will be coming fast and furious. You will have too much to say, too many choices, and too many rhymes. Though getting to this point takes work, it will be well worth the effort. Think of all the times you'll get to say no. No more clichés. No more forced rhymes. No more helpless gratitude that some idea, any idea at all, came along. No more six-hour gigs in Bangor for twenty bucks. Trust me.

Excerpted from *Writing Better Lyrics* © 2009 by **PAT PATTISON**. Used with the kind permission of Writer's Digest Books, an imprint of F+W Media Inc. Visit writersdigestshop.com or call (800)448-0915 to obtain a copy.

SONGWRITING CALENDAR

The best way for songwriters to achieve success is by setting goals. Goals are usually met by songwriters who give themselves or are given deadlines. Something about having an actual date to hit helps create a sense of urgency for most writers. This songwriting calendar is a great place to keep your important deadlines.

Also, this calendar is a good tool for recording upcoming events you'd like to attend or contests you'd like to enter. Or use this calendar to block out time for yourself—to just create.

Of course, you can use this calendar to record other special events, especially if you have a habit of remembering to write but of forgetting birthdays or anniversaries. After all, this calendar is now yours. Do with it what you will.

OCTOBER 2013

SUN	MON	TUE	WED	THURS	FRI	SAT
		1	2	3	4	5
6	7	8	9	10	11	12
13	14	15	16	17	18	19
20	21	22	23	24	25	26
27	28	29	30	31		

Start a blog and make at least one post per week.

NOVEMBER 2013

SUN	MON	TUE	WED	THU	FRI	SAT
					1	2
3	4	5	6	7	8	9
10	11	12	13	14	15	16
17	18	19	20	21	22	23
24	25	26	27	28	29	30

Try sending out one targeted demo per day.

DECEMBER 2013

SUN	MON	TUE	WED	THU	FRI	SAT
1	2	3	4	5	6	7
8	9	10	11	12	13	14
15	16	17	18	19	20	21
22	23	24	25	26	27	28
29	30	31				

Evaluate your 2013 accomplishments and make 2014 goals.

_____

_____

_____

_____

JANUARY 2014

SUN	MON	TUE	WED	THU	FRI	SAT
			1	2	3	4
5	6	7	8	9	10	11
12	13	14	15	16	17	18
19	20	21	22	23	24	25
26	27	28	29	30	31	

Make 2014 your best songwriting year yet!.

FEBRUARY 2014

SUN	MON	TUE	WED	THU	FRI	SAT
						1
2	3	4	5	6	7	8
9	10	11	12	13	14	15
16	17	18	19	20	21	22
23	24	25	26	27	28	

Don't wait until April to file your 2013 taxes.

_____

_____

_____

_____

MARCH 2014

SUN	MON	TUE	WED	THU	FRI	SAT
						1
2	3	4	5	6	7	8
9	10	11	12	13	14	15
16	17	18	19	20	21	22
23	24	25	26	27	28	29
30	31					

Are you on Twitter? Try leaving a meaningful tweet daily.

APRIL 2014

SUN	MON	TUE	WED	THU	FRI	SAT
		1	2	3	4	5
6	7	8	9	10	11	12
13	14	15	16	17	18	19
20	21	22	23	24	25	26
27	28	29	30			

Sign up for a songwriting workshop.

MAY 2014

SUN	MON	TUE	WED	THU	FRI	SAT
				1	2	3
4	5	6	7	8	9	10
11	12	13	14	15	16	17
18	19	20	21	22	23	24
25	26	27	28	29	30	31

Develop one song idea each week..

JUNE 2014

SUN	MON	TUE	WED	THU	FRI	SAT
1	2	3	4	5	6	7
8	9	10	11	12	13	14
15	16	17	18	19	20	21
22	23	24	25	26	27	28
29	30					

Create a social network platform for your songs.

JULY 2014

SUN	MON	TUE	WED	THU	FRI	SAT
		1	2	3	4	5
6	7	8	9	10	11	12
13	14	15	16	17	18	19
20	21	22	23	24	25	26
27	28	29	30	31		

Find a new cowriter to work with.

_____

_____

_____

_____

_____

AUGUST 2014

SUN	MON	TUE	WED	THU	FRI	SAT
					1	2
3	4	5	6	7	8	9
10	11	12	13	14	15	16
17	18	19	20	21	22	23
24	25	26	27	28	29	30
31						

Find a songwriting workshop to attend..

_____

_____

_____

_____

_____

SEPTEMBER 2014

SUN	MON	TUE	WED	THU	FRI	SAT
	1	2	3	4	5	6
7	8	9	10	11	12	13
14	15	16	17	18	19	20
21	22	23	24	25	26	27
28	29	30				

Remember to hit the Save button when you're writing.

OCTOBER 2014

SUN	MON	TUE	WED	THU	FRI	SAT
			1	2	3	4
5	6	7	8	9	10	11
12	13	14	15	16	17	18
19	20	21	22	23	24	25
26	27	28	29	30	31	

If you don't have it yet, find a copy of *2015 Songwriter's Market*.

_____

_____

_____

_____

NOVEMBER 2014

SUN	MON	TUE	WED	THU	FRI	SAT
						1
2	3	4	5	6	7	8
9	10	11	12	13	14	15
16	17	18	19	20	21	22
23	24	25	26	27	28	29
30						

Try an unfamiliar writing style to help you grow as a writer.

_____

_____

_____

_____

DECEMBER 2013

SUN	MON	TUE	WED	THU	FRI	SAT
	1	2	3	4	5	6
7	8	9	10	11	12	13
14	15	16	17	18	19	20
21	22	23	24	25	26	27
28	29	30	31			

Remember to hit the Save button when you're writing.

JANUARY 2015

SUN	MON	TUE	WED	THU	FRI	SAT
				1	2	3
4	5	6	7	8	9	10
11	12	13	14	15	16	17
18	19	20	21	22	23	24
25	26	27	28	29	30	31

Look for a songwriting organization to join, if you haven't already.

FEBRUARY 2015

SUN	MON	TUE	WED	THU	FRI	SAT
1	2	3	4	5	6	7
8	9	10	11	12	13	14
15	16	17	18	19	20	21
22	23	24	25	26	27	28

Attend a show or concert for inspiration.

MUSIC PUBLISHERS

//

Music publishers find songs and then get them recorded. In return for a share of the money made from your songs, they work as an agent for you by plugging your songs to recording artists, taking care of paperwork and accounting, setting you up with co-writers (recording artists or other songwriters), and so on.

HOW DO MUSIC PUBLISHERS MAKE MONEY FROM SONGS?

Music publishers make money by getting songs recorded onto albums, film and TV soundtracks, commercials, etc. While this is their primary function, music publishers also handle administrative tasks such as copyrighting songs; collecting royalties for the songwriter; negotiating and issuing synchronization licenses for use of music in films, television programs and commercials; arranging and administering foreign rights; auditing record companies and other music users; suing infringers; and producing new demos of new songs. In a small, independent publishing company, one or two people may handle all these jobs. Larger publishing companies are more likely to be divided into the following departments: creative (or professional), copyright, licensing, legal affairs, business affairs, royalty, accounting, and foreign.

HOW DO MUSIC PUBLISHERS FIND SONGS?

The *creative department* is responsible for finding talented writers and signing them to the company. Once a writer is signed, it is up to the creative department to develop and nurture the writer so he will write songs that create income for the company. Staff members often put writers together to form collaborative teams. And, perhaps most important, the creative department is responsible for securing commercial recordings of songs and pitching them for use in film and other media. The head of the creative department—usually called the "professional manager"—is charged with locating talented writers for the company.

HOW DO MUSIC PUBLISHERS GET SONGS RECORDED?

Once a writer is signed, the professional manager arranges for a demo to be made of the writer's songs. Even though a writer may already have recorded his own demo, the publisher will often re-demo the songs using established studio musicians in an effort to produce the highest-quality demo possible.

Once a demo is produced, the professional manager begins shopping the song to various outlets. He may try to get the song recorded by a top artist on his or her next album or get the song used in an upcoming film. The professional manager uses all the contacts and leads he has to get the writer's songs recorded by as many artists as possible. Therefore, he must be able to deal efficiently and effectively with people in other segments of the music industry, including A&R personnel, recording artists, producers, distributors, managers, and lawyers. Through these contacts, he can find out what artists are looking for new material, and who may be interested in recording one of the writer's songs.

HOW IS A PUBLISHING COMPANY ORGANIZED?

After a writer's songs are recorded, the other departments at the publishing company come into play.

- The *licensing and copyright departments* are responsible for issuing any licenses for use of the writer's songs in film or TV and for filing various forms with the copyright office.
- The *legal affairs and business affairs departments* work with the professional department in negotiating contracts with its writers.
- The *royalty and accounting departments* are responsible for making sure that users of music are paying correct royalties to the publisher and ensuring the writer is receiving the proper royalty rate as specified in the contract and that statements are mailed to the writer promptly.
- Finally, the *foreign department*'s role is to oversee any publishing activities outside of the United States, to notify sub-publishers of the proper writer and ownership information of songs in the catalogue and update all activity and new releases, and to make sure a writer is being paid for any uses of his material in foreign countries.

LOCATING A MUSIC PUBLISHER

How do you go about finding a music publisher that will work well for you? First, you must find a publisher suited to the type of music you write. If a particular publisher works mostly with alternative music and you're a country songwriter, the contacts he has within the industry will hardly be beneficial to you.

Each listing in this section details, in order of importance, the type of music that publisher is most interested in; the music types appear in **boldface** to make them easier to locate. It's also very important to submit only to companies interested in your level of experience (see A Sample Listing Decoded on page 8). You will also want to refer to the Category Indexes in the back of this book, which list companies by the type of music they work with. Publishers placing music in film or TV will be proceded by an ICON.

Do your research!

It's important to study the market and do research to identify which companies to submit to.

- Many record producers have publishing companies or have joint ventures with major publishers who fund the signing of songwriters and who provide administration services. Since producers have an influence over what is recorded in a session, targeting the producer/publisher can be a useful avenue.
- Since most publishers don't open unsolicited material, try to meet the publishing representative in person (at conferences, speaking engagements, etc.) or try to have an intermediary intercede on your behalf (for example, an entertainment attorney; a manager, an agent, etc.).
- As to demos, submit no more than 3 songs.
- As to publishing deals, co-publishing deals (where a writer owns part of the publishing share through his or her own company) are relatively common if the writer has a well-established track record.
- Are you targeting a specific artist to sing your songs? If so, find out if that artist even considers outside material. Get a copy of the artist's latest album, and see who wrote most of the songs. If they were all written by the artist, he's probably not interested in hearing material from outside writers. If the songs were written by a variety of different writers, however, he may be open to hearing new songs.
- Check the album liner notes, which will list the names of the publishers of each writer. These publishers obviously have had luck pitching songs to the artist, and they may be able to get your songs to that artist as well.
- If the artist you're interested in has a recent hit on the *Billboard* charts, the publisher of that song will be listed in the "Hot 100 A-Z" index. Carefully choosing which publishers will work best for the material you write may take time, but it will only increase your chances of getting your songs heard. "Shotgunning" your demo packages (sending out many packages without regard for music preference or submission policy) is a waste of time and money and will hurt, rather than help, your songwriting career.

Once you've found some companies that may be interested in your work, learn what songs have been successfully handled by those publishers. Most publishers are happy to provide you with this information in order to attract high-quality material. As you're researching music publishers, keep in mind how you get along with them personally. If you can't work with a publisher on a personal level, chances are your material won't be represented as you would like it to be. A publisher can become your most valuable connection to all other segments of the music industry, so it's important to find someone you can trust and feel comfortable with.

Independent or major company?

Also consider the size of the publishing company. The publishing affiliates of the major music conglomerates are huge, handling catalogues of thousands of songs by hundreds of songwriters. Unless you are an established songwriter, your songs probably won't receive enough attention from such large companies. Smaller, independent publishers offer several advantages. First, independent music publishers are located all over the country, making it easier for you to work face-to-face rather than by mail or phone. Smaller companies usually aren't affiliated with a particular record company and are therefore able to pitch your songs to many different labels and acts. Independent music publishers are usually interested in a smaller range of music, allowing you to target your submissions more accurately. The most obvious advantage to working with a smaller publisher is the personal attention they can bring to you and your songs. With a smaller roster of artists to work with, the independent music publisher is able to concentrate more time and effort on each particular project.

SUBMITTING MATERIAL TO PUBLISHERS

When submitting material to a publisher, always keep in mind that a professional, courteous manner goes a long way in making a good impression. When you submit a demo through the mail, make sure your package is neat and meets the particular needs of the publisher. Review each publisher's submission policy carefully, and follow it to the letter. Disregarding this information will only make you look like an amateur in the eyes of the company you're submitting to.

Listings of companies in Canada are preceded by an ICON, and international markets are designated with an ICON. You will find an alphabetical list of these companies at the back of the book, along with an index of publishers by state in the Geographic Index in the back of this book.

PUBLISHING CONTRACTS

Once you've located a publisher you like and he's interested in shopping your work, it's time to consider the publishing contract--an agreement in which a songwriter grants certain rights to a publisher for one or more songs. The contract specifies any advances offered to the writer, the rights that will be transferred to the publisher, the royalties a songwriter is to receive, and the length of time the contract is valid.

- When a contract is signed, a publisher will ask for a 50-50 split with the writer. This is standard industry practice; the publisher is taking that 50% to cover the overhead costs of running his business and for the work he's doing to get your songs recorded.
- It is always a good idea to have a publishing contract (or any music business contract) reviewed by a competent entertainment lawyer.
- There is no "standard" publishing contract, and each company offers different provisions for their writers.

Make sure you ask questions about anything you don't understand, especially if you're new in the business. Songwriter organizations such as the Songwriters Guild of America (SGA) provide contract review services, and can help you learn about music business language and what constitutes a fair music publishing contract. Be sure to read What About Contracts? on page 35 for more information on contracts. See the Organizations section, beginning on page 232 of this book, for more information on the SGA and other songwriting groups.

When signing a contract, it's important to be aware of the music industry's unethical practitioners. The "song shark," as he's called, makes his living by asking a songwriter to pay to have a song published. The shark will ask for money to demo a song and promote it to radio stations; he may also ask for more than the standard 50% publisher's share or ask you to give up all rights to a song in order to have it published. Although none of these practices is illegal, it's certainly not ethical, and no successful publisher uses these methods. *Songwriter's Market* works to list only honest companies interested in hearing new material. (For more on "song sharks," see How Do I Avoid the Rip-Offs? on page 17.)

Icons

For more instructional information on the listings in this book, including explanations of symbols (ICONS), read the article *How To Use Songwriter's Market* on page 2.

① ABEAR PUBLISHING (BMI)/ SONGTOWN PUBLISHING (ASCAP)

5631 Myrtlewood Dr., Nashville TN 37211 United States. **E-mail:** ronhebert@gmail.com.
HOW TO CONTACT Submit MP3 by e-mail. Unsolicited submissions are OK. Prefers 3 songs with lyric sheets. Responds in 1 week if interested.
MUSIC Mostly **country**, **country/pop**, **pop**, **dance**, and **Christian**.

⑨○ ALL ROCK MUSIC

United States. **E-mail:** info@collectorrecords.nl.
Website: www.collectorrecords.nl. **Contact:** Cees Klop, president. Music publisher, record company (Collector Records), and record producer. Estab. 1967. Publishes 40 songs/year; publishes several new songwriters/year. Staff size: 3. Pays standard royalty.

◖ Also see the listings for Collector Records in the Record Companies sections of this book.

AFFILIATES All Rock Music (United Kingdom).
HOW TO CONTACT Submit demo package by mail. Unsolicited submissions are OK. Prefers cassette. SAE and IRC. Responds in 2 months.
MUSIC Mostly **50s rock**, **rockabilly**, and **country rock**; also **piano boogie woogie**. Published *Rock Crazy Baby* (album), written and recorded by Art Adams (1950s rockabilly), released 2004; *Marvin Jackson* (album), by Marvin Jackson (1950s rockers), released 2005; *Western Australian Snake Pit R&R* (album), recorded by various (1950s rockers), released 2005, all on Collector Records.
TIPS "Send only the kind of material we issue/produce as listed."

①❀ ALPHA MUSIC INC.

One International Blvd., Suite 212, Mahwah NJ 07495 United States. **E-mail:** info@trfmusic.com. **Website:** www.trfmusic.com. **Contact:** Michael Nurko, music publisher. Pays standard royalty. Affiliate(s) Dorian Music Publishers, Inc. (ASCAP) and TRF Music Inc.

◖ Also see listing for TRF Production Music Libraries in the Advertising, Audiovisual & Commercial Music Firms section of this book.

HOW TO CONTACT "We accept submissions of new compositions. Submissions are not returnable."
MUSIC **All categories**, mainly **instrumental** and **acoustic** suitable for use as **production music**, including **theme and background music for television and film**. "Have published over 50,000 titles since 1931."

① A NEW RAP JAM PUBLISHING

P.O. Box 683, Lima OH 45802. **E-mail:** jamesmilligan-jr@yahoo.com; newexperiencerecords@yahoo.com. **Contact:** A&R Department. Professional Managers: William Roach (rap, clean); James Milligan (country, 70s music, pop). Music publisher and record company (New Experience/Faze 4 Records, Pump It Up Records, and Rough Edge Records). Publishes 50-100 songs/year; Grind Blocc Records and Touch Tone Digital International Records publishes 5-10 new songwriters/year. Hires staff songwriters. Pays standard royalty.
AFFILIATES Songwriters Party House Publishing (BMI), Creative Star Management, and Rough Edge Records. Distribution through KVZ Distribution and States 51 Distribution.
HOW TO CONTACT *Write first to arrange personal interview or submit demo CD by mail.* Unsolicited submissions are OK. Prefers CD with 3-5 songs and lyric or lead sheet. Include SASE. Responds in 6-8 weeks. "Visit www.myspace.com/newexperiencerecords2 for more information."
MUSIC Mostly **R&B**, **pop**, **blues**, and **rock/rap** (clean); also **contemporary**, **gospel**, **country**, and **soul**. Published "Lets Go Dancing" (single by Dion Mikel), recorded and released 2006 on Faze 4 Records/New Experience Records; "The Broken Hearted" (single) from *The Final Chapter* (album), recorded by T.M.C. the milligan connection (R&B/gospel); James Jr.; "Girl Like You" feat. Terry Zapp Troutman, additional appearances by Kurtis Blow, King MC, Sugarfoot Lead Singer (Ohio Players) Lavel Jackson 2009/10 on New Experience/Pump It Up Records. Other artists include singer-songwriter James Jr. on Faze 4 Records/ Rough Edge Records and Grind Blocc Records.
TIPS "We are seeking hit artists from the 70s, 80s, and 90s who would like to be signed, as well as new talent and female solo artists. Send any available information supporting the group or act. We are a label that does not promote violence, drugs, or anything that we feel is a bad example for our youth. Establish music industry contacts, write and keep writing, and most of all believe in yourself. Use a good recording studio but be very professional. Just take your time and produce the best music possible. Sometimes you only get one chance. Make sure you place your best song on your demo first. This will increase your chances greatly. If you're the owner of your own small label and have a finished product, please send it. And if there is inter-

est we will contact you. Also be on the lookout for new artists on Rough Edge Records and Touch Tone Records. Now reviewing blues and soul music. If you have a developing record label and would like distribution send us your artist listing record label information to be considered and thank you for considering us for your next project."

O ANTELOPE PUBLISHING INC.

P.O. Box 55, Rowayton CT 06853 United States. Publishes 5-10 new songs/year; publishes 3-5 new songwriters/year. Pays standard royalty.

HOW TO CONTACT Submit demo by mail. Unsolicited submissions are OK. Prefers cassette with lead sheet. Does not return material. Responds in 1 month if interested.

MUSIC Only **bebop** and **1940s swing**. Does not want anything electronic. Published "Somewhere Near" (single by Tony LaVorgna) from *Just For My Friends* (album), recorded by Jeri Brown (easy listening); "Cookie Monster" and "The Lady From Mars" (singles by Tony LaVorgna) from *Just For My Friends* (album), recorded by Tony LaVorgna (jazz/easy listening), released 2007 on Antelope.

TIPS "Put your best song first with a short intro."

⊕ BAITSTRING MUSIC

2622 Kirtland Rd., Brewton AL 36426 United States. (251)867-2228. **Contact:** Roy Edwards, president.

AFFILIATES Cheavoria Music Co. (BMI).

HOW TO CONTACT Submit demo by mail. Unsolicited submissions are OK. Prefers CD with 3 songs and lyric sheet. Does not return material. Responds in 1 month.

MUSIC Mostly **R&B, pop,** and **easy listening**; also **country** and **gospel**. Published "Forever and Always," written and recorded by Jim Portwood (pop); and "Make Me Forget" (by Horace Linsley) and "Never Let Me Go" (by Cheavoria Edwards), both recorded by Bobbie Roberson (country), all on Bolivia Records.

TIPS "We need some good gospel."

⊕ BEARSONGS

Box 944, Edgbaston, Birmingham B16 8UTT United Kingdom. +(44)0121-454-7020. **Website:** www. bigbearmusic.com. **Contact:** Jim Simpson, managing director; Russell Fletcher, professional manager. Music publisher and record company (Big Bear Records). Member PRS, MCPS. Publishes 25 songs/year;

publishes 15-20 new songwriters/year. Pays standard royalty.

○ Also see the listing for Big Bear in the Record Producers section of this book.

HOW TO CONTACT Submit demo by mail. Unsolicited submissions are OK. Prefers CD. Does not return material. Responds in 3 months.

MUSIC Mostly **blues, swing,** and **jazz**. Published *Blowing With Bruce* and *Cool Heights* (by Alan Barnes), recorded by Bruce Adams/Alan Barnes Quintet; and *Blues For My Baby* (by Charles Brown), recorded by King Pleasure & The Biscuit Boys, all on Big Bear Records.

TIPS "Have a real interest in jazz, blues, swing."

BIG FISH MUSIC PUBLISHING GROUP

12720 Burbank Blvd., Suite 124, Valley Village CA 91607. (818) 508-9777. **E-mail:** clisag21@yahoo.com. **Contact:** Chuck Tennin. Producer: Gary Black (country, pop, adult contemporary, rock, crossover songs, other styles). Professional Music Manager: Lora Sprague (jazz, New Age, instrumental, pop rock, R&B). Professional Music Manager: B.J. (pop, TV, film, and special projects). Professional Music and Vocal Consultant: Zell Black (country, pop, gospel, rock, blues). Producer, Independent Artists: Darryl Harrelson – Major Label Entertainment (country, pop and other genres). Nashville Music Associate: Ron Hebert (Abear/Songtown Publishing). Songwriter/Consultant: Jerry Zanandrea (Z Best Muzic). Staff Songwriters: Billy O'Hara, Joe Rull, Lisa Faye. Music publisher, record company (California Sun Records) and production company. Publishes 10-20 songs/year; publishes 5-10 new songwriters/year. Staff size: 10. Pays standard royalty. "We also license songs and music copyrights to users of music, especially TV and film, commercials, and recording projects." Member: BMI, ASCAP, CMA, and ACM.

AFFILIATES Big Fish Music (BMI) and California Sun Music (ASCAP).

HOW TO CONTACT *Write first and obtain permission to submit.* Include SASE for reply. "**Please do not call** or e-mail submissions. After permission to submit is confirmed, we will assign and forward to you a submission code number allowing you to submit up to 4 songs maximum, preferably on CD. Include a properly addressed cover letter, signed and dated, with your source of referral (*Songwriter's Market*) with your assigned submission code number and an

SASE for reply and/or return of material. Include lyrics. *Unsolicited material will not be accepted.* This is our submission policy to review outside and new material." Responds in 2 weeks.

FILM & TV Places 6 songs in TV/year. Recently published "Even the Angels Knew" (by Cathy Carlson/Craig Lackey/Marty Axelrod); "Stop Before We Start" (by J.D. Grieco); "Oh Santa" (by Christine Bridges/John Deaver), all recorded by The Black River Girls in *Passions* (NBC); licensed "A Christmas Wish" (by Ed Fry/Eddie Max), used in *Passions* (NBC); "Girls Will Be Girls" (by Cathy Carlson/John LeGrande), recorded by The Black River Girls, used in *All My Children* (ABC); "The Way You're Drivin' Me" and "Ain't No Love 'Round Here" (by Jerry Zanandrea), both recorded by The Black River Girls, used in *Passions* (NBC); "Since You Stole My Heart"(by Rick Colmbra/Jamey Whiting), used in *Passions* (NBC); "Good Time To Fly", "All I Need Is A Highway", and "Eyes Of The Children" (by Wendy Martin), used in *Passions* (NBC); "It's An Almost Perfect Christmas" (by Michael Martin), used in *Passions* (NBC).

MUSIC Country, including **country pop, country A/C,** and **country crossover** with "a cutting edge"; also **pop, rock, pop ballads, adult contemporary, uplifting, praise, worship, spiritual,** and **inspirational adult contemporary gospel** "with a powerful message," **instrumental background and theme music** for TV, film, and commercials, **New Age/instrumental jazz** and **novelty, orchestral classical, R&B,** and **children's music,** for all kinds of commercial use. Published "If Wishes Were Horses" (single by Billy O'Hara); "Purple Bunny Honey" (single by Robert Lloyd/Jim Love); "Leavin' You For Me" (single by J.D. Grieco).

TIPS "Demo should be professional, high quality, clean, simple, dynamic, and must get the song across on the first listen. Good clear vocals, a nice melody, a good musical feel, good musical arrangement, strong lyrics and chorus — a unique, catchy, clever song that sticks with you. Looking for unique country and pop songs with a different edge that can crossover to the mainstream market for ongoing Nashville music projects and songs for hot female Country acts that can crossover to adult contemporary and pop with great lush harmonies. Also, catchy, up-tempo songs with an attitude and a groove, preferably rock, that can be marketed to today's youth."

⃠⊛ BIXIO MUSIC GROUP & ASSOCIATES/IDM MUSIC

111 E. 14th St., Suite 140, New York NY 10003 United States. (212)695-3911. **E-mail:** info@bixio.com. **Website:** www.bixio.com. (ASCAP) Music publisher, record company and rights clearances. Estab. 1985. Publishes a few hundred songs/year; publishes 2 new songwriters/year. Staff size: 6. Pays standard royalty.

HOW TO CONTACT *Does not accept unsolicited material.*

MUSIC Mostly **soundtracks**. Published "La Strada Nel Bosco," included in the TV show *Ed* (NBC); "La Beguine Du Mac," included in the TV show *The Chris Isaac Show* (Showtime); and "Alfonsina Delle Camelie," included in the TV show *UC: Undercover* (NBC).

⃠ BOUQUET-ORCHID PUBLISHING

P.O. Box 1335, Norcross GA 30091 United States. (770)814-2420. Music publisher, record company, record producer (Bouquet-Orchid Enterprises) and artist management. Member: CMA, AFM. Publishes 10-12 songs/year; publishes 3 new songwriters/year. Pays standard royalty.

HOW TO CONTACT Submit demo by mail. Unsolicited submissions are OK. Prefers cassette or CD with 3-5 songs and lyric sheet. "Send biographical information if possible; even a photo helps." Include SASE. Responds in 1 month.

MUSIC Mostly **religious** ("Amy Grant, etc., contemporary gospel"); **country** ("Garth Brooks, Trisha Yearwood-type material"); and **top 100/pop** ("Bryan Adams, Whitney Houston-type material"). Published "Blue As Your Eyes" (single), written and recorded by Adam Day; "Spare My Feelings" (single by Clayton Russ), recorded by Terri Palmer; and "Trying to Get By" (single by Tom Sparks), recorded by Bandoleers, all on Bouquet Records.

⃠ BOURNE CO. MUSIC PUBLISHERS

5 W. 37th St., New York NY 10018 United States. (212)391-4300. **Fax:** (212)391-4306. **E-mail:** bourne@bournemusic.com. **Website:** www.bournemusic.com. Publishes educational material and popular music.

AFFILIATES ABC Music, Ben Bloom, Better Half, Bogat, Burke & Van Heusen, Goldmine, Harborn, Lady Mac, and Murbo Music.

HOW TO CONTACT *Does not accept unsolicited submissions.*

MUSIC Piano/vocal, **band pieces,** and **choral pieces.** Published "Amen" and "Mary's Little Boy Child" (singles by Hairston); "When You Wish Upon a Star" (single by Washington/Harline); and "San Antonio Rose" (single by Bob Willis, arranged John Cacavas).

○ BRANDON HILLS MUSIC, LLC (BMI)

N 3425 Searle County Line Rd., Brandon WI 53919 United States. **E-mail:** martab@centurytel.net. **Website:** www.brandonhillsmusic.com. **Contact:** Marsha L. Brown. Publishes 4 new songwriters/year. Staff size: 2. Pays standard royalty of 50%.

HOW TO CONTACT Submit demo package by mail. Unsolicited submissions are OK. Prefers CD with 1-4 songs and cover letter. Does not return submissions. Responds only if interested.

MUSIC Mostly **country (traditional, modern, country rock), contemporary Christian, blues**; also **children's** and **bluegrass** and **rap**. Published "Let It Rain," recorded by Steff Nevers, written by Larry Migliore and Kevin Gallarello (Universal Records, Norway); "Do You Like My Body," recorded by Ginger-Ly, written by Nisa McCall (SEI Corp and Big Daddy G Music, CA); "Did I Ever Thank You Lord," recorded by Jacob Garcia, written by Eletta Sias (TRW Records); "Honky Tonk In Heaven," recorded by Buddy Lewis, written by Mike Heath and Bob Alexander (Ozark Records).

TIPS "We prefer studio-produced CDs. The lyrics and the CD must match. Cover letter, lyrics, and CD should have a professional look. Demos should have vocals up front and every word should be distinguishable. Please make sure your lyrics match your song. Submit only your best. The better the demo, the better the chance of getting your music published and recorded."

⊘ BUG MUSIC, INC.

7750 Sunset Blvd., Los Angeles CA 90046 United States. (323)969-0988. **Fax:** (323)969-0968. **E-mail:** buginfo@bugmusic.com. **Website:** www.bugmusic.com. **Contact:** Senior Vice President of Creative: Eddie Gomez. Creative Manager: Mara Schwartz. Creative Coordinator: Laura Scott. **Nashville:** 33 Music Square W Suite 104B, Nashville TN 37203. (615)313-7676. **Fax:** (615)313-7670. Director of Creative Services: Ed Williams; Creative Manager: Tyler Pickens. **New York:** 347 W. 36th St., Suite 1203, New York NY 10018. (212)643-0925. **Fax:** (212)643-0897. Senior Vice President: Garry Valletri. Music publisher. "We handle administration."

AFFILIATES Bughouse (ASCAP).

HOW TO CONTACT *Does not accept unsolicited submissions.*

MUSIC All genres. Published "You Were Mine" (by E. Erwin/M. Seidel), recorded by Dixie Chicks on Monument.

○ CALIFORNIA COUNTRY MUSIC

112 Widmar Pl., Clayton CA 94517 United States. **Contact:** Edward J. Brincat, owner. (BMI) Publisher and record company (Roll On Records). Pays standard royalty. Affiliate(s) Sweet Inspirations Music (ASCAP).

HOW TO CONTACT Submit demo by mail. Unsolicited submissions are OK. "Do not call or write. Any calls will be returned collect to caller." Send CD with 3 songs and lyric sheet. Include SASE. Responds in 6 weeks.

MUSIC Mostly **MOR, contemporary country,** and **pop.** Does not want rap, metal, or rock. Published *For Realities Sake* (album by F.L. Pittman/R. Barretta) and *Maddy* (album by F.L. Pittman/M. Weeks), both recorded by Ron Banks & L.J. Reynolds on Life & Bellmark Records; and *Quarter Past Love* (album by Irwin Rubinsky/Janet Fisher), recorded by Darcy Dawson on NNP Records.

❶✦ CHRISTMAS & HOLIDAY MUSIC

26642 Via Noveno, Mission Viejo CA 92691 United States. (949)859-1615. **E-mail:** justinwilde@christmassongs.com. **Website:** www.christmassongs.com. **Contact:** Justin Wilde. Music publisher. Estab. 1980. Publishes 8-12 songs/year; publishes 8-12 new songwriters/year. Staff size: 1. "All submissions must be complete songs (i.e., music and lyrics)." Pays standard royalty.

AFFILIATES Songcastle Music (ASCAP).

HOW TO CONTACT Submit demo CD by mail. Unsolicited submissions are OK. *Do not call. Do not send unsolicited MP3s or links to websites.* See website for submission guidelines. "First Class Mail only. Registered or certified mail not accepted." Prefers CD with no more than 3 songs with lyric sheets. Do not send lead sheets or promotional material, bios, etc." Include SASE but does not return material out of the US. Responds only if interested.

FILM & TV Places 10-15 songs in TV/year. Published Barbara Streisand's "It Must Have Been the Mistletoe."

MUSIC Strictly **Christmas, Halloween, Hanukkah, Mother's Day, Thanksgiving, Father's Day** and **New Year's Eve music** in every style imaginable: easy listening, rock, pop, blues, jazz, country, reggae, rap, children's secular or religious. *Please do not send anything that isn't a holiday song.* Published "It Must Have Been the Mistletoe" (single by Justin Wilde/Doug Konecky) from *Christmas Memories* (album), recorded by Barbara Streisand (pop Christmas), by Columbia; "What Made the Baby Cry?" (single by Toby Keith) and "Mr. Santa Claus" (single by James Golseth) from *Casper's Haunted Christmas* soundtrack (album), recorded by Scotty Blevins (Christmas) on Koch International.

TIPS "We only sign one out of every 200 submissions. Please be selective. If a stranger can hum your melody back to you after hearing it twice, it has 'standard' potential. Couple that with a lyric filled with unique, inventive imagery, that stands on its own, even without music. Combine the two elements, and workshop the finished result thoroughly to identify weak points. Submit to us only when the song is polished to perfection. Submit positive lyrics only. Avoid negative themes like 'Blue Christmas'."

◑ COME ALIVE COMMUNICATIONS, INC. (ASCAP)

348 Valley Rd., Suite A, P.O. Box 436, West Grove PA 19390-0436 United States. (610)869-3660. E-mail: info@comealivemusic.com. **Website:** www.comealiveusa.com. Professional Managers: Joseph L. Hooker (pop, rock, jazz); Bridget G. Hylak (spiritual, country, classical). Music publisher, record producer and record company. Estab. 1985. Publishes 4 singles/year. Staff: 7. Pays standard royalty of 50%.

○ Come Alive Communications received a IHS Ministries Award in 1996, John Lennon Songwriting Contest winner, 2003.

HOW TO CONTACT *Call first to obtain permission to submit a demo.* For song publishing submissions, prefers CD with 3 songs, lyric sheet, and cover letter. Does not return submissions. Responds only if interested.

MUSIC Mostly **pop, easy listening, contemporary Christian**, and **patriotic**; also **country** and **spiritual**. Does not want obscene, suggestive, violent, or morally offensive lyrics. Produced "In Search of America" (single) from *Long Road to Freedom* (album), written and recorded by J. Hooker (patriotic), released 2003 on ComeAliveMusic.com; "Our Priests/Nuestros Sacerdotes," named CMN's official theme song for the

Vatican Designated Year of the Priest (2009-10). See www.ourpriests.com.

⊘ COPPERFIELD MUSIC GROUP/PENNY ANNIE MUSIC (BMI)/TOP BRASS MUSIC (ASCAP)/BIDDY BABY MUSIC (SESAC)

1400 South St., Nashville TN 37212 United States. (615)726-3100. **Fax:** (615)726-3172. **E-mail:** ken@copperfieldmusic.com. **Website:** www.copperfieldmusic.com. **Contact:** Ken Biddy.

HOW TO CONTACT Contact first and obtain permission to submit a demo by e-mail only. Does not return submissions or accept phone calls. Responds only if interested.

MUSIC Mostly **country**; also **modern bluegrass**. Does not want rap or heavy/metal/rock. Recently published "Daddy Won't Sell the Farm" from *Tattoos and Scars* (album), recorded by Montgomery Gentry (country).

○ CORELLI MUSIC GROUP

P.O. Box 2314, Tacoma WA 98401-2314 United States. (253)735-3228. **E-mail:** JerryCorelli@yahoo.com; corellismusicgroup@yahoo.com. **Website:** www.corellimusicgroup.blogspot.com. **Contact:** Jerry Corelli. (BMI/ASCAP) Music publisher, record company (Omega III Records), record producer (Jerry Corelli/Angels Dance Recording Studio), and booking agency (Tone Deaf Booking). Estab. 1996. Publishes 12 songs/year; publishes 6 new songwriters/year. Staff size: 3. Pays standard royalty.

AFFILIATES My Angel's Songs (ASCAP); Corelli's Music Box (BMI).

HOW TO CONTACT Submit demo by mail. Unsolicited submissions are OK. "No phone calls, e-mails, or letters asking to submit." CD only with no more than 3 songs, lyric sheet and cover letter. "*We DO NOT accept MP3s via e-mail.* We want love songs with a message and overtly Christian songs. Make sure all material is copyrighted. *You MUST include SASE or we DO NOT respond!*" Responds in 2 months

MUSIC Mostly **contemporary Christian, Christian soft rock** and **Christmas**; also **love songs, ballads** and **new country**. Does not want songs without lyrics or lyrics without music. Published "I'm Not Dead Yet" (by Jerry Corelli), "Fried Bologna" (by Jerry Corelli), and "His Name is Jesus" (by Jerry Corelli), all from *I'm Not Dead Yet* (album), released 2010 on Omega III Records.

TIPS "Success is obtained when opportunity meets preparation! If a SASE is not sent with demo, we don't even listen to the demo. Be willing to do a rewrite. Don't send material expecting us to place it with a Top Ten artist. Be practical. Do your songs say what's always been said, except differently? Don't take rejection personally. Always send a #10 self-adhesive envelope for your SASE."

THE CORNELIUS COMPANIES/ GATEWAY ENTERTAINMENT, INC.

Dept. SM, 9 Music Square S, Suite 92, Nashville TN 37203 United States. (615)321-5333. **E-mail:** corneliuscompanies@bellsouth.net. **Website:** www.corneliuscompanies.com. (BMI, ASCAP, SESAC) Music publisher and record producer (Ron Cornelius). Publishes 60-80 songs/year; publishes 2-3 new songwriters/year. Occasionally hires staff writers. Pays standard royalty.
AFFILIATES Robin Sparrow Music (BMI), Strummin' Bird Music (ASCAP) and Bridgeway Music (SESAC).
HOW TO CONTACT *Contact by e-mail or call for permission to submit material.* Submit demo package by mail. Unsolicited submissions are OK. "Send demo on CD format only with 2-3 songs." Include SASE. Responds in 2 months.
MUSIC Mostly **country** and **pop**; also **positive country**, **gospel,** and **alternative**. Published songs by Confederate Railroad, Faith Hill, David Allen Coe, Alabama, and over 50 radio singles in the positive Christian/country format.
TIPS "Looking for material suitable for film."

CRINGE MUSIC (PRS, MCPS)

The Cedars, Elvington Lane, Hawkinge, Kent CT18 7AD United Kingdom. (01)(303)893-472. **Fax:** (01) (303)893-833. **E-mail:** info@cringemusic.co.uk. **Website:** www.cringemusic.co.uk. **Contact:** Christopher Ashman. Music publisher and record company (Red Admiral Records). Estab. 1979. Staff size: 2.
HOW TO CONTACT Submit demo package by mail. Unsolicited submissions are OK. CD only with unlimited number of songs and lyric sheet, lead sheet. Submission materials are not returned. Responds if interested.
MUSIC All styles.

THE CROSSWIND CORPORATION

P.O. Box 120816, Nashville TN 37212 United States. (615)467-3860. **Website:** http://crosswindcorporation.com.

CURB MUSIC

48 Music Square East, Nashville TN 37203 United States. (615)321-5080. **Website:** www.curb.com. (ASCAP, BMI, SESAC)
Curb Music only accepts submissions through reputable industry sources and does not accept unsolicited demos.
AFFILIATES Mike Curb Music (BMI); Curb Songs (ASCAP); and Curb Congregation Songs (SESAC).

JOF DAVE MUSIC

1055 Kimball Ave., Kansas City KS 66104 United States. (913)593-3180. **Contact:** David Johnson, CEO. Music publisher, record company (Cymbal Records). Estab. 1984. Publishes 30 songs/year; publishes 12 new songwriters/year. Pays standard royalty.
HOW TO CONTACT *Contact first and obtain permission to submit.* Prefers CD. Include SASE. Responds in 1 month.
MUSIC Mostly **gospel** and **R&B**. Published "The Woman I Love" (single) from *Sugar Bowl* (album), written and recorded by King Alex, released 2001 on Cymbal Records; and "Booty Clap" (single by Johnny Jones) from *Gotta Move On* (album), recorded by Jacuzé, released 2005 on Cymbal Records.

DEFINE SOMETHING IN NOTHING MUSIC

11213 W. Baden Street, Avondale AZ 85323 United States. (360)421-9225. **E-mail:** definesinm@gmail.com. **Website:** http://dsinm.weebly.com. **Contact:** Jaime Reynolds. Music agency. Staff Size: 5. Pays 75% of gross revenue.
HOW TO CONTACT Prefers MP3s sent to e-mail only. "Please do not contact for permission, just send your music." Does not return submissions. Responds in 2 weeks if interested.
MUSIC Interested in all styles. "We welcome everything all over the world."
TIPS "Please e-mail a zip file via yousendit.com. No phone calls or mail, no CDs or cassettes."

DELEV MUSIC COMPANY

7231 Mansfield Ave., Philadelphia PA 19138-1620 United States. (215)276-8861. **E-mail:** delevmusic@msn.com. **Contact:** William Lucas, president/CEO; Darryl Lucas, A&R. (ASCAP, BMI) Music publisher. Publishes 6-10 songs/year; publishes 6-10 new songwriters/year. Pays standard royalty.
AFFILIATES Sign of the Ram Music (ASCAP) and Delev Music (BMI).

HOW TO CONTACT *Does not accept unsolicited material. Write or call first to obtain permission to submit.* Prefers CD format only—no cassettes—with 1-4 songs and lyric sheet. "We will not accept certified mail or SASE." Does not return material. Responds in 1-2 months.

MUSIC Mostly **R&B ballads** and **dance-oriented**; also **pop ballads**, **Christian/gospel**, **crossover** and **country/western**. We do not accept rap song material. Published "Angel Love" (single by Barbara Heston/Geraldine Fernandez) from *The Silky Sounds of Debbie G* (album), recorded by Debbie G (light R&B/easy listening), released 2000 on Blizzard Records; *Variety* (album), produced by Barbara Heston, released on Luvya Records; and "Ever Again" by Bernie Williams, released 2003 on SunDazed Records.

TIPS "Persevere regardless if it is sent to our company or any other company. Most of all, no matter what happens, believe in yourself."

DISNEY MUSIC PUBLISHING

500 S. Buena Vista St., Burbank CA 91521 United States. (818)569-3241. **Fax:** (818)845-9705. **Website:** http://home.disney.go.com/music. (ASCAP, BMI) **AFFILIATES** Seven Peaks Music and Seven Summits Music.

Part of the Buena Vista Music Group.

HOW TO CONTACT *"We cannot accept any unsolicited material."*

DUANE MUSIC, INC.

382 Clarence Ave., Sunnyvale CA 94086 United States. (408)739-6133. Music publisher and record producer. Publishes 10-20 songs/year; publishes 1 new songwriter/year. Pays standard royalty.

AFFILIATES Morhits Publishing (BMI).

HOW TO CONTACT Submit demo by mail. Unsolicited submissions are OK. Prefers CD with 1-2 songs. Include SASE. Responds in 2 months.

MUSIC Mostly **blues**, **country**, **disco**, and **easy listening**; also **rock**, **soul** and **Top 40/pop**. Published "Little Girl" (single), recorded by The Syndicate of Sound & Ban (rock); "Warm Tender Love" (single), recorded by Percy Sledge (soul); and "My Adorable One" (single), recorded by Joe Simon (blues).

ELECTRIC MULE PUBLISHING COMPANY (BMI)/NEON MULE MUSIC (ASCAP)

1019 17th Ave. S, Nashville TN 37212 United States. **E-mail:** emuleme@aol.com.

MUSIC Country, pop.

EMF PRODUCTIONS

1000 E. Prien Lake Rd., Suite D, Lake Charles LA 70601 United States. **Website:** www.emfproductions.com. **Contact:** Ed Fruge, president. (ASCAP) Music publisher and record producer. Estab. 1984. Pays standard royalty.

HOW TO CONTACT Submit demo package by mail. Unsolicited submissions are OK. Prefers CD or DVDs with 3 of your best songs and lyric sheets. Does not return material. Responds in 6 weeks.

MUSIC Mostly **R&B**, **pop** and **rock**; also **country** and **gospel**.

EMI CHRISTIAN MUSIC PUBLISHING

P.O. Box 5084, Brentwood TN 37024 United States. (615)371-4300. **Website:** www.emicmg.com. (ASCAP, BMI, SESAC) Music publisher. Publishes more than 100 songs/year. Represents more than 35,000 songs and over 300 writers. Hires staff songwriters. Pays standard royalty.

AFFILIATES Birdwing Music (ASCAP), Sparrow Song (BMI), His Eye Music (SESAC), Ariose Music (ASCAP), Straightway Music (ASCAP), Shepherd's Fold Music (BMI), Songs of Promise (SESAC), Dawn Treader Music (SESAC), Meadowgreen Music Company (ASCAP), River Oaks Music Company (BMI), Stonebrook Music Company (SESAC), Bud John Songs, Inc. (ASCAP), Bud John Music, Inc. (BMI), Bud John Tunes, Inc. (SESAC), WorshipTogether Songs, ThankYou Music, Thirst Moon River.

HOW TO CONTACT *"We do not accept unsolicited submissions."*

MUSIC Published Chris Tomlin, Toby Mac, David Crowder, Jeremy Camp, Stephen Curtis Chapman, Delirious, Tim Hughes, Matt Redman, Demon Hunter, Underoath, Switchfoot, Third Day, Casting Crowns, and many others.

TIPS "Do what you do with passion and excellence and success will follow; just be open to new and potentially more satisfying definitions of what 'success' means."

EMI MUSIC PUBLISHING

75 Ninth Ave., 4th Floor, New York NY 10011 United States. (212)492-1200. **Fax:** (212)492-1865. **Website:** www.emimusicpub.com. See website for global offices.

HOW TO CONTACT *EMI does not accept unsolicited material.*

MUSIC Published "All Night Long" (by F. Evans/R. Lawrence/S. Combs), recorded by Faith Evans featuring Puff Daddy on Bad Boy; "You" (by C. Roland/J. Powell), recorded by Jesse Powell on Silas; and "I Was" (by C. Black/P. Vassar), recorded by Neal McCoy on Atlantic.

TIPS "Don't bury your songs. Less is more—we will ask for more if we need it. Put your strongest song first."

◑ EMSTONE MUSIC PUBLISHING

Box 398, Hallandale FL 33008 United States. **E-mail:** webmaster@emstonemusicpublishing.com. **Website:** www.emstonemusicpublishing.com. **Contact:** Mitchell Stone; Madeline Stone. (BMI)

HOW TO CONTACT Submit demo CD by mail with any number of songs. Unsolicited submissions are OK. Does not return material. Responds only if interested. "Also check our sister company at SongwritersBestSong.com."

MUSIC All types. Published *Greetings from Texas* (2009) (album), by Greetings From Texas; "Gonna Recall My Heart" (written by Dan Jury) from *No Tears* (album), recorded by Cole Seaver and Tammie Darlene, released on CountryStock Records; and "I Love What I've Got" (single by Heather and Paul Turner) from *The Best of Talented Kids* (compilation album) recorded by Gypsy; "My Christmas Card to You" (words and music by Madeline and Mitchell Stone); and "Your Turn to Shine" (words and music by Mitchell Stone).

TIPS "Keep the materials inside your demo package as simple as possible. Just include a brief cover letter (with your contact information) and lyric sheets. Avoid written explanations of the songs; if your music is great, it'll speak for itself. We only offer publishing contracts to writers whose songs exhibit a spark of genius. Anything less can't compete in the music industry."

FATT CHANTZ MUSIC

2535 Winthrope Way, Lawrenceville GA 30044 United States. (770)982-7055. **Website:** www.jeromepromotions.com. **Contact:** Bill Jerome, president. (BMI) Staff size: 3. Pays standard royalty of 50%.

HOW TO CONTACT Contact first and obtain permission to submit a demo. Include CD or MP3 and cover letter. Does not return submissions. Responds in 1 week.

MUSIC **Top 40, alt country.** Also **alternative,** crossover **R&B,** and **hip-hop.** Does not want rap, gospel, country. Published "She's My Girl," written by Lefkowith/Rogers, recorded by Hifi on Red/Generic (2009).

◐ ◑ ✪ FIRST TIME MUSIC (PUBLISHING) U.K.

Sovereign House, 12 Trewartha Rd., Praa Sands, Penzance, Cornwall TR20 9ST United Kingdom. +44(01736)762826. **Fax:** +44(01736)763328. **E-mail:** panamus@aol.com. **Website:** www.panamamusic. co.uk. Music publisher, record company (Digimix Records Ltd www.digimaxrecords.com, Rainy Day Records, Mohock Records, Pure Gold Records). Estab. 1986. Publishes 500-750 songs/year; 20-50 new songwriters/year. Staff size: 6. Hires staff writers. Pays standard royalty; "50-60% to established and up-and-coming writers with the right attitude."

AFFILIATES Scamp Music Publishing, Panama Music Library, Musik Image Library, Caribbean Music Library, PSI Music Library, ADN Creation Music Library, Promo Sonor International, Eventide Music, Melody First Music Library, Piano Bar Music Library, Corelia Music Library, Panama Music Ltd, Panama Music Productions, Digimix Worldwide Digital Distribution Services.

HOW TO CONTACT Submit demo package by mail. Unsolicited submissions are OK. Submit on CD only, "of professional quality" with unlimited number of songs/instrumentals and lyric or lead sheets. Responds in 1 month. SAE and IRC required for reply.

FILM & TV Places 200 songs in film and TV/year. "Copyrights and phonographic rights of Panama Music Limited and its associated catalogue have been used and subsist in many productions broadcasts and adverts produced by major and independent production companies, television, film/video companies, radio broadcasters (not just in the UK, but in various countries world-wide) and by commercial record companies for general release and sale. In the UK & Republic of Ireland they include the BBC networks of national/regional television and radio, ITV network programs and promotions (Channel 4, Border TV, Granada TV, Tyne Tees TV, Scottish TV, Yorkshire TV, HTV, Central TV, Channel TV, LWT, Meridian TV, Grampian TV, GMTV, Ulster TV, Westcountry TV, Channel TV, Carlton TV, Anglia TV, TV3, RTE (Ireland), Planet TV, Rapido TV, VT4 TV, BBC

Worldwide, etc.), independent radio stations, satellite Sky Television (BskyB), Discovery Channel, Learning Channel, National Geographic, Living Channel, Sony, Trouble TV, UK Style Channel, Hon Cyf, CSI, etc., and cable companies, GWR Creative, Premier, Spectrum FM, Local Radio Partnership, Fox, Manx, Swansea Sound, Mercury, 2CRFM, Broadland, BBC Radio Collection, etc. Some credits include copyrights in programs, films/videos, broadcasts, trailers and promotions such as *Desmond's*, *One Foot in the Grave*, *EastEnders*, *Hale and Pace*, *Holidays from Hell*, *A Touch of Frost*, *999 International*, and *Get Away*."

MUSIC All styles. Published "I Get Stoned" (hardcore dance), recorded by AudioJunkie & Stylus, released by EMI records (2009) on *Hardcore Nation 2009*; "Long Way to Go" (country/MOR) on *Under Blue Skies*, recorded by Charlie Landsborough, released on Rosette Records (2008); "Mr Wilson" (folk) from *Only the Willows are Weeping*, released on Digimix Records (2009); "Blitz" (progressive rock/goth rock), recorded by Bram Stoker on *Rock Paranoia*, released by Digimix Records, and many more.

TIPS "Have a professional approach—present well produced demos. First impressions are important and may be the only chance you get. Writers are advised to join the Guild of International Songwriters and Composers in the United Kingdom (www.songwriters-guild.co.uk and www.myspace.com/guildofsongwriters)."

FRICON MUSIC COMPANY

11 Music Square E, Nashville TN 37203 United States. (615)826-2288. **Fax:** (615)826-0500. **E-mail:** fricon@ comcast.net. **Website:** http://friconent.com. **Contact:** Terri Fricon, president; Madge Benson, professional manager. Publishes 25 songs/year; publishes 1-2 new songwriters/year. Staff size: 6. Pays standard royalty.

AFFILIATES Fricout Music Company (ASCAP) and Now and Forever Songs (SESAC).

HOW TO CONTACT *Contact first and obtain permission to submit.* Prefers CD with 3-4 songs and lyric or lead sheet. "Prior permission must be obtained or packages will be returned." Include SASE. Responds in 2 months.

MUSIC Mostly **country**.

GLAD MUSIC CO.

14340 Torrey Chase, Suite 380, Houston TX 77014 United States. (281)397-7300. **Fax:** (281)397-6206. **E-mail:** hwesdaily@gladmusicco.com. **Website:** www.

gladmusicco.com. **Contact:** Wes Daily; Don Daily. Music publisher, record company and record producer. Publishes 3 songs/year; publishes 2 new songwriters/year. Staff size: 2. Pays standard royalty.

AFFILIATES Bud-Don (ASCAP), Rayde (SESAC), and Glad Music (BMI).

HOW TO CONTACT Submit via CD or MP3 with 3 songs maximum, lyric sheet and cover letter. Lyric sheet should be folded around CD and submitted in a rigid case and secured with rubber band. Does not return material. Responds in 6 weeks. SASE or e-mail address for reply.

MUSIC Mostly **country**. Does not want weak songs. Published *Love Bug* (album by C. Wayne/W. Kemp), recorded by George Strait, released 1995 on MCA; *Walk Through This World With Me* (album), recorded by George Jones; and *Race Is On* (album by D. Rollins), recorded by George Jones, both released 1999 on Asylum.

G MAJOR PUBLISHING

P.O. Box 3331, Fort Smith AR 72913 United States. **E-mail:** Alex@Gmajor.org. **Website:** https://sites.google. com/a/gmajor.org/www/. **Contact:** Alex Hoover.

HOW TO CONTACT *No unsolicited submissions.* Submit inquiry by mail with SASE. Prefers CD or MP3. Submit up to 3 songs with lyrics. Include SASE. Responds in 4-6 weeks.

MUSIC Mostly **country** and **contemporary Christian**. Published *Set The Captives Free* (album by Chad Little/Jeff Pitzer/Ben Storie), recorded by Sweeter Rain (contemporary Christian), for Cornerstone Television; "Hopes and Dreams" (single by Jerry Glidewell), recorded by Carrie Underwood (country), released on Star Rise; and "Be Still" (single by Chad Little/Dave Romero/Bryan Morse/Jerry Glidewell), recorded by CO3 (contemporary Christian), released on Flagship Records.

TIPS "We are looking for 'smash hits' to pitch to the Country and Christian markets."

GOODNIGHT KISS MUSIC

10153 1/2 Riverside Dr. #239, Toluca Lake CA 91602 United States. (831)479-9993. **Website:** www.goodnightkiss.com. (BMI, ASCAP) Publishes 6-8 songs/year; publishes 4-5 new songwriters/year. Pays standard royalty.

Goodnight Kiss Music specializes in placing music in movies and TV.

AFFILIATES Scene Stealer Music (ASCAP).

HOW TO CONTACT "Check our website or subscribe to newsletter (www.goodnightkiss.com) to see what we are looking for and to obtain codes. Packages must have proper submission codes, or they are discarded." Only accepts material that is requested on the website. Does not return material. Responds in 6 months.

FILM & TV Places 3-5 songs in film/year. Published "I Do, I Do, Love You" (by Joe David Curtis), recorded by Ricky Kershaw in Road Ends; "Bee Charmer's Charmer" (by Marc Tilson) for the MTV movie *Love Song*; "Right When I Left" (by B. Turner/J. Fisher) in the movie *Knight Club*.

MUSIC All modern styles. Published and produced *Addiction: Highs & Lows* (CD), written and recorded by various artists (all styles), released 2004; *Tall Tales of Osama Bin Laden* (CD), written and recorded by various artists (all styles parody), released 2004; and *Rythm of Honor* (CD), written and recorded by various artists (all styles), slated release 2005, all on Goodnight Kiss Records.

TIPS "The absolute best way to keep apprised of the company's needs is to subscribe to the online newsletter. Only specifically requested material is accepted, as listed in the newsletter (what the industry calls us for is what we request from writers). We basically use an SGA contract, and there are never fees to be considered for specific projects or albums. However, we are a real music company, and the competition is just as fierce as with the majors."

○ L.J. GOOD PUBLISHING

33 Appleway Rd., Okanogan WA 98840 United States. (509)422-1400. **E-mail:** ljgood@wingsforchrist.com. **Website:** www.wingsforchrist.com. **Contact:** Lonnie Good. (ASCAP) Publishes 5 songs/year. Publishes 1 new songwriters/year. Staff size: 1. Pays standard royalty of 50%.

AFFILIATES L.J. Good Publishing (ASCAP).

HOW TO CONTACT Prefers CD or MP3 with 3 songs and lyric sheet, cover letter. Does not e-mailed MP3s. Does not return submissions.

MUSIC Mostly **country, blues, soft rock, contemporary Christian/Praise and Worship**.

GREEN MEADOWS PUBLISHING (BMI)

414 S. Main St., Beaver Dam KY 42320. (270)775-5431. **Contact:** Robert Bailey, executive director. Promotes 5 songs/year; 5 new songwriters/year. Works with composers and lyricists. Pays standard royalty.

Write or call first to obtain permission to submit. Prefers CDs with 5 songs or cassettes with lyric sheets. Does not return unsolicited material. Responds in 2 months. Music: Promotes and publishes Gospel Music. Published *Land up High,* written and recorded by Robert Bailey on Beatle Records.

☺ ⊘ HICKORY LANE PUBLISHING AND RECORDING

19854 Butternut Lane, Pitt Meadows BC V3Y 2S7 Canada. (604)465-1258. **E-mail:** kobzar@telus.net. **Website:** http://chrisurbanski.weebly.com. **Contact:** Chris Urbanski. (ASCAP, SOCAN) Music publisher, record company and record producer. Estab. 1988. Hires staff writers. Publishes 30 songs/year; publishes 5 new songwriters/year. Pays standard royalty.

HOW TO CONTACT *Does not accept unsolicited submissions.*

MUSIC Mostly **country** and **country rock**. Published "Just Living For Today" (single by Chris Urbanski), recorded by Chris Michaels (country), released 2005 on Hickory Lane Records; "This is My Sons" (single by Tyson Avery/Chris Urbanski/Alex Bradshaw), recorded by Chris Michaels (country), released 2005 on Hickory Lane Records; "Stubborn Love" (single by Owen Davies/Chris Urbanski/John Middleton), recorded by Chris Michaels (country), released 2005 on Hickory Lane Records.

TIPS "Send us a professional quality demo with the vocals upfront. We are looking for hits, and so are the major record labels we deal with. Be original in your approach, don't send us a cover tune."

○ HITSBURGH MUSIC CO.

P.O. Box 1431, 233 N. Electra, Gallatin TN 37066 United States. (615)452-0324. Publishes 12 songs/year. Staff size: 4. Pays standard royalty.

AFFILIATES 7th Day Music (BMI).

HOW TO CONTACT Submit demo by mail. Unsolicited submissions are OK. Prefers cassette or quality videocassette with 2-4 songs and lead sheet. Prefers studio produced demos. Include SASE. Responds in 6 weeks.

MUSIC Mostly **country gospel** and **MOR**. Published "That Kind'a Love" (single by Kimolin Crutchet and Dan Serafini), from *Here's Cissy* (album), recorded by Cissy Crutcher (MOR), released 2005 on Vivaton; "Disorder at the Border" (single), written and recorded by Donald Layne, released 2001 on Southern City; and "Blue Tears" (single by Harold Gilbert/Elaine

Harmon), recorded by Hal, released 2006 (reissue) on Southern City.

○ HOME TOWN HERO'S PUBLISHING (BMI)

304 E. Bois D'arc, Leonard TX 75452 United States. (903)587-2767. **Website:** www.myspace.com/hometownheroespublishing1. **Contact:** Tammy Wood, owner. Submit demo by mail. Unsolicited submissions are OK. Prefers CD with 3-6 songs, lyric sheet, and cover letter. Does not return submissions. Responds only if interested.

MUSIC Mostly **country (all styles)**, **pop**, **Southern rock**; also **ballads**, **gospel**, and **blues**. Does not want heavy metal and rap.

TIPS "Most of all, believe in yourself. The best songs come from the heart. Don't get discouraged, be tough, keep writing, and always think positive. Songwriters, no calls please. I will contact you if interested. Send me your best."

IDOL PUBLISHING

P.O. Box 720043, Dallas TX 75372 United States. (214)321-8890. **E-mail:** info@idolrecords.com. **Website:** www.IdolRecords.com. **Contact:** Erv Karwelis, president. Record publisher. Estab. 1992. Releases 30 singles, 80 LPs, 20 EPs and 10-15 CDs/year. Pays negotiable royalty to artists on contract; negotiable rate to publisher per song on record.

HOW TO CONTACT See website at www.IdolRecords.com for submission policy. No phone calls or e-mail follow-ups.

MUSIC Mostly **rock**, **pop**, and **alternative**. Released *The Boys Names Sue - The Hits Vol. Sue!* (album), The O's - *We are the Os* (album), Little Black Dress - *Snow in June* (album), *The Man* recorded by Sponge (alternative); *Movements* (album) recorded by Black Tie Dynasty (alternative); *In Between Days* (album), recorded by Glen Reynolds (rock), all released 2006/2006 on Idol Records. Other artists include Flickerstick, DARYL, Centro-matic, The Deathray Davies, GBH, PPT, The Crash that Took Me, Shibboleth, Trey Johnson.

●○ INSIDE RECORDS/OK SONGS

St.-Jacobsmarkt 76 (B1), 2000, Antwerp Belgium. 32+(0)3-226-77-19. **Fax:** 32+(0)3-226-78-05. **E-mail:** info@inside-records.be. **Website:** www.inside-records.be. Music publisher and record company. Estab. 1989. Publishes 50 songs/year; publishes 30-40 new songwriters/year. Hires staff writers. Royalty varies "depending on teamwork."

HOW TO CONTACT Submit demo by mail. Unsolicited submissions are OK. Prefers cassette with complete name, address, telephone and fax number. SAE and IRC. Responds in 2 months.

MUSIC Mostly **dance**, **pop**, and **MOR contemporary**; also **country**, **reggae**, and **Latin**. Published *Fiesta De Bautiza* (album by Andres Manzana); *I'm Freaky* (album by Maes-Predu'homme-Robinson); and *Heaven* (album by KC One-King Naomi), all on Inside Records.

●○⊛ INTOXYGENE SARL

283 rue du Fbg St. Antoine, Paris 75011 France. **E-mail:** infos@intoxygene.com. **Website:** www.intoxygene.com or www.theyounggods.com. **Contact:** Patrick Jammes. Music publisher and record company. Estab. 1990. Staff size: 1. Publishes 30 songs/year. Pays 50% royalty.

HOW TO CONTACT *Does not accept unsolicited submissions.*

FILM & TV Places 3/5 songs in film and in TV/year.

MUSIC Mostly **new industrial** and **metal**, **lounge**, **electronic**, and **ambient**. Publisher for Peepingtom (trip-hop), Djaimin (house), Missa Furiosa by Thierry Zaboitzeff (progressive), The Young Gods (alternative), Alex Carter, Love Motel, Steve Tallis, and lo'n, amongst others.

●○ ISLAND CULTURE MUSIC PUBLISHERS

E-mail: islandking@islandkingrecords.com. (BMI) Music publisher and record company (Island King Records). Estab. 1996. Publishes 10 songs/year; publishes 3 new songwriters/year. Hires staff songwriters. Staff size: 3. Pays standard royalty.

HOW TO CONTACT Submit demo package by mail. Unsolicited submissions are OK. Prefers CD with 8 songs and lyric sheet. Send bio and 8×10 glossy. Does not return material. Responds in 1 month.

MUSIC Mostly **reggae**, **calypso**, and **zouk**; also **house**. Published *De Paris a Bohicon* (album), recorded by Rasbawa (reggae), released 2006 on Island King Records; "Jah Give Me Life" (single by Chubby) from *Best of Island King* (album), recorded by Chubby (reggae), released 2003 on Island King Records; "When People Mix Up" (single by Lady Lex/L. Monsanto/Chubby) and "I Am Real" (single by L. Monsanto) from *Best of Island King* (album), recorded by Lady Lex (reggae), released 2003 on Island King Records.

○ IVORY PEN ENTERTAINMENT

P.O. Box 1097, Laurel MD 20725 United States. **E-mail:** ivorypen@comcast.net. (ASCAP) Professional Managers: Steven Lewis (R&B, pop/rock, inspirational); Sonya Lewis (A/C, dance) Wandaliz Colon (Latin, ethnic); Cornelius Roundtree (gospel/inspirational). Music publisher. Publishes 10 songs/year. Staff size: 4. Pays standard royalty.

HOW TO CONTACT E-mail electronic press kit or MP3 no less than 128k. Unsolicited submissions are OK. Prefers CD with 3-5 songs and cover letter. Does not return material. Responds in 4 months. "Don't forget contact info with e-mail address for faster response! Always be professional when you submit your work to any company. Quality counts."

MUSIC Mostly **R&B, dance, pop/rock, Latin, adult contemporary**, and **inspirational**. Published Ryan Vetter (single), written and recorded by Alan Johnson (pop/rock), released on Ivory Pen Entertainment; and "Mirror" (single), by Angel Demone, on Vox Angel Inc./Ivory Pen Entertainment.

TIPS "Learn your craft. Always deliver high quality demos. 'Remember, if you don't invest in yourself, don't expect others to invest in you. Ivory Pen Entertainment is a music publishing company that caters to the new songwriter, producer, and aspiring artist. We also place music tracks (no vocals) with artists for release."

◐ JANA JAE MUSIC

P.O. Box 35726, Tulsa OK 74153 United States. (918)786-8896. **E-mail:** janajae@janajae.com. **Website:** www.janajae.com. **Contact:** Kathleen Pixley, secretary. Music publisher, record company (Lark Record Productions, Inc.) and record producer (Lark Talent and Advertising). Publishes 5-10 songs/year; publishes 1-2 new songwriters/year. Staff size: 8. Pays standard royalty.

HOW TO CONTACT Submit demo by mail. Unsolicited submissions are OK. Prefers CD or DVD with 3-4 songs and typed lyric and lead sheet if possible. Does not return material. Responds only if accepted for use.

MUSIC Mostly **country, bluegrass, jazz** and **instrumentals (classical** or **country)**. Published *Mayonnaise* (album by Steve Upfold), recorded by Jana Jae; and *Let the Bible Be Your Roadmap* (album by Irene Elliot), recorded by Jana Jae, both on Lark Records.

○ JERJOY MUSIC

P.O. Box 1264, Peoria IL 61654 United States. (309)673-5755. **Website:** www.unitedcyber.com. **Contact:** Jerry Hanlon, professional manager. (BMI) Music publisher and record company (UAR Records). Estab. 1978. Publishes 10+ songs/year; publishes numerous new songwriters/year. Staff size: 3. Pays standard royalty.

Also see the listing for Kaysarah Music in this section and UAR Records in the Record Companies section of this book.

AFFILIATES Kaysarah Music (ASCAP); Abilite Music (BMI).

HOW TO CONTACT *Write first and obtain permission to submit.* "*WE DO NOT RESPOND TO TELEPHONE CALLS.* Unsolicited submissions are OK, but be sure to send SASE and/or postage or mailing materials if you want a reply and/or a return of all your material. *WE DO NOT OFFER CRITIQUES OF YOUR WORK UNLESS SPECIFICALLY ASKED.* Simple demos—vocal plus guitar or keyboard—are acceptable. We DO NOT require a major demo production to interpret the value of a song." Prefers CD with 4-8 songs and lyric sheet. Responds in 2 weeks.

MUSIC Mostly **American country, Irish country** and **religious**. Published "Philomena From Ireland," "I Wanted You for Mine," and "Lisa, Dance with Me" written by The Heggarty Twins of Northern Ireland (recorded by The Heggarty Twins and Jerry Hanlon, country), and "Things My Daddy Used to Do" written by Mark Walton (recorded by Jerry Hanlon, country); "That Little Irish Church" written and recorded by Jerry Hanlon, country gospel Irish). "I'd Better Stand Up" written by Gene Gillen and Will Herring (recorded by The Heggarty Twins and Jerry Hanlon, country); "Rainbow" written by Dwight Howell (recorded by The Heggarty Twins and Jerry Hanlon, Irish country). "All Your Little Secrets" and "The Girl from Central High" written by Ron Czikall (recorded by Tracy Wells, country); all released on UAR Records.

TIPS "Don't submit any song that you don't honestly feel is well constructed and strong in commercial value. Be critical of your writing efforts. Be sure you use each and every one of your lyrics to its best advantage. 'Think Big!' Make your songs tell a story and don't be repetitious in using the same or similar ideas or words in each of your verses. Would your musical creation stand up against the major hits that are making the charts today? Think of great hooks you can work into your song ideas."

⊘ QUINCY JONES MUSIC

6671 Sunset Blvd., #1574A, Los Angeles CA 90028 United States. (323)957-6601. **Fax:** (323)962-5231. **E-mail:** info@quincyjonesmusic.com. **Website:** www. quincyjonesmusic.com. (ASCAP)

HOW TO CONTACT *Quincy Jones Music does not accept unsolicited submissions.*

MUSIC The Quincy Jones Music Publishing catalogue is home to over 1,600 titles spanning five decades of music covering numerous musical genres including Jazz, R&B, Pop, Rock-n-Roll, Brazilian, Alternative and Hip-Hop. Over the years, such legendary performers as Frank Sinatra, Count Basie, Sarah Vaughan, Louis Jordan, Lesley Gore, Barbara Streisand, Billy Eckstine and Tony Bennett have recorded our songs. We remain a presence in today's market by way of such artists as Michael Jackson, 98°, Tevin Campbell, K-Ci & Jo Jo, George Benson, Ivan Lins, S.W.V., Vanessa Williams, Patti Austin, The Manhattan Transfer, James Ingram, Barry White, and Ray Charles. Our current roster of talent includes lyricists, composers, musicians, performers, and producers.

○ KAUPPS & ROBERT PUBLISHING CO.

P.O. Box 5474, Stockton CA 95205 United States. (209)948-8186. **E-mail:** kauppsrobertbmi@yahoo. com. (BMI) Melissa Glenn, A&R coordinator (all styles). Production Manager (country, pop, rock): Rick Webb. Professional Manager (country, pop, rock): Bruce Bolin. President: Nancy L. Merrihew. Music publisher, record company (Kaupp Records), manager, and booking agent (Merri-Webb Productions and Most Wanted Bookings). Estab. 1990. Publishes 15-20 songs/year; publishes 5 new songwriters/year. Pays standard royalty.

HOW TO CONTACT *Write first and obtain permission to submit.* Prefers cassette or VHS videocassette (if available) with 3 songs maximum and lyric sheet. "If artist, send PR package." Include SASE. Responds in 6 months.

MUSIC Mostly **country**, **R&B**, and **A/C rock**; also **pop**, **rock** and **gospel**. Published "Rushin' In" (single by N. Merrihew/B. Bolin), recorded by Valerie; "Goin Postal" (single by N. Merrihew/B. Bolin), recorded by Bruce Bolin (country/rock/pop); and "I Gotta Know" (single by N. Merrihew/B. Bolin), recorded by Cheryl (country/rock/pop), all released on Kaupp Records.

TIPS "Know what you want, set a goal, focus in on your goals, be open to constructive criticism, polish tunes and keep polishing."

○ KAYSARAH MUSIC

P.O. Box 1264, 6020 W. Pottstown Rd., Peoria IL 61654-1264 United States. (309)673-5755. **Fax:** (309)673-7636. **E-mail:** jerryhanlon33@yahoo.com. **Website:** www.unitedcyber.com. (ASCAP, BMI) Music Publisher, record company (UAR Records), and record producer. Estab. 2000. Publishes 2 new songwriters/year. Staff size: 3. Pays standard royalty.

○ Also see the listing for Jerjoy Music in this section and UAR Records in the Record Companies section of this book.

AFFILIATES Jerjoy Music (BMI); Abilite Music (BMI).

HOW TO CONTACT *Write first and obtain permission to submit.* "WE DO NOT RESPOND TO TELEPHONE CALLS. Unsolicited submissions are OK, but be sure to send SASE and/or postage or mailing materials if you want a reply and/or a return of all your material. WE DO NOT OFFER CRITIQUES OF YOUR WORK UNLESS SPECIFICALLY ASKED." Prefers CD with 4 songs and lyric sheet and cover letter. Include SASE. Responds in 2 weeks.

MUSIC Mostly **traditional country** and **country gospel**; also **Irish country**, **Irish ballads,** and **Irish folk/traditional**.

TIPS "Be honest and self-critical of your work. Make every word in a song count. Attempt to create work that is not over 2:50 minutes in length. Compare your work to the songs that seem to be what you hear on the radio. A good A&R person or professional recording artist with a creative mind can determine the potential value of a song simply by hearing a melody line (guitar or keyboard) and the lyrics. DON'T convince yourself that your work is outstanding if you feel that it will not be able to compete with the tough competition of today 's market."

○ LITA MUSIC

P.O. Box 40251, Nashville TN 37204 United States. (615)269-8682. **Fax:** (615)269-8929. **E-mail:** justinpeters@songsfortheplanet.com; songsfortheplanet@songsfortheplanet.com. **Website:** http://songsfortheplanet.com. **Contact:** Justin Peters. (ASCAP)

AFFILIATES Justin Peters Music, Platinum Planet Music and Tourmaline (BMI).

HOW TO CONTACT Submit demo package by mail. Unsolicited submissions are OK. Prefers CD with 5 songs and lyric sheet. Does not return material. "Place code '2011' on each envelope submission."

MUSIC Mostly **country**, **classic rock**, **Southern rock**, **inspirational AC Pop**, **Southern gospel/Christi**-**an**and **worship songs**. Published "The Bottom Line" recorded by Charley Pride on Music City Records (written by Art Craig, Drew Bourke, and Justin Peters); "No Less Than Faithful" (single by Don Pardoe/Joel Lyndsey), recorded by Ann Downing on Daywind Records, Jim Bullard on Genesis Records and Melody Beizer (#1 song) on Covenant Records; "No Other Like You" (single by Mark Comden/Paula Carpenter), recorded by Twila Paris and Tony Melendez (#5 song) on Starsong Records; "Making A New Start" and "Invincible Faith" (singles by Gayle Cox), recorded by Kingdom Heirs on Sonlite Records; "I Don't Want To Go Back" (single by Gayle Cox), recorded by Greater Vision on Benson Records; and "He Had Mercy On Me" (by Constance and Justin Peters) recorded by Shining Grace.

☉◐ MANY LIVES MUSIC PUBLISHERS (SOCAN)

RR #1, Kensington PE C0B 1M0 Canada. (902)836-4571. **E-mail:** musicpublisher@amajorsound.com. **Website:** www.amajorsound.com/manylivespublishers.html. **Contact:** Paul C. Milner, publisher. "Owners of Shell Lane Studio www.shelllanestudio.com complete in-house production facility. Many Lives Music Publishers was also involved in the production and recording of all projects listed below." Pays standard royalty.

HOW TO CONTACT Submit demo by mail, Myspace, or SonicBids. Unsolicited submissions are OK. Prefers CD and lyric sheet (lead sheet if available). Does not return material. Responds in 3 months if interested.

MUSIC All styles. *Six Pack EP* and *Colour*(album), written and recorded by Chucky Danger (Pop/Rock), released 2005 on Landwash Entertainment. Chucky Danger's *Colour* album was named Winner Best Pop Recording at the East Coast Music Awards 2006, "Sweet Symphony" was nominated for Single of the Year, and Chucky Danger was nominated for Best New Group. Released *Temptation* (album by various writers), arrangement by Paul Milner, Patrizia, Dan Cutrona (rock/opera), released 2003 on United One Records; *The Edge Of Emotion* (album by various writers), arrangement by Paul Milner, Patrizia, Dan Cutrona (rock/opera), released 2006 on Nuff entertain-ment /United One Records. The Single "Temptation" won a SOCAN #1 award. *Saddle River Stringband* (album) written and recorded by The Saddle River Stringband (Bluegrass) released on Panda Digital/Save As Music 2007. Winners of best Bluegrass recording East Coast Music Awards 2007. *Pat Deighan and the Orb Weavers* (album) "In A Fever In A Dream" (alternative) written by Pat Deighan, released on Sandbar Music April 2008.

MATERIAL WORTH PUBLISHING

46 First St., Walden NY 12586. (845)778-7768. **E-mail:** materialworthpub@aol.com. **Website:** www.material-worth.com. **Contact:** Frank Sardella, owner. (ASCAP) Music publisher. Staff size: 3. Pays standard royalty of 50%.

HOW TO CONTACT *E-mail or visit website for how to obtain permission to submit. Must have permission before sending.* Do not call first. Prefers MP3 or online player. CD, lyric sheet, and cover letter are also accepted; "no cassette tapes please." Does not return submissions. Responds in 6-8 weeks.

MUSIC Mostly **female pop** or **pop/country crossover**, **singer-songwriter, male pop alternative rock**.

◐ MCCLURE & TROWBRIDGE PUBLISHING, LTD (ASCAP, BMI)

P.O. Box 148548, Nashville TN 37214 United States. (615)902-0509. **E-mail:** manager@trowbridgeplanetearth.com. **Website:** http://trowbridgeplanetearth.com. Music publisher, record label (JIP Records), and production company (George McClure, producer). Publishes 35 songs/year. Publishes 5 new songwriters/year. Staff size: 8. Pays standard royalty of 50%.

HOW TO CONTACT *Follow directions ONLINE ONLY—obtain Control Number to submit a demo via US Mail.* Requires CD with 1-5 songs, lyric sheet, and cover letter. Does not return submissions. Responds in 3 weeks if interested.

MUSIC **Pop, country, gospel, Latin** and **swing**. Publisher of Band of Writers (BOW) series. Published *Experience (Should Have Taught Me)* (album) 2010 on JIP Records; *The Lights Of Christmas* (album); "PlayboySwing," released 2008 on JIP Records; "Miles Away" (single) on DiscoveryChannel's "The Deadliest Catch"; and "I'm A Wild One" (single), recorded by Veronica Leigh, released 2006 on Artist Choice CD.

○ JIM MCCOY MUSIC

25 Troubadour Lane, Berkeley Springs WV 25411 United States. (304)258-9381 or (304)258-8314. **Web-**

site: www.troubadourlounge.com. (BMI) **E-mail:** mccoytroubadour@aol.com. **Website:** www.troubadourlounge.com. **Contact:** Bertha and Jim McCoy, owners. Music publisher, record company (Winchester Records) and record producer (Jim McCoy Productions). Estab. 1973. Publishes 20 songs/year; publishes 3-5 new songwriters/year. Pays standard royalty.

AFFILIATES New Edition Music (BMI).

HOW TO CONTACT Submit demo by mail with lyric sheet. Unsolicited submissions are OK. Prefers cassette or CD with 6 songs. Include SASE. Responds in 1 month.

MUSIC Mostly **country, country/rock** and **rock**; also **bluegrass** and **gospel**. Published *Jim McCoy and Friends Remember Ernest Tubb*; "She's the Best" recorded by Matt Hahn on Troubadour Records (written by Jim McCoy); "Shadows on My Mind" recorded by Sandy Utley (written by Jim McCoy), "Rock and Roll Hillbilly Redneck Girl" recorded by Elaine Arthur (written by Jim McCoy), released in 2007.

⊘⊛ MCJAMES MUSIC INC.

1724 Stanford St., Suite B, Santa Monica CA 90404 United States. (310)712-1916. **Fax:** (419)781-6644. **E-mail:** tim@mcjamesmusic.com; steven@mcjamesmusic.com. **Website:** www.mcjamesmusic.com. **Contact:** Tim Jame; Steven McClintock. (ASCAP) Writers include: Pamela Phillips Oland, Stephen Petree, Jeremy Dawson, Chad Petree, Brian Stoner, Tom Templeman, Cathy-Anne McClintock, Tim James, Steven McClintock, Ryan Lawhon. Publishes 50 songs/year. Staff size: 4. Pays standard royalty. Does administration and collection for all foreign markets for publishers and writers.

AFFILIATES 37 Songs (ASCAP) and McJames Music, Inc. (BMI).

HOW TO CONTACT *Only accepts material referred by a reputable industry source.* Prefers CD with 2 songs and cover letter. Does not return material. Responds in 6 months.

FILM & TV Places 2 songs in film and 3 songs in TV/year. Music Supervisor: Tim James/Steven McClintock. *Blood and Chocolate, 3 Day Weekend, Dirty Sexy Money, Brothe3rs and Sisters, Dancing With the Stars, Dexter, It's Always Sunny in Philadelphia, America's Top Model.* Commercials include Honda Australia, Scion California, Motorola Razr 2 worldwide.

MUSIC Mostly **modern rock, country, pop, jazz** and **euro dance**; also **bluegrass** and **alternative**. Will ac-

cept some mainstream rap but no classical. Published "Le Disko"; "You are the One"; "Rainy Monday" (singles from Shiny Toy Guns on Universal), "Be Sure"; "What It Is" (singles from Cris Barber), "Keeps Bringing Me Back" (from Victoria Shaw on Taffita), "Christmas Needs Love to be Christmas" (single by Andy Williams on Delta), recent cover by ATC on BMG/Universal with "If Love is Blind"; single by new Warner Bros. act Sixwire called "Look at me Now."

TIPS "Write a song we don't have in our catalogue or write an undeniable hit. We will know it when we hear it."

⊘⊛ MIDI TRACK PUBLISHING (BMI)

P.O. Box 1545, Smithtown NY 11787 United States. (718)767-8995. **E-mail:** info@allrsmusic.com. **Website:** www.allrsmusic.com. **Contact:** Renee Silvestri-Bushey, president; F.John Silvestri, founder; Leslie Migliorelli, director of operations. Music publisher, record company (MIDI Track Records), music consultant, artist management, record producer. Voting member of NARAS/National Academy of Recording Arts and Sciences (The Grammy Awards), voting member of the Country Music Association (CMA Awards); SGMA/Southern Gospel Music Association, SGA/Songwriters Guild of America (Diamond Member). Estab. 1994. Staff size: 6. Publishes 3 songs/year; publishes 2 new songwriters/year. Pays standard royalty.

AFFILIATES ALLRS Music Publishing Co. (ASCAP).

HOW TO CONTACT "Write or e-mail first to obtain permission to submit. We do not accept unsolicited submissions." Prefers CD with 3 songs, lyric sheet and cover letter. Does not return material. Responds in 6 months only if interested.

FILM & TV Places 1 song in film/year. Published "Why Can't You Hear My Prayer" (single by F. John Silvestri/Leslie Silvestri), recorded by Iliana Medina in a documentary by Silvermine Films.

MUSIC Mostly **country, gospel, Top 40, R&B, MOR,** and **pop**. Does not want showtunes, jazz, classical or rap. Published "Why Can't You Hear My Prayer" (single by F. John Silvestri/Leslie Silvestri), recorded by eight-time Grammy nominee Huey Dunbar of the group DLG (Dark Latin Groove), released on MIDI Track Records (including other multiple releases); "Chasing Rainbows" (single by F. John Silvestri/Leslie Silvestri/Darin Kelly), recorded by Tommy Cash (country), released on MMT Records (including other multiple releases); "Because of You" (single by F. John Silvestri/Leslie Silvestri), recorded by Iliana Medina, released 2002 on MIDI Track Records (including other multiple releases also recorded by Grammy nominee Terri Williams, of Always, Patsy Cline, Grand Ole Opry member Ernie Ashworth), released on KMA Records and including other multiple releases; "My Coney Island" (single by F. John Silvestri/Leslie Silvestri), recorded by eight-time Grammy nominee Huey Dunbar, released 2005-2009 on MIDI Track Records.

TIPS "Attend workshops, seminars, and visit our blog on our website for advise, tips, and info on the music industry."

☺● MONTINA MUSIC

P.O. Box 32, Montreal QC H3X 3T3 Canada. (SOCAN) Music publisher and record company (Monticana Records). Estab. 1963. Pays negotiable royalty.

AFFILIATES Saber-T Music (SOCAN).

HOW TO CONTACT Unsolicited submissions are OK. Prefers CD. SAE and IRC. Responds in 3 months.

MUSIC Mostly **Top 40**; also **bluegrass, blues, country, dance-oriented, easy listening, folk, gospel, jazz, MOR, progressive, R&B, rock,** and **soul.** Does not want heavy metal, hard rock, jazz, classical, or New Age.

TIPS "Maintain awareness of styles and trends of your peers who have succeeded professionally. Understand the markets to which you are pitching your material. Persevere at marketing your talents. Develop a network of industry contacts, first locally, then regionally, nationally, and internationally."

⊘ THE MUSIC ROOM PUBLISHING GROUP

525 S. Francisca Ave., Redondo Beach CA 90277 United States. (310)316-4551. **E-mail:** mrp@aol.com. **Website:** http://musicroomonline.com; www.musicroom.us. **Contact:** John Reed. (ASCAP)/MRP MUSIC (BMI) Music publisher and record producer. Estab. 1982. Pays standard royalty.

AFFILIATES MRP Music (BMI).

HOW TO CONTACT *Not accepting unsolicited material.*

MUSIC Mostly **pop/rock/R&B** and **crossover.** Published "That Little Tattoo," "Mona Lisa" and "Sleepin' with an Angel" (singles by John E. Reed) from *Rock With an Attitude* (album), recorded by Rawk Dawg (rock), released 2002; "Over the Rainbow" and "Are You Still My Lover" (singles) from *We Only Came to Rock* (album), recorded by Rawk Dawg, released 2004 on Music Room Productions.

◉ MUST HAVE MUSIC

P.O. Box 361326, Los Angeles CA 90036 United States. (323)932-9524. **E-mail:** info@musthavemusic.com. **Website:** www.musthavemusic.com. (ASCAP, BMI) Music publisher and music library. Estab. 1990. Pays standard royalty.

AFFILIATES Must Have More Music (ASCAP); Must Have Music (BMI).

HOW TO CONTACT Submit demo by mail with a personal e-mail address included for director's response. Unsolicited submissions are OK. Prefers CD with lyric sheet and cover letter. Does not return submissions. Responds in 2 months.

FILM & TV Music supervisor: Ken Klar, managing director.

MUSIC Mostly **pop/R&B, pop/country,** and **rock;** also **AAA, adult contemporary,** and **contemporary Christian/gospel.** Does not want instrumental music. "We only work with completed songs with lyric and vocal."

TIPS "Write what you know and what you believe. Then re-write it!"

☻○ NERVOUS PUBLISHING

5 Sussex Crescent, Northolt, Middlesex UB5 4DL United Kingdom. +44(020) 8423 7373. **Fax:** +44(020) 8423 7773. **E-mail:** info@nervous.co.uk. **Website:** www.nervous.co.uk. **Contact:** Roy Williams, owner. Music publisher, record company (Nervous Records) and record producer. MCPS, PRS and Phonographic Performance Ltd. Publishes 100 songs/year; publishes 25 new songwriters/year. Pays standard royalty; royalties paid directly to US songwriters.

⊖   Nervous Publishing's record label, Nervous Records, is listed in the Record Companies section.

HOW TO CONTACT Submit demo by mail. Unsolicited submissions are OK. Prefers CD with 3-10 songs and lyric sheet. "Include letter giving your age and mentioning any previously published material." SAE and IRC. Responds in 3 weeks.

MUSIC Mostly **psychobilly, rockabilly,** and **rock** (impossibly fast music—e.g.: Stray Cats but twice as fast); also **blues, country, R&B** and **rock** ('50s style). Published *Trouble* (album), recorded by Dido Bonneville (rockabilly); *Rockabilly Comp* (album), recorded by various artists; and *Nervous Singles Collection* (album), recorded by various artists, all on Nervous Records.

TIPS "Submit *no* rap, soul, funk—we want *rockabilly*."

● NEWBRAUGH BROTHERS MUSIC

228 Morgan Lane, Berkeley Springs WV 25411 United States. (304)261-0228. **E-mail:** Nbtoys@verizon. net. (ASCAP, BMI) Music publisher, record company (NBT Records, BMI/ASCAP). Estab. 1967. Publishes 124 songs/year. Publishes 14 new songwriters/year. Staff size: 1. Pays standard royalty.

AFFILIATES NBT Music (ASCAP) and Newbraugh Brothers Music (BMI).

HOW TO CONTACT Submit demo by mail. Unsolicited submissions are OK. Prefers cassette or CD with any amount of songs, a lyric sheet and a cover letter. Include SASE. Responds in 6 weeks. "Please don't call for permission to submit. Your materials are welcomed."

MUSIC Mostly **rockabilly**, **hillbilly**, **folk** and **bluegrass**; also **rock**, **country**, and **gospel**. "We will accept all genres of music except songs with vulgar language." Published *"Ride the Train Series Vol. 25; Layin' It On the Line"* by Night Drive (2009); "Love Notes" The Sisters Two; "The Country Cowboy" by Jack Long; "Original Praise Songs" by Russ and Donna Miller.

TIPS "Find out if a publisher/record company has any special interest. NBT, for instance, is always hunting 'original' train songs. Our 'registered' trademark is a train and from time to time we release a compilation album of all train songs. We welcome all genres of music for this project."

● NEWCREATURE MUSIC

P.O. Box 1444, Hendersonville TN 37077 United States. (615)585-9301. **E-mail:** ba@landmarkcommunicationsgroup.com. **Website:** www.landmark-communicationsgroup.com. **Contact:** Bill Anderson Jr., president; G.L. Score, professional manager. Music publisher, record company, record producer (Landmark Communications Group), and radio and TV syndicator. Publishes 25 songs/year; publishes 2 new songwriters/year. Pays standard royalty.

AFFILIATES Mary Megan Music (ASCAP).

HOW TO CONTACT *Contact first and obtain permission to submit.* Prefers CD or videocassette with 4-10 songs and lyric sheet. Include SASE. Responds in 6 weeks.

MUSIC Mostly **country**, **gospel**, **jazz**, **R&B**, **rock**, and **Top 40/pop**. Published *Let This Be the Day* by C.J.

Hall; *When a Good Love Comes Along* by Gail Score; *The Wonder of Christmas* by Jack Mosley.

❷❀ OLD SLOWPOKE MUSIC

P.O. Box 52626, Utica Square Station, Tulsa OK 74152 United States. (918)742-8087. **Fax:** (888)878-0817. **E-mail:** ryoung@oldslowpokemusic.com. **Website:** http://oldslowpokemusic.com. **Contact:** Rodney Young, president. (BMI) Music publisher and record producer. Estab. 1977. Publishes 10- 20 songs/year; publishes 2 new songwriters/year. Staff size: 2. Pays standard royalty.

HOW TO CONTACT CDs only, no cassettes.

FILM & TV Places 1 song in film/year. Recently published "Samantha," written and recorded by George W. Carroll in *Samantha*. Placed two songs for Tim Drummond in movies, "Hound Dog Man" in *Loving Lu Lu* and "Fur Slippers" in a CBS movie *Shake, Rattle & Roll*.

MUSIC Mostly **rock**, **country** and **R&B**; also **jazz**. Published *Promise Land* (album), written and recorded by Richard Neville on Cherry Street Records (rock).

TIPS "Write great songs. We sign only artists who play an instrument, sing, and write songs."

❷ PEERMUSIC

2397 Shattuck Ave., Suite 202, Berkeley CA 94704 United States. (510)848-7337. **Fax:** (510)848-7355. **E-mail:** sfcorp@peermusic.com. **Website:** www.peermusic.com. Music publisher and artist development promotional label. Estab. 1928. Hires staff songwriters. "All deals negotiable."

AFFILIATES Songs of Peer Ltd. (ASCAP) and Peermusic III Ltd. (BMI).

HOW TO CONTACT "We do NOT accept unsolicited submissions. We only accept material through agents, attorneys and managers." Prefers CD and lyric sheet. Does not return material.

MUSIC Mostly **pop**, **rock** and **R&B**. Published music by David Foster (writer/producer, pop); Andrew Williams (writer/producer, pop); Christopher "Tricky" Stewart (R&B, writer/producer).

❷● PEGASUS MUSIC

Otago 2564 New Zealand. **Website:** www.myspace.com/pegasusmusicpublishing. Professional Managers: Errol Peters (country, rock); Ginny Peters (gospel, pop). Music publisher and record company. Estab. 1981. Publishes 20-30 songs/year; publishes 5 new songwriters/year. Pays standard royalty.

HOW TO CONTACT Submit demo package by mail. Unsolicited submissions are OK. Prefers CD with 3-5 songs and lyric sheet. SAE and IRC. Responds in 1 month.

MUSIC Mostly **country**; also **bluegrass**, **easy listening**, and **Top 40/pop**. Published "Beyond the Reason," written and recorded by Ginny Peters (Pegasus Records); "I Only See You," written by Ginny Peters, recorded by Dennis Marsh (Rajon Records, New Zealand); "The Mystery of God," written and recorded by Ginny Peters (NCM Records, England).

TIPS "Get to the meat of the subject without too many words. Less is better."

⊘ PERLA MUSIC

134 Parker Ave., Easton PA 18042 United States. (212)957-9509. **Fax:** (917)338-7596. **E-mail:** PM@PM-Records.org. **Website:** www.pmrecords.org. **Contact:** Gene Perla. (ASCAP) Music publisher, record company (PMRecords.org), record producer (Perla.org), studio production (TheSystemMSP.com), and Internet Design (CCINYC.com). Estab. 1971. Publishes 5 songs/year. Staff size: 5.

HOW TO CONTACT *E-mail first and obtain permission to submit.*

MUSIC Mostly **jazz** and **rock**.

○ JUSTIN PETERS MUSIC

P.O. Box 40251, Nashville TN 37227 United States. (615)269-8682. **Fax:** (615)269-8929. **E-mail:** justinpeters@songsfortheplanet.com; songsfortheplanet@songsfortheplanet.com. **Website:** http://songsfortheplanet.com. **Contact:** Justin Peters. (BMI) Music publisher. Estab. 1981.

AFFILIATES Platinum Planet Music(BMI), Tourmaline (BMI) and LITA Music (ASCAP).

HOW TO CONTACT Submit demo package by mail. Unsolicited submissions are OK. Prefers CD with 5 songs and lyric sheet. Does not return material. "Place code '2010' on each envelope submission."

MUSIC Mostly **pop**, **reggae**, **country** and **comedy**. Published "Saved By Love" (single), recorded by Amy Grant on A&M Records; "From the Center of my Heart," by Shey Baby on JAM Records; "A Gift That She Don't Want" (single), recorded by Bill Engvall on Warner Brother Records; "The Bottom Line," recorded by Charley Pride on Music City Records, cowritten by Justin Peters; "Heaven's Got to Help Me Shake These Blues" (single), written by Vickie Shaub and Justin Peters, recorded by B.J. Thomas; "Virginia Dreams"

and "Closer to You" (Jimmy Fortune/Justin Peters), recorded by Jimmy Fortune.

⊘ PHOEBOB MUSIC

5181 Regent Dr., Nashville TN 37212 United States. (615)832-4199. **Contact:** Phoebe Binkley. (BMI)

HOW TO CONTACT "We do not want unsolicited submissions." Music Mostly **country**, **Christian**, and **theatre**.

○ PLATINUM PLANET MUSIC, INC.

P.O. Box 40251, Nashville TN 37204 United States. (615)269-8682. **Fax:** (615)269-8929. **E-mail:** justinpeters@songsfortheplanet.com. **Website:** http://songsfortheplanet.com. **Contact:** Justin Peters. (BMI) Music publisher. Estab. 1997.

AFFILIATES Justin Peters Music (BMI), Tourmaline (BMI) and LITA Music (ASCAP).

HOW TO CONTACT Submit demo package by mail. Unsolicited submissions are OK. Prefers CD with 5 songs and lyric sheet. Does not return material. "Place code '2011' on each envelope submission."

MUSIC Mostly **R&B**, **reggae**, **sports themes**, **dance**, and **country**; also represents many **Christian** artists/writers. Published "Happy Face" (single by Dez Dickerson/Jordan Dickerson), recorded by Squirt on Absolute Records; "Buena Vida" (Daron Glenn and Justin Peters), recorded by Daron Glenn on PPMI; "Love's Not a Game" (single), written by Art Craig and J. Peters and recorded by Kashief Lindo on Heavybeat Records; "Place Called Heaven" written by Armond Morales and Kevin Wicker and released by the Imperials; "Love Won't Let Me Leave" (Art Craig and Justin Peters), recorded by Jason Rogers on Independent; and "Loud" (single), written and recorded by These Five Down on Absolute Records.

⊘ PORTAGE MUSIC (BMI)

16634 Gannon Ave. W., Rosemount MN 55068 United States. (952)432-5737. **E-mail:** olrivers@earthlink.net. **Contact:** Larry LaPole, president. Music publisher. Publishes 0-5 songs/year. Pays standard royalty.

HOW TO CONTACT *Call or e-mail first for permission to submit.*

MUSIC Mostly **country** and **country rock**. Published "Lost Angel," "Think It Over," and "Congratulations to Me" (by L. Lapole), all recorded by Trashmen on Sundazed.

TIPS "Keep songs short, simple and upbeat with positive theme."

○⊛ QUARK, INC.

P.O. Box 452, Newtown CT 06470 United States. (917)687-9988. **E-mail:** quarkent@aol.com. Music publisher, record company (Quark Records) and record producer (Curtis Urbina). Estab. 1984. Publishes 12 songs/year; 2 new songwriters/year. Staff size: 4. Pays standard royalty.

AFFILIATES Quarkette Music (BMI), Freedurb Music (ASCAP), and Quark Records.

HOW TO CONTACT Prefers CD only with 2 songs. No cassettes. Include SASE. Responds in 2 months.

FILM & TV Places 10 songs in film/year. Music Supervisor: Curtis Urbina.

MUSIC Pop. Does not want anything short of a hit.

○⊛ RAINBOW MUSIC CORP.

45 E. 66 St., New York NY 10021 United States. (212)988-4619. **E-mail:** fscam45@aol.com. **Contact:** Fred Stuart. Music publisher. Estab. 1990. Publishes 25 songs/year. Staff size: 2. Pays standard royalty.

AFFILIATES Tri-Circle (ASCAP).

HOW TO CONTACT *Only accepts material referred by a reputable industry source.* Prefers CD with 2 songs and lyric sheet. Include SASE. Responds in 1 week.

FILM & TV Published "You Wouldn't Lie To An Angel, Would Ya?" (single by Diane Lampert/Paul Overstreet) from *Lady of the Evening* (album), recorded by Ben te Boe (country), released 2003 on Mega International Records; "Gonna Give Lovin' A Try" (single by Cannonball Adderley/Diane Lampert/Nat Adderley) from *The Axelrod Chronicles* (album), recorded by Randy Crawford (jazz), released 2003 on Fantasy Records; "Breaking Bread" (single by Diane Lampert/Paul Overstreet) from *Unearthed* (album), recorded by Johnny Cash (country), released 2003 on Lost Highway Records; "Gonna Give Lovin' a Try" (single by Cannonball Adderley/Diane Lampert/Nat Adderley) from *Day Dreamin'* (album), recorded by Laverne Butler (jazz), released 2002 on Chesky Records; "Nothin' Shakin' (But the Leaves on the Trees)" (single by Diane Lampert; John Gluck, Jr./Eddie Fontaine/Cirino Colcrai) recorded by the Beatles, from *Live at the BBC* (album).

MUSIC Mostly **pop**, **R&B** and **country**; also **jazz**. Published "Break It to Me Gently" (single by Diane Lampert/Joe Seneca) from *TIME/LIFE* compilations *Queens of Country* (2004), *Classic Country* (2003),

and *Glory Days of Rock 'N Roll* (2002), recorded by Brenda Lee.

○○⊛ RANCO MUSIC PUBLISHING

(formerly Lilly Music Publishing), 61 Euphrasia Dr., Toronto ON M6B 3V8 Canada. **E-mail:** panfilo@sympatico.ca; obbiemusic@sympatico.ca. **Website:** www.myspace.com/rancorecords; www.obbiemusic.com. **Contact:** Panfilo Di Matteo, president. Music publisher and record company (P. & N. Records). Publishes 20 songs/year; publishes 8 new songwriters/year. Staff size: 3. Pays standard royalty.

AFFILIATES San Martino Music Publishing and Paglieta Music Publishing (CMRRA).

HOW TO CONTACT Submit demo by mail. Unsolicited submissions are OK. Prefers CD (or videocassette if available) with 3 songs and lyric and lead sheets. "We will contact you only if we are interested in the material." Responds in 1 month.

FILM & TV Places 12 songs in film/year.

MUSIC Mostly **dance**, **ballads**, and **rock**; also **country**. Published "I'd Give It All" (single by Glenna J. Sparkes), recorded by Suzanne Michelle (country crossover), released on Lilly Records.

RAZOR & TIE ENTERTAINMENT

214 Sullivan St., Suite 4A, New York NY 10012 United States. (212)598-2259. **Fax:** (212)473-9173. **E-mail:** bprimont@razorandtie.com. **Website:** www.razorandtiemusicpublishing.com.

HOW TO CONTACT *Does not accept unsolicited material.*

MUSIC Songwriters represented include Natalie Grant, Phillip LaRue, Matisyahu, Drive-By Truckers, Dave Barnes, Melinda Watts, and many more.

○ RED SUNDOWN RECORDS

1920 Errel Dowlen Rd, Pleasant View TN 37146 United States. (615)746-0844. **E-mail:** rsdr@bellsouth.net. (BMI)

HOW TO CONTACT *Does not accept unsolicited submissions.* Submit CD and cover letter. Does not return submissions.

MUSIC **Country**, **rock**, and **pop**. Does not want rap or hip-hop. Published "Take a Heart" (single by Kyle Pierce) from *Take Me With You* (album), recorded by Tammy Lee (country) released in 1998 on Red Sundown Records.

⊘ RONDOR MUSIC INTERNATIONAL/ALMO/IRVING MUSIC, A UNIVERSAL MUSIC GROUP COMPANY

Part of Universal Music Publishing Group, 2440 Sepulveda Blvd., Suite 119, Los Angeles CA 90064 United States. (310)235-4800. **Fax:** (310)235-4801. **E-mail:** rondorla@umusic.com. **Website:** www.universalmusicpublishing.com. (ASCAP, BMI)

AFFILIATES Almo Music Corp. (ASCAP) and Irving Music, Inc. (BMI).

HOW TO CONTACT *Does not accept unsolicited submissions.*

⊙ RUSTIC RECORDS, INC. PUBLISHING

6337 Murray Lane, Brentwood TN 37027 United States. (615)371-0646. **E-mail:** rusticrecordsam@aol.com. **Website:** www.rusticrecordsinc.com. (ASCAP,BMI,SESAC) **Contact:** Jack Schneider, president. Vice President: Claude Southall. Office Manager: Nell Tolson. Music publisher, record company (Rustic Records Inc.) and record producer. Estab. 1984. Publishes 20 songs/year. Pays standard royalty.

AFFILIATES Covered Bridge Music (BMI), Town Square Music (SESAC), Iron Skillet Music (ASCAP).

HOW TO CONTACT Submit demo by mail. Unsolicited submissions are OK. Prefers CD with 3-4 songs and lyric sheet. Include SASE. Responds in 3 months.

MUSIC Mostly **country**. Published "In Their Eyes" (single by Jamie Champa); "Take Me As I Am" (single by Bambi Barrett/Paul Huffman); and "Yesterday's Memories" (single by Jack Schneider), recorded by Colte Bradley (country), released 2003.

TIPS "Send three or four traditional country songs, novelty songs 'foot-tapping, hand-clapping' gospel songs with strong hook for male or female artist of duet. Enclose SASE (manilla envelope)."

⊙ SABTECA MUSIC CO. (ASCAP)

P.O. Box 10286, Oakland CA 94610 United States. **E-mail:** sabtecarecords@aol.com. **Website:** http://sabtecamusiccompany.com. **Contact:** Duane Herring, owner; Romare Herring, representative. Music publisher and record company (Sabteca Record Co., Andre Romare). Estab. 1980. Publishes 8-10 songs/year; 1-2 new songwriters/year. Pays standard royalty.

AFFILIATES Toyiabe Publishing (BMI).

HOW TO CONTACT *Write first and obtain permission to submit.* Prefers cassette with 2 songs and lyric sheet. Include SASE. Responds in 1 month.

MUSIC Mostly **R&B**, **pop** and **country**. Published "Walking My Baby Home" (single by Reggie Walker) from *Reggie Walker* (album), recorded by Reggie Walker (pop), 2002 on Andre Romare Records/Sabteca; "Treat Me Like a Dog" (single by Duane Herring/Thomas Roller), recorded by John Butterworth (pop), released 2004 Sabteca Music Co; "Sleeping Beauty", recorded by C Haynace, released 2008, Sabteca Music Co.

TIPS "Listen to music daily, if possible. Keep improving writing skills."

⊙ SANDALPHON MUSIC PUBLISHING

P.O. Box 542407, Grand Prairie TX 75054. **E-mail:** jackrabbit01@comcast.net. **Contact:** Ruth Otey. Music publisher, record company (Sandalphon Records), and management agency (Sandalphon Management). Staff size: 2. Pays standard royalty of 50%.

HOW TO CONTACT Submit demo by mail. Unsolicited submissions are fine. Prefers CD with 1-5 songs, lyric sheet, and cover letter. Include SASE or SAE and IRC for outside United States. Responds in 6-8 weeks.

MUSIC Mostly **rock**, **country**, and **alternative**; also **pop**, **blues**, and **gospel**.

⊙ SILICON MUSIC PUBLISHING CO.

222 Tulane St., Garland TX 75043 United States. **E-mail:** support@siliconmusic.us. **Website:** http://siliconmusic.us. Public Relations: Steve Summers. Music publisher and record company (Front Row Records). Estab. 1965. Publishes 10-20 songs/year; publishes 2-3 new songwriters/year. Pays standard royalty.

HOW TO CONTACT Submit demo package by mail. Unsolicited submissions are OK. Prefers cassette with 1-2 songs. Does not return material. Responds ASAP.

MUSIC Mostly **rockabilly** and **50s material**; also **old-time blues/country** and **MOR**. Published "Rockaboogie Shake" (single by James McClung) from *Rebels and More* (album), recorded by Lennerockers (rockabilly), released 2002 on Lenne (Germany); "Be-Bop City" (single by Dan Edwards), "So" (single by Dea Summers/Gene Summers), and "Little Lu Ann" (single by James McClung) from *Do Right Daddy* (album), recorded by Gene Summers (rockabilly/'50s rock and roll), released 2004 on Enviken (Sweden).

TIPS "We are very interested in 50s rock and rockabilly original masters for release through overseas affiliates. If you are the owner of any 50s masters, contact us first! We have releases in Holland, Switzerland, United Kingdom, Belgium, France, Sweden, Norway and Australia. We have the market if you have the tapes! Our staff writers include James McClung, Gary Mears (original Casuals), Robert Clark, Dea Summers, Shawn Summers, Joe Hardin Brown, Bill Becker and Dan Edwards."

⊘⊛ SILVER BLUE MUSIC/OCEANS BLUE MUSIC

3940 Laurel Canyon Blvd., Suite 441, Studio City CA 91604. (818)980-9588. **E-mail:** jdiamond20@aol. com. **Contact:** Joel Diamond. (ASCAP, BMI) Music publisher and record producer (Joel Diamond Entertainment). Estab. 1971. Publishes 50 songs/year. Pays standard royalty.

HOW TO CONTACT *Does not accept unsolicited material.* "No tapes returned."

FILM & TV Places 4 songs in film and 6 songs in TV/year.

MUSIC Mostly **pop** and **R&B**; also **rap** and **classical**. Produced and managed The 5 Browns-3 #1 CDs on Sony. Published "After the Lovin'" (by Bernstein/Adams), recorded by Engelbert Humperdinck; "This Moment in Time" (by Alan Bernstein/Ritchie Adams), recorded by Engelbert Humperdinck. Other artists include David Hasselhoff, Kaci (Curb Records), Ike Turner, Andrew Dice Clay, Gloria Gaynor, Tony Orlando, Katie Cassidy, and Vaneza.

◑ SIZEMORE MUSIC

P.O. Box 210314, Nashville TN 37221 United States. E-mail: americanabooks@comcast.net. **Website:** www. sizemoremusic.com. Music publisher, record company (Willowind) and record producer (G.L. Rhine). Estab. 1960. Publishes 5 songs/year; 1 new songwriter/year. Pays standard royalty.

HOW TO CONTACT Submit demo by mail. Unsolicited submissions are OK. Prefers CD with 2 songs and lyric sheets. Does not return material. Responds in 3 months.

MUSIC Mostly **hip-hop**, **soul**, **blues**, and **country**. Published "Liquor and Wine" and "The Wind," written and recorded by K. Shackleford (country), released on Heart Records.

◑ SME PUBLISHING GROUP

P.O. Box 1150, Tuttle OK 73089 United States. (405)381-3754. **E-mail:** smemusic@juno.com. **Website:** www.smepublishinggroup.com. (ASCAP,BMI) Professional Managers: Cliff Shelder (southern gospel); Sharon Kinard (country gospel). Music publisher.

Estab. 1994. Publishes 6 songs/year; publishes 2 new songwriters/year. Staff size: 2. Pays standard royalty.
AFFILIATES Touch of Heaven Music (ASCAP) and SME Music (BMI).

HOW TO CONTACT Submit demo package by mail. Unsolicited submissions are OK. Prefers CD with 3 songs and lyric sheet. Make sure tapes and CDs are labeled and include song title, writer's name, e-mail address, and phone number. Do not send SASE. Does not return or critique material. Responds only if interested.

MUSIC Mostly **Southern gospel**, **country gospel** and **Christian country**. Does not want Christian rap, rock and roll, or hard-core country. Released "I Love You Son" (single), by Jeff Hinton and Quint Randle, from *My Oasis* (album), recorded by the Crist Family (Southern gospel) on Crossroads Records; "Look Who's in the Ship" (Single by Mike Spanhanks) from *How I Picture Me* (album), recorded by the Skyline Boys (Southern Gospel) on Journey Records; "My Oasis" from *My Oasis* (album), recorded by the Crist Family (Southern gospel) on Crossroads Records.

TIPS "Always submit good quality demos. Never give up."

◑ SOUND CELLAR MUSIC

703 N. Brinton Ave., Dixon IL 61021 United States. (815)297-2800. **E-mail:** revelators@cellarrecords.com. **Website:** www.cellarrecords.com. **Contact:** Todd Anthony Joos. (BMI) **Contact:** Todd Joos (country, pop, Christian), president. Professional Managers: James Miller (folk, adult contemporary); Mike Thompson (metal, hard rock, alternative). Music publisher, record company (Sound Cellar Records), record producer and recording studio. Estab. 1987. Publishes 15-25 songs/year. Publishes 5 or 6 new songwriters/year. Staff size: 7. Pays standard royalty.

HOW TO CONTACT Submit demo by mail. Unsolicited submissions are OK. Prefers CD with 3 or 4 songs and lyric sheet. Does not return material. "We contact by phone in 3-4 weeks only if we want to work with the artist."

MUSIC Mostly **metal**, **country,** and **rock**; also **pop** and **blues**. Published "Problem of Pain" (single by Shane Sowers) from *Before the Machine* (album), recorded by Junker Jorg (alternative metal/rock), released 2000; "Vaya Baby" (single by Joel Ramirez) from *It's About Time* (album), recorded by Joel Ramirez and the All-Stars (Latin/R&B), released

2000; and "X" (single by Jon Pomplin) from *Project 814* (album), recorded by Project 814 (progressive rock), released 2001, all on Cellar Records. "Vist our website for up-to-date releases."

⊘✪ STILL WORKING MUSIC GROUP

1625 Broadway, Suite 200, Nashville TN 37203 United States. (615)242-0567. **Website:** www.myspace.com/stillworkingmusic. (ASCAP, BMI, SESAC) Music publisher and record company (Orby Records, Inc.). Estab. 1994.

AFFILIATES Still Working for the Woman Music (ASCAP), Still Working for the Man Music (BMI) and Still Working for All Music (SESAC).

HOW TO CONTACT *Does not accept unsolicited submissions.*

FILM & TV Published "First Noel," recorded by The Kelions in *Felicity.*

MUSIC Mostly **rock**, **country** and **pop**; also **dance** and **R&B**. Published "If You See Him/If You See Her" (by Tommy Lee James), recorded by Reba McIntire/Brooks & Dunn; "Round About Way" (by Wil Nance), recorded by George Strait on MCA; and "Wrong Again" (by Tommy Lee James), recorded by Martina McBride on RCA (country).

TIPS "If you want to be a country songwriter you need to be in Nashville where the business is. Write what is in your heart."

◉ SUPREME ENTERPRISES INT'L CORP.

P.O. Box 1373, Agoura Hills CA 91376 United States. (818)707-3481. **E-mail:** seicorp@earthlink.net. **Website:** www.seicorp.ne. (ASCAP, BMI) Music publisher, record company and record producer. Publishes 20-30 songs/year; publishes 2-6 new songwriters/year. Pays standard royalty.

AFFILIATES Fuerte Suerte Music (BMI), Big Daddy G. Music (ASCAP).

HOW TO CONTACT *No phone calls.* Submit demo by mail. Unsolicited submissions are OK. Prefers CD. Does not return material and you must include an e-mail address for a response. "Please copyright material before submitting and include e-mail." Responds in 12-16 weeks if interested.

MUSIC Mostly **reggae**, **rap**, and **dance**. Published "Paso La Vida Pensando," recorded by Jose Feliciano on Universal Records; "Cucu Bam Bam" (single by David Choy), recorded by Kathy on Polydor Records (reggae/pop); "Volvere Alguna Vez" recorded by Matt

Monro on EMI Records and "Meneaito" (single), recorded by Gaby on SEI Records.

TIPS "A good melody is a hit in any language."

◉ T.C. PRODUCTIONS/ETUDE PUBLISHING CO.

121 Meadowbrook Dr., Hillsborough NJ 08844 United States. (908)359-5110. **Fax:** (908)359-1962. **E-mail:** tony@tcproductions2005.com. **Website:** www.tony-camillo.com. (BMI) Music publisher and record producer. Estab. 1992. Publishes 25-50 songs/year; publishes 3-6 new songwriters/year. Pays negotiable royalty.

AFFILIATES We Iz It Music Publishing (ASCAP), Etude Publishing (BMI), and We B Records (BMI).

HOW TO CONTACT *Write or call first and obtain permission to submit.* Prefers CD or cassette with 3-4 songs and lyric sheet. Include SASE. Responds in 1 month.

MUSIC Mostly **R&B** and **dance**; also **country** and **outstanding pop ballads**. Published "I Just Want To Be Your Everything" (single) from *A Breath of Fresh Air* (album), recorded by Michelle Parto (spiritual), released 2006 on Chancellor Records; and *New Jersey Jazz* (album).

TIPS "Michelle Parto will soon be appearing in the film musical *Sing Out*, directed by Nick Castle and written by Kent Berhard."

◉✪ THISTLE HILL (BMI)

P.O. Box 707, Hermitage TN 37076 United States. (615)320-6071. **E-mail:** billyherzig@hotmail.com; wendy@greyhousestudio.com.

HOW TO CONTACT Submit demo by mail. Unsolicited submissions OK. Prefers CD with 3-10 songs. *No lyric sheets.* Responds only if interested.

MUSIC **Country**, **pop**, and **rock**; also **songs for film/TV**. Published "Angry Heart " (single) from *See What You Wanna See* (album), recorded by Radney Foster (Americana); and "I Wanna Be Free" (single) from *I Wanna Be Free* (album), recorded by Jordon MyCoskie (Americana), released 2003 on Ah! Records; "Que Vamos Hacer" (single) from *Rachel Rodriguez* (album), recorded by Rachel Rodriguez.

◯ TIKI STUDIOS-O'NEAL PRODUCTIONS (ASCAP, BMI)

195 S. 26th St., San Jose CA 95116 United States. (408)286-9840. **E-mail:** onealprod@gmail.com. **Website:** www.onealprod.net. **Contact:** Gradie O'Neal, president. Professional Manager: Jeannine O'Neil.

Music publisher, record company (Rowena Records) and record producer (Jeannine O'Neal and Gradie O'Neal). Estab. 1967. Publishes 40 songs/year; publishes 12 new songwriters/year. Staff size: 3. Pays standard royalty.

AFFILIATES Tooter Scooter Music (BMI), Janell Music (BMI) and O'Neal & Friend (ASCAP).

HOW TO CONTACT Submit demo by mail. Unsolicited submissions are OK. Prefers CD with 3 songs and lyric or lead sheets. Include SASE. Responds in 2 weeks.

MUSIC Mostly **country**, **Mexican**, **rock/pop**, **gospel**, **R&B** and **New Age**. Does not want atonal music. Published "You're Looking Good To Me" (single) from *A Rock 'N' Roll Love Story* (album), written and recorded by Warren R. Spalding (rock 'n' roll), released 2003-2004; "I Am Healed" (single) from *Faith On The Front Lines* (album), written and recorded by Jeannine O'Neal (praise music), released 2003-2004; and "It Amazes Me" (single by David Davis/Jeannine O'Neal) from *The Forgiven Project* (album), recorded by David Davis and Amber Littlefield, released 2003, all on Rowena Records.

TIPS "For up-to-date published titles, review our website. Keep writing and sending songs in. Never give up—the next hit may be just around the bend."

◐ TOURMALINE MUSIC, INC.

2831 Dogwood Place, Nashville TN 37204 United States. (615)269-8682. **Fax:** (615)269-8929. **E-mail:** justinpeters@songsfortheplanet.com. **Website:** http://songsfortheplanet.com. **Contact:** Justin Peters. (BMI) Music publisher. Estab. 1980.

AFFILIATES Justin Peters Music (BMI), LITA Music (ASCAP), and Platinum Planet Music (BMI).

HOW TO CONTACT Submit demo package by mail. Unsolicited submissions are OK. Prefers CD with 5 songs and lyric sheet. Does not return material. "Place code '2011' on each envelope submissions."

MUSIC Mostly **rock and roll**, **classy alternative**, **adult contemporary**, **classic rock**, **country**, **Spanish gospel**, and some **Christmas music**. Published "Making War In The Heavenlies," written by George Searcy, recorded by Ron Kenoly (Integrity); "The Hurt Is Worth the Chance," by Justin Peters/Billy Simon, recorded by Gary Chapman on RCA/BMG Records, and "The Bottom Line," by Art Craig, Drew Bourke, and Justin Peters, recorded by Charley Pride (Music City Records).

◐ ❀ TOWER MUSIC GROUP

19 Music Square W, Suite U-V-W, Nashville TN 37203 United States. (615)401-7111. **Fax:** (615)401-7111. **E-mail:** Towermanagementgroup@castleRecords.com. **Website:** www.castlerecords.com. **Contact:** Dave Sullivan. (ASCAP, BMI) Professional Managers: Ed Russell; Eddie Bishop. Music publisher, record company (Castle Records) and record producer. Estab. 1969. Publishes 50 songs/year; publishes 10 new songwriters/year. Staff size: 15. Pays standard royalty.

AFFILIATES Cat's Alley Music (ASCAP) and Alley Roads Music (BMI).

HOW TO CONTACT See submission policy on website. Prefers CD with 3 songs and lyric sheet. Does not return material. "You may follow up via e-mail." Responds in 3 months only if interested.

FILM & TV Places 2 songs in film and 26 songs in TV/year. Published "Run Little Girl" (by J.R. Jones/Eddie Ray), recorded by J.R. Jones in Roadside Prey.

MUSIC Mostly **country** and **R&B**; also **blues**, **pop** and **gospel**. Published "If You Broke My Heart" (single by Condrone) from *If You Broke My Heart* (album), recorded by Kimberly Simon (country); "I Wonder Who's Holding My Angel Tonight" (single) from *Up Above* (album), recorded by Carl Butler (country); and "Psychedelic Fantasy" (single by Paul Sullivan/Priege) from *The Hip Hoods* (album), recorded by The Hip Hoods (power/metal/y2k), all released 2001 on Castle Records. "Visit our website for an up-to-date listing of published songs."

TIPS "Please follow our Submission Policy at our web site www.CastleRecords.com."

◐ TRANSITION MUSIC CORPORATION

P.O. Box 2586, Toluca Lake CA 91610 United States. (323)860-7074. **E-mail:** submissions@transitionmusic.com. **Website:** www.transitionmusic.com. Publishes 250 songs/year; publishes 50 new songwriters/year. Variable royalty based on song placement and writer.

AFFILIATES Pushy Publishing (ASCAP), Creative Entertainment Music (BMI) and One Stop Shop Music (SESAC).

HOW TO CONTACT Submit one song (make it your best) online only to submissions@transitionmusic.com. We accept all genres and unsolicited music. **Responses will not be given due to the high volume of submissions daily. Please do not call/email to in-**

quire about us receiving your submission. TMC will only contact who they intend on signing.

FILM & TV "TMC provides music for all forms of visual media. Mainly television." Music—all styles.

MUSIC TMC is a music library and publishing company generating over 95,000 performances in film, TV, commercials, games, internet, and webisodes over the past year. In the last few months, TMC launched its newest division, Ultimate Exposure, exposing new independent artists to the world of visual media.

TIPS "Supply master quality material with great songs."

⊘ TRIO PRODUCTIONS, INC/ SONGSCAPE MUSIC, LLC

1026 15th Ave. S., Nashville TN 37212 United States. **E-mail:** info@trioproductions.com; robyn@trioproductions.com. **Website:** www.trioproductions.com.

AFFILIATES ASCAP, BMI, SESAC, Harry Fox Agency, CMA, WMBA, IPA

HOW TO CONTACT Contact first by e-mail to obtain permission to submit demo. *Unsolicited material will not be listened to or returned.* Submit CD with 3-4 songs and lyric sheet. Submit via MP3 once permission to send has been received. Include a lyric sheet.

MUSIC Country, pop, and **Americana**.

⊘ UNIVERSAL MUSIC PUBLISHING

2100 Colorado Ave., Santa Monica CA 90404 United States. (310)235-4700. **Fax:** (310)235-4900. **Website:** www.umusicpub.com. (ASCAP, BMI, SESAC)

HOW TO CONTACT *Does not accept unsolicited submissions.*

◑ UNKNOWN SOURCE MUSIC (ASCAP)

120-4d Carver Loop, Bronx NY 10475 United States. **E-mail:** unknownsourcemusic@hotmail.com. **Website:** www.unknownsourcemusic.com. Music publisher, record company (Smokin Ya Productions) and record producer. Estab. 1993. Publishes 5-10 songs/year; publishes 5-10 new songwriters/year. Hires staff songwriters. Staff size: 10. Pays standard royalty.

AFFILIATES Sundance Records (ASCAP), Critique Records, WMI Records, and Cornell Entertainment.

HOW TO CONTACT *Send e-mail first then mail.* Unsolicited submissions are OK. Prefers MP3s. Responds within 6 weeks.

MUSIC Mostly **rap/hip-hop**, **R&B**, and **alternative**. Published "LAH" recorded by Force Dog; "Changed My World" recorded by Crysto.

TIPS "Keep working with us, be patient, be willing to work hard. Send your very best work."

◑ VAAM MUSIC GROUP

P.O. Box 29550, Hollywood CA 90029 United States. **E-mail:** request@vaammusic.com. **Website:** www.vaammusic.com. **Contact:** Pete Martin, president. (BMI) Music publisher and record producer (Pete Martin/Vaam Productions). Estab. 1967. Publishes 9-24 new songs/year. Pays standard royalty.

AFFILIATES Pete Martin Music (ASCAP).

HOW TO CONTACT Send CD with 2 songs and lyric sheet. Include SASE. Responds in 1 month. "Small packages only."

MUSIC Mostly **Top 40/pop**, country. "Submitted material must have potential of reaching top 5 on charts."

TIPS "Study the top 10 charts in the style you write. Stay current and up-to-date with today's market."

◑ VINE CREEK MUSIC

P.O. Box 171143, Nashville TN 37217 United States. **E-mail:** vinecreek1@aol.com. **Website:** www.myspace.com/vinecreekmusic; www.darleneaustin.com. **Contact:** Darlene Austin. (ASCAP) Administration: Jayne Negri. Creative Director: Brenda Madden.

HOW TO CONTACT *Vine Creek Music does not accept unsolicited submissions.* "Only send material of good competitive quality. We do not return tapes/CDs unless SASE is enclosed."

○ WALKERBOUT MUSIC GROUP

P.O. Box 24454, Nashville TN 37202 United States. (615)269-7074. **Fax:** (888)894-4934. **E-mail:** matt@walkerboutmusic.com. **Website:** www.walkerboutmusic.com. **Contact:** Matt Watkins, director of operations. (ASCAP, BMI, SESAC) Publishes 50 songs/year; 5-10 new songwriters/year. Pays standard royalty.

AFFILIATES Goodland Publishing Company (ASCAP), Marc Isle Music (BMI), Gulf Bay Publishing (SESAC), Con Brio Music (BMI), Wiljex Publishing (ASCAP), Concorde Publishing (SESAC).

HOW TO CONTACT "Please see website for submission information."

MUSIC Mostly **country/Christian** and **adult contemporary**.

◔⊘ WARNER/CHAPPELL MUSIC, INC.

10585 Santa Monica Blvd., Los Angeles CA 90025 United States. (310)441-8600. **Fax:** (310)470-8780. **Website:** www.warnerchappell.com.

HOW TO CONTACT *Warner/Chappell does not accept unsolicited material.*

● WEAVER OF WORDS MUSIC

2239 Bank St., Baltimore MD 21231 United States. (276)970-1583. **E-mail:** weaverofwordsmusic@gmail.com. **Website:** www.weaverofwordsmusic.com. **Contact:** H.R. Cook, president. (BMI) Music publisher and record company (Fireball Records). Estab. 1978. Publishes 12 songs/year. Pays standard royalty.

AFFILIATES Weaver of Melodies Music (ASCAP).

HOW TO CONTACT Submit demo by mail. Unsolicited submissions are OK. Prefers CD with 3 songs and lyric or lead sheets. "We prefer CD submissions but will accept MP3s—limit 2." Include SASE. Responds in 3 weeks.

MUSIC Mostly **country**, **pop**, **bluegrass**, **R&B**, **film and television** and **rock**. Published "Zero To Love" (single by H. Cook/Brian James Deskins/Rick Tiger) from *It's Just The Night* (album), recorded by Del McCoury Band (bluegrass), released 2003 on McCoury Music; "Muddy Water" (Alan Johnston) from *The Midnight Call* (album), recorded by Don Rigsby (blue-grass), released 2003 on Sugar Hill; "Ol Brown Suit-case" (H.R. Cook) from *Lonesome Highway* (album), recorded by Josh Williams (bluegrass), released 2004 on Pinecastle; and "Mansions of Kings" from *Cherry Holmes II* (album), recorded by IBMA 2005 Entertainer of the Year Cherry Holmes (bluegrass), released 2007 on Skaggs Family Records.

● WILCOM PUBLISHING

248 Deano Road, Branson MO 65616 United States. (417)559-5256. **E-mail:** william@wilcompublishing.com. **Contact:** William Clark, owner. (ASCAP) Music publisher. Estab. 1989. Publishes 10-15 songs/year; publishes 1-2 new songwriters/year. Staff size: 2. Pays standard royalty.

HOW TO CONTACT *Write or call first and obtain permission to submit.* Prefers CD with 1-2 songs and lyric sheet. Include SASE. Responds in 3 weeks.

MUSIC Mostly **R&B**, **pop** and **rock**; also **country**. Does not want rap. Published "Girl Can't Help It" (single by W. Clark/D. Walsh/P. Oland), recorded by Stage 1 on Rockit Records (top 40). Also produced a cover of "D'yer M'aker" by Mylo Bigsby on MGL Records.

RECORD
COMPANIES

///

Record companies release and distribute records, CDs, and digital albums—the "tangible" products of the music industry. They sign artists to recording contracts, decide what songs those artists will record, and determine which songs to release. They are also responsible for providing recording facilities, securing producers and musicians, and overseeing the manufacture, distribution and promotion of new releases.

MAJOR LABELS & INDEPENDENT LABELS

Major labels and independent labels—what's the difference between the two?

The majors

As of this writing, there are three major record labels, commonly referred to as the "Big 3":

• **Sony BMG** (Columbia Records, Epic Records, RCA Records, Arista Records, J Records, Provident Label Group, and recently absorbed The EMI Group, which included Capitol Music Group, Angel Music Group, Astralwerks, Chrysalis Records, etc.)

• **Universal Music Group** (Universal Records, Interscope/Geffen/A&M, Island/Def Jam, Dreamworks Records, MCA Nashville Records, Verve Music Group, etc.)

• **Warner Music Group** (Atlantic Records, Bad Boy, Asylum Records, Warner Bros. Records, Maverick Records, Sub Pop, etc.)

Each of the "Big 3" is a large publicly-traded corporation beholden to shareholders and quarterly profit expectations. This means the major labels have greater financial resources and promotional muscle than a smaller "indie" label, but it's also harder to get signed to a major. A big major label may also expect more contractual control over an artist or band's sound and image.

As shown in the above list, they also each act as umbrella organizations for numerous other well-known labels—former major labels in their own right, well-respected former independent/boutique labels, as well as subsidiary "vanity" labels fronted by successful major label recording artists. Each major label also has its own related worldwide product distribution system, and many independent labels will contract with the majors for distribution into stores.

If a label is distributed by one of these major companies, you can be assured any release coming out on that label has a large distribution network behind it.

The independents

Independent labels go through smaller distribution companies to distribute their product. They usually don't have the ability to deliver records in massive quantities as the major distributors do. However, that doesn't mean independent labels aren't able to have hit records just like their major counterparts. A record label's distributors are found in the listings after the **Distributed by** heading.

Which do I submit to?

Many of the companies listed in this section are independent labels. They are usually the most receptive to receiving material from new artists. Major labels spend more money than most other segments of the music industry; the music publisher, for instance, pays only for items such as salaries and the costs of making demos. Record companies, at great financial risk, pay for many more services, including production, manufacturing and promotion. Therefore, they must be very selective when signing new talent. Also, the continuing fear of copyright infringement suits has closed avenues to getting new material heard by the majors. Most don't listen to unsolicited submissions, period. Only songs recommended by attorneys, managers and producers who record company employees trust and respect are being heard by A&R people at major labels (companies with a referral policy have an ICON preceding their listing). But that doesn't mean all major labels are closed to new artists. With a combination of a strong local following, success on an independent label (or strong sales of an independently produced and released album) and the right connections, you could conceivably get an attentive audience at a major label.

But the competition is fierce at the majors, so you shouldn't overlook independent labels. Since they're located all over the country, indie labels are easier to contact and can be important in building a local base of support for your music (consult the Geographic Index at the back of the book to find out which companies are located near you). Independent labels usually concentrate on a specific type of music, which will help you target those companies your submissions should be sent to. And since the staff at an indie label is smaller, there are fewer channels to go through to get your music heard by the decision makers in the company.

HOW RECORD COMPANIES WORK

Independent record labels can run on a small staff, with only a handful of people running the day-to-day business. Major record labels are more likely to be divided into the following departments: A&R, sales, marketing, promotion, product management, artist development, production, finance, business/legal and international.

- The *A&R department* is staffed with A&R representatives who search out new talent. They go out and see new bands, listen to demo tapes, and decide which artists to sign. They also look for new material for already signed acts, match producers with artists and oversee recording projects. Once an artist is signed by an A&R rep and a record is recorded, the rest of the departments at the company come into play.
- The *sales department* is responsible for getting a record into stores. They make sure record stores and other outlets receive enough copies of a record to meet consumer demand.
- The *marketing department* is in charge of publicity, advertising in magazines and other media, promotional videos, album cover artwork, in-store displays, and any other means of getting the name and image of an artist to the public.
- The *promotion department*'s main objective is to get songs from a new album played on the radio. They work with radio programmers to make sure a product gets airplay.
- The *product management department* is the ringmaster of the sales, marketing and promotion departments, assuring that they're all going in the same direction when promoting a new release.
- The *artist development department* is responsible for taking care of things while an artist is on tour, such as setting up promotional opportunities in cities where an act is performing.
- The *production department* handles the actual manufacturing and pressing of the record and makes sure it gets shipped to distributors in a timely manner.
- People in the *finance department* compute and distribute royalties, as well as keep track of expenses and income at the company.
- The *business/legal department* takes care of contracts, not only between the record company and artists but with foreign distributors, record clubs, etc.
- And finally, the *international department* is responsible for working with international companies for the release of records in other countries.

LOCATING A RECORD LABEL

With the abundance of record labels out there, how do you go about finding one that's right for the music you create? First, it helps to know exactly what kind of music a record label releases. Become familiar with the records a company has released, and see if they fit in with what you're doing. Each listing in this section details the type of music a particular record company is interested in releasing. You will want to refer to the Category Index in the back of this book to help you find those companies most receptive to the type of music you write. You should only approach companies open to your level of experience (see A Sample Listing Decoded on page 8). Visiting a company's website can also provide valuable information about a company's philosophy, the artists on the label and the music they work with.

NETWORKING

Recommendations by key music industry people are an important part of making contacts with record companies. Songwriters must remember that talent alone does not guarantee success in the music business. You must be recognized through contacts, and the only way to make contacts is through networking. Networking is the process of building an interconnecting web of acquaintances within the music business. The more industry people you meet, the larger your contact base becomes, and the better are your chances of meeting someone with the clout to get your demo into the hands of the right people. If you want to get your music heard by key A&R representatives, networking is imperative.

Networking opportunities can be found anywhere industry people gather. A good place to meet key industry people is at regional and national music conferences and workshops. There are many held all over the country for all types of music (see the Workshops and Conferences section for more information). You should try to attend at least one or two of these events each year; it's a great way to increase the number and quality of your music industry contacts.

Creating a buzz

Another good way to attract A&R people is to make a name for yourself as an artist. By starting your career on a local level and building it from there, you can start to cultivate a following and prove to labels that you can be a success. A&R people figure if an act can be successful locally, there's a good chance they could be successful nationally. Start getting booked at local clubs, and start a mailing list of fans and local media. Once you gain some success on a local level, branch out. All this attention you're slowly gathering, this "buzz" you're generating, will not only get to your fans but to influential people in the music industry as well.

SUBMITTING TO RECORD COMPANIES

When submitting to a record company, major or independent, a professional attitude is imperative. Be specific about what you are submitting and what your goals are. If you are strictly a songwriter and the label carries a band you believe would properly present your song, state that in your cover letter. If you are an artist looking for a contract, showcase your strong points as a performer. Whatever your goals are, follow submission guidelines closely, be as neat as possible and include a top-notch demo. If you need more information concerning a company's requirements, write or call for more details. (For more information on submitting your material, see the article *Where Should I Send My Songs?* on page 5 and Demo Recordings on page 9.)

RECORD COMPANY CONTRACTS

Once you've found a record company that is interested in your work, the next step is signing a contract. Independent label contracts are usually not as long and complicated as major label ones, but they are still binding, legal contracts. Make sure the terms are in the best interest of both you and the label. Avoid anything in your contract that you feel is too restrictive. It's important to have your contract reviewed by a competent entertainment lawyer. A basic recording contract can run from 40 to 100 pages, and you need a lawyer to help you understand it. A lawyer will also be essential in helping you negotiate a deal that is in your best interest.

Recording contracts cover many areas, and just a few of the things you will be asked to consider will be: What royalty rate is the record label willing to pay you? What kind of advance are they offering? How many records will the company commit to? Will they offer tour support? Will they provide a budget for video? What sort of a recording budget are they offering? Are they asking you to give up any publishing rights? Are they offering you a publishing advance? These are only a few of the complex issues raised by a recording contract, so it's vital to have an entertainment lawyer at your side as you negotiate.

The Case for Independents

If you're interested in getting a major label deal, it makes sense to look to independent record labels to get your start. Independent labels are seen by many as a stepping stone to a major recording contract. Very few artists are signed to a major label at the start of their careers; usually, they've had a few independent releases that helped build their reputation in the industry. Major labels watch independent labels closely to locate up-and-coming bands and new trends. In the current economic atmosphere at major labels—with extremely high overhead costs for developing new bands and the fact that only 10% of acts on major labels actually make any profit—they're not willing to risk everything on an unknown act. Most major labels won't even consider signing a new act that hasn't had some indie success.

But independents aren't just farming grounds for future major label acts; many bands have long term relationships with indies, and prefer it that way. While they may not be able to provide the extensive distribution and promotion that a major label can (though there are exceptions), indie labels can help an artist become a regional success, and may even help the performer to see a profit as well. With the lower overhead and smaller production costs an independent label operates on, it's much easier to "succeed" on an indie label than on a major.

Icons

For more instructional information on the listings in this book, including explanations of symbols (ICONS), read the article *How To Use Songwriter's Market* on page 2.

4AD

17-19 Alma Road, London SW18 1AA United Kingdom. **E-mail:** 4AD@4AD.com. **Website:** www.4ad.com.

HOW TO CONTACT Submit demo (CD or vinyl only) by mail, attention A&R, 4AD. "Sadly, there just aren't enough hours in the day to respond to everything that comes in. We'll only get in touch if we really like something."

MUSIC Mostly **rock, indie/alternative**. Current artists include Blonde Redhead, Bon Iver, Camera Obscura, The Breeders, The National, TV On The Radio, and more.

ALTERNATIVE TENTACLES

P.O. Box 419092, San Francisco CA 94141. (510)596-8981. **Fax:** (510)596-8982. **E-mail:** jb@alternativetentacles.com; promo@alternativetentacles.com. **Website:** www.alternativetentacles.com.

DISTRIBUTED BY Lumberjack/Mordam Records.

HOW TO CONTACT Unsolicited submissions OK. Prefers CD or cassette. Does not return material. Responds only if interested. "*We accept demos by postal mail ONLY! We do not accept MP3s sent to us.* We will not go out and listen to your MP3s on websites. If you are interested in having ATR hear your music, you need to send us a CD, tape or vinyl. We cannot return your demos either, so please don't send us your originals or ask us to send them back. Sometimes Jello replies to people submitting demos; sometimes he doesn't. There is no way for us to check on your 'status', so please don't ask us."

MUSIC Mostly **punk rock**, **spoken word**, **Brazilian hardcore**, **bent pop**, **faux-country**, and **assorted rock & roll**. Released *It's Not the Eat, It's the Humidity* (album), recorded by the Eat (punk); *Fuck World Trade* (album), recorded by Leftover Crack (punk); *Live from the Armed Madhouse* (album), recorded by Greg Palast (spoken word); *Dash Rip Rock* (album), recorded by Hee Haw Hell (southern country punk); *Homem Inimigo Do Homem* (album), recorded by Ratos De Parao (Brazilian hardcore). Other artists include Jello Biafra, The (International) Noise Conspiracy, Subhumans, Butthole Surfers, Dead Kennedys, DOA, Pansy Division, and Melvins.

ANGEL RECORDS

150 Fifth Ave., 6th Floor, New York NY 10011. (212)786-8600. **E-mail:** EMIClassicsUS@gmail.com. **Website:** www.angelrecords.com.

Angel Records is a subsidiary of the EMI Group, one of the "Big 4" major labels. EMI is a British-based company.

DISTRIBUTED BY EMI Music Distribution.

HOW TO CONTACT *Angel/EMI Records does not accept unsolicited submissions.*

MUSIC Artists include Sarah Brightman, Sir Paul McCartney, and Bernadette Peters.

ARIANA RECORDS

1312 S. Avenida Polar, #A-8, Tucson AZ 85710. (520)790-7324. **E-mail:** jtiom@aol.com. **Website:** www.arianarecords.net. **Contact:** James M. Gasper, president; Tom Dukes, vice president (pop, rock); Tom Privett (funk, experimental, rock) and Scott Smith (pop, rock, AOR), partners. Record company, music publisher (Myko Music/BMI) and record producer. Estab. 1980. Releases 5 CDs a year and 1 compilation/year. Pays negotiable rates.

DISTRIBUTED BY LoneBoy Records London, The Yellow Record Company in Germany, and Groovetune Music distributors in Alberta, Canada. Started talks with RCD Records for German distribution in early 2012.

HOW TO CONTACT "Send finished masters only. No demos! Unsolicited material okay."

MUSIC Mostly rock, funk, jazz, anything weird, strange, or lo-fi (must be mastered to CD). Released *Rustling Silk* (electronic) by BuddyLoveBand; *PornMuzik 2* (ambient); *T.G.I.F4* (electronica); *UnderCover Band*; *2010* (pop rock and funk); *Catch the Ghost* (hard rock). New releases *Musika* 2011 CD compilation, *Fun and Games* EP by Alien Workshop, and the single, "Hey Mr. President" by the Bailout Boys. Recently signed Perfect Paris (an electronic duo) and A Thousand Poets (an industrial/electronic duo).

TIPS "Keep on trying."

ARKADIA ENTERTAINMENT CORP.

11 Reservoir Rd., Saugerties NY 12477. (845)246-9955. **Fax:** (845)246-9966. **E-mail:** info@view.com. **Website:** www.arkadiarecords.com. A&R Song Submissions, acquisitions@view.com. Labels include Arkadia Jazz and Arkadia Chansons. Record company, music publisher (Arkadia Music), record producer (Arkadia Productions), and Arkadia Video. Estab. 1995.

HOW TO CONTACT *Write or call first and obtain permission to submit.*

MUSIC Mostly **jazz**, **classical**, and **pop/R&B**; also **world**.

ASTRALWERKS

101 Avenue of the Americas, 10th Floor, New York NY 10013. **E-mail:** astralwerks@astralwerks.net; A&R@astralwerks.net. **Website:** www.astralwerks.com.

○ Astralwerks is a subsidiary of the EMI Group, one of the "Big 4" major labels. EMI is a British-based company.

HOW TO CONTACT Send submissions to: "A&R Dept." to address above. No unsolicited phone calls please. Prefers CD. "Please include any pertinent information, including your group name, track titles, names of members, bio background, successes, and any contact info. Do not send e-mail attachments."

MUSIC Mostly **alternative/indie/electronic**. Artists include VHS or BETA, Badly Drawn boy, The Beta Band, Chemical Brothers, Turin Breaks, and Fatboy Slim.

TIPS "We are open to artists of unique quality and enjoy developing artists from the ground up. We listen to all types of 'alternative' music regardless of genre. It's about the aesthetic and artistic quality first. We send out rejection letters so do not call to find out what's happening with your demo."

○ ATLAN-DEC/GROOVELINE RECORDS

2529 Green Forest Court, Snellville GA 30078-4183. (877)751-5169. **E-mail:** atlandec@prodigy.net. **Website:** www.atlan-dec.com. **Contact:** Wileta J. Hatcher, art director. This company has grown to boast a roster of artists representing different genres of music. "Our artists' diversity brings a unique quality of musicianship to our CDs and tapes. This uniqueness excites our listeners and has gained us the reputation of releasing only the very best in recorded music." Atlan-Dec/Grooveline Records CDs and tapes are distributed worldwide through traditional and virtual online retail stores. Record company, music publisher and record producer. Staff size: 2. Releases 3-4 singles, 3-4 LPs and 3-4 CDs/year. Pays 10-25% royalty to artists on contract; statutory rate to publisher per song on record.

DISTRIBUTED BY C.E.D. Entertainment Dist.

HOW TO CONTACT Submit demo package by mail. Unsolicited submissions are OK. Prefers CD with lyric sheet. Does not return material. Responds in 3 months.

MUSIC Mostly **R&B/urban, hip-hop/rap,** and **contemporary jazz;** also **soft rock, gospel, dance,** and **new country.** Released "Temptation" by Shawree, re-

leased 2004 on Atlan-Dec/Grooveline Records; *Enemy of the State* (album), recorded by Lowlife (rap/hip-hop); *I'm The Definition* (album), recorded by L.S. (rap/hip-hop), released 2007; "AHHW" (single), recorded by LeTebony Simmons (R&B), released 2007. Other artists include Furious D (rap/hip-hop), Mark Cocker (new country), and Looka, "From the Top" (rap/hip-hop) recorded in 2008.

○○ ATLANTIC RECORDS

1290 Avenue of the Americas, New York NY 10104. (212)707-2000. **Fax:** (212)581-6414. **E-mail:** contact@atlanticrecords.com. **Website:** www.atlanticrecords.com. Labels include Big Beat Records, LAVA, Nonesuch Records, Atlantic Classics, and Rhino Records. Record company. Pays negotiable royalty to artists on contract; negotiable rate to publisher per song on record.

○ Atlantic Records is a subsidiary of Warner Music Group, one of the "Big 4" major labels.

DISTRIBUTED BY WEA.

HOW TO CONTACT *Does not accept unsolicited material.* "No phone calls please."

MUSIC Artists include Missy Elliott, Simple Plan, Lupe Fiasco, Phil Collins, B.O.B., Jason Mraz, and Death Cab For Cutie.

○ AVITA RECORDS

P.O. Box 764, Hendersonville TN 37077-0764. (615)824-1435. **E-mail:** tachoir@bellsouth.net. **Website:** www.tachoir.com.

○ Also see the listing for Riohcat Music in the Managers & Booking Agents section of this book.

HOW TO CONTACT *Contact first and obtain permission to submit.* "We only accept material referred to us by a reputable industry source." Prefers CD, cassette, or DAT. Does not return materials. Responds only if interested.

MUSIC Mostly **jazz.** Recently released *Travels* by the Jerry Tachoir Group. Other artists include Van Manakas and Marlene Tachoir.

○○ AWAL UK LIMITED

Sheffield Technology Park, Arundel St., Sheffield S1 2NS United Kingdom. **E-mail:** info@awal.com. **Website:** www.awal.com.

DISTRIBUTED BY Primarily distributes via digital downloads but physical distribution available.

HOW TO CONTACT Submit demo by mail. Unsolicited submissions are OK. Prefers CD with 5 songs, lyric sheet, cover letter and press clippings. Does not return materials.

MUSIC Mostly **pop**, **world**, and **jazz**; also **techno**, **teen**, and **children's**. Released *Go Cat Go* (album by various), recorded by Carl Perkins on ArtistOne.com; *Bliss* (album), written and recorded by Donna Delory (pop); and *Shake A Little* (album), written and recorded by Michael Ruff, both on Awal Records.

⊘ AWARE RECORDS

1316 Sherman Ave., #215, Evanston IL 60201. (847)424-2000. **E-mail:** awareinfo@awaremusic.com. **Website:** www.awaremusic.com.

HOW TO CONTACT *Does not accept unsolicited submissions.*

MUSIC Mostly **rock/pop**. Artists include Mat Kearney and Guster.

◑ BLACKHEART RECORDS

636 Broadway, New York NY 10012. (212)353-9600. **Fax:** (212)353-8300. **E-mail:** blackheart@blackheart. com. **Website:** www.blackheart.com.

HOW TO CONTACT Unsolicited submissions are OK. Prefers CD with 1-3 songs and lyric sheets. Include SASE. Responds only if interested.

MUSIC Mostly **rock**. Artists include Joan Jett & the Blackhearts, The Dollyrots, The Vacancies, Girl In A Coma, and The Eyeliners.

BOUQUET-ORCHID ENTERPRISES

P.O. Box 1335, Norcross GA 30091. (770)339-9088. **Contact:** Bill Bohannon, president. Management firm, booking agency, music publisher (Orchid Publishing/BMI) and record company (Bouquet Records). Represents individuals and groups; currently handles 3 acts. Receives 10-15% commission. Reviews material for acts.

HOW TO CONTACT Submit demo package by mail. Unsolicited submissions are OK. Prefers cassette, CD or videocassette with 3-5 songs, song list and lyric sheet. Include brief résumé. If seeking management, press kit should include current photograph, 2-3 media clippings, description of act, and background information on act. Include SASE. Responds in 1 month.

MUSIC Mostly **country**, **rock** and **Top 40/pop**; also **gospel** and R&B. Works primarily with vocalists and groups. Current acts include Susan Spencer, Jamey Wells, Adam Day and the Bandoleers.

● CAMBRIA RECORDS & PUBLISHING

P.O. Box 374, Lomita CA 90717. (310)831-1322. **Fax:** (310)833-7442. **E-mail:** cambriamus@aol.com. **Website:** http://cambriamus.com.

DISTRIBUTED BY Albany Distribution.

HOW TO CONTACT *Write first and obtain permission to submit.* Prefers cassette. Include SASE. Responds in 1 month.

MUSIC Mostly **classical**. Released *Songs of Elinor Remick Warren* (album) on Cambria Records. Other artists include Marie Gibson (soprano), Leonard Pennario (piano), Thomas Hampson (voice), Mischa Lefkowitz (violin), Leigh Kaplan (piano), North Wind Quintet, and Sierra Wind Quintet.

● CANTILENA RECORDS

740 Fox Dale Ln., Knoxville TN 37934. **Website:** www. cantilenarecords.com. Record company. Estab. 1993. Releases 3 CDs/year. Pays Harry Fox standard royalty to artists on contract; statutory rate to publishers per song on record.

HOW TO CONTACT *Write first and obtain permission to submit or to arrange personal interview.* Prefers CD. Does not return material.

MUSIC Classical, jazz. Released "Caliente!" (single by Christopher Caliendo) from *Caliente! World Music for Flute & Guitar* (album), recorded by Laurel Zucker and Christopher Caliendo! (world crossover); *Suites No. 1 & 2 For Flute & Jazz Piano Trio* (album by Claude Bolling), recorded by Laurel Zucker, Joe Gilman, David Rokeach, Jeff Neighbor (jazz); and *HOPE! Music for Flute, Soprano, Guitar* (album by Daniel Akiva, Astor Piazzolla, Haim Permont, Villa-Lobos) (classical/world), recorded by Laurel Zucker, Ronit Widmann-Levy, Daniel Akiva, all released in 2004 by Cantilena Records. Other artists include Tim Gorman, Prairie Prince, Dave Margen, Israel Philharmonic, Erkel Chamber Orchestra, Samuel Magill, Renee Siebert, Robin Sutherland, and Gerald Ranch.

⊘ CAPITOL RECORDS

1750 N. Vine St., Hollywood CA 90028. (323)462-6252. **Fax:** (323)469-4542. **Website:** www.hollywoodandvine.com. Labels include Blue Note Records, Grand Royal Records, Pangaea Records, The Right Stuff Records and Capitol Nashville Records. Record company.

〇 Capitol Records is a subsidiary of the EMI Group.

DISTRIBUTED BY EMD.

HOW TO CONTACT *Capitol Records does not accept unsolicited submissions.*

MUSIC Artists include Coldplay, The Decemberists, Beastie Boys, Katy Perry, Interpol, Lily Allen, and Depeche Mode.

◐✾ CAPP RECORDS

P.O. Box 150871, San Rafael CA 94915-0871. (415)457-8617. **Website:** www.capprecords.com.

HOW TO CONTACT Submit demo package by mail. Unsolicited submissions are OK. Prefers CD or NTSC videocassette with 3 songs and cover letter. "E-mail (on website) us in advance for submissions, if possible." Include SASE. Only responds if interested.

FILM & TV Places 20 songs in film and 7 songs in TV/year. Music Supervisors: Dominique Toulon (pop, dance, New Age). "Currently doing music placement for television—MTV, VH1, Oprah, A&E Network, and Discovery Channel."

MUSIC Mostly **pop**, **dance**, and **techno**; also **New Age**. Does not want country. Released "It's Not a Dream" (single by Cary August/Andre Pessis), recorded by Cary August on CAPP Records (dance). "Visit our website for new releases."

☾◯ COLLECTOR RECORDS

P.O. Box 1200, 3260 AE Oud Beijerland The Netherlands. (31)186 604266. **E-mail:** info@collectorrecords.nl. **Website:** www.collectorrecords.nl.

HOW TO CONTACT Submit demo package by mail. Unsolicited submissions are OK. Prefers cassette. SAE and IRC. Responds in 2 months.

MUSIC Mostly **50s rock**, **rockabilly**, **hillbilly boogie** and **country/rock**; also **piano boogie woogie**. Released *Rock Crazy Baby* (album), by Art Adams (1950s rockabilly), released 2005; *Marvin Jackson* (album), by Marvin Jackson (1950s rockers), released 2005; *Western Australian Snake Pit R&R* (album), recorded by various (1950s rockers), released 2005, all on Collector Records. Other artists include Henk Pepping, Rob Hoeke, Eric-Jan Overbeek, and more. "See our website."

⊘ COLUMBIA RECORDS

550 Madison Ave., 10th Floor, New York NY 10022. (212)833-4000. **Fax:** (212)833-4389. **E-mail:** sonymusiconline@sonymusic.com. **Website:** www.columbiarecords.com. **Santa Monica:** 2100 Colorado Ave., Santa Monica CA 90404. (310)449-2100. **Fax:** (310)449-2743. **Nashville:** 34 Music Square E., Nashville TN 37203. (615)742-4321. **Fax:** (615)244-2549. Record company.

◔ Columbia Records is a subsidiary of Sony BMG, one of the "Big 4" major labels.

DISTRIBUTED BY Sony.

HOW TO CONTACT *Columbia Records does not accept unsolicited submissions.*

MUSIC Artists include Aerosmith, Marc Anthony, Beyonce, Bob Dylan, and Patti Smith.

⊘ COSMOTONE RECORDS

2951 Marina Bay Dr., Suite 130, PMB 501, League City TX 77573-2733. **E-mail:** marianland@earthlink.net. **Website:** www.marianland.com/music.html; www.cosmotonerecords.com. Record company, music publisher (Cosmotone Music, ASCAP), and record producer (Rafael Brom).

DISTRIBUTED BY marianland.com

HOW TO CONTACT "Sorry, we do not accept material at this time." Does not return materials.

MUSIC Mostly **Christian pop/rock**. Released *Rafael Brom I*, *Padre Pio* by Lord Hamilton, *Dance for Padre Pio*, *Peace of Heart*, *Music for Peace of Mind*, *The Sounds of Heaven*, *The Christmas Songs*, *Angelophany*, *The True Measure of Love*, *All My Love to You Jesus* (albums), and *Rafael Brom Unplugged* (live concert DVD), *Life is Good*, *Enjoy it While You Can*, *Change*, by Rafael Brom, *Refugee from Socialism* by Rafael Brom, and *Move Your Ass*, by Rafael Brom, *Peanut Regatta* by Rafael Brom, and *Best of Rafael Brom*, Volume I, II, III and IV.

◯ CREATIVE IMPROVISED MUSIC PROJECTS (CIMP) RECORDS

Cadence Building, Redwood NY 13679. (315)287-2852. **Fax:** (315)287-2860. **Website:** www.cimprecords.com. Labels include Cadence Jazz Records. Record company and record producer (Robert D. Rusch). Releases 25-30 CDs/year. Pays negotiable royalty to artists on contract; pays statutory rate to publisher per song on record. Distributed by North Country Distributors.

◔ CIMP specializes in jazz and creative improvised music.

HOW TO CONTACT Submit demo by mail. Unsolicited submissions are OK. Prefers cassette or CD. "We are not looking for songwriters but recording artists." Include SASE. Responds in 1 week.

MUSIC Mostly **jazz** and **creative improvised music**. Released *The Redwood Session* (album), recorded by Evan Parker, Barry Guy, Paul Lytton, and Joe McPhee;

Sarah's Theme (album), recorded by the Ernie Krivda Trio, Bob Fraser, and Jeff Halsey; and *Human Flowers* (album), recorded by the Bobby Zankel Trio, Marily Crispell, and Newman Baker, all released on CIMP (improvised jazz). Other artists include Arthur Blythe, Joe McPhee, David Prentice, Anthony Braxton, Roswell Rudd, Paul Smoker, Khan Jamal, Odean Pope, etc.

TIPS "CIMP Records are produced to provide music to reward repeated and in-depth listenings. They are recorded live to two-track which captures the full dynamic range one would experience in a live concert. There is no compression, homogenization, eq-ing, post-recording splicing, mixing, or electronic fiddling with the performance. Digital recording allows for a vanishingly low noise floor and tremendous dynamic range. This compression of the dynamic range is what limits the 'air' and life of many recordings. Our recordings capture the dynamic intended by the musicians. In this regard these recordings are demanding. Treat the recording as your private concert. Give it your undivided attention and it will reward you. CIMP Records are not intended to be background music. This method is demanding not only on the listener but on the performer as well. Musicians must be able to play together in real time. They must understand the dynamics of their instrument and how it relates to the others around them. There is no fix-it-in-the-mix safety; either it works or it doesn't. What you hear is exactly what was played. Our main concern is music not marketing."

CURB RECORDS

49 Music Square E., Nashville TN 37203. (615)321-5080. **Fax:** (615)327-1964. **Website:** www.curb.com.

HOW TO CONTACT *Curb Records does not accept unsolicited submissions; accepts previously published material only. Do not submit without permission.*

MUSIC Released *Everywhere* (album), recorded by Tim McGraw; *Sittin' On Top of the World* (album), recorded by LeAnn Rimes; and *I'm Alright* (album), recorded by Jo Dee Messina, all on Curb Records. Other artists include Mary Black, Merle Haggard, David Kersh, Lyle Lovett, Tim McGraw, Wynonna, and Sawyer Brown.

DEEP SOUTH ENTERTAINMENT

P.O. Box 17737, Raleigh NC 27619-7737. (919)844-1515. **Fax:** (919)847-5922. **E-mail:** info@deepsouth-

entertainment.com. **Website:** www.deepsouthentertainment.com.

DISTRIBUTED BY Redeye Distribution, Valley, Select-O-Hits, City Hall, AEC/Bassin, Northeast One Stop, Pollstar, and Koch International.

HOW TO CONTACT Submit demo by mail. Unsolicited submissions are OK. Prefers cassette or CD with 3 songs, cover letter, and press clippings. Does not return material. Responds only if interested.

MUSIC Mostly **pop**, **modern rock**, and **alternative**; also **swing**, **rockabilly**, and **heavy rock**. Does not want rap or R&B. Artists include Bruce Hornsby, Little Feat, Mike Daly, SR-71, Stretch Princess, Darden Smith, and Vienna Teng.

DENTAL RECORDS

P.O. Box 20058 DHCC, New York NY 10017. (212)486-4513. **E-mail:** rsanford@dentalrecords.com. **Website:** www.dentalrecords.com.

HOW TO CONTACT "Check website to see if your material is appropriate." *Not currently accepting unsolicited submissions.*

MUSIC **Pop-derived structures**, **jazz-derived harmonies**, and **neo-classic-wannabee-pretenses**. Claims no expertise, nor interest, in urban, heavy metal, or hardcore. Released *Perspectivism* (album), written and recorded by Rick Sanford (instrumental), released 2003 on Dental Records. Other artists include Les Izmor.

DRUMBEAT INDIAN ARTS, INC.

4143 N. 16th St., Suite 1, Phoenix AZ 85016. (602)266-4823.

Note that Drumbeat Indian Arts is a very specialized label, and only wants to receive submissions by Native American artists.

HOW TO CONTACT *Call first and obtain permission to submit.* Include SASE. Responds in 2 months.

MUSIC **Music by American Indians**—any style (must be enrolled tribal members). Does not want New Age "Indian style" material. Released *Pearl Moon* (album), written and recorded by Xavier (native Amerindian). Other artists include Black Lodge Singers, R. Carlos Nakai, Lite Foot, and Joanne Shenandoah.

TIPS "We deal only with American Indian performers. We do not accept material from others. Please include tribal affiliation."

EARACHE RECORDS

4402 11th St., #507A, Long Island City NY 11101. (718)786-1707. **Fax:** (718)786-1756. **E-mail:** usaproduction@earache.com. **Website:** www.earache.com. **MUSIC Rock, industrial, heavy metal techno, death metal, grindcore**. Artists include Municipal Waste, Dillinger Escape Plan, Bring Me the Horizon, Deicide, Oceano, and more.

⊘ ELEKTRA RECORDS

75 Rockefeller Plaza, 17th Floor, New York NY 10019. **Website:** www.elektra.com.

◖   Elektra Records is a subsidiary of Warner Music Group.

DISTRIBUTED BY WEA.

HOW TO CONTACT *Elektra does not accept unsolicited submissions.*

MUSIC Mostly alternative/modern rock. Artists include Bruno Mars, Cee Lo, Justice, Little Boots, and others appearing on *True Blood*.

⊘ EPIC RECORDS

550 Madison Ave., 22nd Floor, New York NY 10022. (212)833-8000. **Fax:** (212)833-4054. **Website:** www.epicrecords.com. Labels include Beluga Heights, Daylight Records and E1 Music. Record company.

◖   Epic Records is a subsidiary of Sony BMG.

DISTRIBUTED BY Sony Music Distribution.

HOW TO CONTACT *Write or call first and obtain permission to submit* (New York office only). Does not return material. Responds only if interested. *Santa Monica and Nashville offices do not accept unsolicited submissions.*

MUSIC Artists include Sade, Shakira, Modest Mouse, The Fray, Natasha Bedingfield, Sean Kingston, Incubus, and The Script.

TIPS "Do an internship if you don't have experience or work as someone's assistant. Learn the business and work hard while you figure out what your talents are and where you fit in. Once you figure out which area of the record company you're suited for, focus on that, work hard at it and it shall be yours."

⊘ EPITAPH RECORDS

2798 Sunset Blvd., Los Angeles CA 90026. (213)355-5000. **E-mail:** publicity@epitaph.com. **Website:** www.epitaph.com. **Contact:** Jessica Giordano. Record company. Contains imprints Hellcat Records and Anti. "Epitaph Records was founded by Bad Religion guitarist Brett Gurewitz with the aim of starting an artist-friendly label from a musician's point of view. Perhaps most well known for being the little indie from L.A. that spawned the 90s punk explosion."

HOW TO CONTACT "Post your demos online at one of the many free music portals, then simply fill out the Demo Submission-form" on the website.

MUSIC Artists include Social Distortion, Alkaline Trio, Rancid, The Weakerthans, Weezer, Bad Religion, and Every Time I Die.

FAT WRECK CHORDS

P.O. Box 193690, San Francisco CA 94119. **E-mail:** mailbag@fatwreck.com. **Website:** www.fatwreck.com.

MUSIC Punk, rock, alternative. Artists include NOFX, Rise Against, The Lawrence Arms, Anti-Flag, Me First and the Gimme Gimmes, Propagandhi, Dillinger Four, Against Me!, and more.

FEARLESS RECORDS

13772 Goldenwest St. #545, Westminster CA 92683. **E-mail:** todd@fearlessrecords.com. **Website:** www.fearlessrecords.com.

HOW TO CONTACT Send all demos to mailing address. "Do not e-mail us about demos or with links to MP3s."

MUSIC Alternative, pop, indie, rock, metal. Artists include Plain White T's, At The Drive-in, The Maine, Mayday Parade, Sugarcult, Every Avenue, Alesana, Blessthefall, Breathe Carolina, Artist Vs Poet, and more.

◑ FIREANT

2009 Ashland Ave., Charlotte NC 28205. **E-mail:** lewh@fireantmusic.com. **Website:** www.fireantmusic.com.

DISTRIBUTED BY eMusic.com.

HOW TO CONTACT Submit demo by mail. Unsolicited submissions are OK. Prefers cassette, DAT, or videocassette. Does not return material.

MUSIC Mostly **progressive**, **traditional**, and **musical hybrids**. "Anything except New Age and MOR." Released *Loving the Alien: Athens Georgia Salutes David Bowie* (album), recorded by various artists (rock/alternative/electronic), released 2000 on Fireant; and *Good Enough* (album), recorded by Zen Frisbee. Other artists include Mr. Peters' Belizean Boom and Chime Band.

FLYING HEART RECORDS

4015 NE 12th Ave., Portland OR 97212. **E-mail:** flyheart@teleport.com. **Website:** http://home.teleport.com/~flyheart.

DISTRIBUTED BY Burnside Distribution Co.

HOW TO CONTACT Submit demo by mail. Unsolicited submissions are OK. Prefers cassette with 1-10 songs and lyric sheets. Does not return material. "SASE required for *any* response." Responds in 3 months.

MUSIC Mostly **R&B**, **blues**, and **jazz**; also **rock**. Released *Vexatious Progr.* (album), written and recorded by Eddie Harris (jazz); *Juke Music* (album), written and recorded by Thara Memory (jazz); and *Lookie Tookie* (album), written and recorded by Jan Celt (blues), all on Flying Heart Records. Other artists include Janice Scroggins, Tom McFarland, Thara Memory, and Snow Bud & The Flower People.

FRESH ENTERTAINMENT

1315 Joseph E. Boone Blvd., NW, Suite 5, Atlanta GA 30314. **E-mail:** whunter1122@yahoo.com. **Contact:** Willie W. Hunter, managing director. Record company and music publisher (Hserf Music/ASCAP, Blair Vizzion Music/BMI). Releases 5 singles and 2 LPs/year. Pays 7-10% royalty to artists on contract; statutory rate to publisher per song on record.

DISTRIBUTED BY Ichiban International and Intersound Records.

HOW TO CONTACT Submit demo package by mail. Unsolicited submissions are OK. Prefers cassette or VHS videocassette with at least 3 songs and lyric sheet. Include SASE. Responds in 2 months.

MUSIC Mostly **R&B**, **rock** and **pop**; also **jazz**, **gospel** and **rap**. Released in 2008: *Nubian Woman* by Bob Miles (jazz); Lissen (R&B/hip-hop); *You Know I'm From the A* by Joe "Da Bingo" Bing (rap); Future's *Pluto* CD album, 3 tracks): "Tony Montana," "Astronaut Chick", and "Fishscale."

FUELED BY RAMEN

1290 Avenue of the Americas, New York NY 10104. **E-mail:** john@fueledbyramen.com. **Website:** www.fueledbyramen.com.

HOW TO CONTACT Send demos by mail to address above.

MUSIC **Alternative, rock, indie**. Artists include The Academy Is..., Cobra Starship, Gym Class Heroes, Panic! at the Disco, Paramore, Sublime with Rome, This Providence, and more.

MARTY GARRETT ENTERTAINMENT

320 W. Utica Place, Broken Arrow OK 74011. (800)210-4416. **E-mail:** musicbusiness@telepath.com. **Website:** http://martygarrettentertainment.com; www.musicbusinessmoney.com. **Contact:** Marty R. Garrett, president. Labels include MGE Records and Lonesome Wind Records. Record company, record producer, music publisher, and entertainment consultant. Releases 1-2 EPs and 1 CD/year. Pays negotiable royalty to artists on contract; statutory rate to publisher per song on record.

HOW TO CONTACT *Call or check Internet site first and obtain permission to submit.* Prefers CD with 4-5 songs and lyric or lead sheet with chord progressions listed. Does not return material. No press packs or bios, unless specifically requested. Responds in 4-6 weeks.

MUSIC Mostly **honky tonk**, **traditional country**, or **scripture-based gospel**. Released *We're All in the Same Boat* (album) by Marty Garrett on MGE Records. Released singles include "He Bought Me Back Again," "My Father Made The Jailhouse Rock," "Drinking the New Wine," "Get Myself Off My Mind," and "What Would God Say Then"; "Peace From the Rock"; "Were All in the Same Boat"; all singles released on MGE Records.

TIPS "We help artists secure funding to record and release major label quality CD products to the public for sale through 1-800 television and radio advertising and on the Internet. Although we do submit finished products to major record companies for review, our main focus is to establish and surround the artist with their own long-term production, promotion and distribution organization. Professional studio demos are not required, but make sure vocals are distinct, up-front and up-to-date. I personally listen and respond to each submission received, so check the website to see if we are reviewing for an upcoming project."

GOTHAM RECORDS

P.O. Box 7185, Santa Monica CA 90406. **E-mail:** ar@gothamrecords.com; info@gothamrecords.com. **Website:** www.gothamrecords.com. Releases 8 LPs and 8 CDs/year. Pays negotiable royalty to artists on contract; statutory rate to publisher per song on record. "Gotham Music Placement is Gotham Records' main focus. Gotham Music Placement places recorded material with motion picture, TV, advertising, and video game companies. GMP supervises full feature films and releases full soundtracks, and represents artists from all over the world and all types of genres."

DISTRIBUTED BY Sony RED.

HOW TO CONTACT Submit demo by mail "in a padded mailer or similar package." Unsolicited submissions are OK. Prefers CD and bios, pictures, and touring information. Does not return material.

MUSIC All genres. Artists include SLANT, Red Horizon, The Day After…, and The Vicious Martinis.

TIPS "Send all submissions in regular packaging. Spend your money on production and basics, not on fancy packaging and gift wrap."

○ HACIENDA RECORDS & RECORDING STUDIO

1236 S. Staples St., Corpus Christi TX 78404. (361)882-7066. **Fax:** (361)882-3943. **E-mail:** info@haciendarecords.com. **Website:** www.haciendarecords.com.

HOW TO CONTACT Submit demo package by mail. Unsolicited submissions are OK. Prefers CD with cover letter. Does not return material. Responds in 6 weeks.

MUSIC Mostly **tejano**, **regional Mexican**, **country** (Spanish or English), and **pop**. Released "Chica Bonita" (single), recorded by Albert Zamora and D.J. Cubanito, released 2001 on Hacienda Records; "Si Quieres Verme Llorar" (single) from *Lisa Lopez con Mariachi* (album), recorded by Lisa Lopez (mariachi), released 2002 on Hacienda; "Tartamudo" (single) from *Una Vez Mas* (album), recorded by Peligro (norteno); and "Miento" (single) from *Si Tu Te Vas* (album), recorded by Traizion (tejano), both released 2001 on Hacienda. Other artists include, Gary Hobbs, Steve Jordan, Grammy Award nominees Mingo Saldivar and David Lee Garza, Michelle, Victoria Y Sus Chikos, and La Traizion.

● HEADS UP INT., LTD.

23309 Commerce Park Rd., Cleveland OH 44122. (216)765-7381. **Fax:** (216)464-6037. **E-mail:** dave@headsup.com. **Website:** www.headsup.com. Staff size: 57. Releases 13 LPs/year. Pays negotiable royalty to artists on contract.

DISTRIBUTED BY Universal Fontana (domestically).

HOW TO CONTACT Submit demo by mail. Unsolicited submissions are OK. Prefers CD. Does not return material. Responds to all submissions.

MUSIC Mostly **jazz**, **R&B**, **pop** and **world**. Does not want anything else. Released *Long Walk to Freedom* (album), recorded by Ladysmith Black Mambazo (world); *Pilgrimage* (album), recorded by Michael Brecker (contemporary jazz); *Rizing Sun* (album), recorded by Najee (contemporary jazz). Other artists include Diane Schuur, Mateo Parker, Victor Wooten, Esperanza Spalding, Incognito, George Doke, Take 6, Fourplay.

⊘ HEART MUSIC, INC.

P.O. Box 160326, Austin TX 78716-0326. (512)795-2375. **E-mail:** info@heartmusic.com. **Website:** www.heartmusic.com. **Contact:** Tab Bartling, president. Record company and music publisher (Coolhot Music). "Studio available for artists." Staff size: 2. Releases 1-2 CDs/year. Pays statutory rate to publisher per song on record.

HOW TO CONTACT *Not interested in new material at this time.* Does not return material. Responds only if interested.

MUSIC Mostly **Folk-rock, pop**, and **jazz**; also **blues** and **contemporary folk**. Libby Kirkpatrick's *Heroine* in early 2011; released *The Fisherman* (album), recorded by Darin Layne/Jason McKensie; *Collaborations* (album), recorded by Will Taylor and Strings Attached, featuring Eliza Gilkyson, Shawn Colvin, Patrice Pike, Ian Moore, Guy Forsyth, Ruthie Foster, Libby Kirkpatrick, Jimmy LaFave, Slaid Cleaves, and Barbara K., released 2006; *Goodnight Venus* (album), recorded by Libby Kirkpatrick, released in 2003, and *Be Cool Be Kind* (album), recorded by Carla Helmbrecht (jazz), released January 2001.

HOLOGRAPHIC RECORDING COMPANY

Longworth Hall, 700 West Pete Rose Way, Suite 390, P.O. Box 18, Cincinnati OH 45203. (513)442-3886. **Fax:** (513)834-9390. **E-mail:** info@holographicrecords.com. **Website:** http://holographicrecords.com.

HOW TO CONTACT Call first and obtain permission to submit.

MUSIC **Jazz, progressive**. Current acts include Acumen (progressive jam rock), John Novello (fusion), Alex Skolnick Trio (progressive jazz), Jeff Berlin (jazz), Poogie Bell Band (urban jazz), Dave LaRue (fusion), Mads Eriksen (fusion).

○ HOTTRAX RECORDS

1957 Kilburn Dr. NE, Atlanta GA 30324. **E-mail:** hotwax@hottrax.com. **Website:** www.hottrax.com.

DISTRIBUTED BY Get Hip Inc., DWM Music and Super D.

HOW TO CONTACT *E-mail first to obtain permission to submit.* Prefers an e-link to songs and lyrics in the e-mail. Does not return CDs or printed material. Responds in 6 months. "When submissions get extremely heavy, we do not have the time to respond/return material we pass on. We do notify those sending the most promising work we review, however. Current economic conditions may also affect song acceptance and response."

MUSIC Mostly **blues/blues rock**, some **Top 40/pop**, **rock**, and **country**; also **hardcore punk** and **jazz-fusion**. Released *Power Pop Deluxe* (album), by Secret Lover featuring Delanna Protas, *Some of My Best Friends Have the Blues* (album), by Big Al Jano, *Hot to Trot* (album), written and recorded by Starfoxx (rock); *Lady That Digs The Blues* (album), recorded by Big Al Jano's Blues Mafia Show (blues rock); and *Vol. III, Psychedelic Era. 1967-1969* (album), released 2002 on Hottrax. Other artists include Big Al Jano, Sammy Blue, and Sheffield & Webb. Released in 2010: *So Much Love* (album), by Michael Rozakis & Yorgos; Beyond the Shadows--Then and Now, by Little Phil. Scheduled: *Rare Pidgeon* (CD) by Rick Ware.

IDOL RECORDS

P.O. Box 140344, Dallas TX 75214. (214)370-5417. **E-mail:** info@idolrecords.com. **Website:** www.idolrecords.com. **Contact:** Erv Karwelis, president. Releases 30 singles, 80 LPs, 20 EPs and 10-15 CDs/year. Pays negotiable royalty to artists on contract; negotiable rate to publisher per song on record.

DISTRIBUTED BY Super D (SDID).

HOW TO CONTACT See website at www.IdolRecords.com for submission policy. No phone calls or e-mail follow-ups.

MUSIC Mostly **rock**, **pop**, and **alternative**; also some **hip-hop**. The O's - *Between The Two* (album), Here Holy Spain - *Division* (album), Calhoun - *Heavy Sugar* (album), Little Black Dress - *Snow in June* (album), all released 2009-12 on Idol Records. Other artists include Flickerstick, DARYL, Centro-matic, The Deathray Davies, GBH, PPT, The Crash that Took Me, Shibboleth, Trey Johnson, Black Tie Dynasty, Old 97's.

INTERSCOPE/GEFFEN/A&M RECORDS

2220 Colorado Ave., Santa Monica CA 90404. (310)865-1000. **Fax:** (310)865-7908. **Website:** www.interscoperecords.com. Labels include Blackground Records, Cherrytree Records, will.i.am music group and Aftermath Records. Record company.

Interscope/Geffen/A&M is a subsidiary of Universal Music Group.

HOW TO CONTACT *Does not accept unsolicited submissions.*

MUSIC Released *Worlds Apart*, recorded by ...And You Will Know Us By The Trail Of Dead; and *Guero*, recorded by Beck. Other artists include U2, M.I.A, Keane, and Lady Gaga.

ISLAND/DEF JAM MUSIC GROUP

825 Eighth Ave., New York NY 10019. (212)333-8000. **Fax:** (212)603-7654. **Website:** www.islanddefjam.com.

Island/Def Jam is a subsidiary of Universal Music Group.

HOW TO CONTACT *Island/Def Jam Music Group does not accept unsolicited submissions. Do not send material unless requested.*

MUSIC Artists include Bon Jovi, Fall Out Boy, Kanye West, Rihanna, The Killers, Jay-Z, and Ludacris.

JEROME PROMOTIONS & MARKETING INC.

2535 Winthrope Way, Lawrenceville GA 30044. (770)982-7055. **Fax:** (770)982-1882. **E-mail:** hitcd@bellsouth.net. **Website:** www.jeromepromotions.com.

HOW TO CONTACT Contact first and obtain permission to submit a demo. Include CD with 5 songs and cover letter. Does not return submissions. Responds in 1 week.

MUSIC Mostly interested in **Top 40**, **adult contemporary**, **hot AC**; also **R&B, alternative** and **hip-hop crossover**. Does not want rap, country, gospel, hard rock.

J RECORDS

745 Fifth Ave., 6th Floor, New York NY 10151. (212)833-8000. **Website:** www.jrecords.com. Part of Arista Records.

HOW TO CONTACT *J Records does not accept unsolicited submissions.*

MUSIC Artists include Alicia Keys, Rod Stewart, and Pitbull.

KAUPP RECORDS

Box 5474, Stockton CA 95205. **Contact:** Melissa Glenn. Record company, music publisher (Kaupps and Robert Publishing Co./BMI), management firm (Merri-Webb Productions) and record producer (Merri-Webb Productions). Estab. 1990. Releases 1 single and 4 LPs/year. Pays standard royalty to artists on contract; statutory rate to publisher per song on record.

DISTRIBUTED BY Merri-Webb Productions and Cal-Centron Distributing Co.

HOW TO CONTACT *Write first and obtain permission to submit or to arrange personal interview.* Prefers cassette or VHS videocassette with 3 songs. Include SASE. Responds in 3 months.

MUSIC Mostly **country**, **R&B**, and **A/C rock**; also **pop**, **rock**, and **gospel**. Mostly **country**, **R&B** and **A/C rock**; also **pop**, **rock**, and **gospel**. Published "Rushin' In" (single by N. Merrihew/B. Bolin), recorded by Valerie; "Goin Postal" (single by N. Merrihew/B. Bolin), recorded by Bruce Bolin (country/rock/pop); and "I Gotta Know" (single by N. Merrihew/B. Bolin), recorded by Cheryl (country/rock/pop), all released on Kaupp Records.

◑ KILL ROCK STARS

WA **Website:** www.killrockstars.com.

DISTRIBUTED BY Redeye Distribution.

HOW TO CONTACT *Does not accept or listen to demos sent by mail.* Will listen to links online only if in a touring band coming through Portland. "If you are not touring through Portland, don't send us anything." Prefers link to webpage or EPK. Does not return material.

MUSIC Mostly **punk rock**, **neo-folk** or **anti-folk** and **spoken word**. Artists include Deerhoof, Xiu Xiu, Mary Timony, The Gossip, Erase Errata, and Two Ton Boa.

TIPS "We will only work with touring acts, so let us know if you are playing Olympia, Seattle or Portland. Particularly interested in young artists with indie-rock background."

○ LANDMARK COMMUNICATIONS GROUP

P.O. Box 1444, Hendersonville TN 37077. **E-mail:** lmarkcom@bellsouth.net. **Website:** www.landmark-communicationsgroup.com. Labels include Jana and Landmark Records. Record company, record producer, music publisher (Newcreature Music/BMI and Mary Megan Music/ASCAP) and management firm (Landmark Entertainment). Releases 6 singles, 8 CDs/year. Pays 5-7% royalty to artists on contract; statutory rate to publisher for each record sold.

HOW TO CONTACT Submit demo tape by mail. Unsolicited submissions are OK. Prefers MP3 or CD with 2-4 songs and lyric sheet. Responds in 1 month.

MUSIC Mostly **country/crossover**, **Christian**. Recent projects: *Smoky Mountain Campmeeting* by Various Artists; *The Pilgrim & the Road* by Tiffany Turner; *Fallow Ground* by C.J. Hall; *Prince Charming is Dead* by Kecia Burcham.

TIPS "Be professional in presenting yourself."

◑ LARK RECORD PRODUCTIONS, INC.

P.O. Box 35726, Tulsa OK 74153. (918)786-8896. **Fax:** (918)786-8897. **E-mail:** janajae@janajae.com. **Website:** www.janajae.com.

HOW TO CONTACT Submit demo by mail. Unsolicited submissions are OK. Prefers CD or DVD with 3 songs and lead sheets. Does not return material. Responds only if interested.

MUSIC Mostly **country**, **bluegrass**, and **classical**; also **instrumentals**. Released "Fiddlestix" (single by Jana Jae); "Mayonnaise" (single by Steve Upfold); and "Flyin' South" (single by Cindy Walker), all recorded by Jana Jae on Lark Records (country). Other artists include Sydni, Hotwire, and Matt Greif.

◑ MAGNA CARTA RECORDS

A-1 Country Club Rd., East Rochester NY 14445. (585)381-5224. **E-mail:** info@magnacarta.net. **Website:** www.magnacarta.net.

HOW TO CONTACT Contact first and obtain permission to submit. *No unsolicited material.*

MUSIC Mostly **progressive metal**, **progressive rock**, and **progressive jazz**.

⊘ MATADOR RECORDS

304 Hudson St., 7th Floor, New York NY 10013. (212)995-5882. **Fax:** (212)995-5883. **E-mail:** info@matadorrecords.com. **Website:** www.matadorrecords.com.

HOW TO CONTACT "We are sorry to say that we *no longer accept unsolicited demo submissions*."

MUSIC **Alternative rock**. Artists include Lou Reed, Pavement, Belle and Sebastian, Cat Power, Jay Reatard, Sonic Youth, Yo La Tengo, Mogwai, The New Pornographers, and more.

◑⊘ MCA NASHVILLE

1904 Adelicia St., Nashville TN 37212. (615)340-5400. **Fax:** (615)340-5491. **Website:** www.umgnashville.com.

○ MCA Nashville is a subsidiary of Universal Music Group.

HOW TO CONTACT *MCA Nashville cannot accept unsolicited submissions.*

MUSIC Artists include Tracy Byrd, George Strait, Vince Gill, Sugarland, The Mavericks, and Shania Twain.

○ MEGAFORCE RECORDS

P.O. Box 63584, Philadelphia PA 19147. (215)922-4612. **Fax:** (509)757-8602. **Website:** www.megaforcerecords.com.

DISTRIBUTED BY Red/Sony Distribution.

HOW TO CONTACT *Contact first and obtain permission to submit.* Submissions go to the Philadelphia office.

MUSIC Mostly **rock**. Artists include Truth and Salvage, The Meat Puppets, and The Disco Biscuits.

◐ METAL BLADE RECORDS

5737 Kanan Rd. #143, Agoura Hills CA 91301. (805)522-9111. **Fax:** (805)522-9380. **E-mail:** metalblade@metalblade.com. **Website:** www.metalblade.com.

HOW TO CONTACT Submit demo through website form. Does not accept physical copies of demos. Unsolicited submissions are OK. Response time varies, but "be patient."

MUSIC Mostly **heavy metal** and **industrial**; also **hardcore**, **gothic** and **noise**. Released *Gallery of Suicide*, recorded by Cannibal Corpse; *Voo Doo*, recorded by King Diamond; and *A Pleasant Shade of Gray*, recorded by Fates Warning, all on Metal Blade Records. Other artists include As I Lay Dying, The Red Chord, The Black Dahlia Murder, and Unearth.

TIPS "Metal Blade is known throughout the underground for quality metal-oriented acts."

○ MODAL MUSIC, INC.

P.O. Box 6473, Evanston IL 60204-6473. (847)864-1022. **E-mail:** info@modalmusic.com. **Website:** www.modalmusic.com.

HOW TO CONTACT Submit demo package by mail. Unsolicited submissions are OK. Prefers CD with bio, PR, brochures, any info about artist and music. Does not return material. Responds in 4 months.

MUSIC Mostly **ethnic** and **world**. Released "St. James Vet Clinic" (single by T. Doehrer/Z. Doehrer) from *Wolfpak Den Recordings* (album), recorded by Wolfpak, released 2005; "Dance The Night Away" (single

by T. Doehrer) from *Dance The Night Away* (album), recorded by Balkan Rhythm Band™; "Sid Beckerman's Rumanian" (single by D. Jacobs) from *Meet Your Neighbor's Folk Music*™ (album), recorded by Jutta & The Hi-Dukes™; and *Hold Whatcha Got* (album), recorded by Razzemetazz™, all on Modal Music Records. Other artists include Ensemble M'chaiya™, Nordland Band™ and Terran's Greek Band™.

TIPS "Please note our focus is primarily traditional and traditionally-based ethnic which is a very limited, non-mainstream market niche. You waste your time and money by sending us any other type of music. If you are unsure of your music fitting our focus, please call us before sending anything. Put your name and contact info on every item you send!"

◔○ NERVOUS RECORDS

5 Sussex Crescent, Northolt, Middx UB5 4DL United Kingdom. 44(020)8423 7373. **Fax:** 44(020)8423 7713. **E-mail:** info@nervous.co.uk. **Website:** www.nervous.co.uk. **Contact:** R. Williams. Record company (Nervous Records), record producer and music publisher (Nervous Publishing and Zorch Music). Member: MCPS, PRS, PPL, ASCAP, NCB. Releases 2 albums/year. Pays 8-12% royalty to artists on contract; statutory rate to publisher per song on records. Royalties paid directly to US songwriters and artists or through US publishing or recording affiliate.

○ Nervous Records' publishing company, Nervous Publishing, is listed in the Music Publishers section.

HOW TO CONTACT Unsolicited submissions are OK. Prefers CD with 4-15 songs and lyric sheet. SAE and IRC. Responds in 3 weeks.

MUSIC Mostly **psychobilly** and **rockabilly**. "No heavy rock, AOR, stadium rock, disco, soul, pop—only wild rockabilly and psychobilly." Released *Extra Chrome*, written and recorded by Johnny Black; *It's Still Rock 'N' Roll to Me*, written and recorded by The Jime. Other artists include Restless Wild and Taggy Tones.

● OGLIO RECORDS

P.O. Box 404, Redondo Beach CA 90277. (310)791-8600. **Fax:** (310)791-8670. **E-mail:** getinfo4@oglio.com. **Website:** http://oglio.com.

HOW TO CONTACT *No unsolicited demos.*

MUSIC Mostly **alternative rock** and **comedy**. Released *Shine* (album), recorded by Cyndi Lauper (pop); *Live At The Roxy* (album), recorded by Brian Wilson (rock); *Team Leader* (album), recorded by George Lopez (comedy).

ⓘ OUTSTANDING RECORDS

P.O. Box 2111, Huntington Beach CA 92647. **Website:** www.outstandingrecords.com.

DISTRIBUTED BY All full CDs listed on the website can be ordered directly through the website. Most of them are now available via download through iTunes, Napster, Rhapsody, Amazon/MP3, Emusic, or Yahoo. Whenever wholesale distributors contact me for specific orders, I am happy to work with them, especially distributors overseas.

HOW TO CONTACT Submit demo by mail. Unsolicited submissions are OK. Prefers CD (full albums), lyric sheet, photo and cover letter. Include SASE. Responds in 3 weeks.

MUSIC Mostly **jazz**, **rock** and **country**; also **everything else, especially Latin**. Does not want music with negative, anti-social or immoral messages. "View our website for a listing of all current releases."

TIPS "We prefer to receive full CDs, rather than just three numbers. A lot of submitters suggest we release their song in the form of singles, but we just can't bother with singles at the present time. Especially looking for performers who want to release their material on my labels. Some songwriters are pairing up with performers and putting out CDs with a 'Writer Presents the Performer' concept. No dirty language. Do not encourage listeners to use drugs, alcohol or engage in immoral behavior. I'm especially looking for upbeat, happy, danceable music."

ⓧⓘ THE PANAMA MUSIC GROUP OF COMPANIES

12 Trewartha Rd., Praa Sands, Penzance, Cornwall TR20 9ST England. +44 (0)1736 762826. **Fax:** +44 (0)1736 763328. **E-mail:** panamus@aol.com. **Website:** www.songwriters-guild.co.uk; www.panamamusic.co.uk. **Contact:** Roderick G. Jones, CEO, A&R. Labels include Pure Gold Records, Panama Music Library, Rainy Day Records, Panama Records, Mohock Records, Digimix Records Ltd. (www.digimixrecords.com and www.myspace.com/digimixrecords). Registered members of Phonographic Performance Ltd. (PPL). Record company, music publisher, production and development company (Panama Music Library, Melody First Music Library, Eventide Music Library, Musik Image Music Library, Promo Sonor International Music Library, Caribbean Music Library, ADN Creation Music Library, Piano Bar Music Library, Corelia Music Library, PSI Music Library, Scamp Music, First Time Music Publishing U.K.), Digimix Music Publishing, registered members of the Mechanical Copyright Protection Society (MCPS) and the Performing Right Society (PRS) (London, England UK), management firm and record producer (First Time Management & Production Co.). Staff size: 6. Pays variable royalty to artists on contract; statutory rate to publisher per song on record subject to deal.

DISTRIBUTED BY Media U.K. Distributors and Digimix Worldwide Digital Distribution.

HOW TO CONTACT Submit demo package by mail. Unsolicited submissions are OK. CD only with unlimited number of songs/instrumentals and lyric or lead sheets where necessary. "We do not return material so there is no need to send return postage. We will, due to volume of material received only respond to you if we have any interest. Please note: no MP3 submissions, attachments, downloads, or referrals to Web sites in the first instance via e-mail. Do not send anything by recorded delivery or courier as it will not be signed for. If we are interested, we will follow up for further requests and offers as necessary."

MUSIC All styles. Published by Scamp Music: "F*ck Me I'm Famous" written by Paul Clarke & Matthew Dick (film/DVD & single & album track), released worldwide in *Get Him to the Greek*, Universal films Hollywood, starring Russell Brand, recorded by Dougal & Gammer, released as an album track by Gut Records Ltd. and as a single by Essential Platinum Records in 2010. Also published "The River" (soul/R&B), recorded by Leonie Parker, released by Digimix Records Ltd; "The Huffle Shuffle Band" (country), recorded by The Glen Kirton Country Band on Digimix Records Ltd, published by Scamp Music; "Break It" (hardcore), recorded by Dougal & Gammer, released by Universal Records/All Around the World; published by Scamp Music: "I Get Stoned" (hardcore dance) recorded by AudioJunkie & Stylus, released by EMI records on *Hardcore Nation 2009*, published by Panama Music Library; "Everytime I Hear Your Name" (pop dance), recorded by Cascada, released by All Around The World/Universal Records, published by Scamp Music; *Summer* 9-track album (mind, body, & soul) by Kevin Kendle, released by Eventide Music and Digimix Records Ltsd, published by Panama Music Library, and many more.

PAPER + PLASTICK

E-mail: rey@reybee.com. **Website:** http://paperand-plastick.com.

MUSIC Rock, punk, and more. Artists include: Dopamines, Andrew Dost, Coffee Project, Foundation, Gatorface, Blacklist Royals, Landmines, We are the Union, and more.

◑ PARLIAMENT RECORDS

357 S. Fairfax Ave. #430, Los Angeles CA 90036. (323)653-0693. **Fax:** (323)653-7670. **Website:** www.parliamentrecords.com.

◒ Also see the listings for Audio MusiC Publishers and Queen Esther Music Publishing in the Music Publishers section and Weisman Production Group in the Record Producers section.

HOW TO CONTACT Submit demo package by mail. Unsolicited submissions are OK. Prefers CD with 3-10 songs and lyric sheet. Include SASE. "Mention *Songwriter's Market.* Please make return envelope the same size as the envelopes you send material in, otherwise we cannot send everything back." Responds in 6 weeks.

MUSIC Mostly **R&B**, **soul**, **dance**, and **top 40/pop**; also **gospel** and **blues**. Arists include Rapture 7 (male gospel group), Wisdom Gospel Singers (male gospel group), Chosen Gospel Recovery (female gospel group), Jewel With Love (female gospel group), Apostle J. Dancy (gospel), TooMiraqulas (rap), The Mighty Voices of Joy (male gospel group) and L'Nee (hip hop/soul).

TIPS "Parliament Records will also listen to 'tracks' only. If you send tracks, please include a letter stating what equipment you record on—ADAT, Pro Tools or Roland VS recorders."

◑ QUARK RECORDS

P.O. Box 452, Newtown CT 06470. (917)687-9988. **E-mail:** quarkent@aol.com. **Contact:** Curtis Urbina. Record company and music publisher (Quarkette Music/BMI and Freedurb Music/ASCAP). Releases 3 singles and 3 LPs/year. Pays negotiable royalty to artists on contract; 3/4 statutory rate to publisher per song on record.

HOW TO CONTACT Prefers CD with 2 songs (max). Include SASE. "Must be an absolute 'hit' song!" Responds in 6 weeks.

MUSIC Pop and electronica music only.

◒ RADICAL RECORDS

77 Bleecker St., New York NY 10012. (212)475-1111. **Fax:** (212)475-3676. **E-mail:** info@radicalrecords.com; keith@radicalrecords.com. **Website:** www.radicalrecords.com. **Contact:** Keith Masco, president; Bryan Mechutan, general manager/sales and marketing. "We do accept unsolicited demos, however please allow ample time for a response. Also please note that we deal almost exclusively with punk rock. Feel free to send us your Hip-Hop, Folk, Jazz Fusion, demo but don't be surprised when we don't show up at your door with a contract. Please make sure you have an email address clearly printed on the disc or case. Most importantly, don't call us, we'll call you."

DISTRIBUTED BY City Hall, Revelation, Select-O-Hits, Choke, Southern, Carrot Top, and other indie distributors.

HOW TO CONTACT *E-mail first for permission to submit demo.* Prefers CD. Does not return material. Responds in 1 month.

MUSIC Mostly **punk**, **hardcore**, **glam** and **rock**.

TIPS "Create the best possible demos you can and show a past of excellent self-promotion."

◒◒ RANCO RECORDS

61 Euphrasia Dr., Toronto ON M6B 3V8 Canada. (416)782-5768. **Fax:** (416)782-7170. **E-mail:** panfilo@sympatico.ca. **Contact:** Panfilo Di Matteo, president, A&R. Record company, record producer, and music publisher (Lilly Music Publishing). Staff size: 2. Releases 10 singles, 20 12" singles, 15 LPs, 20 EPs ,and 15 CDs/year. Pays 25-35% royalty to artists on contract; statutory rate to publisher per song on record.

HOW TO CONTACT Submit demo by mail. Unsolicited submissions are OK. Prefers CD or videocassette with 3 songs and lyric or lead sheet. Does not return material. Responds in 1 month only if interested.

MUSIC Mostly **dance**, **ballads**, and **rock**. Released *Only This Way* (album), written and recorded by Angelica Castro; *The End of Us* (album), written and recorded by Putz, both on P&N Records (dance); and "Lovers" (single by Marc Singer), recorded by Silvana (dance), released on P&N Records.

◒ RAVE RECORDS, INC.

Attn: Production Dept., 13400 W. Seven Mile Rd., Detroit MI 48235. **E-mail:** info@raverecords.com. **Website:** www.raverecords.com. **Contact:** Carolyn and Derrick, production managers. Record company and music publisher (Magic Brain Music/ASCAP).

Staff size: 2. Releases 2-4 singles and 2 CDs/year. Pays various royalty to artists on contract; statutory rate to publisher per song on record.

DISTRIBUTED BY Action Music Sales.

HOW TO CONTACT *"We do not accept unsolicited submissions."* Submit demo package by mail. Prefers CD with 3 songs, lyric sheet. "Include any bios, fact sheets, and press you may have. We will contact you if we need any further information." Does not return materials.

MUSIC Mostly **alternative rock** and **dance**. Artists include Cyber Cryst, Dorothy, Nicole, and Bukimi 3.

RCA RECORDS

550 Madison Ave., New York NY 10022. **Website:** www.rcarecords.com. Labels include RCA Records Nashville and RCA Victor. Record company.

○ RCA Records is a subsidiary of Sony BMG.

DISTRIBUTED BY BMG.

HOW TO CONTACT *RCA Records does not accept unsolicited submissions.*

MUSIC Artists include The Strokes, Dave Matthews Band, Christina Aguilera, and Foo Fighters.

RED ADMIRAL RECORDS LLP

The Cedars, Elvington Lane, Hawkinge, Folkestone, Kent CT18 7AD United Kingdom. (01) (303) 893-472. **E-mail:** info@redadmiralrecords.com. **Website:** www.redadmiralrecords.com. **Contact:** Chris Ashman. Registered members of MCPS, PRS, and PPL. Record company and music publisher (Cringe Music [MCPS/PRS]).

HOW TO CONTACT Submit demo package by mail. Unsolicited submissions are OK. Submit CD only with unlimited number of songs. Submission materials are not returned. Responds if interested.

MUSIC All styles.

RED ONION RECORDS

8377 Westview, Houston TX 77055. (713)464-4653. **E-mail:** jeffwells@soundartsrecording.com. **Website:** www.soundartsrecording.com. **Contact:** Jeff Wells.

DISTRIBUTED BY Earth Records.

HOW TO CONTACT Submit demo by mail. Unsolicited submissions are OK. Prefers CD with 4 songs and lyric sheet. Does not return material. Responds in 6 weeks.

MUSIC Mostly **country**, **blues** and **pop/rock**. Released *Glory Baby* (album), recorded by Tony Vega Band (blues); *Two For Tuesday* (album), recorded by

Dr. Jeff and the Painkilllers (blues), all released 2007 on Red Onion Records.

REPRISE RECORDS

3300 Warner Blvd., 4th Floor, Burbank CA 91505. (818)846-9090. **Website:** www.warnerbrosrecords. com.

○ Reprise Records is a subsidiary of Warner Music Group.

DISTRIBUTED BY WEA.

HOW TO CONTACT *Reprise Records does not accept unsolicited submissions.*

MUSIC Artists include Eric Clapton, My Chemical Romance, Michael Bublé, The Used, Green Day, Alanis Morissette, Fleetwood Mac, and Neil Young.

RISE RECORDS

421 SW 6th Ave., Suite 1400, Portland OR 97204. **E-mail:** Matthew@RiseRecords.com. **Website:** www. riserecords.com. **Contact:** Matthew Gordner.

HOW TO CONTACT E-mail a link to music, either on Purevolume or MySpace. "Please save your money and don't mail a press kit."

MUSIC Rock, metal, alternative. Artists include Dance Gavin Dance, Emarose, The Devil Wears Prada, Of Mice & Men, and more.

ROADRUNNER RECORDS

902 Broadway, 8th Floor, New York NY 10010. **Website:** www.roadrunnerrecords.com.

HOW TO CONTACT Submit demo by e-mail at signmeto@roadrunnerrecords.com. Submissions are currently open.

MUSIC Rock, metal, alternative. Artists include Korn, Killswitch Engage, Opeth, Nickelback, Lenny Kravitz, Lynyrd Skynyrd, Megadeth, Slipknot, and more.

ROBBINS ENTERTAINMENT LLC

35 Worth St., 4th Floor, New York NY 10013. (212)675-4321. **Fax:** (212)675-4441. **E-mail:** info@robbinsent. com. **Website:** www.robbinsent.com.

DISTRIBUTED BY Sony/BMG.

HOW TO CONTACT Accepts unsolicited radio edit demos as long as it's dance music. Prefers CD with 2 songs or less. "Make sure everything is labeled with the song title information and your contact information. This is important in case the CD and the jewel case get separated.

MUSIC Commercial **dance** only. Released top 10 pop smashes, "Heaven" (single), recorded by DJ Sammy;

"Everytime We Touch" (single), recorded by Cascada; "Listen To Your Heart" (single), recored by DHT; as well as Billboard Hot 100 records from Rockell, Lasgo, Reina and K5. Other artists includel September, Andain, Judy Torres, Jenna Drey, Marly, Dee Dee, Milky, Kreo and many others.

TIPS "Do not send your package 'Supreme-Overnight-Before-You-Wake-Up' delivery. Save yourself some money. Do not send material if you are going to state in your letter that, 'If I had more (fill in the blank) it would sound better.' We are interested in hearing your best and only your best. Do not call us and ask if you can send your package. The answer is yes. We are looking for dance music with crossover potential."

ROTTEN RECORDS

P.O. Box 56, Upland CA 91786. (909)920-4567. **Fax:** (909)920-4577. **E-mail:** rotten@rottenrecords.com. **Website:** www.rottenrecords.com. **Contact:** Ron Peterson, president.

DISTRIBUTED BY RIOT (Australia), Sonic Rendezvous (NL), RED (US) and PHD (Canada).

HOW TO CONTACT Submit demo package by mail. Unsolicited submissions are OK. Prefers CD or MySpace link. Does not return material.

MUSIC Mostly **rock**, **alternative** and **commercial**; also **punk** and **heavy metal**. Released *Paegan Terrorism* (album), written and recorded by Acid Bath; *Kiss the Clown* (album by K. Donivon), recorded by Kiss the Clown; and *Full Speed Ahead* (album by Cassidy/Brecht), recorded by D.R.T., all on Rotten Records.

TIPS "Be patient."

◐ ROUGH TRADE RECORDS

66 Golborne Rd., London W10 5PS United Kingdom. **Website:** www.roughtraderecords.com.

HOW TO CONTACT Demos should be marked for attention of Paul Jones.

MUSIC Alternative. Artists include Super Furry Animals, Jarvis Cocker, The Hold Steady, Emiliana Torrini, British Sea Power, The Libertines, My Morning Jacket, Jenny Lewis, The Strokes, The Mystery Jets, The Decemberists, and more.

◑ RUSTIC RECORDS

6337 Murray Lane, Brentwood TN 37027. (615)371-0646. **E-mail:** rusticrecordsam@aol.com. **Contact:** Jack Schneider, president and founder; Nell Schneider; Brien Fisher.

DISTRIBUTED BY CDBaby.com and available on iTunes, MSN Music, Rhapsody, and more.

HOW TO CONTACT Submit professional demo package by mail. Unsolicited submissions are OK. CD only; no MP3s or e-mails. Include no more than 4 songs with corresponding lyric sheets and cover letter. Include appropriately-sized SASE. Responds in 4 weeks.

MUSIC Good combination of traditional and modern **country**. 2008-09 releases: *Ready to Ride*—debut album from Nikki Britt, featuring "C-O-W-B-O-Y," "Do I Look Like Him," "Star in My Car," and "You Happened"; *Hank Stuff* from DeAnna Cox—featuring "I'm a Long Gone Mama," and "I'm so Lonesome I Could Cry."

TIPS "Professional demo preferred."

◯ SANDALPHON RECORDS

P.O. Box 542407, Grand Prairie TX 75054. (972)333-0876.

DISTRIBUTED BY "We are currently negotiating for distribution."

HOW TO CONTACT Submit demo package by mail. Unsolicited submissions are fine. Prefers CD with 1-5 songs with lyric sheet and cover letter. Returns submissions if accompanied by a SASE or SAE and IRC for outside the United States. Responds in 6-8 weeks.

MUSIC Mostly **rock**, **country**, and **alternative**; also **pop**, **gospel**, and **blues**.

SILVER WAVE RECORDS

P.O. Box 7943, Boulder CO 80306. (303)443-5617. **Fax:** (303)443-0877. **E-mail:** valerie@silverwave.com. **Website:** www.silverwave.com. **Contact:** Valerie Sanford, art director.

MUSIC Mostly **Native American** and **world**.

SIMPLY GRAND MUSIC INC

P.O. Box 770208, Memphis TN 38177-0208. (901)763-4787. **E-mail:** info@simplygrandmusic.com. **Website:** www.simplygrandmusic.com. **Contact:** Linda Lucchesi, president. Record company (Simply Grand Music) and music publisher (Beckie Publishing Company). Staff size: 2. Released 9 CDs last year. Royalties are negotiable. Distributed by Ace Records and various others.

HOW TO CONTACT Contact first and obtain permission to submit a demo. Include CD with 1-3 songs and lyric sheet. Returns submissions if accompanied by an SASE with ample postage. Responds in 3 months.

MUSIC Mostly interested in **country, soul/R&B, pop**; also interested in **top 40, soft rock**. Recently published "Get Your Praise On", written by Corey Lee Barker and Jody Harris, recorded by Suzette Michaels (Christian) for *Stronger Every Day* (album) on High Mountain Records; "Pity A Fool", written by Dan Greer, recorded by Barbara & The Browns (soul), featured in *Against The Wall* on USA Network; "I Love You," written by Charles Chalmers and Domingo Samudio, performed by Richard & Walter (soul), featured in *Happy and Bleeding* movie; "Can't Find Happiness," written by Charlie Chalmers and Paul Selph, Jr., recorded by Barbara & The Browns (soul) for *Can't Find Happiness* (album) on Ace Records.

SKELETON CREW

NJ **E-mail:** info@skeletoncrewonline.com; publicity@skeletoncrewonline.com. **Website:** www.skeletoncrewonline.com.

HOW TO CONTACT E-mail or send message through MySpace page for directions on sending material.

MUSIC **Punk, indie, rock, alternative**. Artists include David Costa, The Architects, New Tomorrow, The Mean Reds, and more.

● SMALL STONE RECORDS

P.O. Box 02007, Detroit MI 48202. (248)219-2613. **Fax:** (248)541-6536. **E-mail:** sstone@smallstone.com. **Website:** www.smallstone.com.

DISTRIBUTED BY A EC, Allegro/Nail, Carrot Top.

HOW TO CONTACT Submit CD/CD Rom by mail. Unsolicited submissions are OK. Does not return material. Responds in 2 months.

MUSIC Mostly **alternative, rock** and **blues**; also **funk (not R&B)**. Released *Fat Black Pussy Cat*, written and recorded by Five Horse Johnson (rock/blues); *Wrecked & Remixed*, written and recorded by Morsel (indie rock, electronica); and *Only One Division*, written and recorded by Soul Clique (electronica), all on Small Stone Records. Other artists include Acid King, Perplexa, and Novadriver.

TIPS "Looking for esoteric music along the lines of Bill Laswell to Touch & Go/Thrill Jockey records material. Only send along material if it makes sense with what we do. Perhaps owning some of our records would help."

SMOG VEIL RECORDS

1658 N. Milwaukee Ave. #284, Chicago IL 60647. (773)706-0450. **Fax:** (312)276-0450. **E-mail:** franklise@aol.com. **Website:** www.smogveil.com.

HOW TO CONTACT Submit CD or CD-R to Frank Mauceri by mail. Does not accept submissions by e-mail or links to website. Submissions must inlcude a contact, press kit, and plans for touring. Response time is slow. "Note that if your band is playing the Chicago area, we cannot help with booking, but may be interested in seeing you perform live. Therefore, please email gig details. Demo submissions cannot be returned to the submitter."

MUSIC Artists include Batusis, David Thomas, Thor, This Moment in Black History, Butcher Boys, and Prisoners.

○ SONIC UNYON RECORDS CANADA

P.O. Box 57347, Jackson Station, Hamilton ON L8P 4X2 Canada. (905)777-1223. **Fax:** (905)777-1161. **E-mail:** jerks@sonicunyon.com. **Website:** www.sonicunyon.com. **Contact:** Tim Potocic and Mark Milne, co-owners.

DISTRIBUTED BY Caroline Distribution.

HOW TO CONTACT *Call first and obtain permission to submit.* Prefers CD or cassette. "Research our company before you send your demo. We are small; don't waste my time and your money." Does not return material. Responds in 4 months.

MUSIC Mostly **rock, heavy rock** and **pop rock**. Released *Doberman* (album), written and recorded by Kittens (heavy rock); *What A Life* (album), written and recorded by Smoother; and *New Grand* (album), written and recorded by New Grand on sonic unyon records (pop/rock). Other artists include Ad Astra Per Aspera, Wooden Stars, The Ghost is Dancing, The Nein, Simply Saucer, Raising the Fawn, and Aereogramme.

TIPS "Know what we are about. Research us. Know we are a small company. Know signing to us doesn't mean that everything will fall into your lap. We are only the beginning of an artist's career."

⊘ SONY BMG

550 Madison Ave., New York NY 10022. **Website:** www.sonymusic.com.

○ Sony BMG is one of the primary "Big 4" major labels.

HOW TO CONTACT For specific contact information see the listings in this section for Sony subsidiaries Columbia Records, Epic Records, Sony Music Nashville, RCA Records, J Records, Arista, and American Recordings.

⊘ SONY MUSIC NASHVILLE

1400 18th Ave. S, Nashville TN 37212-2809. Labels include Columbia Nashville, Arista Nashville, RCA, BNA, and Provident Music Group.

🖰 Sony Music Nashville is a subsidiary of Sony BMG,.

HOW TO CONTACT *Sony Music Nashville does not accept unsolicited submissions.*

⊘ SUGAR HILL RECORDS

NC **E-mail:** info@sugarhillrecords.com. **Website:** www.sugarhillrecords.com.

🖰 Welk Music Group acquired Sugar Hill Records in 1998.

HOW TO CONTACT *No unsolicited submissions.* "If you are interested in having your music heard by Sugar Hill Records or the Welk Music Group, we suggest you establish a relationship with a manager, publisher, or attorney that has an ongoing relationship with our company. We do not have a list of such entities."

MUSIC Mostly **Americana**, **bluegrass**, and **country**. Artists include Nitty Gritty Dirt Band, Sarah Jarosz, Donna the Buffalo, The Infamous Stringdusters, Joey + Rory, and Sam Bush.

🖰 TEXAS MUSIC CAFE

3004 Franklin Ave., Waco TX 76710. **E-mail:** info@texasmusiccafe.com. **Website:** www.texasmusiccafe.com. **Contact:** Richard Paul Thomas, booking. Television show. Staff size: 10. Releases 26 TV programs/year. Pay: quality recording and opportunity to perform on international television. Original music only.

DISTRIBUTED BY PBS in high definition and surround sound.

HOW TO CONTACT Submit demo by mail or e-mail a link. Unsolicited submissions are OK. Does not return material. Responds only if interested.

TIPS "Must be willing to travel to Texas at your expense to be taped. Let us know if you are traveling near central Texas."

⊘ TOMMY BOY ENTERTAINMENT LLC

120 Fifth Ave., 7th Floor, New York NY 10011. **E-mail:** info@tommyboy.com. **Website:** www.tommyboy.com.

DISTRIBUTED BY WEA, Subway Records.

HOW TO CONTACT E-mail to obtain current demo submission policy.

MUSIC Artists include Chavela Vargas, Afrika Bambaataa, Biz Markie, Kool Keith, and INXS.

🖰 TOPCAT RECORDS

P.O. Box 670234, Dallas TX 75367. (972)484-4141. **Website:** www.topcatrecords.com.

DISTRIBUTED BY City Hall.

HOW TO CONTACT *Call first and obtain permission to submit.* Prefers CD. Does not return material. Responds in 1 month.

MUSIC Mostly **blues**, **swing**, **rockabilly**, **Americana**, **Texana** and **R&B**. Released *If You Need Me* (album), written and recorded by Robert Ealey (blues); *Texas Blueswomen* (album by 3 Female Singers), recorded by various (blues/R&B); and *Jungle Jane* (album), written and recorded by Holland K. Smith (blues/swing), all on Topcat. Released CDs: *Jim Suhler & Alan Haynes-Live*; Bob Kirkpatrick *Drive Across Texas*; *Rock My Blues to Sleep* by Johnny Nicholas; *Walking Heart Attack*, by Holland K. Smith; *Dirt Road* (album), recorded by Jim Suhler; *Josh Alan Band* (album), recorded by Josh Alan; *Bust Out* (album), recorded by Robin Sylar. Other artists include Grant Cook, Muddy Waters, Big Mama Thornton, Big Joe Turner, George "Harmonica" Smith, J.B. Hutto and Bee Houston. "View our website for an up-to-date listing of releases."

TIPS "Send me blues (fast, slow, happy, sad, etc.) or good blues oriented R&B. No pop, hip-hop, or rap."

TOUCH AND GO/QUARTERSTICK RECORDS

P.O. Box 25520, Chicago IL 60625. (773)388-8888. **Fax:** (773)388-3888. **E-mail:** info@tgrec.com. **Website:** www.tgrec.com.

HOW TO CONTACT Mail to one or the other (staffed by same people, no need to send to both labels). "Demos are listened to by any and all staffers who want to or have time to listen to them. Do not call or e-mail us about your demo." Do not e-mail MP3s or web URLs.

MUSIC **All Styles**. Artists include Therapy?, TV on the Radio, Pinback, Naked Raygun, Blonde Redhead, Henry Rollins, Yeah Yeah Yeahs, Girls Against Boys, and more.

🖰 TRANSDREAMER RECORDS

P.O. Box 1955, New York NY 10113. **Website:** www.transdreamer.com. "We wanted the name, Transdreamer, to symbolize artists and projects that attempt to transcend normal genre conventions. Transdreamer also distributes and finances many projects with the same devotion to quality like The Rapture, Das Racist, Joseph Arthur and others."

○ Also see the listing for Megaforce in this section of the book.

DISTRIBUTED BY Red/Sony.

HOW TO CONTACT *Contact first and obtain permission to submit.*

MUSIC Mostly **alternative/rock**. Artists include The Delgados, Arab Strap, Dressy Bessy, The Dig, and Holly Golightly.

○ UAR RECORDS

Box 1264, 6020 W. Pottstown Rd., Peoria IL 61654-1264. (309)673-5755. **Fax:** (309)673-7636. **Website:** www.unitedcyber.com/uarltd.

○ Also see the listings for Kaysarah Music (ASCAP) and Jerjoy Music BMI) in the Music Publishers section of this book.

HOW TO CONTACT "If you are an artist seeking a record deal, please send a sample of your vocal and/or songwriting work-guitar and vocal is fine, no more than 4 songs. Fully produced demos are NOT necessary. Also send brief information on your background in the business, your goals, etc. If you are NOT a songwriter, please send 4 songs maximum of cover tunes that we can use to evaluate your vocal ability. If you wish a reply, please send a SASE, otherwise, you will not receive an answer. If you want a critique of your vocal abilities, please so state as we do not routinely offer critiques. Unsolicited submissions are OK. If you wish all of your material returned to you, be sure to include mailing materials and postage. WE DO NOT RETURN PHONE CALLS."

MUSIC Mostly **American** and **Irish country**. Released "When Jackie Sang The Walking Talking Dolly," "Far Side Banks of Jordan," "There's You," all recorded by Jerry Hanlon. "Lisa Dance With Me," "Philomena From Ireland," "Rainbow," "I'd Better Stand Up," all recorded by the Heggarty Twins from Northern Ireland and Jerry Hanlon. "An Ordinary Woman," "All Your Little Secrets," recorded by Anne More.

TIPS "We are a small independent company, but our belief is that every good voice deserves a chance to be heard and our door is always open to new and aspiring artists."

○ UNIVERSAL MOTOWN RECORDS

1755 Broadway, #6, New York NY 10019. (212)373-0600. **Fax:** (212)373-0726. **Website:** www.universalmotown.com.

○ Universal Motown Records is a subsidiary of Universal Music Group.

HOW TO CONTACT *Does not accept unsolicited submissions.*

MUSIC Artists include Lil' Wayne, Erykah Badu, Days Difference, Kem, Paper Route, and Kelly Rowland.

VAGRANT RECORDS

2118 Wilshire Blvd. #361, Santa Monica CA 90403. **E-mail:** publicity@vagrant.com; info@vagrant.com. **Website:** www.vagrant.com.

HOW TO CONTACT Send demos to demosubmissions@vagrant.com.

MUSIC **Rock, alternative**. Artists include Black Rebel Motorcycle Club, Electric Owls, J Roddy Walston and The Business, Murder by Death, Protest the Hero, School of Seven Bells, Senses Fail, Stars, The Hold Steady, Thrice, and more.

○ ⊘ THE VERVE MUSIC GROUP

1755 Broadway, 3rd Floor, New York NY 10019. (212)331-2000. **E-mail:** contact@vervemusicgroup.com. **Website:** www.vervemusicgroup.com. Record company. Labels include Verve, GRP, and Impulse! Records.

○ Verve Music Group is a subsidiary of Universal Music Group.

HOW TO CONTACT *The Verve Music Group does not accept unsolicited submissions.*

MUSIC Artists include Boney James, Diana Krall, Ledisi, Herbie Hancock, Queen Latifah, and Bruce Hornsby & The Noisemakers.

VICTORY RECORDS

346 N. Justine St., 5th Floor, Chicago IL 60607. **Website:** www.victoryrecords.com.

HOW TO CONTACT Submit demo using online submission manager.

MUSIC **Alternative, metal, rock**. Artists include The Audition, Bayside, Catch 22, Funeral For A Friend, Otep, Hawthorne Heights, Ringworm, Secret Lives of the Freemasons, Silverstein, The Tossers, Voodoo Glow Skulls, William Control, Streetlight Manifesto, and more.

⊘ VIRGIN MUSIC GROUP

5750 Wilshire Blvd., Los Angeles CA 90036. (323)462-6252. **Fax:** (310)278-6231. **Website:** www.virginrecords.com.

○ Virgin Records is a subsidiary of the EMI Group.

DISTRIBUTED BY EMD.

HOW TO CONTACT *Virgin Music Group does not accept recorded material or lyrics unless submitted by a reputable industry source.* "If your act has received positive press or airplay on prior independent releases, we welcome your written query. Send a letter of introduction accompanied by all pertinent artist information. Do not send a tape until requested. All unsolicited materials will be returned unopened."

MUSIC Mostly **rock** and **pop**. Artists include Lenny Kravitz, Placebo, Joss Stone, Ben Harper, Iggy Pop, and Gorillaz.

◑ WAREHOUSE CREEK RECORDING CORP.

P.O. Box 102, Franktown VA 23354. **E-mail:** warehousecreek@verizon.net. **Website:** www.warehousecreek.com.

DISTRIBUTED BY City Hall Records.

HOW TO CONTACT Submit demo by mail. Unsolicited submissions are OK. Prefers cassette, CD, or VHS videocassette with lyric sheet. Does not return material.

MUSIC Mostly **R&B**, **blues** and **gospel**. Released *Nothin' Nice* (album), recorded by Guitar Slim Jr. (blues); *Frank Town Blues* (album), recorded by the Crudup Brothers (blues); *Hi-Fi Baby* (album), recorded by Greg "Fingers" Taylor (blues), all released on Warehouse Creek Records.

WARNER BROS. RECORDS

3300 Warner Blvd., Burbank CA 91505. (818)953-3361; (818)846-9090. **Fax:** (818)953-3232. **Website:** www.wbr.com.

DISTRIBUTED BY WEA.

HOW TO CONTACT *Warner Bros. Records does not accept unsolicited material.* "All unsolicited material will be returned unopened. Those interested in having their tapes heard should establish a relationship with a manager, publisher or attorney that has an ongoing relationship with Warner Bros. Records."

MUSIC Released *Van Halen 3* (album), recorded by Van Halen; *Evita* (soundtrack); and *Dizzy Up the Girl* (album), recorded by Goo Goo Dolls, both on Warner Bros. Records. Other artists include Faith Hill, Tom Petty & the Heartbreakers, Jeff Foxworthy, Porno For Pyros, Travis Tritt, Yellowjackets, Bela Fleck and the Flecktones, Al Jarreau, Joshua Redmond, Little Texas, and Curtis Mayfield.

⊘ WATERDOG RECORDS

329 W. 18th St., #313, Chicago IL 60616. (312)421-7499. **E-mail:** waterdog@waterdogmusic.com. **Website:** www.waterdogmusic.com. **Contact:** Rob Gillis.

○ "At present Waterdog Music is solely concentrating on the career of Ralph Covert and his Bad Examples, Ralph's World and theatrical music projects."

HOW TO CONTACT "Not accepting unsolicited materials, demos at this time. If submission policy changes, it will be posted on our website."

MUSIC Mostly **rock** and **pop**. *Smash Record*, by The Bad Examples, released 2011. Other artists have included Middle 8, Al Rose & The Transcendos, Kat Parsons, Torben Floor (Carey Ott), MysteryDriver, Joel Frankel, Dean III, Suzy Brack & the New Jack Lords and Matt Pingel

TIPS "Ralph Covert's children's music (Ralph's World) (past releases will be reissued on Waterdog in 2013). We are not looking for any other children's music performers or composers."

◑ WINCHESTER RECORDS

25 Troubadour Lane, Berkeley Springs WV 25411. **E-mail:** info@winchesterrecords.com. **Website:** http://winchesterrecords.com.

HOW TO CONTACT *Write first and obtain permission to submit.* Prefers CD with 5-10 songs and lead sheet. Include SASE. Responds in 1 month.

MUSIC Mostly **bluegrass**, **church/religious**, **country**, **folk**, **gospel**, **progressive** and **rock**.

⊘ WIND-UP ENTERTAINMENT

72 Madison Ave., 7th Floor, New York NY 10016. **Website:** www.winduprecords.com. Wind-up Records is a privately-owned, full-service music entertainment firm founded in 1997. The company has successfully launched numerous multi-platinum artists, including Evanescence, Creed, Seether, and Finger Eleven and has further built on the successes of Five for Fighting and O.A.R. In addition to these marquee acts, Wind-up has scouted and developed several award-winning, newer artists, such as Civil Twilight, Company of Thieves, and Thriving Ivory.

Since its inception nearly 15 years ago, the company has shipped over 60 million units worldwide generating over $700 million in gross revenue. Wind-up has garnered seven multi-platinum albums (including one diamond—sales over 10 million) and seven gold albums. The Company has licensed music to high-profile television shows and motion pictures and has released several motion picture soundtracks, most notably, the platinum selling, *Walk the Line* and *Daredevil*, which went on to sell over 700,000 copies. Combining a team of creative A&R scouts, in-house writers, and engineers with its own recording studio and housing in New York City, Wind-up cultivates a fluid and collaborative recording process with its artists, independent of points in their career.

DISTRIBUTED BY BMG.

HOW TO CONTACT *Write first and obtain permission to submit.* Prefers CD or DVD. Does not return material or respond to submissions.

MUSIC Mostly **rock**, **folk** and **hard rock**. Artists include Seether, Evanescence, Finger Eleven, Creed, and People In Planes.

TIPS "We rarely look for songwriters as opposed to bands, so writing a big hit single would be the rule of the day."

◯ WORLD BEATNIK RECORDS

121 Walnut Lane, Rockwall TX 75032. **Phone/fax:** (972)771-3797. **E-mail:** tropikalproductions@gmail. com. **Website:** www.tropikalproductions.com. Record company and record producer (Jimi Towry). Staff size: 4. Releases 6 singles, 6 LPs, 6 EPs and 6 CDs/year. Pays negotiable royalty to artists on contract; statutory rate to publisher per song on record.

DISTRIBUTED BY Midwest Records, Southwest Wholesale, Reggae OneLove, Ejaness Records, Ernie B's, and CD Waterhouse.

HOW TO CONTACT Submit demo tape by mail. Unsolicited submissions are OK. Prefers CD with lyric sheet. Include SASE. Responds in 2 weeks.

MUSIC Mostly **world beat**, **reggae** and **ethnic**; also **jazz**, **hip-hop/dance**, and **pop**. Released *Alive Mon-*

tage by Watusi; *Pura Vida* by Wave; *Jamma* by Panorama; *I and I* (album by Abby I/Jimbe), recorded by Abby I (African pop); *Rastafrika* (album by Jimbe/ Richard Ono), recorded by Rastafrika (African roots reggae); and *Vibes* (album by Jimbe/Bongo Cartheni), recorded by Wave (worldbeat/jazz), all released 2001/2002 on World Beatnik. Other artists include Ras Richi (Cameroon), Wisdom Ogbor (Nigeria), Joe Lateh (Ghana), Dee Dee Cooper, Ras Lyrix (St. Croix), Ras Kumba (St. Kitts), Gary Mon, Darbo (Gambia), Ricki Malik (Jamaica), Arik Miles, Narte's (Hawaii), Gavin Audagnotti (South Africa), and Bongo (Trinidad).

◑ XEMU RECORDS

2 E. Broadway, Suite 901, New York NY 10038. (212)807-0290. **E-mail:** XemuRecord@aol.com. **Website:** www.xemu.com.

DISTRIBUTED BY Redeye Distribution.

HOW TO CONTACT *Write first and obtain permission to submit.* Prefers CD with 3 songs. Does not return material. Responds in 2 months.

MUSIC Mostly **alternative**. Released *Happy Suicide, Jim!* (album) by The Love Kills Theory (alternative rock); *Howls From The Hills* (album) by Dead Meadow; *The Fall* (album), recorded by Mikki James (alternative rock); *A is for Alpha* (album), recorded by Alpha Bitch (alternative rock); *Hold the Mayo* (album), recorded by Death Sandwich (alternative rock); *Stockholm Syndrome* (album), recorded by Trigger Happy (alternative rock) all released on Xemu Records. Other artists include Morning After Girls, Spindrift, and Rumpleville.

◑ XL RECORDINGS

One Codrington Mews, London W11 2EH United Kingdom. **Website:** www.xlrecordings.com.

MUSIC Alternative rock. Artists include Adele, Basement Jaxx, Radiohead, Beck, M.I.A, Peaches, Sigur Ros, The Horrors, The Raconteurs, The White Stripes, Thom Yorke, Vampire Weekend, and more.

RECORD PRODUCERS

//

The independent producer can best be described as a creative coordinator, and is often the one with the most creative control over a recording project and is ultimately responsible for the finished product. Some record companies have in-house producers who work with the acts on that label (although, in more recent years, such producer-label relationships are often non-exclusive). Today, most record companies contract out-of-house, independent record producers on a project-by-project basis.

WHAT RECORD PRODUCERS DO

Producers play a large role in deciding what songs will be recorded for a particular project and are always on the lookout for new songs for their clients. They can be valuable contacts for songwriters because they work so closely with the artists whose records they produce. They usually have a lot more freedom than others in executive positions and are known for having a good ear for potential hit songs. Many producers are songwriters and musicians themselves. Since they wield a great deal of influence, a good song in the hands of the right producer at the right time stands a good chance of being cut. And even if a producer is not working on a specific project, he is well-acquainted with record company executives and artists and can often get material through doors not open to you.

SUBMITTING MATERIAL TO PRODUCERS

It can be difficult to get your tapes to the right producer at the right time. Many producers write their own songs and even if they don't write, they may be involved in their own publishing companies so they have instant access to all the songs in their catalogues. Also, some genres are more dependent on finding outside songs than others. A producer working with a rock group or a singer-songwriter will rarely take outside songs.

It's important to understand the intricacies of the producer/publisher situation. If you pitch your song directly to a producer first, before another publishing company publishes the song, the producer may ask you for the publishing rights (or a percentage thereof) to your song. You must decide whether the producer is really an active publisher who will try to get the song recorded again and again or whether he merely wants the publishing rights because it means extra income for him from the current recording project. You may be able to work out a co-publishing deal, where you and the producer split the publishing of the song. That means he will still receive his percentage of the publishing income, even if you secure a cover recording of the song by other artists in the future. Even though you would be giving up a little bit initially, you may benefit in the future.

Some producers will offer to sign artists and songwriters to "development deals." These can range from a situation where a producer auditions singers and musicians with the intention of building a group from the ground up, to development deals where a producer signs a band or singer-songwriter to his production company with the intention of developing the act and producing an album to shop to labels (sometimes referred to as a "baby record deal").

You must carefully consider whether such a deal is right for you. In some cases, such a deal can open doors and propel an act to the next level. In other worst-case scenarios, such a deal can result in loss of artistic and career control, with some acts held in contractual bondage for years at a time. Before you consider any such deal, be clear about your goals, the producer's reputation, and the sort of compromises you are willing to make to reach those goals. If you have any reservations whatsoever, don't do it.

The listings that follow outline which aspects of the music industry each producer is involved in, what type of music he is looking for, and what records and artists he's recently produced. Study the listings carefully, noting the artists each producer works with, and consider if any of your songs might fit a particular artist's or producer's style. Then determine whether they are open to your level of experience (see the A Sample Listing Decoded on page 8).

Consult the Category Index in the back of this book to find producers who work with the type of music you write, and the Geographic Index at the back of the book to locate producers in your area.

ADDITIONAL RECORD PRODUCERS

There are **more record producers** located in other sections of the book! Review the index at that back of this book to find listings within other sections who are also record producers.

Icons

For more instructional information on the listings in this book, including explanations of symbols (ICONS), read the article *How To Use Songwriter's Market* on page 2.

WILLIAM ACKERMAN

P.O. Box 419, Bar Mills ME 04004. **E-mail:** will@williammackerman.com. **Website:** www.williammackerman.com.

MUSIC Acoustic, alternative, instrumental. Has worked with George Winston, Michael Hedges, Heidi Anne Breyer, Fiona Joy Hawkins, Devon Rice, Erin Aas.

⊘ ADR STUDIOS

250 Taxter Rd., Irvington NY 10533. (914)591-5616. **Fax:** (914)591-5617. **E-mail:** adrstudios@adrinc.org. **Website:** www.adrinc.org. **Contact:** Stuart J. Allyn. Produces 6 singles and 3-6 CDs/year. Fee derived from sales royalty and outright fee from recording artist and record company.

○ *Does not accept unsolicited submissions.*

MUSIC Mostly **pop**, **rock**, **jazz**, and **theatrical**; also **R&B** and **country**. Produced *Thad Jones Legacy* (album), recorded by Vanguard Jazz Orchestra (jazz), released on New World Records. Other artists include Billy Joel, Aerosmith, Carole Demas, Michael Garin, The Magic Garden, Bob Stewart, The Dixie Peppers, Nora York, Buddy Barnes and various video and film scores.

ALLRS MUSIC PUBLISHING CO. (ASCAP)

P.O. Box 1545, Smithtown NY 11787. (718)767-8995. **E-mail:** info@allrsmusic.com. **Website:** www.allrsmusic.com. **Contact:** Renee Silvestri-Bushey, president. Music publisher, record company (MIDI Track Records), music consultant, artist management, record producer. Voting member of: NARAS (The Grammy Awards); the Country Music Association (The CMA Awards); SGMA; and Songwriters Guild of America (Diamond member). Staff size: 5. Publishes 3 songs/year; publishes 2 new songwriters/year. Pays standard royalty.

AFFILIATE Midi-Track Publishing Co. (BMI).

HOW TO CONTACT "Write/e-mail to obtain permission to submit. *We do not accept unsolicited submissions.*" Prefers CD with 3 songs, lyric sheet and cover letter. Responds via e-mail in 6 months only if interested.

MUSIC Mostly **country**, **gospel**, **Top 40**, **R&B**, **MOR**, and **pop**. Does not want showtunes, jazz, classical or rap. Published "Why Can't You Hear My Prayer" (single by F. John Silvestri/Leslie Silvestri), recorded by 10-time Grammy nominee Huey Dunbar of the group DLG (Dark Latin Groove) released on Midi-Track

Records including other multiple releases); "Chasing Rainbows" (single by F. John Silvestri/Leslie Silvestri), recorded by Tommy Cash (country), released on MMT Records (including other multiple releases).

TIPS "Attend workshops, seminars, and visit our blog on our website for advise and info on the music industry."

○ ◑ A MAJOR SOUND CORPORATION

RR # 1, Kensington PE COB 1MO Canada. (902)836-1051. **E-mail:** info@amajorsound.com; musicpublisher@amajorsound.com. **Website:** www.amajorsound.com. **Contact:** Paul Milner, producer/engineer/mixer. Record producer and music publisher. Produces 8 CDs/year. Fee derived in part from sales royalty when song or artist is recorded, and/or outright fee from recording artist or record company, or investors. Submit demo package by mail. Unsolicited submissions are OK. Prefers CD with 5 songs and lyric sheet (lead sheet if available). Does not return material. Responds only if interested in 3 months.

MUSIC Mostly **rock**, **A/C**, **alternative** and **pop**; also **Christian** and **R&B**. Produced *COLOUR* (album written by J. MacPhee/R. MacPhee/C. Buchanan/D. MacDonald), recorded by The Chucky Danger Band (pop/rock); winner of ECMA award; *Something In Between* (album, written by Matt Andersen), recorded by Matt Andersen and Friends (Blues), released on Weatherbox / Andersen; *In A Fever In A Dream* (album, written by Pat Deighan), recorded by Pat Deighan and The Orb Weavers (Rock), released on Sandbar Music; *Saddle River String Band* (album, written by Saddle River String band), recorded by Saddle River Stringband (Bluegrass) released on Save As Music; winner of ECMA award.

TIM ANDERSEN

(651)271-0515. **E-mail:** tandersen2005@yahoo.com. **Website:** www.timandersenrecordingengineer.com. "Can offer all those techniques to make your project rise above "the usual" to something extraordinary, the way real records are made."

MUSIC Has worked with House of Pain, Shaq, Judgement Night, SDTRK, De Jef, Patti LaBelle, Temptations, Hiroshima, Krazy Bone, Snoop Dogg. **Music:** rock, r&b, hip-hop, rap, acoustic.

◑ AUDIO 911

P.O. Box 212, Haddam CT 06438. (860)916-9947. **E-mail:** request@audio911.com. **Website:** www.audio911.com. Produces 4-8 singles, 3 LPs, 3 EPs and

4 CDs/year. Fee derived from outright fee from recording artist or record company. Submit demo by mail. Unsolicited submissions are OK. Prefers CD or VHS videocassette with several songs and lyric or lead sheet. "Include live material if possible." Does not return material. Responds in 3 months.

MUSIC Mostly **rock**, **pop**, **top 40** and **country/acoustic**. Produced *Already Home* (album), recorded by Hannah Cranna on Big Deal Records (rock); *Under the Rose* (album), recorded by Under the Rose on Utter Records (rock); and *Sickness & Health* (album), recorded by Legs Akimbo on Joyful Noise Records (rock). Other artists include King Hop!, The Shells, The Gravel Pit, G'nu Fuz, Tuesday Welders and Toxic Field Mice.

WILLIE BASSE

Los Angeles CA (818)731-9116. **E-mail:** williebasse@gmail.com. **Website:** www.williebasse.com. **Contact:** James Wright.

MUSIC **rock**, **blues**, **heavy metal**. Has worked with: Canned Heat, Finis Tasby, Frank Goldwasser, Paul Shortino, Jeff Nothrup, Black Sheep.

EVAN BEIGEL

5618 Vineland Ave., N. Hollywood CA 91601. (818)321-5472. **E-mail:** mail@evanjbeigel.com. **Website:** www.evanjbeigel.com.

MUSIC **rock**, **indie**, **alternative** . Has worked with Ray Kurzweil, Badi Assad, Ted Nugent, EightStopSeven, Test Your Reflex, Ford, Budweiser.

◐ BIG BEAR

P.O. Box 944, Edgbaston, Birmingham, B16 8UT United Kingdom. (0)(121)454-7020. **Fax:** (0)(121)454-9996. **E-mail:** jim@bigbearmusic.com. **Website:** www.bigbearmusic.com. **Contact:** Jim Simpson, managing director. Record producer, music publisher (Bearsongs) and record company (Big Bear Records). Produces 10 LPs/year. Fee derived from sales royalty. *Write first about your interest, then submit demo tape and lyric sheet.* Does not return material. Responds in 2 weeks.

MUSIC **Blues**, **swing**, and **jazz**.

◯ BLUES ALLEY RECORDS

Rt. 1, Box 288, Clarksburg WV 26301. (304)598-2583. **E-mail:** info@bluesalleymusic.com. **Website:** www.bluesalleymusic.com. Record producer, record company and music publisher (Blues Alley Publishing/BMI). Produces 4-6 LPs and 2 EPs/year. Fee derived from sales royalty when song or artist is recorded.

Submit demo package by mail. Unsolicited submissions are OK. Will only accept CDs with lead sheets and typed lyrics. Does not return material. Responds in 6 weeks.

MUSIC Mostly **country**, **pop**, **Christian**, and **rock**. Produced *Monongalia*, recorded by The New Relics (country), 2009; *Chasing Venus*, recorded by The New Relics (acoustic rock), 2006; *Sons of Sirens*, recorded by Amity (rock), 2004; and *It's No Secret*, recorded by Samantha Caley (pop country), 2004.

CLIFF BRODSKY

Beverly Hills CA **E-mail:** cliff@brodskyentertainment.com. **Website:** www.cliffbrodsky.com.

MUSIC **indie**, **pop**, **rock**. Has worked with Rose Rossi, Jason Kirk, Warner Brothers, Universal, Sony, MCA, Virgin, Interscope.

⊘ CABIN-ON-THE-LAKE MUSIC

4120 Dale Rd., Suite J-8 #180, Modesto CA 95356. (608)239-4121. **Fax:** (209)409-8343 (call first). **E-mail:** jmiksche@cabin-on-the-lake.com. **Website:** www.cabin-on-the-lake.com. **Contact:** Jim Miksche.

MUSIC Mostly interested in **singer/songwriters**, **folk**; also **country/crossover**, **blues rock**. Does not want rap, hard rock, hip-hop, or jazz. Produced "The Legend of Coby Gill" (single by Chris Lawrence) from *The Legend of Coby Gill* (album), recorded by Coby Gill (folk/country); "Give Me a Call" (single by Chris Lawrence), from *The Legend of Coby Gill* (album), recorded by Coby Gill (folk/country); "I Could Swear" written and recorded by Tom Davis.

◯ JAN CELT MUSICAL SERVICES

4015 NE 12th Ave., Portland OR 97212. **E-mail:** flyheart@teleport.com. **Website:** http://home.teleport.com/~flyheart. Record producer, music producer and publisher (Wiosna Nasza Music/BMI) and record company (Flying Heart Records). Submit demo tape by mail. Unsolicited submissions are OK. Prefers high-quality cassette with 1-10 songs and lyric sheet. "SASE required for any response." Does not return materials. Responds in 4 months.

◔   Also see the listing for Flying Heart Records in the Record Companies section of this book.

MUSIC Mostly **R&B**, **rock** and **blues**; also **jazz**. Produced "Vexatious Progressions" (single), written and recorded by Eddie Harris (jazz); "Bong Hit" (single by Chris Newman), recorded by Snow Bud & the Flower People (rock); and "She Moved Away" (single by Chris Newman), recorded by Napalm Beach, all on Flying

Heart Records. Other artists include The Esquires and Janice Scroggins.

COACHOUSE MUSIC

P.O. Box 1308, Barrington IL 60011. (847)382-7631. E-mail: michael@coachousemusic.com. **Website:** http://coachousemusic.com.

MUSIC Mostly **rock**, **pop** and **blues**; also **alternative rock** and **country/Americana/roots**. Produced *Casque Nu* (album), written and recorded by Charlelie Couture on Chrysalis EMI France (contemporary pop); *Time Will Tell* (album), recorded by Studebaker John on Blind Pig Records (blues); *Where Blue Begins* (album by various/D. Coleman), recorded by Deborah Coleman on Blind Pig Records (contemporary blues); *A Man Amongst Men* (album), recorded by Bo Diddley (blues); and *Voodoo Menz (album),* recorded by Corey Harris and Henry Butler. Two WC Handy nominations; produced *Pinetop Perkins & Friends* on Telarc recorded by Pinetop Perkins--Grammy nominated. Other artists include Paul Chastain, Candi Station, Eleventh Dream Day, Magic Slim, The Tantrums, The Pranks, The Bad Examples, Mississippi Heat and Sherri Williams.

TIPS "Be honest, be committed, strive for excellence."

ERIC CORNE

Los Angeles CA (310)500-8831. **E-mail:** eric@ericcornemusic.com. **Website:** www.ericcornemusic.com. **Contact:** Eric Corne, producer.

MUSIC **rock, indie, Americana, country, blues, jazz, folk.** Has worked with Glen Campbell, Michelle Shocked, DeVotchKa, Instant Karma..

CREATIVE SOUL

Nashville TN 37179. (615)400-3910. **E-mail:** firstcontact@creativesoulrecords.com. **Website:** www.creativesoulonline.com. Record producer. Produces 5-10 singles and 8-15 albums/year. Fee derived from outright fee from recording artist or company. Other services include consulting/critique/review services. *Contact first by e-mail to obtain permission to submit demo.* Prefers CD with 2-3 songs and lyric sheet and cover sheet. Does not return submissions. Responds only if interested.

MUSIC Contemporary, **Christian, jazz,** and **instrumental**; also **R&B** and **pop/rock**. "If you are a Christian jazz or instrumentalist, then all the better!" Produced *Cedars Gray*, recorded by Cedars Gray (contemporary Christian); *It Is Of You*, recorded by Matt Pitzl (contemporary Christian); *Fairytale Life*, recorded by

Stephanie Newton (contemporary Christian); all released on Creative Soul Records. Other artists include Brett Rush, Frances Drost, Kristyn Leigh, Tom Dolan, and Canopy Red.

TIPS "Contact us first by e-mail; we are here in Nashville for you. We offer monthly information and special consults in Nashville for artists and writers. We want to meet you and talk with you about your dreams. E-mail us and let's start talking about your music and ministry!"

MARC DESISTO

Sherman Oaks CA (818)522-0214. **E-mail:** marcd-mix@gmail.com. **Website:** www.marcdesisto.com. **MUSIC** **rock, alternative, pop, indie** . Has worked with Stevie Nicks, Michelle Branch, Unwritten Law, Melissa Ethridge, Rick Knowles, Don Henley, Patti Smith, Mark Opitz, Tom Petty, U2.

JEANNIE DEVA

P.O. Box 4636, Sunland CA 91041. (818)446-0932. **E-mail:** sing@jeanniedeva.com. **Website:** www.jeanniedeva.com. **Contact:** Jeannie Deva.

MUSIC all contemporary styles. Has worked with Rounder Records, Charisse Arrington, MCA, Dar Williams, Razor and Tie Records, Alldaron West.

JOEL DIAMOND ENTERTAINMENT

3940 Laurel Canyon Blvd., Suite 441, Studio City CA 91604. (818)980-9588. **E-mail:** jdiamond20@aol.com. **Website:** www.joeldiamond.com. **Contact:** Joel Diamond, president and CEO. Record producer, music publisher and manager. Fee derived from sales royalty when song is recorded or outright fee from recording artist or record company.

Also see the listing for Silver Blue Music/Oceans Blue Music in the Music Publishers section of this book.

MUSIC Mostly **dance**, **R&B**, **soul**, and **Top 40/pop**. The 5 Browns—3 number 1 CDs for Sony/BMG, David Hasselhoff; produced "One Night In Bangkok" (single by Robey); "I Think I Love You," recorded by Katie Cassidy (daughter of David Cassidy) on Artemis Records; "After the Loving" (single), recorded by E. Humperdinck; "Forever Friends," recorded by Vaneza (featured on Nickelodeon's *The Brothers Garcia*); and "Paradise" (single), recorded by Kaci.

LES DUDEK

EFLAT Productions, P.O. Box 726, Auburndale FL 33823-0726. **Website:** www.lesdudek.com.

MUSIC southern rock. Has worked with Stevie Nicks, Steve Miller Band, Cher, Dave Mason, The Allman Brothers, Mike Finnigan, Bobby Whitlock.

● FINAL MIX INC.

2219 W. Olive Ave., Suite 102, Burbank CA 91506. **E-mail:** rob@finalmix.com. **Website:** www.finalmix.com. Releases 12 singles and 3-5 LPs and CDs/year. Fee derived from sales royalty when song or artist is recorded.

○ *Does not accept unsolicited submissions.*

MUSIC Primarily **pop**, **rock**, **dance**, **R&B**, and **rap**. Produced and/or mixer/remixer for Mary Mary, New Boyz, Kirk Franklin, Charlie Wilson, LeAnn Rimes, Charice, Train, Aaliyah, Hilary Duff, Jesse McCartney, Christina Aguilera, American Idol, Ray Charles, Quincy Jones, Michael Bolton, K-Ci and Jo Jo, Will Smith, and/or mixer/remixer for Janet Jackson, Ice Cube, Queen Latifah, Jennifer Paige, and The Corrs.

RICHARD FINK IV

P.O. Box 127, Bergen NY 14416. (646)233-3393. **E-mail:** voice@richardiv.com. **Website:** www.richardiv.com.

MUSIC **pop**, **rock**, **alternative**, **hard rock**, **metal**, **R&B**. Has worked with Carmireli, Meredith Haight, Scattered Ink, Johnny Cummings, Krista Marie.

MAURICE GAINEN

4470 Sunset Blvd., Suite 177, Hollywood CA 90027. (323)662-3642. **E-mail:** info@mauricegainen.com. **Website:** www.mauricegainen.com. "We provide complete start to finish CD Production, including help in choosing songs and musicians through CD mastering. We also pride ourselves on setting a budget and keeping to it."

MUSIC **R&B**, **jazz**, **alternative**, **rock**, **pop**. Has worked with Stacy Golden, Yuka Takara, Donna Loren, James Webber, Andy McKee, Rafael Moreira, Alex Skolnick Trio, Metro, Mel Elias, Shelly Rudolph, Kenny Tex, Rachael Owens.

BRIAN GARCIA

Los Angeles CA (626)487-0410. **E-mail:** record@wt.net. **Website:** www.briangarcia.net.

MUSIC **rock, pop, indie**. "Producer-Mixer-Engineer Brian Garcia specializes in the genres of rock and pop. He has been part of 22 million records sold, debuts at No. 1 in 30 countries, a Grammy winning album, and a No. 1 single on iTunes as a co-writer/producer/mixer. Brian has taken artists from development to secur-

ing record deals and producing albums for EMI and Sony/BMG." Has worked with Our Lady Peace, Earshot, Until June, Galactic Cowboys, Avril Lavigne, Kelly Clarkson, Michelle Branch, Dizmas, Chantal Kreviazuk, King's X, Diana Degarmo, The Library, Pushmonkey, The Daylights, Precious Death, Joy Drop.

MCKAY GARNER

c/o Bounce Inventive Audio, 1873 Eighth Ave. Suite A, San Francisco CA 94122. (323)912-9119. **E-mail:** info@mckaygarner.com. **Website:** www.mckaygarner.com.

MUSIC Has worked with Red Hot Chili Peppers, Styles of Beyond, Flogging Molly, Valencia, Mike Shinoda, Michael Buble, Sara Melson, Elyzium.

CARMEN GRILLO

Big Surprise Music, 1616 Ventura Blvd. Suite 522, Encino CA 91436. (818)905-7676. **E-mail:** info@carmengrillo.com. **Website:** www.carmengrillo.com.

MUSIC **R&B, pop, rock, jazz, blues**. Has worked with Manhattan, Transfer, Chicago, Bill Champlin, Mike Finnigan, Tower of Power..

● HEART CONSORT MUSIC

410 First St. SW, Mt. Vernon IA 52314. **E-mail:** mail@heartconsortmusic.com. **Website:** www.heartconsortmusic.com. **Contact:** James Kennedy. Produces 2-3 CDs/year. Fee derived from sales royalty when song or artist is recorded. Submit demo package by mail. Unsolicited submissions are OK. Prefers CD with 3 songs and 3 lyric sheets. Include SASE. Responds in 3 months.

MUSIC Mostly **jazz**, **New Age** and **contemporary**. Produced *New Faces* (album), written and recorded by James Kennedy on Heart Consort Music (world/jazz).

TIPS "We are interested in jazz/New Age artists with quality demos and original ideas. We aim for an international audience."

HEATHER HOLLEY

New York NY **E-mail:** info@heatherholley.com. **Website:** http://heatherholley.com. "Heather Holley is a New York-based multi-platinum songwriter/arranger/producer whose credits have yielded combined sales of over 29 million, and climbing."

MUSIC **pop, dance, indie, R&B**. Has worked with Christina Aguilera, Katie Costello, Holly Brook, Caitlin Moe.

JIMMY HUNTER

Hollywood CA (323)655-0615. **E-mail:** jimmy@jimmyhunter.com. **Website:** www.jimmyhunter.com. "When you work with Jimmy Hunter, you find a fellow artist who will help you to achieve and refine your vision. He has the experience and tools to get the ultimate sound for your music and bring out the very best in you."

MUSIC rock, pop, R&B. Has worked with Cher, Savannah Phillips, Smoove, Jared Justice, Lisa Rine, Lynn Tracy, Mark R. Kent, Della Reese, Lisa Gold, Jamie Palumbo, The Ramblers.

SIMON ILLA

Atlanta GA **E-mail:** info@simonilla.com. **Website:** www.simonilla.com.

MUSIC hip-hop, R&B, pop, folk, rock, gospel, emo. Has worked with Onyx, Vivian Green, Floetry, Roscoe P. Coldchain, The Answer.

❶ INTEGRATED ENTERTAINMENT

1815 JFK Blvd., #1612, Philadelphia PA 19103. **Website:** www.gelboni.com. 1815 JFK Blvd., #1612, Philadelphia, PA 19103. (267)408-0659. **E-mail:** lawrence@gelboni.com. **Website:** www.gelboni.com. **Contact:** Gelboni, president. Record producer. Estab. 1991. Produces up to 6 projects/year. Compensation is derived from outright fee from recording artist or record company and sales royalties.

HOW TO CONTACT Submit demo package by mail. Solicited submissions only. CD only with 3 songs. "Draw a guitar on the outside of envelope so we'll know it's from a songwriter." Will respond if interested.

MUSIC Mostly **rock** and **pop**. Produced *Gold Record* (album), written and recorded by Dash Rip Rock (rock) on Ichiban Records and many others.

CHRIS JULIAN

4872 Topanga Canyon Blvd., Suite 406, Woodland Hills CA 91364. (310)924-7849. **E-mail:** chris@ChrisJulian.com. **Website:** www.chrisjulian.com. "Owned and operated solely by engineer/producer Chris Julian, the studio is oriented toward personal service."

MUSIC R&B, pop, rock, soul, hip-hop, jazz. Has worked with David Bowie, Vanessa Williams, Jimmy Webb, De La Soul, Queen Latifah, Biz Markie, A Tribe Called Quest, Fat Joe, Peter Moffitt, Danielle Livingston, Bobbi Humphrey, Mint, Just James, Brenda K. Star, Naughty By Nature.

❶ KAREN KANE PRODUCER/ENGINEER

(910)681-0220. **E-mail:** karenkane@mixmama.com. **Website:** www.mixmama.com. **Contact:** Karen Kane. Record producer and recording engineer. Produces 3-5 CDs/year. Fee derived from sales royalty when song or artist is recorded or outright fee from recording artist or record company. *E-mail first and obtain permission to submit. Unsolicited submissions are not OK.* "Please note: I am not a song publisher. My expertise is in album production." Does not return material. Responds in 1 week.

MUSIC Mostly **acoustic music of any kind**, **rock**, **blues**, **pop**, **alternative**, **R&B/reggae**, **country**, and **bluegrass**. Produced *Good to Me* (album), recorded by Nina Repeta; *Topless* (Juno-nominated album), recorded by Big Daddy G, released on Reggie's Records; *Mixed Wise and Otherwise* (Juno-nominated album), recorded by Harry Manx (blues). Other artists include Tracy Chapman (her first demo), Katarina Bourdeaux, Crys Matthews, Laura Bird, L Shape Lot, The Hip Hop Co-op, Barenaked Ladies (live recording for a TV special), and The Coolidge Band.

TIPS "Get proper funding to be able to make a competitive, marketable product."

TIM DAVID KELLY

Los Angeles CA (818)601-7047. **E-mail:** info@timdavidkelly.com. **Website:** www.timdavidkelly.com.

MUSIC alternative, metal, Americana, rock, acoustic pop. Has worked with Kicking Harold, Shiny Toy Guns, Dokken.

❶ L.A. ENTERTAINMENT, INC.

7095 Hollywood Blvd., #826, Hollywood CA 90028. **E-mail:** info@warriorrecords.com. **Website:** www.warriorrecords.com. Record producer, record company (Warrior Records) and music publisher (New Entity Music/ASCAP, New Copyright Music/BMI, New Euphonic Music/SESAC). Fee derived from sales royalty when song or artist is recorded. Submit demo package by mail. Unsolicited submissions are OK. Prefers CD and/or videocassette with original songs, lyric and lead sheet if available. "We do not review Internet sites. Do not send MP3s, unless requested. All written submitted materials (e.g., lyric sheets, letter, etc.) should be typed." Does not return material unless SASE is included. Responds in 2 months only via e-mail or SASE.

MUSIC All styles. "All genres are utilized with our music supervision company for Film & TV, but our original focus is on **alternative rock** and **urban genres** (e.g., **R&B**, **rap**, **gospel**).

○ LANDMARK COMMUNICATIONS GROUP

P.O. Box 1444, Hendersonville TN 37077. (615)585-9301. **E-mail:** ba@landmarkcommunicationsgroup.com. **Website:** www.landmarkcommunications-group.com. **Contact:** Bill Anderson Jr., producer. Record producer, record company, music publisher (Newcreature Music/BMI) and TV/radio syndication. Produces 6 singles and 6 LPs/year. Fee derived from sales royalty. *Write first and obtain permission to submit.* Prefers CD, MP3 with 4-10 songs and lyric sheet. Include SASE.

○   Also see the listings for Landmark Communications Group in the Record Companies section of this book.

MUSIC Country crossover. Recent projects: *Smoky Mountain Campmeeting* by Various Artists; *The Pilgrim & the Road* by Tiffany Turner; *Fallow Ground* by C.J. Hall; *Prince Charming is Dead* by Kecia Burcham.

○ LINEAR CYCLE PRODUCTIONS

P.O. Box 2608, North Hills CA 91393. **E-mail:** accessiblyliveoffline@gmail.com. **Website:** www.linearcycle-productions.com.

MUSIC Mostly **rock/pop**, **R&B/blues** and **country**; also **gospel** and **comedy**. Produced "Giving it All to Me" (single by Pandanceski/Katz/Purewhite), recorded by Monea Later (pop/dance), released on Tozic Googh Sounds. "P for the Bits" (G Glix) (single by Hyram Yip Pea) from his *Last Sound Collection*, recorded and released on "Swip" brand MP3s; and "Back into the Box Sho Nuff" (single by Blyma/Warmwater/Posh) recorded by Mister Quit.

TIPS "We only listen to songs and other material recorded on quality tapes and CDs. We will not accept any submissions via e-mail. If your demo is recorded on an MP3 or AIFF sound file, you must either burn the file onto a CD, or download the sound file into an MP3 player and send the player with the songs to our attention. Otherwise, anything sent via e-mail will be disposed of and will not be considered."

BOB LUNA

Los Angeles CA (310)202-8043 or (310)508-1356. **E-mail:** bobluna@earthlink.net. **Website:** http://bobluna music.net.

MUSIC live and midi orchestration.

PETER MALICK

Los Angeles CA (866)884-9919, ext. 2. **E-mail:** petermalick@gmail.com. **Website:** www.petermalick.com. **MUSIC indie, rock, roots, Americana**. Has worked with Fast Heart Mart, Henry Gummer, Chelsea Williams, Hope Waits, Norah Jones, Kirsten Proffit, Whitey Conwell, Free Dominguez, Suzanne Santos.

⊘ COOKIE MARENCO

P.O. Box 874, Belmont CA 94002. (650)595-8475. **E-mail:** info@bluecoastrecords.com. **Website:** http://cookiemarenco.com.

HOW TO CONTACT *"No speculative projects." Does not accept unsolicited material.* Must have budget.

MUSIC Mostly acoustic, high resolution, live-performance oriented **alternative modern rock**, **country**, **folk**, **rap**, **ethnic**, and **avante-garde**; also **classical**, **pop**, and **jazz**. Produced *Winter Solstice II* (album), written and recorded by various artists for Windham Hill Records (instrumental). Artists include Tony Furtado, Brain, Buckethead, Alex Degrassi, Turtle Island String Quartet, Praxis, Oregon, Mary Chapin Carpenter, Max Roach and Charle Haden & Quartet West.

TIPS "Specialist in high quality ANALOG recording. Mixing to 1/2" or DSD digital. Full service mastering and dynamic website development."

◑ PETE MARTIN/VAAM MUSIC PRODUCTIONS

P.O. Box 29550, Hollywood CA 90029-0550. **E-mail:** pmarti3636@aol.com. **Website:** www.vaammusic.com. **Contact:** Pete Martin. "Looking for uptempo, positive country and country crossover songs, both for male and female artists. Please no sad, crying in your beer, she left me songs. Must be positive uplifting songs with intelligent lyrics ready for publishing."

HOW TO CONTACT Send CD or cassette with 2 songs and a lyric sheet. Send small packages only. Include SASE. Responds in 1 month.

MUSIC Mostly **Top 40/pop**, **country** and **R&B**.

TIPS "Study the market in the style that you write. Songs must be capable of reaching top 5 on charts."

⊙○ SCOTT MATHEWS, D/B/A HIT OR MYTH PRODUCTIONS INC.

246 Almonte Blvd., Mill Valley CA 94941. **E-mail:** scott@scottmathews.com. **Website:** www.scottmathews.com. Record producer, "song doctor", studio owner, and professional consultant. Produces 6-9

CDs/year. Fee derived from recording artist or record company (with royalty points).

○ Scott Mathews has several gold and platinum awards for sales of more than 15 million records. He has worked with more than 60 Rock & Roll Hall of Fame inductees and on several Grammy and Oscar-winning releases. He is currently working primarily with emerging artists while still making music with his legendary established artists. The pan-Asian pop group he is working with, Blush, had a #1 Billboard dance hit in early 2012.

HOW TO CONTACT "No publishing submissions, please. We do not place songs with artists because we work with artists who write their own material." Submit artist demo for production consideration with a CD by mail or an MP3 by e-mail. "Unsolicited submissions are often the best ones and readily accepted. Include SASE if e-mail is not an option. Also include your e-mail address on your demo CD as all early stage business is handled by e-mail." Responds in 2 months.

MUSIC Mostly **rock/pop**, **alternative** and **singer/songwriters of all styles**. Produced 4 tracks on *Anthology* (best of), recorded by John Hiatt (rock/pop), released on Hip-O. In 2004 Mathews earned a gold album for *Smile* by Brian Wilson. He has produced Elvis Costello, Roy Orbison, Rosanne Cash, Jerry Garcia, Huey Lewis, Sammy Hagar, and many more. He has recorded classics with Barbara Streisand, John Lee Hooker, Keith Richards, George Harrison, Mick Jagger, Van Morrison, Bonnie Raitt, Brian Wilson, Zac Brown, Chris Isaak, and Eric Clapton.

TIPS "These days if you are not independent, you are dependent. The new artists that are coming up and achieving success in the music industry are the ones that prove they have a vision and can make incredible records without the huge financial commitment of a major label. When an emerging artist makes great product for the genre they are in, they are in the driver's seat to be able to make a fair and equitable deal for distribution, be it with a major or independent label. My philosophy is to go where you are loved. The truth is, a smaller label that is completely dedicated to you and shares your vision may help your career far more than a huge label that will not keep you around if you don't sell millions of units. Perhaps no label is needed at all, if you are up for the challenge of wearing a lot of hats. I feel too much pressure is put on the emerging artist when they have to pay huge sums back to the label in order to see their first royalty check. We all know those records can be made for a fraction of that cost without compromising quality or commercial appeal. I still believe in potential and our company is in business to back up that belief. It is up to us as record makers/visionaries to take that potential into the studio and come out with music that can compete with anything else on the market. Discovering, developing and producing artists that can sustain long careers is our main focus at Hit or Myth Productions. We are proud to be associated with so many legendary and timeless artists and our track record speaks for itself. If you love making music, don't let anyone dim that light. We look forward to hearing from you if you are an emerging artist looking for production to kick your career into high gear. (Please check out www.scottmathews.com for more info, and also www.allmusic.com-keyword; Scott Mathews.) Accept no substitutes!"

◑ MEGA TRUTH RECORDS

P.O. Box 4988, Culver City CA 90231. **E-mail:** jonbare@aol.com. **Website:** www.jonbare.net. **Contact:** Jon Bare, CEO. Submit demo package by mail. Unsolicited submissions are OK. Prefers CD. "We specialize in recording world-class virtuoso musicians and bands with top players." Does not return material. Responds in 2 weeks only if interested.

MUSIC Mostly **rock**, **blues** and **country rock**; also **swing**, **dance** and **instrumental**. Produced *Party Platter* recorded by Hula Monsters (swing); and *Killer Whales*, *Shredzilla* and *Orcastra* (by Jon Bare and the Killer Whales) (rock), all on Mega Truth Records. Other artists include The Rich Harper Blues Band, Aeon Dream & the Dream Machine and Techno Dudes.

TIPS "Create a unique sound that blends great vocals and virtuoso musicianship with a beat that makes us want to get up and dance."

BILL METOYER

16209 Victor Blvd. #132, Lake Balboa CA 91406. (818)780-5394. **E-mail:** bill@skullseven.com. **Website:** www.billmetoyer.com.

MUSIC Has worked with Salyer, W.A.S.P., Fates Warning, Six Feet Under, Armored Saint, Tourniquet, Skrew, Rigor Mortis, Sacred Steel, Cement. **Music:** hard rock, metal.

BILLY MITCHELL

P.O. Box 284, S. Pasadena CA 91031. (626)574-5040. **Fax:** (626)446-2584. **E-mail:** billymitchell2k@aol.com. **Website:** www.billy-mitchell.com.

MUSIC contemporary jazz, pop. Has worked with Chartmaker Records, Vista Records, PRC Records, USA Music Group.

ADAM MOSELEY

Los Angeles CA (323)316-4932. **E-mail:** adammoseley@mac.com. **Website:** www.adammoseley.com.

MUSIC rock, alternative, electronica, acoustic. Has worked with Claudio Valenzuela, Lisbeth Scott, Wolfmother, Nikka Costa, Abandoned Pools, John Cale, AJ Croce, Lucybell, The Cure, KISS, Rush, Roxette, Maxi Priest.

O MUSICJONES RECORDS

P.O. Box 5163, Chatsworth CA 91313. (818)920-8058. **E-mail:** mike@musicjones.com. **Website:** www.musicjones.com.

MUSIC Mostly **country**, **folk** and **pop**; also **rock**. Recent album releases: *The Highway* featuring Mike Jones and "Oops My Bad" Featuring Ginger Granger. Also produced "Lonelyville," and "Alabama Slammer" (singles), both written and recorded by Wake Eastman; and "Good Looking Loser" (single), written and recorded by Renee Rubach, all on Sound Works Records (country). Other artists include Matt Dorman, Steve Gilmore, The Tackroom Boys, The Las Vegas Philharmonic, and J.C. Clark.

TIPS "Put your ego on hold. Don't take criticism personally. Advice is meant to help you grow and improve your skills as an artist/songwriter. Be professional and business-like in all your dealings."

◐ MUSTROCK PRODUCTIONZ WORLDWIDE

167 W. 81st St., Suite 5C, New York NY 10024-7200. **E-mail:** recordmode@hotmail.com.

HOW TO CONTACT *E-mail first and obtain permission to submit.* Prefers MP3, CD, DVD and lyric sheet. Does not return material. Responds in 2 months. "Unless booking our services, only opinion will be given-—we do not shop deals."

MUSIC Mostly **hip-hop**, **R&B** and **pop**; also **soul, ballads** and **soundtracks**. Produced "Poor Georgie" (by MC Lyte/DJ DOC), recorded by MC Lyte on Atlantic Records (rap). Other artists include Caron Wheeler, The Hit Squad, The Awesome II, Black Steel Music, Underated Productions, EPMD, Redman, Dr. Dre &

Ed-Lover, Das-EFX, Biz Markie, BDP, Eric B & Rakim, The Fugees, The Bushwackass, Shai and Pudgee, Alisha Keys, 50 cent, Tiro de Garcia, etc.

TIPS "Services provided include ProTools production (pre/post/co), digital tracking, mixing, remixing, live show tapes, jingles, etc. For additinal credits, go to www.allmusic.com, type 'Ivan Doc Rodriguez' under 'artist' and enter, or send e-mail."

XAVIER NATHAN

524 Raymond Ave. #4, Santa Monica CA 90405. (818)339-3238. **E-mail:** zave2004@yahoo.com. **Website:** http://xavierjnathan.com.

MUSIC Has worked with Headsandwich, Sahaloop, The Joy House, Dan Bern, Indya, Edouardo Torres. **Music:** rock, blues, R&B, funk, acoustic, hard rock.

O NEU ELECTRO PRODUCTIONS

P.O. Box 1582, Bridgeview IL 60455. (630)257-6289. **E-mail:** neuelectro@email.com. **Website:** www.neuelectro.com. **Contact:** Bob Neumann.

MUSIC Mostly **dance**, **house**, **techno**, **rap**, and **rock**; also **experimental**, **New Age**, and **Top 40**. Produced "Juicy" (single), written and recorded by Juicy Black on Dark Planet International Records (house); "Make Me Smile" (single), written and recorded by Roz Baker (house); *Reactovate-6* (album by Bob Neumann), recorded by Beatbox-D on N.E.P. Records (dance); and *Sands of Time* (album), recorded by Bob Neumann (New Age). Other artists include Skid Marx and The Deviants.

◑ NEW EXPERIENCE RECORDS/FAZE 4 RECORDS/PUMP IT UP RECORDS/TOUCH TONE RECORDS

P.O. Box 683, Lima OH 45802. **E-mail:** just_chilling_2002@yahoo.com; newexperiencerecords@yahoo.com. **Contact:** James L. Milligan Jr., president, CEO, and music publisher. Record producer, music publisher (A New Rap Jam Publishing/ASCAP), management firm (Creative Star Management) and record company (New Experience Records, Rough Edge Records, Grand-Slam Records, and Pump It Up Records). Produces 15-30 12" singles, 3 EPs, and 2-5 CDs/year. Fee derived from sales royalty when song or artist is recorded or outright fee from record company, "depending on services required." Distributed by KVZ Distribution and States 51 Distribution.

❑ Also see the listings for A New Rap Jam Publishing (ASCAP) in the Music Publishers section of this book.

HOW TO CONTACT Contact A&R Department or write first to arrange personal interview. Address material to A&R Department or Talent Coordinator. Prefers CD with a minimum of 3 songs and lyric or lead sheet (if available). "If CDs are to be returned, proper postage should be enclosed and all CDs and letters should have SASE for faster reply." Responds in 6-8 weeks.

MUSIC Mostly **pop**, **R&B**, and **rap**; also **gospel**, **soul**, **contemporary gospel** and **rock**. Produced "The Son of God" (single by James Milligan/Anthony Milligan/Melvin Milligan) from *The Final Chapter* (album), recorded by T.M.C. Milligan Conection (R&B, Gospel), released 2002 on New Experience/Pump It Up Records. Other artists include Dion Mikel, Paulette Mikel, Melvin Milligan and Venesta Compton.

TIPS "Do your homework on the music business. Be aware of all the new sampling laws. There are too many soundalikes. Be yourself. I look for what is different, vocal ability, voice range and sound stage presence, etc. Be on the lookout for our new blues label Rough Edge Records/Rough Edge Entertainment. Blues material is now being reviewed. Send your best studio recorded material. Also be aware of the new digital downloading laws. People are being jailed and fined for recording music that has not been paid for. Do your homework. Labels: New Experience Records, Touch Tone Records, Grind Blocc Records, Pump It Up Records; now we can better serve our customers with great distribution. We are reviewing hip-hop and rap material that is positive, clean, and commercial; please no Gangsta rap if you want a deal with us as well as airplay. Also reviewing gospel music, gospel rap and anything with commercial appeal."

O NIGHTWORKS RECORDS

355 W. Potter Dr., Anchorage AK 99518. (907)562-3754. **E-mail:** surrealstudiosak@gmail.com. **Website:** www.surrealstudios.com. **Contact:** Kurt Riemann, owner/engineer.

HOW TO CONTACT Submit demo package by mail. Unsolicited submissions are OK. Prefers CD with 2-3 songs "produced as fully as possible. Send jingles and songs on separate CDs." Does not return material. Responds in 1 month.

MUSIC Produces a variety of music from **native Alaskan** to **Techno** to **Christmas**.

CARLA OLSON

11684 Ventura Blvd. Suite 583, Studio City CA 91604. **E-mail:** carlawebsite@aol.com. **Website:** www.carlaolson.com.

MUSIC Has worked with Paul Jones, Jake Andrews, Davis Gaines, Joe Louis Walker, Astrella Celeste, Youngblood Hart, Billy Joe Royal, Kim Wilson.

PLATINUM STUDIOS

Los Angeles CA (818)994-5368. **E-mail:** paulhilton123@sbcglobal.net. **Website:** www.paulhiltonmusic.com. "Platinum sound at affordable rates."

MUSIC **Latin, rock, blues**. Has worked with Janet Klein, Matt Zane & Society 1, Bon Jovi, Spencer Davis, Big Joe Turner, Billy Vera, Metallica, Ratt, Motley Crue, Morgana King, Jack Mack & the Heart Attack, Rodney O & Joe Cooley, WASP, Carlos Rico, Mera, Sam Glaser.

WILL RAY

P.O. Box 9222, Asheville NC 28815. (828)296-0107. **E-mail:** will@willray.biz. **Website:** www.willray.biz.

MUSIC **country, folk, blues**. Has worked with The Hellecasters, Solomon Burke, Wylie & the Wild West Show, Candye Kane, Jeffrey Steele, Clay DuBose, The Buzzards, Carrie James.

TODD ROSENBERG

Los Angeles CA (310)926-5059. **E-mail:** todd@toddrosenberg.net. **Website:** www.toddrosenberg.net.

MUSIC **indie, rock, Americana, country, ska, punk**.. Has worked with Pressure 45, Devil Driver, Mad Caddies, Motograter, Honda, Mitsubishi, Panasonic, Grooveworks.

O STEVE SATKOWSKI RECORDINGS

P.O. Box 3403, Stuart FL 34995. (772)225-3128. **Website:** www.clearsoulproductions.com/SteveSatkowski.html.

HOW TO CONTACT Submit demo by mail. Unsolicited submissions are OK. Prefers CD or cassette. Does not return material. Responds in 2 weeks.

MUSIC Mostly **classical**, **jazz** and **big band**. Produced recordings for National Public Radio and affiliates. Engineered recordings for Steve Howe, Patrick Moraz, Kenny G, and Michael Bolton.

MARK SAUNDERS

Beat 360 Studios, 630 Ninth Ave., Suite 710, New York NY 10036. (212)262-4932. **E-mail:** ollie@rocketmusic.com. **Website:** www.marksaunders.com. **Contact:** Ollie Hammett.

MUSIC Has worked with The Cure, Tricky, Depeche Mode, Marilyn Manson, David Byrne, Shiny Toy Guns, Yaz, The Sugarcubes, Gravity Kills, Neneh Cherry. **Music**: electronic, rock.

◐ SOUND ARTS RECORDING STUDIO

8377 Westview Dr., Houston TX 77055. (713)464-4653. **E-mail:** brianbaker@soundartsrecording.com; nickcooper@soundartsrecording.com. **Website:** www.soundartsrecording.com. **Contact:** Brian Baker; Nick Cooper.

◐ Also see the listing for Earthscream MusiC Publishing in the Music Publishers section of this book.

MUSIC Mostly **pop/rock**, **country** and **blues**. Produced Texas Johnny Brown (album), written and recorded by Texas Johnny Brown on Quality (blues); and "Sheryl Crow" (single), recorded by Dr. Jeff and the Painkillers. Other artists include Tim Nichols, Perfect Strangers, B.B. Watson, Jinkies, Joe "King" Carasco (on Surface Records), Mark May (on Icehouse Records), The Barbara Pennington Band (on Earth Records), Tempest, Atticus Finch, Tony Vega Band (on Red Onion Records), Saliva (Island Records), Earl Gillian, Blue October (Universal Records), and The Wiggles.

CHRIS STAMEY

Modern Recording, Chapel Hill NC (919)929-5008. **E-mail:** info@chrisstamey.com. **Website:** www.chrisstamey.com. "The central philosophy behind my production and mixing these days is that the best records combine the recording of transcendent musical moments with the structuring of the carefully considered arrangement details that frame those moments. And the point of recording is to add new entries to that select list of best records." See website for rates.
MUSIC rock, indie, alternative. Has worked with Alejandro Excovedo, Ryan Adams, Amy Ray, Squirrel Nut Zippers, Patrick Park, Jeremy Larson, Chatham Country Line.

◐ STUART AUDIO SERVICES

Houndog Recording, 134 Mosher Rd., Gorham ME 04038. (207)892-0960. **E-mail:** js@stuartaudio.com. **Website:** http://stuartaudio.com.
HOW TO CONTACT *Write or call first and obtain permission to submit or to arrange a personal interview.* Prefers CD with 4 songs and lyric sheet. Include SASE. Responds in 2 months.

MUSIC Mostly **alternative folk-rock**, **rock** and **country**; also **contemporary Christian**, **children's** and **unusual**. Produced *One of a Kind* (by various artists), recorded by Elizabeth Boss on Bosco Records (folk); *Toad Motel*, written and recorded by Rick Charrette on Fine Point Records (children's); and *Holiday Portrait*, recorded by USM Chamber Singers on U.S.M. (chorale). Other artists include Noel Paul Stookey, Beavis and Butthead (Mike Judge), Don Campbell, Jim Newton and John Angus.

◯ STUDIO SEVEN

417 N. Virginia, Oklahoma City OK 73106. (405)236-0643. **Website:** www.lunacyrecords.com.
HOW TO CONTACT *Contact first and obtain permission to submit.* Prefers CD or cassette with lyric sheet. Include SASE. Responds in 6 weeks.
MUSIC Mostly **rock**, **jazz-blues**, **country**, and **Native American**.

RANDALL MICHAEL TOBIN

2219 W. Olive Ave. Suite 226, Burbank CA 91506. (818)955-5888. **E-mail:** rmt@rmtobin.com. **Website:** www.rmtobin.com; www.thetasound.com.
MUSIC pop, rock, R&B, jazz, alternative, country. Has worked with Mel Carter, Bettie Ross, Isla St. Clair, Margaret MacDonald, Katheryne Levin.

DAVE TOUGH

5801 Tee Pee Dr., Nashville TN 37013. (615)554-6693. **E-mail:** dave@davetough.com. **Website:** www.davetough.com.
HOW TO CONTACT See website for rates.
MUSIC country, pop. Has worked with Come & Go, Cindy Alter, Matt Heinecke, Craig Winquist.

BIL VORNDICK

6090 Fire Tower Rd., Nashville TN 37221. (615)352-1227. **E-mail:** bilinstudio@comcast.net. **Website:** www.bilvorndick.com. "Helping artists realize their dreams."
MUSIC Has worked with Alison Krauss, Rhonda Vincent, Jerry Douglas, Bela Fleck, Jim Lauderdale, Ralph Stanley, Lynn Anderson, Bob Dylan, John Oates.

DICK WAGNER

Desert Dreams Books & Music, 10645 N. Tatum Blvd., Suite 200, Phoenix AZ 85028. (888)458-7900. **E-mail:** wagnerrocks@gmail.com. **Website:** www.wagnermusic.com.
MUSIC rock, pop, modern country, spiritual. Has worked with Wensday, Robert Wagner, Chris de Mar-

co, Bleedstreet, Janis Leigh, DWB, Matt Besey, Darin Scott, Skinner Rat, Gwen Goodman, Adam Smith.

DAVE WATERBURY

Laurel Canyon and Magnolia, Valley Village CA 91607. **E-mail:** davewaterbury91607@yahoo.com. **Website:** www.davewaterbury.net.

MUSIC Has worked with The XOTX, Robbie Krieger, Pink, Mark Krendal, David Eagle, Irv Kramer. **Music:** rock, dance, electronica, pop.

ⓒ WESTWIRES RECORDING USA

1042 Club Ave., Allentown PA 18109. (610)435-1924. **E-mail:** westwires@aol.com. **Website:** www.westwires.com.

MUSIC Mostly **rock**, **R&B**, **dance**, **alternative**, **folk** and **eclectic**. Produced Ye Ren (Dimala Records), Weston (Universal/Mojo), Zakk Wylde (Spitfire Records). Other artists include Ryan Asher, Paul Rogers, Anne Le Baron, and Gary Hassay

TIPS "We are interested in singer/songwriters and alternative artists living in the mid-Atlantic area. Must have steady gig schedule and established fan base."

ⓒ WLM MUSIC/RECORDING

2808 Cammie St., Durham NC 27705-2020. (919)471-3086. **Fax:** (919)471-4326. **E-mail:** wlm-musicrecording@nc.rr.com; wlm-band@nc.rr.com. **Contact:** Watts Lee Mangum, owner. Record producer. Fee derived from outright fee from recording artist. "In some cases, an advance payment requested for demo production."

HOW TO CONTACT Submit demo by mail. Unsolicited submissions are OK. Prefers CD with 2-4 songs and lyric or lead sheet (if possible). Include SASE. Responds in 6 months.

MUSIC Mostly **country**, **country/rock**, and **blues/rock**; also **pop**, **rock**, **blues**, **gospel** and **bluegrass**. Produced "911," and "Petals of an Orchid" (singles), both written and recorded by Johnny Scoggins (country); and "Renew the Love" (single by Judy Evans), recorded by Bernie Evans (country), all on Independent. Other artists include Southern Breeze Band and Heart Breakers Band.

MICHAEL WOODRUM

(818)848-3393. **E-mail:** michael@woodrumproductions.com. **Website:** www.woodrumproductions.com. "Michael Woodrum is a producer who's also an accomplished engineer. He gets sounds faster than you can think them up. You won't sit around waiting for something to sound right."

MUSIC rock, pop, R&B, rap, hip-hop, alternative, acoustic, indie, Americana, country, soul. Has worked with 3LW, Juvenile, 2Pac, Linkin Park, MC Lyte, Mary J. Blige, Eric Clapton, Joss Stone, Snoop Dogg, Bobby Rydell, B2K, Rocio Banquells, Queen Latifah, JoJo, Dr. Dre, John Guess, Tiffany Evans, Samantha Jade.

ⓒ WORLD RECORDS

5450 Harris Rd., Traverse City MI 49684. **E-mail:** jack@worldrec.org. **Website:** www.worldrec.org. "We produce and distribute CD recordings from a limited number of outstanding musicians."

MUSIC Mostly **classical**, **folk**, and **jazz**. Produced *Mahler, Orff, Collins* (album), recorded by Traverse Symphony Orchestra (classical); *Reflections on Schubert* (album) recorded by Michael Coonrod (classical). Other artists include Jeff Haas and The Camerata Singers.

ⓒ ZIG PRODUCTIONS

P.O. Box 120931, Arlington TX 76012. **E-mail:** billyherzig@hotmail.com. **Website:** www.zigproductions.com. "Occasionally I produce a single that is recorded separate from a full CD project." Produces 6-10 albums. Fee derived from sales royalty when song or artist is recorded and/or outright fee from recording artist. "Sometimes there are investors."

MUSIC Mostly **country**, **Americana**, and **rock**; also **pop**, **r&b**, and **alternative**. Produced "Ask Me to Stay" (single by King Cone/Josh McDaniel) from *Gallery*, recorded by King Cone (Texas country/Americana). released on King Cone; "A Cure for Awkward Silence" (single), recorded by Tyler Stock (acoustic rock), released on Payday Records; "Take Me Back" (single) from *Peace, Love & Crabs*, written and recorded by Deanna Dove (folk-rock), released on Island Girl. Also produced Robbins & Jones (country), Jordan Mycoskie (country), Carla Rhodes (comedy), Four Higher (alternative), Charis Thorsell (country), Shane Mallory (country), Rachel Rodriguez (blues-rock), Jessy Daumen (country), Frankie Moreno (rock/r&b), Shawna Russell (country), and many others.

SAUL ZONANA

606 Stone Mill Circle, Murfreesboro TN 37130. (914)610-5342. **E-mail:** zonana@comcast.net. **Website:** http://saulzonana.com.

MUSIC rock, electronica. Has worked with Crash Test Dummies, Adrian Belew, Blue Oyster Cult, Nicole McKenna, Ace Frehley.

MANAGERS & BOOKING AGENTS

//

Before submitting to a manager or booking agent, be sure you know exactly what you need. If you're looking for someone to help you with performance opportunities, the booking agency is the one to contact. They can help you book shows either in your local area or throughout the country. If you're looking for someone to help guide your career, you need to contact a management firm. Some management firms may also handle booking; however, it may be in your best interest to look for a separate booking agency. A manager should be your manager—not your agent, publisher, lawyer, or accountant.

MANAGERS

Of all the music industry players surrounding successful artists, managers are usually the people closest to the artists themselves. The artist manager can be a valuable contact, both for the songwriter trying to get songs to a particular artist and for the songwriter/performer. A manager and his connections can be invaluable in securing the right publishing deal or recording contract if the writer is also an artist. Getting songs to an artist's manager is yet another way to get your songs recorded, since the manager may play a large part in deciding what material his client uses. For the performer seeking management, a successful manager should be thought of as the foundation for a successful career.

The relationship between a manager and his client relies on mutual trust. A manager works as the liaison between you and the rest of the music industry, and he must know exactly what you want out of your career in order to help you achieve your goals. His handling of publicity, promotion and finances, as well as the contacts he has within the industry, can make or break your career. You should never be afraid to ask questions about any aspect of the relationship between you and a prospective manager.

Always remember that a manager works *for the artist*. A good manager is able to communicate his opinions to you without reservation, and should be willing to explain any confusing terminology or discuss plans with you before taking action. A manager needs to be able to communicate successfully with all segments of the music industry in order to get his client the best deals possible. He needs to be able to work with booking agents, publishers, lawyers and record companies.

Keep in mind that you are both working together toward a common goal: success for you and your songs. Talent, originality, professionalism and a drive to succeed are qualities that will attract a manager to an artist—and a songwriter.

BOOKING AGENTS

The function of the booking agent is to find performance venues for their clients. They usually represent many more acts than a manager does, and have less contact with their acts. A booking agent charges a commission for his services, as does a manager. Managers usually ask for a 15-20% commission on an act's earnings; booking agents usually charge around 10%. In the area of managers and booking agents, more successful acts can negotiate lower percentage deals than the ones set forth above.

SUBMITTING MATERIAL TO MANAGERS & BOOKING AGENTS

The firms listed in this section have provided information about the types of music they work with and the types of acts they represent. You'll want to refer to the Category Index in the back of this book to find out which companies deal with the type of music you write, and the Geographic Index at the back of the book to help you locate companies near where you live. Then determine whether they are open to your level of experience (see A Sample Listing Decoded on page 8). Each listing also contains submission requirements and information about what items to include in a press kit and will also specify whether the company is a management firm or a booking agency. Remember that your submission represents you as an artist, and should be as organized and professional as possible.

ADDITIONAL MANAGERS & BOOKING AGENTS

There are **more managers & booking agents** located in other sections of the book! Review the index in the back of this book to find listings within other sections who are also managers/booking agents.

Icons

For more instructional information on the listings in this book, including explanations of symbols (ICONS), read the article *How To Use Songwriter's Market* on page 2.

⊙❶ ALERT MUSIC INC.

305-41 Britain St., Suite 305, Toronto ON M5A 1R7 Canada. (416)364-4200. **Fax:** (416)364-8632. **E-mail:** contact@alertmusic.com. **Website:** www.alertmusic. com. **Contact:** W. Tom Berry, president. Management firm, record company and recording artist. Represents local and regional individual artists and groups; currently handles 3 acts. Reviews material for acts.

HOW TO CONTACT *Write first and obtain permission to submit.* Prefers CD. If seeking management, press kit should include finished CD, photo, press clippings, and bio. Include SASE.

MUSIC All types. Works primarily with bands and singer/songwriters. Current acts include Holly Cole (jazz vocalist), Kim Mitchell (rock singer/songwriter), and Michael Kaeshammer (pianist/singer).

❶ MICHAEL ALLEN ENTERTAINMENT DEVELOPMENT

P.O. Box 111510, Nashville TN 37222. (615)754-0059. **E-mail:** gmichaelallen@comcast.net. **Website:** www. gmichaelallen.com. **Contact:** Michael Allen. Management firm and public relations. Represents individual artists, groups and songwriters. Receives 15-25% commission. Reviews material for acts.

HOW TO CONTACT Submit demo package by mail. Unsolicited submissions are OK. Prefers CD/DVD with 3 songs and lyric or lead sheets. If seeking management, press kit should include photo, bio, press clippings, letter and CD/DVD. Include SASE. Responds in 3 months.

MUSIC Mostly **country** and **pop**; also **rock** and **gospel**. Works primarily with vocalists and bands. Currently doing public relations for Brenda Lee, The Imperials, Ricky Lynn Gregg, Kyle Rainer, and Lee Greenwood.

◯ AMERICAN BANDS MANAGEMENT

3300 S. Gessner, Suite 207, Houston TX 77063. (713)785-3700. **Fax:** (713)785-4641. **E-mail:** americanbandmgmt@aol.com. **Contact:** John Blomstrom Sr., CEO; Cheryl Blomstrom, vice president and CFO. Represents groups from anywhere. Receives 15-25% commission. Reviews material for acts.

HOW TO CONTACT Submit demo package by mail prior to making phone contact. Unsolicited submissions are OK. Prefers live videos. If seeking management, press kit should include cover letter, bio, photo, demo tape/CD, press clippings, video, résumé, and

professional references with names and numbers. Does not return material. Responds in 1 month.

MUSIC Mostly **rock (all forms)** and **modern country**. Works primarily with bands. Current acts include The Scars Heal In Time, Trey Gadler & Dead Man's Hand, Kenny Cordrey & Love Street, The Standells, Paul Cotton (from Poco), and Pearl (Janis Joplin tribute).

❶ BILL ANGELINI ENTERPRISES/ BOOKYOUREVENT.COM

P.O. Box 132, Seguin TX 78155. (830)401-0061. **Fax:** (830)401-0069. **E-mail:** bill@bookyourevent.com. **Website:** www.bookyourevent.com. **Contact:** Bill Angelini, owner. Management firm and booking agency. Represents individual artists and groups from anywhere. Receives 10-15% commission. Reviews material for acts.

HOW TO CONTACT Submit demo package by mail or EPK. Unsolicited submissions are OK. Press kit should include pictures, bio, and discography. Does not return material. Responds in 1 month.

MUSIC Mostly **Latin American**, **Tejano**, and **International**; also **Norteno** and **country**. Current acts include Jay Perez (Tejano), Ram Herrera (Tejano), Michael Salgado (Tejano), Electric Cowboys (tex-mex), Los Caporales (Tejano), Grupo Solido (Tejano), and Texmaniacs (Tex-Mex).

❶ APODACA PROMOTIONS INC.

717 E. Tidwell Rd., Houston TX 77022. (713)691-6677. **Fax:** (713)692-9298. **E-mail:** houston@apodacapromotions.com. **Website:** www.apodacapromotions. com. **Contact:** Domingo A. Barrera, manager. Management firm, booking agency, and music publisher (Huina Publishing, Co. Inc.). Represents songwriters and groups from anywhere; currently handles 40 acts. Reviews material for acts.

HOW TO CONTACT Submit demo package by mail. Unsolicited submissions are OK. Prefers CD and lyric and lead sheet. Include SASE. Responds in 2 months.

MUSIC Mostly **international** and **Hispanic**; also **rock**. Works primarily with bands and songwriters. Current acts include Alicia Villarreal, Boby Pulldo, Fanny Lu, Elephant, Angel Y Khriz, Golden Horse, and Ninel Conde.

❶ ARTIST REPRESENTATION AND MANAGEMENT

1257 Arcade St., St. Paul MN 55106. (651)483-8754. **Fax:** (651)776-6338. **E-mail:** ra@armentertainment. com; jdr@armentertainment.com. **Website:** www.

armentertainment.com. **Contact:** Roger Anderson, agent/manager. Management firm and booking agency. Estab. 1983. Represents artists from USA/Canada. Receives 15% commission. Reviews material for acts.

HOW TO CONTACT Submit CD and DVD (preferable) by mail. Unsolicited submissions are OK. Please include minimum 3 songs. If seeking management, current schedule, bio, photo, and press clippings should also be included. "Priority is placed on original artists with product who are currently touring." Does not return material. Responds only if interested within 30 days.

MUSIC Mostly **melodic rock**. Current acts include Alannah Myles, Warrant, Firehouse, Winger, Skid Row, Head East, Frank Hannon of Tesla, LA Guns featuring Phil Lewis, Dokken, Adler's Appetite, and Vince Neil.

◑ BACKSTREET BOOKING

Longworth Hall Office Complex, 700 W. Pete Rose Way, Lobby B, 3rd Floor, Suite 390, Cincinnati OH 45203. (513)442-4405. **Fax:** (513)834-9390. **E-mail:** jimbb@backstreetbooking.com; info@backstreet-booking.com. **Website:** www.backstreetbooking.com. **Contact:** Jim Sfarnas, president. Represents individual artists and groups from anywhere; currently handles 30 acts. Receives 10-15% commission. Reviews material for acts.

HOW TO CONTACT Call first and obtain permission to submit. Accepts only signed acts with product available nationally and/or internationally.

MUSIC Mostly **niche-oriented music**. Current acts include Bobby Womack (soul), 500 Miles To Memphis (country punk), Niacin (fusion), John Novello (fusion), Novello B3 Soul (Urban Jazz), Jeff Berlin (jazz), Greg Howe (fusion), and Cares Of Steel (tribute to Rush).

TIPS "Build a base on your own."

◑ BLOWIN' SMOKE PRODUCTIONS/ RECORDS

7438 Shoshone Ave., Van Nuys CA 91406-2340. (818)881-9888. **Fax:** (818)881-0555. **E-mail:** blowin-smokeband@ktb.net. **Website:** www.blowinsmoke-band.com. **Contact:** Larry Knight, president. Management firm and record producer. Estab. 1990. Represents local and West Coast individual artists and groups; currently handles 6 acts. Receives 15-20% commission. Reviews material for acts.

HOW TO CONTACT Write or call first and obtain permission to submit. Prefers cassette or CD. If seeking management, press kit should include cover letter, demo tape/CD, lyric sheets, press clippings, video if available, photo, bios, contact telephone numbers and any info on legal commitments already in place. Include SASE. Responds in 1 month.

MUSIC Mostly **R&B**, **blues**, and **blues-rock**. Works primarily with single and group vocalists and a few R&B/blues bands. Current acts include Larry "Fuzzy" Knight (blues singer/songwriter), King Floyd (R&B artist), The Blowin' Smoke Rhythm & Blues Band, The Fabulous Smokettes, Joyce Lawson, Sky King (rock/blues), and Guardians of the Clouds (alternative rock).

● THE BLUE CAT AGENCY

P.O. Box 4036, San Rafael CA 94913-4036. **E-mail:** bluecat_agency@yahoo.com. **Contact:** Karen Kindig, owner/agent. Management firm and booking agency. Estab. 1989. Represents established individual artists and/or groups from anywhere; currently handles 5 acts. Receives 10-15% commission. Reviews material for acts.

HOW TO CONTACT E-mail only for permission to submit. Prefers cassette or CD. If seeking management, press kit should include CD or tape, bio, press clippings and photo. SASE. Responds in 2 months.

MUSIC Mostly **rock/pop "en espanol"** and **jazz/ Latin jazz**. Works primarily with bands (established performers only). Current acts include Ylonda Nickell, Kai Eckhardt, Alejandro Santos, Ania Paz, Gabriel Rosati.

○ BREAD & BUTTER PRODUCTIONS

P.O. Box 1539, Wimberley TX 78676. (512)301-7117. **E-mail:** sgladson@gmail.com. **Contact:** Steve Gladson, managing partner. Management firm and booking agency. Represents individual artists, songwriters and groups from anywhere; currently handles 6 acts. Receives 10-20% commission. Reviews material for acts.

HOW TO CONTACT Submit demo package by e-mail or mail. Unsolicited submissions OK. Prefers e-mail. If seeking management, press kit should include cover letter, demo tape/CD, lyric sheets, press clippings, video, résumé, picture, and bio or a list of your social networking sites. Does not return material. Responds in 1 month.

MUSIC Mostly **alternative rock**, **country**, and **R&B**; also **classic rock**, **folk** and **Americana**. Works primarily with singer/songwriters and original bands.

Current acts include Lou Cabaza (songwriter/producer/manager), Duck Soup (band) and Gaylan Ladd (songwriter/singer/producer).

TIPS "Remember why you are in this biz. The art comes first."

● BROTHERS MANAGEMENT ASSOCIATES

141 Dunbar Ave., Fords NJ 08863. (732)738-0880. **Fax:** (732)738-0970. **E-mail:** bmaent@yahoo.com. **Website:** www.bmaent.com. **Contact:** Allen A. Faucera, president. Management firm and booking agency. Represents artists, groups and songwriters; currently handles 25 acts. Receives 15-20% commission. Reviews material for acts.

HOW TO CONTACT *Write first and obtain permission to submit.* Prefers CD or DVD with 3-6 songs and lyric sheets. Include photographs and résumé. If seeking management, include photo, bio, tape, and return envelope in press kit. Include SASE. Responds in 2 months.

MUSIC Mostly **pop**, **rock**, **MOR**, and **R&B**. Works primarily with vocalists and established groups. Current acts include Nils Lofgren of the E Street Band, Cover Girls, Harold Melvin's Blue Notes, and Gloria Gaynor.

TIPS "Submit very commercial material—make demo of high quality."

●● ● CIRCUIT RIDER TALENT & MANAGEMENT CO.

123 Walton Ferry Rd., Hendersonville TN 37075. . (615)824-1947. **Fax:** (615)264-0462. **E-mail:** dotwool@ bellsouth.net. **Contact:** Linda S. Dotson, president. Consultation and deal negotiation firm, booking agency and music publisher (Channel Music, Cordial Music, Dotson & Dotson Music Publishers, Shalin Music Co.). Represents individual artists, songwriters and actors; currently handles 10 acts. Works with a large number of recording artists, songwriters, actors, and producers. (Includes the late multi-Grammy-winning producer/writer Skip Scarborough.) Receives 10-15% commission as booking agent (union rates). Reviews material for acts (free of charge) as publisher.

HOW TO CONTACT *E-mail or call first and obtain permission to submit.* Prefers DVD or CD with 3 songs and lyric sheet. If seeking consultation, press kit should include bio, cover letter, résumé, lyric sheets if original songs, photo and CD or DVD with 3 songs.

"Full press kit or EPK to my e-mail address required of artist's submissions." Include SASE. Responds "ASAP, sometimes 8 weeks, but if by EPK or internet, will be more timely."

MUSIC Mostly **Latin blues**, **pop**, **country** and **gospel**; also **R&B** and **comedy**. Works primarily with vocalists, special concerts, movies and TV. Current acts include Razzy Bailey (award winning blues artist/writer), Clint Walker (actor/recording artist), Ben Colder (comedy/novelty), and Freddy Weller (formerly Paul Revere & The Raiders/hit songwriter), and Dickie Lee.

TIPS "Artists, have your act together. Have a full press kit, videos and be professional. Attitudes are a big factor in my agreeing to work with you (no egotists). This is a business, and we will be building your career."

● CLASS ACT PRODUCTIONS/ MANAGEMENT/PETER KIMMEL'S MUSIC CATALOG

P.O. Box 55252, Sherman Oaks CA 91413. (818)980-1039. **E-mail:** peter.kimmel@sbcglobal.net. **Contact:** Peter Kimmel, president. Management firm; independent music licensing professional and composer rep. Currently represents music material of artists for licensing to media; must have broadcast-quality, mastered recordings. Receives 50/50 split of licensing fees income from placements onto soundtracks of motion pictures, TV shows, commercials, etc.

HOW TO CONTACT "Music artists: Submit broadcast-quality, mastered recordings via mail or high quality MP3s derived from your mastered recordings, via e-mail. Unsolicited submissions are OK. For mail, include CD, cover letter (mentioning *Songwriter's Market*), lyric sheets (mandatory) or submit electronic press kit by e-mail. Responds in 1 month.

MUSIC **All styles**. Represents select first rate music material to music supervisors of films, television, commercials, etc.

TIPS "We cannot use song lyrics only. Songwriting must be professional quality, music must be highly accomplished, and recordings must be professional, broadcast-quality and mastered."

● CLOUSHER PRODUCTIONS

P.O. Box 1191, Mechanicsburg PA 17055. (717)766-7644. **Fax:** (717)766-1490. **E-mail:** cpinfo@msn.com. **Website:** www.clousherentertainment.com. **Contact:** Fred Clousher, owner. Booking agency and production company. Represents groups from anywhere; currently handles over 100 acts.

HOW TO CONTACT Submit demo package by mail. Please, no electronic press kits. Unsolicited submissions are OK. Prefers CDs or DVD. Press kit should include bio, credits, pictures, song list, references, and your contact information. Does not return material. "Performer should check back with us!"

MUSIC Mostly **country, oldies rock & roll,** and **ethnic** (German, Hawaiian, etc.); also **dance bands** (regional), **Dixieland,** and **classical musicians**. "We work mostly with country, old time R&R, regional variety dance bands, tribute acts, and all types of variety acts." Current acts include Jasmine Morgan (country/pop vocalist), Robin Right (country vocalist and Tammy Wynette tribute artist) and Brian Keith Jazz Trio.

TIPS "The songwriters we work with are entertainers themselves, which is the aspect we deal with. They usually have bands or do some sort of show, either with tracks or live music. We engage them for stage shows, concerts, etc. We do not review songs you've written. We do not publish music, or submit performers to recording companies for contracts. We strictly set up live performances for them."

CONCEPT 2000 INC.

P.O. Box 2950, Columbus OH 43216-2950. (614)276-2000. **Fax:** (614)275-0163. **E-mail:** info2k@concept2k.com. **Website:** www.concept2k.com. **Contact:** Brian Wallace, president. Management firm and booking agency. Represents international individual artists, groups and songwriters. Receives 20% commission. Reviews material for acts.

HOW TO CONTACT Submit demo by mail. Unsolicited submissions are OK. Prefers CD with 4 songs. If seeking management, include demo tape, press clips, photo and bio. Does not return material. Responds in 2 weeks.

MUSIC Mostly **rock, country, pop,** and **contemporary gospel**. Current acts include Satellites Down (rock); Gene Walker (jazz); Endless Summer (show group); Thomas Wynn and the Believers (country).

TIPS "Send quality songs with lyric sheets. Production quality is not necessary."

CRAWFISH PRODUCTIONS

P.O. Box 5412, Buena Park CA 90620 United States. **Producer:** Leo J. Eiffert, Jr. Management firm, music publisher (Young Country/BMI), record producer (Leo J. Eiffert, Jr.) and record company (Plain Country Records). Estab. 1968. Represents local and international individual artists and songwriters; currently

handles 4 acts. Commission received is open. Reviews material for acts.

HOW TO CONTACT Submit demo tape by mail. Unsolicited submissions are OK. Prefers cassette with 2-3 songs and lyric sheet. Include SASE. Responds in 3 weeks.

MUSIC Mostly **country** and **gospel**. Works primarily with vocalists. Current acts include Pigeons, Southern Spirit and Nashville Snakes.

DAS COMMUNICATIONS, LTD.

83 Riverside Dr., New York NY 10024. (212)877-0400. **Fax:** (212)595-0176. Management firm. Estab. 1975. Represents individual artists, groups and producers from anywhere; currently handles 25 acts. Receives 20% commission.

HOW TO CONTACT *Does not accept unsolicited submissions.*

MUSIC Mostly **rock, pop, R&B, alternative** and **hiphop**. Current acts include Joan Osborne (rock), Wyclef Jean (hip-hop), Black Eyed Peas (hip-hop), John Legend (R&B), Spin Doctors (rock), and The Bacon Brothers (rock).

DCA PRODUCTIONS

676A 9th Ave., #252, New York NY 10036. (800)659-2063. **Fax:** (609)259-8260. **E-mail:** info@dcaproductions.com. **Website:** www.dcaproductions.com. **Contact:** Suzanne Perrotta, office manager. Management firm. Represents individual artists, groups, and songwriters from anywhere.

HOW TO CONTACT If seeking management, press kit should include cover letter, bio, photo, demo tape/CD, and video. Prefers cassette or DVD with 2 songs. "All materials are reviewed and kept on file for future consideration. Does not return material. We respond only if interested."

MUSIC Mostly **acoustic, rock,** and **mainstream**; also **cabaret** and **theme**. Works primarily with acoustic singer/songwriters, Top 40 or rock bands. Current acts include And Jam Band (soulful R&B), Lorna Bracewell (singer/songwriter), and Jimmy and The Parrots (Jimmy Buffett cover band). "Visit our website for a current roster of acts."

TIPS "Please do not call for a review of material."

DIVINE INDUSTRIES

(formerly Gangland Artists), Unit 191, #101-1001 W. Broadway, Vancouver BC V6H 4E4 Canada. (604)737-0091. **Fax:** (604)737-3602. **E-mail:** divine@divineindustries.com. **Website:** www.divineindustries.com. **Contact:** Allen Moy. Management firm, production house and music publisher. Represents artists and songwriters; currently handles 5 acts. Reviews material for acts.

HOW TO CONTACT *Write first and obtain permission to submit.* Prefers audio links. "Videos are not entirely necessary for our company. It is certainly a nice touch. If you feel your audio cassette is strong--send the video upon later request." Does not return material. Responds in 2 months.

MUSIC **Rock**, **pop**, and **roots**. Works primarily with rock/left-of-center folk show bands. Current acts include 54-40 (rock/pop), Blackie & The Rodeo Kings (folk rock), Ridley Bent, John Mann (of Spirit of the West).

○ SCOTT EVANS PRODUCTIONS

P.O. Box 814028, Hollywood FL 33081-4028. (954)963-4449. **E-mail:** evansprod@hotmail.com; evansprod@aol.com. **Website:** www.theentertainmentmall.com. **Contact:** Jeffrey Birnbaum, new artists; Jeanne K., Internet marketing and sales. Management firm and booking agency. Represents local, regional or international individual artists, groups, songwriters, comedians, novelty acts and dancers; currently handles over 200 acts. Receives 10-50% commission. Reviews material for acts.

HOW TO CONTACT New artists can make submissions through the "Auditions" link located on the website. Unsolicited submissions are OK. "Please be sure that all submissions are copyrighted and not your original copy as we do not return material."

MUSIC Mostly **pop**, **R&B**, and **Broadway**. Deals with "all types of entertainers; no limitations." Current acts include Scott Evans and Company (variety song and dance), Dorit Zinger (female vocalist), Jeff Geist, Actors Repertory Theatre, Entertainment Express, Joy Deco (dance act), Flashback (musical song and dance revue), and Around the World (international song and dance revue).

TIPS "Submit a neat, well put together, organized press kit."

○◐ S.L. FELDMAN & ASSOCIATES & MACKLAM FELDMAN MANAGEMENT

200-1505 W. 2nd Ave., Vancouver BC V6H 3Y4 Canada. (604)734-5945. **Fax:** (604)732-0922. **E-mail:** info@mfmgt.com; feldman@slfa.com. **Website:** www. mfmgt.com; www.slfa.com. Booking agency and art-

ist management firm. Agency represents mostly established Canadian recording artists and groups.

HOW TO CONTACT *Write or call first to obtain permission to submit a demo.* Prefers CD, photo and bio. If seeking management, contact Watchdog for consideration and include video in press kit. SAE and IRC. Responds in 2 months.

MUSIC Current acts include The Chieftains, Diana Krall, Elvis Costello, Pink Martini, James Taylor, Colin James, Ry Cooder, Tommy LiPuma, and Melody Gardot.

○◐ B.C. FIEDLER MANAGEMENT

53 Seton Park Rd., Toronto ON M3C 3Z8 Canada. (416)421-4421. **Fax:** (416)421-0442. **E-mail:** info@bcfiedler.com. **Website:** www.bcfiedler.com. **Contact:** B.C. Fiedler. Management firm, music publisher (B.C. Fiedler Publishing) and record company (Sleeping Giant Music Inc.). Represents individual artists, groups and songwriters from anywhere. Receives 20-25% or consultant fees. Reviews material for acts.

HOW TO CONTACT *Call first and obtain permission to submit.* Prefers CD or VHS videocassette with 3 songs and lyric sheet. If seeking management, press kit should include bio, list of concerts performed in past 2 years including name of venue, repertoire, reviews and photos. Does not return material. Responds in 2 months.

MUSIC Mostly **classical/crossover**, **voice** and **pop**. Works primarily with classical/crossover ensembles, instrumental soloists, operatic voice and pop singer/songwriters. Current acts include Gordon Lightfoot, Dan Hill, Quartetto Gelato, and Patricia O'Callaghan.

TIPS "Invest in demo production using best quality voice and instrumentalists. If you write songs, hire the vocal talent to best represent your work. Submit CD and lyrics. Artists should follow up 6-8 weeks after submission."

◑◐ FIRST TIME MANAGEMENT

Sovereign House, 12 Trewartha Rd., Praa Sands-Penzance, Cornwall TR20 9ST United Kingdom. (01736)762826. **Fax:** (01736)763328. **E-mail:** panamus@aol.com. **Website:** www.songwriters-guild.co.uk. **Contact:** Roderick G. Jones, managing director. Management firm, record company (Digimix Records Ltd www.digimixrecords.com, Rainy Day Records, Mohock Records, Pure Gold Records), and music publisher (Panama Music Library, Melody First Music Library, Eventide Music Library, Musik' Image Music

Library, Promo Sonor International Music Library, Caribbean Music Library, ADN Creation Music Library, Piano Bar Music Library, Corelia Music Library, PSI Music Library, Scamp Music Publishing, First Time Music [Publishing] U.K. [www.panamamusic. co.uk and www.myspace.com/scampmusicpublishing] —registered members of the Mechanical Copyright Protection Society [MCPS] and the Performing Right Society [PRS]). Represents local, regional, and international individual artists, groups, composers, DJs, and songwriters. Receives 15-25% commission. Reviews material for acts.

○ Also see the listings for First Time Music (Publishing) in the Music Publishers section of this book.

HOW TO CONTACT Submit demo package by mail. Unsolicited submissions are OK. Prefers CD with 3 songs, lyric sheets and also complete album projects where writer/performer has finished masters. If seeking management, press kit should include cover letter, bio, photo, demo tape/CD, press clippings and anything relevant to make an impression. Does not return material. Responds in 1 month only if interested.

MUSIC All styles. Works primarily with songwriters, composers, DJs, rappers, vocalists, bands, groups and choirs. Current acts include Leonie Parker (soul), The Glen Kirton Country Band (country), Bram Stoker (prog rock/gothic rock group), Kevin Kendle (New Age, holistic) Peter Arnold (folk/roots), David Jones (urban/R&B), Shanelle (R&B/dance), AudioJunkie & Stylus (dance/hardcore/funky house/electro house) Ray Guntrip (jazz); DJ Gammer (hardcore/hardhouse/dance).

TIPS "Become a member of the Guild of International Songwriters and Composers (www.songwriters-guild. co.uk). Keep everything as professional as possible. Be patient and dedicated to your aims and objectives."

◑ BILL HALL ENTERTAINMENT & EVENTS

138 Frog Hollow Rd., Churchville PA 18966-1031. (215)357-5189. **Fax:** (215)357-0320. **E-mail:** billhallevents@verizon.net. **Contact:** William B. Hall III, owner/president. Booking agency and production company. Represents individuals and groups. Receives 15% commission. Reviews material for acts.

HOW TO CONTACT Submit demo package by mail. Unsolicited submissions are OK. Prefers CD, cassette, or videocassette of performance with 2-3 songs "and

photos, promo material, and CD, record, or tape. We need quality material, preferably before a 'live' audience." Does not return material. Responds only if interested.

MUSIC Marching band, **circus**, and **novelty**. Works primarily with "unusual or novelty attractions in musical line, preferably those that appeal to family groups." Current acts include Fralinger and Polish-American Philadelphia Championship Mummers String Bands (marching and concert group), "Mr. Polynesian" Show Band and Hawaiian Revue (ethnic group), the "Phillies Whiz Kids Band" of Philadelphia Phillies Baseball team, Mummermania Musical Quartet, Philadelphia German Brass Band (concert band), Vogelgesang Circus Calliope, Kromer's Carousel Band Organ, Reilly Raiders Drum & Bugle Corps, Hoebel Steam Calliope, Caesar Rodney Brass Band, Philadelphia Police & Fire Pipes Band, Tim Laushey Pep & Dance Band, Larry Stout (show organist/keyboard player), Jersey Surf Drum & Bugle Corp, Caesar Rodney Brass Marching Band, Corporales San Simon Bolivian Dancers, Robinson's Grandmaster Concert Band Organ, and Bobby Burnett, vocalist/comedian.

TIPS "Please send whatever helps us to most effectively market the attraction and/or artist. Provide something that gives you a clear edge over others in your field!"

○ HARDISON INTERNATIONAL ENTERTAINMENT CORPORATION

P.O. Box 1732, Knoxville TN 37901-1732. (865)360-0155 (prefers e-mail contact). **E-mail:** dennishardison@bellsouth.net. **Website:** www.dynamoreckless. com. **Contact:** Dennis K. Hardison, CEO/founder; Dennis K. Hardison II, president; Travis J. Hardison, president, Denlatrin Record (a division of Hardison International Entertainment Corp.). Management firm, booking agency, music publisher (Denlatrin Music) BMI, record label (Denlatrin Records), and record producer. Represents individual artists from anywhere; currently handles 3 acts. Receives 20% commission. Reviews material for acts. "We are seeking level-minded and patient individuals. Our primary interests are established recording acts with prior major deals."

○ This company has promoted many major acts and unsigned acts for over 38 years.

HOW TO CONTACT Submit demo package by mail. Unsolicited submissions are OK. Prefers CD with 3 songs only. If seeking management, press kit should include bio, promo picture, and CD. Does not return materials. Responds in 6 weeks to the "best material". Critiques available via dennishardison@bellsouth.net.

MUSIC Mostly **R&B**, **hip-hop**, and **rap**. Current acts include Dynamo (hip-hop), The Nafro Queens of Lagos, Nigeria, Triniti (record producer, Universal Music, Public Enemy, Dynamo, among others; current engineer for Chuck D), and RapStation artists.

TIPS "We respond to the hottest material, so make it hot!"

⊘ M. HARRELL & ASSOCIATES

5444 Carolina, Merrillville IN 46410 United States. (219)887-8814. **Fax:** (480)345-2255. **E-mail:** mharrell@promos@gmail.com. **Contact:** Mary Harrell, owner. Booking agency. Estab. 1984. Represents individual artists, groups, songwriters, all talents--fashion, dancers, etc.; currently handles 30-40 acts. Receives 10-20% commission. Reviews material for acts.

HOW TO CONTACT *Call first and obtain permission to submit.* Submit demo by mail. Prefers CD or DVD with 2-3 songs. Send résumé, bio, photo, CD and press clippings. "Keep it brief and current." Does not return material. Responds in 1 month.

MUSIC country, **R&B**, **jazz**, **gospel**, **Big Band**, **light rock** and **reggae**. Current acts include Manny B (showact), Michael Essany (celebrity talk show host), Bill Shelton & 11th Avenue ('50s rock & roll), Bang (R&B/jazz), Julian Michaels (singer-songwriter/pop), and David Bacon, musician, theater director.

TIPS "The bands listed can and do tour in the U.S. and Europe (variety, mostly R&B, jazz and Top 40) as well as the Chicagoland area. They get steady work and repeat business, because they are good and beat their competition."

⊘ INTERNATIONAL ENTERTAINMENT BUREAU

3612 N. Washington Blvd., Indianapolis IN 46205-3592. (317)926-7566. **E-mail:** ieb@prodigy.net. **Contact:** David Leonards. Booking agency. Represents individual artists and groups from anywhere; currently handles 145 acts. Receives 20% commission.

HOW TO CONTACT *No unsolicited submissions.*

MUSIC Mostly **rock**, **country**, and **A/C**; also **jazz**, **nostalgia**, and **ethnic**. Works primarily with bands, comedians and speakers. Current acts include Five Easy Pieces (A/C), Scott Greeson (country), and Cool City Swing Band (variety).

◐ JANA JAE ENTERPRISES

P.O. Box 35726, Tulsa OK 74153. (918)786-8896. **Fax:** (918)786-8897. **E-mail:** janajae@janajae.com. **Website:** www.janajae.com. **Contact:** Kathleen Pixley, agent. Booking agency, music publisher (Jana Jae Publishing/BMI) and record company (Lark Record Productions, Inc.). Represents individual artists and songwriters; currently handles 12 acts. Receives 15% commission. Reviews material for acts.

◖ Also see the listings for Jana Jae Music in the Music Publishers section, Lark Record Productions in the Record Companies section of this book.

HOW TO CONTACT Submit demo by mail. Unsolicited submissions are OK. Prefers CD or DVD of performance. If seeking management, press kit should include cover letter, bio, photo, demo tape/CD, lyric sheets and press clippings. Does not return material.

MUSIC Mostly **country**, **classical**, and **jazz instrumentals**; also **pop**. Works with vocalists, show and concert bands, solo instrumentalists. Represents Jana Jae (country singer/fiddle player), Matt Greif (classical guitarist), Sydni (solo singer) and Hotwire (country show band).

◑ KENDALL WEST AGENCY

P.O. Box 1673, Colleyville TX 76034. **E-mail:** Michelle@KendallWestAgency.com. **Contact:** Michelle Vellucci. Booking agency and television producer. Represents individual artists and groups from anywhere. Receives 20% commission. Reviews material for acts.

HOW TO CONTACT *Write first and obtain permission to submit or write to arrange personal interview.* Prefers CD with 5 songs and lead sheet. If seeking management, press kit should include bio, photo, cover letter, CD and resume. Include SASE. Responds in 1 month.

MUSIC Mostly **country**, **blues/jazz**, and **rock**; also **trios**, **dance** and **individuals**. Works primarily with bands. Current acts include Chris & the Roughnecks (Texas music), Shawna Russell (southern rock), Ty England (country), and Jaz-Vil (jazz/blues).

◯ KUPER PERSONAL MANAGEMENT/ RECOVERY RECORDINGS

515 Bomar St., Houston TX 77006. (713)520-5791. **E-mail:** info@recoveryrecordings.com. **Website:** www.recoveryrecordings.com. **Contact:** Koop Kuper, owner. Management firm, music publisher (Kuper-Lam

Music/BMI, Uvula Music/BMI, and Meauxtown Music/ASCAP), and record label (Recovery Recordings). Represents individual artists, groups, and songwriters from Texas. Receives 20% commission. Reviews material for acts.

HOW TO CONTACT Submit demo package by mail. Unsolicited submissions are OK. Prefers CD. If seeking management, press kit should include cover letter, press clippings, photo, bio (1 page) tearsheets (reviews, etc.) and demo CD. Does not return material. Responds in 2 months.

MUSIC Mostly **singer/songwriters**, **AAA**, **roots rock**, and **Americana**. Works primarily with self-contained and self-produced artists. Current acts include Philip Rodriguez (singer/songwriter), David Rodriguez (singer/songwriter), and Def Squad Texas (hip-hop). U.S. representative for the group The Very Girls (Dutch vocal duo).

TIPS "Create a market value for yourself, produce your own master tapes, and create a cost-effective situation."

◑ LEVINSON ENTERTAINMENT VENTURES INTERNATIONAL, INC.

1440 Veteran Ave., Los Angeles CA 90024. (323)663-6940. **E-mail:** leviinc@aol.com. **Contact:** Jed Leland, Jr.. Management firm. Represents national individual artists, groups and songwriters. Receives 15-25% commission. Reviews material for acts.

HOW TO CONTACT *Write first and obtain permission to submit.* Prefers CD, DVD, cassette, or VHS videocassette with 6 songs and lead sheet. If seeking management, press kit should include bio, pictures and press clips. Include SASE. Responds in 1 month.

MUSIC Mostly **rock**, **MOR**, **R&B**, and **country**. Works primarily with rock bands, and vocalists.

TIPS "Should be a working band, self-contained and, preferably, performing original material."

● RICK LEVY MANAGEMENT

4250 A1AS, D-11, St. Augustine FL 32080. (904)806-0817. **Fax:** (904)460-1226. **E-mail:** rick@ricklevy.com. **Website:** www.ricklevy.com. **Contact:** Rick Levy, president. Management firm, music publisher (Flying Governor Music/BMI), and record company (Luxury Records). Voting member of the Grammys. Represents local, regional, or international individual artists and groups; currently handles 5 acts. Also provides worldwide music promotion services. Receives 15-20% commission. Reviews material for acts.

HOW TO CONTACT *Write or call first and obtain permission to submit.* Prefers CD or DVD with 3 songs and lyric sheet. If seeking management, press kit should include cover letter, bio, demo tape/CD, DVD demo, photo and press clippings. Include SASE. Responds in 2 weeks.

MUSIC Mostly **R&B** (no rap), **pop**, **country**, and **oldies**. Current acts include Jay & the Techniques ('60s hit group), The Limits (pop), Freddy Cannon ('60s), The Fallin Bones (Blues/rock), Tommy Roe ('60s), Wax (rock).

TIPS "If you don't have 200% passion and commitment, don't bother. Be sure to contact only companies that deal with your type of music."

○ LOGGINS PROMOTION

5018 Franklin Pike, Nashville TN 37220. (615)323-2200. **E-mail:** staff@LogginsPromotion.com. **Website:** www.logginspromotion.com. **Contact:** Paul Loggins, CEO. Management firm and radio promotion. Represents individual artists, groups and songwriters from anywhere; currently handles 6 acts. Receives 20% commission. Reviews material for acts.

HOW TO CONTACT If seeking management, press kit should include picture, short bio, cover letter, press clippings and CD (preferred). "Mark on CD which cut you, as the artist, feel is the strongest." Does not return material. Responds in 2 weeks.

MUSIC Mostly **adult**, **Top 40** and **AAA**; also **urban**, **rap**, **alternative**, **college**, **smooth jazz** and **Americana**. Works primarily with bands and solo artists.

● MANAGEMENT BY JAFFE

68 Ridgewood Ave., Glen Ridge NJ 07028. (973)743-1075. **Fax:** (973)743-1075. **E-mail:** jerjaf@aol.com. **Contact:** Jerry Jaffe, president. Management firm. Represents individual artists and groups from anywhere. Receives 20% commission. Reviews material for acts "rarely." Reviews for representation "sometimes."

HOW TO CONTACT *Write or call first to arrange a personal interview.* Prefers CD or DVD with 3-4 songs and lyric sheet. Does not return material. Responds in 2 months.

MUSIC Mostly **rock/alternative**, **pop**, and **Hot AC**. Works primarily with groups and singers/songwriters.

TIPS "If you are influenced by Jesus & Mary Chain, please e-mail. Create some kind of 'buzz' first."

◑◐ THE MANAGEMENT TRUST, LTD.

411 Queen St. W., 3rd Floor, Toronto ON M5V 2A5 Canada. (416)979-7070. **Fax:** (416)979-0505. **Website:** www.mgmtrust.ca. **Contact:** Shelley Stertz, director/artist manager. Management firm. Represents individual artists and/or groups.

HOW TO CONTACT Submit demo package by mail (Attn: A&R Dept.). Unsolicited submissions are OK. If seeking management, press kit should include CD, bio, cover letter, photo and press clippings. Does not return material. Responds in 2 months.

MUSIC All types.

○ RICK MARTIN PRODUCTIONS

125 Fieldpoint Rd., Greenwich CT 06830. **Website:** www.rickmartinproductions.com; www.myspace.com/rickmartinproductions. **Contact:** Rick Martin, president. Personal manager and independent producer. Held the Office of Secretary of the National Conference of Personal Managers for 22 years. Represents vocalists; currently produces pop and country crossover music artists in private project studio and looking for a female vocalist in the general area of Greenwich, CT, for production project. Receives 15% commission as a personal manager and/or customary production and publishing distributions.

HOW TO CONTACT "Please e-mail for initial contact with your web link. Do not submit unless permission received to do so."

MUSIC Any genre but hip-hop or rap.

TIPS "Your demo does not have to be professionally produced to submit to producers, publishers, or managers. In other words, save your money. It's really not important what you've done. It's what you can do now that counts."

◐ PHIL MAYO & COMPANY

P.O. Box 304, Bomoseen VT 05732 United States. (802)468-2554. **Fax:** (802)468-2554. **E-mail:** pmcamgphil@aol.com. **Contact:** Phil Mayo, President. Management firm and record company (AMG Records). Estab. 1981. Represents individual artists, groups and songwriters from anywhere; currently handles 4 acts. Receives 15-20% commission. Reviews material for acts.

HOW TO CONTACT *Contact first and obtain permission to submit.* Prefers CD with 3 songs (professionally recorded) and lyric or lead sheet. If seeking management, include bio, photo and lyric sheet in press kit. Does not return material. Responds in 2 months.

MUSIC Mostly **contemporary Christian pop**. Current and past acts have included John Hall, Guy Burlage, Jonell Mosser, Pam Buckland, Orleans, Gary Nicholson, and Jon Pousette-Dart.

○ MID-COAST, INC.

1002 Jones Rd., Hendersonville TN 37075. (615)400-4664. **E-mail:** mid-co@ix.netcom.com. **Contact:** Bruce Andrew Bossert, managing director. Management firm and music publisher (MidCoast, Inc./BMI). Represents individual artists, groups, and songwriters. Reviews material for acts.

HOW TO CONTACT Submit demo package by mail. Unsolicited submissions are OK. Prefers CD, cassette, VHS videocassette, or DAT with 2-4 songs and lyric sheet. If seeking management, press kit should include cover letter, "short" bio, tape, video, photo, press clippings, and announcements of any performances in the Nashville area. Does not return material. Responds in 6 weeks if interested.

MUSIC Mostly **rock**, **pop**, and **country**. Works primarily with original rock and country bands and artists.

● NOTEWORTHY PRODUCTIONS

124 1/2 Archwood Ave., Annapolis MD 21401. (410)268-8232. **Fax:** (410)268-2167. **E-mail:** mcshane@mcnote.com. **Website:** www.mcnote.com. **Contact:** McShane Glover, president. Management firm and booking agency. Represents individual artists, groups, and songwriters from everywhere. Receives 15-20% commission. Reviews material for acts.

HOW TO CONTACT *Write first and obtain permission to submit.* Prefers CD/CD-R with lyric sheet. If seeking management, press kit should include CD, photo, bio, venues played and press clippings (preferably reviews). "Follow up with a phone call 3-5 weeks after submission." Does not return material. Responds in 2 months.

MUSIC Mostly **Americana**, **folk**, and **Celtic**. Works primarily with performing singer/songwriters. Current acts include Toby Walker (blues) and Vicki Genfan (folk/jazz/soul).

○ ON THE LEVEL MUSIC!

P.O. Box 508, Owego NY 13827. P.O. Box 508, Owego NY 13827. **E-mail:** fredny2020@yahoo.com. **Contact:** Fred Gage, CEO/president. Management firm, booking agency and music publisher (On The Level Music! Publishing). Estab. 1970. Represents individual artists, groups and songwriters from anywhere; currently handles 30 acts. Receives 15% commission. Reviews material for acts.

HOW TO CONTACT Submit demo tape by mail. Unsolicited submissions are OK. Prefers CDs, DAT or VHS videocassette with 4 songs and lyric or lead sheet. If seeking management, press kit should include cover letter, bio, demo tape/CD, lyric sheets, press clippings, 8×10 photo and video. Does not return material. Responds in 1 month.

MUSIC Mostly **rock**, **alternative** and **jazz**; also **blues**. Current acts include Ice River Blues and Summer Jam.

◖ PARADIGM TALENT AGENCY

360 N. Crescent Dr., North Bldg., Beverly Hills CA 90210. (310)288-8000. **Fax:** (310)288-2000. **Website:** www.paradigmagency.com. **Nashville:** 124 12th Ave. S., Suite 410, Nashville TN 37203. (615)251-4400. **Fax:** (615)251-4401. **New York:** 260 Park Ave. S., 16th Floor, New York, NY 10010. (212)897-6400. **Fax:** (212)764-8941. **Monterey:** 404 W. Franklin St., Monterey, CA 93940. (831)375-4889. **Fax:** (831)375-2623. Booking agency. Represents individual artists and groups from anywhere. Receives 10% commission. Reviews material for acts.

HOW TO CONTACT *Write or call first to arrange a personal interview.*

MUSIC Current acts include Ricky Skaggs, Junior Brown, Toby Keith, Kasey Chambers, Umphrey's McGee, Black Eyed Peas, Kirk Franklin, Lily Allen, My Chemical Romance, and Lauryn Hill.

◖ PRIME TIME ENTERTAINMENT

2430 Research Dr., Livermore CA 94550. (925)449-1724. **Fax:** (925)605-0379. **E-mail:** info@primetimeentertainment.com. **Website:** www.primetimeentertainment.com. Management firm and booking agency. Represents individual artists, groups and songwriters from anywhere. Receives 10-20% commission. Reviews material for acts.

HOW TO CONTACT Submit demo package by mail. Unsolicited submissions are OK. Prefers CD with 3-5 songs. If seeking management, press kit should include 8x10 photo, reviews, and CDs/tapes. Include SASE. Responds in 1 month.

MUSIC Mostly **jazz**, **country**, and **alternative**; also **ethnic**.

TIPS "It's all about the song."

◖ RAINBOW TALENT AGENCY LLC

146 Round Pond Lane, Rochester NY 14626. (585)723-3334. **E-mail:** carl@rainbowtalentagency.com; info@rainbowtalentagency.com. **Website:** www.rainbowtalentagency.com. **Contact:** Carl Labate, president. Management firm and booking agency. Represents artists and groups. Receives 15-25% commission.

HOW TO CONTACT Submit demo package by mail. Unsolicited submissions are OK. Prefers CD with minimum 3 songs. May send DVD if available; "a still photo and bio of the act; if you are a performer, it would be advantageous to show yourself or the group performing live. Theme videos are not helpful." If seeking management, include photos, bio, markets established, and CD/DVD. Does not return material. Responds in 1 month.

MUSIC Mostly **blues**, **rock**, and **R&B**. Works primarily with touring bands and recording artists. Current acts include Russell Thompkins Jr. & The New Stylistics (R&B), Josie Waverly (country), and Spanky Haschmann Swing Orchestra (high energy swing).

TIPS "My main interest is with groups or performers that are currently touring and have some product. And are at least 50% original. Strictly songwriters should apply elsewhere."

○ RASPBERRY JAM MUSIC

(formerly Endangered Species Artist Management), 4 Berachah Ave., South Nyack NY 10960-4202. (845)353-4001. **Fax:** (845)353-4332. **E-mail:** muzik@verizon.net. **Website:** www.musicandamerica.com or www.anyamusic.com. President: Fred Porter. Vice President: Suzanne Buckley. Management firm. Estab. 1979. Represents individual artists, groups and songwriters from anywhere; currently handles 3 acts. Receives 20% commission. Reviews material for acts.

HOW TO CONTACT *Call first and obtain permission to submit.* Prefers CD with 3 or more songs and lyric sheet. "Please include a demo of your music, a clear, recent photograph, current press, if any, and a cover letter indicating at what stage in your career you are and expectations for your future. Please label the cassette and/or CD with your name and address as well as the song titles." If seeking management, press kit should include cover letter, bio, photo, demo/CD, lyric sheet and press clippings. Include SASE. Responds in 6 weeks.

MUSIC Mostly **pop**, **rock** and **world**; also **Latin/heavy metal**, **R&B**, **jazz** and **instrumental**. Current acts include Jason Wilson & Tabarruk (pop/reggae, nominated for Juno award 2001), and Anya (pop singer).

TIPS "Listen to everything, classical to country, old to contemporary, to develop an understanding of many writing styles. Write with many other partners to keep the creativity fresh. Don't feel your style will be ruined by taking a class or a writing seminar. We all process moods and images differently. This leads to uniqueness in the music."

○ REIGN MUSIC AND MEDIA, LLC

P.O. Box 2394, New York NY 10185. **E-mail:** online@reignmm.com. **Website:** www.reignmm.com. **Contact:** Talent Relations Department. Multimedia/artist development firm. Promotes/develops primarily local and regional vocalists, producers, and songwriters. Receives 20-25% commission. Reviews material for artists.

HOW TO CONTACT Submit demo package by mail or e-mail. Unsolicited submissions are OK. Prefers CD, MP3, or video. Standard hard copy press kit or EPK should include cover letter, press clippings and/or reviews, bio, demo (in appropriate format), picture, and accurate contact telephone number. Include SASE. Usually responds in 3 weeks.

MUSIC Mostly **pop**, **R&B**, **club/dance**, and **hip-hop/rap**; some **Latin**. Works primarily with singer/songwriters, producers, rappers, and bands.

① RIOHCAT MUSIC

P.O. Box 764, Hendersonville TN 37077-0764. (615)824-1435. **E-mail:** tachoir@bellsouth.net. **Website:** www.tachoir.com. **Contact:** Robert Kayne, manager. Management firm, booking agency, record company (Avita Records) and music publisher. Represents individual artists and groups. Receives 15-20% commission.

○ Also see the listing for Avita Records in the Record Companies section of this book.

HOW TO CONTACT *Contact first and obtain permission to submit.* Prefers CD and lead sheet. If seeking management, press kit should include cover letter, bio, photo, demo tape/CD, and press clippings. Does not return material. Responds in 6 weeks.

MUSIC Mostly **contemporary jazz** and **fusion**. Works primarily with jazz ensembles. Current acts include Group Tachoir (jazz), Tachoir/Manakas Duo (jazz) and Jerry Tachoir (jazz vibraphone artist).

●○ ROBERTSON ENTERTAINMENT

106 Harding Road Kendenup 6323, Western Australia Australia. (618)9851-4311. **Fax:** (618)9851-4225. **E-mail:** info@robertsonentertainment.com. **Website:** www.robertsonentertainment.com. **Contact:** Eddie Robertson. Booking agency. Represents individual artists and/or groups; currently handles 50 acts. Receives 20% commission. Reviews material for acts.

HOW TO CONTACT *Write first and obtain permission to submit.* Unsolicited submissions are OK. Prefers cassette or videocassette with photo, information on style and bio. If seeking management, press kit should include photos, bio, cover letter, press clippings, video, demo, lyric sheets and any other useful information. Does not return material. Responds in 1 month.

MUSIC Mostly **Top 40/pop**, **jazz**, and **'60s-'90s**; also **reggae** and **blues**. Works primarily with show bands and solo performers. Current acts include Faces (dance band), Heart & Soul (easy listening), and Ruby Tuesday (contemporary pop/rock/classics).

TIPS "Send as much information as possible. If you do not receive a call after 4-5 weeks, follow up with a letter or phone call."

① SA'MALL MANAGEMENT

468 N. Camden Dr., Suite 200, Beverly Hills CA 90210. (818)506-8533. **Fax:** (310)860-7400. **E-mail:** pplzmi@aol.com. **Website:** www.pplentertainmentgroup.com. **Contact:** Ted Steele, vice president of talent. Management firm, music publisher (Pollybyrd Publications) and record company (PPL Entertainment Group). Represents individual artists, groups and songwriters worldwide; currently handles 10 acts. Receives 10-25% commission. Reviews material for acts.

HOW TO CONTACT *E-mail first and obtain permission to submit.* "Only professional full-time artists who tour and have a fan base need apply. No weekend warriors, please." Prefers CD or cassette. If seeking management, press kit should include picture, bio and tape. Include SASE. Responds in 2 months.

MUSIC **All types**. Current acts include Riki Hendrix (rock), Buddy Wright (blues), Fhyne, Suzette Cuseo, The Band AKA, LeJenz, B.D. Fuoco, MoBeatz, and Kenyatta Jarrett (Prince Ken).

●✸ SERGE ENTERTAINMENT GROUP

P.O. Box 5147, Canton GA 30114. (678)880-8207. **Fax:** (678)494-9289. **E-mail:** sergeent@aol.com. **Website:** www.sergeentertainmentgroup.com. **Contact:** Sandy Serge, president. Management and PR firm and song publishers. Represents individual artists, groups, songwriters from anywhere; currently handles 20 acts. Receives 20% commission for management. Monthly fee required for PR acts.

HOW TO CONTACT *E-mail first for permission to submit.* Submit demo package by mail. Unsolicited submissions are OK. Prefers CD with 4 songs and lyric sheet. If seeking management, press kit should include 8x10 photo, bio, cover letter, lyric sheets, max of 4 press clips, DVD, performance schedule and CD. "All information submitted must include name, address and phone number on each item." Does not return material. Responds in 6 weeks if interested.

MUSIC Mostly **rock**, **pop**, and **country**; also **New Age**. Works primarily with singer/songwriters and bands. Current acts include Asia featuring John Payne (prog rock), Erik Norlander (prog rock), and Lana Lane (prog rock).

◐ ● SIEGEL ENTERTAINMENT LTD.

1736 W. 2nd Ave, Vancouver BC V6J 1H6 Canada. (604)736-3896. **Fax:** (604)736-3464. **E-mail:** siegelent@telus.net. **Website:** www.siegelent.com. **Contact:** Robert Siegel, president. Management firm and booking agency. Represents individual artists, groups and songwriters from anywhere; currently handles more than 100 acts (for bookings). Receives 15-20% commission. Reviews material for acts.

HOW TO CONTACT *Does not accept unsolicited submissions. E-mail or write for permission to submit.* Does not return material. Responds in 1 month.

MUSIC Mostly **rock**, **pop**, and **country**; also **specialty** and **children's**. Current acts include Johnny Ferreira & The Swing Machine, Lee Aaron, Kenny Blues Boss Wayne (boogie) and Tim Brecht (pop/children's).

○ GARY SMELTZER PRODUCTIONS

P.O. Box 201112, Austin TX 78720-11112. (512)478-6020. **Fax:** (512)478-8979. **E-mail:** info@garysmeltzerproductions.com. **Website:** www.garysmeltzerproductions.com. **Contact:** Gary Smeltzer, president. Management firm and booking agency. Represents individual artists and groups from anywhere. Currently handles 20 acts. "We book about 100 different bands each year—none are exclusive." Receives 20% commission. Reviews material for acts.

HOW TO CONTACT Submit demo package by mail. Unsolicited submissions are OK. Prefers CD or DVD. If seeking management, press kit should include cover letter, résumé, CD/DVD, bio, picture, lyric sheets, press clippings, and video. Does not return material. Responds in 1 month.

MUSIC Mostly **alternative**, **R&B** and **country**. Current acts include Rotel & the Hot Tomatoes (nostalgic '60s showband).

TIPS "We prefer performing songwriters who can gig their music as a solo or group."

◑ SOUTHEASTERN ATTRACTIONS

1025 23rd St. S., Suite 302, Birmingham AL 35205. (205)307-6790. **Fax:** (205)307-6798. **E-mail:** info@seattractions.com. **Website:** www.seattractions.com. **Contact:** Agent. Booking agency. Represents groups from anywhere. Receives 20% commission.

HOW TO CONTACT Submit demo package by mail. Unsolicited submissions are OK. Prefers CD or DVD. Does not return material. Responds in 2 months.

MUSIC Mostly **rock**, **alternative**, **oldies**, **country**, and **dance**. Works primarily with bands. Current acts include The Undergrounders (variety to contemporary), The Connection (Motown/dance), andRollin' in the Hay (bluegrass).

◑ STAIRCASE PROMOTION

P.O. Box 211, East Prairie MO 63845 United States. (573)649-2211. **Contact:** Tommy Loomas, president. Vice President: Joe Silver. Management firm, music publisher (Lineage Publishing) and record company (Capstan Record Production). Estab. 1975. Represents individual artists and groups from anywhere; currently handles 6 acts. Receives 25% commission. Reviews material for acts.

HOW TO CONTACT Submit demo by mail. Unsolicited submissions are OK. Prefers cassette with 3 songs and lyric sheet. If seeking management, press kit should include bio, photo, audio cassette and/or video and press reviews, if any. "Be as professional as you can." Include SASE. Responds in 2 months.

MUSIC Mostly **country**, **pop** and **easy listening**; also **rock**, **gospel** and **alternative**. Current acts include Skidrow Joe (country comedian, on Capstan Records), Vicarie Arcoleo (pop singer, on Treasure Coast Records) and Scarlett Britoni (pop singer on Octagon Records).

◑ STARKRAVIN' MANAGEMENT

11135 Weddington St., Suite 424, North Hollywood CA 91601. (818)587-6801. **Fax:** (818)587-6802. **E-mail:** bcmclane@aol.com. **Website:** www.benmclane.com.

Contact: B.C. McLane, Esq. Management and law firm. Estab. 1994. Represents individual artists, groups and songwriters. Receives 20% commission (management); $300/hour as attorney.

HOW TO CONTACT Submit demo package by mail. Unsolicited submissions are OK. Prefers CDs. Does not return material. Responds in 1 month if interested.

MUSIC Mostly **rock**, **pop** and **R&B**. Works primarily with bands.

○ ST. JOHN ARTISTS

P.O. Box 619, Neenah WI 54957-0619. (920)722-2222. **Fax:** (920)725-2405. **E-mail:** jon@stjohn-artists.com. **Website:** www.stjohn-artists.com. **Contact:** Jon St. John and Gary Coquoz, agents. Booking agency. Represents local and regional individual artists and groups; currently handles 20 acts. Receives 15-20% commission. Reviews material for acts.

HOW TO CONTACT *Call first and obtain permission to submit.* Prefers CD or DVD. If seeking management, press kit should include cover letter, bio, photo, demo tape/CD, video and résumé. Include SASE.

MUSIC Mostly **rock** and **MOR**. Current acts include Boogie & the Yo-Yo's ('60s to 2000s), Vic Ferrari (Top 40 '80s-2000s), Little Vito & the Torpedoes (variety '50s-2000s), and Da Yoopers (musical comedy/novelty).

❶ TAS MUSIC CO./DAVID TASSÉ ENTERTAINMENT

N2467 Knollwood Dr., Lake Geneva WI 53147. (888)554-9898; (262)245-1335. **E-mail:** info@baybreezerecords.com. **Website:** www.baybreezerecords.com. **Contact:** David Tassé. Booking agency, record company and music publisher. Represents artists, groups, and songwriters; currently handles 21 acts. Receives 10-20% commission. Reviews material for acts.

HOW TO CONTACT Submit demo tape by mail. Unsolicited submissions are OK. Prefers CD with 2-4 songs and lyric sheet. Include performance videocassette if available. If seeking management, press kit should include tape, bio and photo. Does not return material. Responds in 3 weeks.

MUSIC Mostly **pop** and **jazz**; also **dance, MOR, rock, soul**, and **Top 40**. Works primarily with show and dance bands. Current acts include Maxx Kelly (pop rock) and Glenn Davis (blues band).

❶ T.L.C. BOOKING AGENCY

37311 N. Valley Rd., Chattaroy WA 99003. (509)292-2201. **Fax:** (509)292-2205. **E-mail:** tlcagent@ix.netcom.com. **Website:** www.tlcagency.com. **Contact:** Tom or Carrie Lapsansky, agent/owners. Booking agency. Represents individual artists and groups from anywhere. Receives 10-15% commission. Reviews material for acts.

HOW TO CONTACT *Call first and obtain permission to submit.* Prefers CD with 3-4 songs. Does not return material. Responds in 3 weeks.

MUSIC Mostly **rock**, **country**, and **variety**; also **comedians** and **magicians**. Works primarily with bands, singles and duos. Current acts include Nobody Famous (variety/classic rock), Mr. Happy (rock), and Jimmy Buffett Review.

○ UNIVERSAL MUSIC MARKETING

P.O. Box 2297, Universal City TX 78148. **Phone/fax:** (210)653-3989. **Website:** www.universalmusicmarketing.net. **Contact:** Frank Wilson, president. Management firm, record company (BSW Records), booking agency, music publisher and record producer (Frank Wilson). Represents individual artists and groups from anywhere. Receives 15% commission. Reviews material for acts.

HOW TO CONTACT Submit demo package by mail. Unsolicited submissions are OK. Prefers CD or DVD with 3 songs and lyric sheet. If seeking management, include tape/CD, bio, photo and current activities. Include SASE. Responds in 6 weeks.

MUSIC Mostly **country** and **light rock**; also **blues** and **jazz**. Works primarily with vocalists, singer/songwriters and bands.

TIPS "Visit our website for an up-to-date listing of current acts."

❶ CHERYL K. WARNER PRODUCTIONS

P.O. Box 179, Hermitage TN 37076. (615)429-7849. **E-mail:** cherylkwarner@tds.net (primary); cherylkwarner@comcast.net (secondary). **Website:** www.cherylkwarner.com; www.cherylkwarner.net. **Contact:** Cheryl K. Warner. Recording and stage production, music consulting, music publisher, record label, A&R. Currently works with 2 acts with expansion in the works. Reviews material for acts.

HOW TO CONTACT Submit demo package by mail or e-mail. Unsolicited submissions are OK. Prefers CD or DVD, but will accept CD with 3 best songs, lyric or lead sheet, bio, and picture. Press kit should include CD, DVD with up-to-date bio, cover letter, lyric sheets, press clippings, and picture. Does not return material. Responds in 6 weeks if interested.

MUSIC Mostly **country/traditional and contemporary, Christian/gospel**, and **A/C/pop/rock**. Works primarily with singer/songwriters and bands with original and versatile style. Current acts include Cheryl K. Warner (recording artist/entertainer) and Cheryl K. Warner Band (support/studio).

◑ WORLDSOUND, LLC

17837 1st Ave. South, Suite 3, Seattle WA 98148. (206)444-0300. **Fax:** (206)244-0066. **E-mail:** a-r@worldsound.com. **Website:** www.worldsound.com. **Contact:** Warren Wyatt, A&R manager. Management firm. Represents individual artists, groups and songwriters from anywhere. Receives 20% commission. Reviews material for acts.

HOW TO CONTACT "Online, send us an e-mail containing a link to your website where your songs can be heard and the lyrics are available; **please do not e-mail song files!** By regular mail, unsolicited submissions are OK." Prefers CD with 2-10 songs and lyric sheet. "If seeking management, please send an e-mail with a link to your website--your site should contain song samples, band biography, photos, video (if available), press and demo reviews. By mail, please send the materials listed above and include SASE." Responds in 1 month.

MUSIC Mostly **rock**, **pop**, and **world**; also **heavy metal**, **hard rock**, and **top 40**. Works primarily with pop/rock/world artists.

TIPS "Always submit new songs/material, even if you have sent material that was previously rejected; the music biz is always changing."

◑ ZANE MANAGEMENT, INC.

One Liberty Place, 1650 Market St., 56th Floor, Philadelphia PA 19103. (215)575-3803. **Fax:** (215)575-3801. **Website:** www.zanemanagement.com. **Contact:** Lloyd Z. Remick, Esq., president.. Entertainment/sports consultants and managers. Represents artists, songwriters, producers and athletes; currently handles 7 acts. Receives 10-15% commission.

HOW TO CONTACT Submit demo tape by mail. Unsolicited submissions are OK. Prefers CD and lyric sheet. If seeking management, press kit should include cover letter, bio, photo, demo tape and video. Does not return material. Responds in 3 weeks.

MUSIC Mostly **dance**, **easy listening**, **folk**, **jazz (fusion)**, **MOR**, **rock (hard and country)**, **soul** and **top 40/pop**. Current acts include Bunny Sigler (disco/funk), Peter Nero and Philly Pops (conductor), Pieces of a Dream (jazz/crossover), Don't Look Down (rock/pop), Christian Josi (pop-swing), Bishop David Evans (gospel), Kevin Roth (children's music), and Rosie Carlino (standards/pop).

MUSIC FIRMS

//

ADVERTISING, AUDIOVISUAL & COMMERCIAL

It's happened a million times—you hear a jingle on the radio or television and can't get it out of your head. That's the work of a successful jingle writer, writing songs to catch your attention and make you aware of the product being advertised. But the field of commercial music consists of more than just memorable jingles. It also includes background music that many companies use in videos for corporate and educational presentations, as well as films and TV shows.

SUBMITTING MATERIAL

More than any other market listed in this book, the commercial music market expects composers to have made an investment in the recording of their material before submitting. A sparse, piano/vocal demo won't work here; when dealing with commercial music firms, especially audiovisual firms and music libraries, high quality production is important. Your demo may be kept on file at one of these companies until a need for it arises, and it may be used or sold as you sent it. Therefore, your demo tape or reel must be as fully produced as possible.

The presentation package that goes along with your demo must be just as professional. A list of your credits should be a part of your submission, to give the company an idea of your experience in this field. If you have no experience, look to local television and radio stations to get your start. Don't expect to be paid for many of your first jobs in the commercial music field; it's more important to get the credits and exposure that can lead to higher-paying jobs.

Commercial music and jingle writing can be a lucrative field for the composer/songwriter with a gift for writing catchy melodies and the ability to write in many different music styles. It's a very competitive field, so it pays to have a professional presentation package that makes your work stand out.

Three different segments of the commercial music world are listed here: advertising agencies, audiovisual firms, and commercial music houses/music libraries. Each looks for a different type of music, so read these descriptions carefully to see where the music you write fits in.

ADVERTISING AGENCIES

Ad agencies work on assignment as their clients' needs arise. Through consultation and input from the creative staff, ad agencies seek jingles and music to stimulate the consumer to identify with a product or service.

When contacting ad agencies, keep in mind they are searching for music that can capture and then hold an audience's attention. Most jingles are short, with a strong, memorable hook. When an ad agency listens to a demo, it is not necessarily looking for a finished product so much as for an indication of creativity and diversity. Many composers put together a reel of excerpts of work from previous projects, or short pieces of music that show they can write in a variety of styles.

AUDIOVISUAL FIRMS

Audiovisual firms create a variety of products, from film and video shows for sales meetings, corporate gatherings and educational markets, to motion pictures and TV shows. With the increase of home video use, how-to videos are a big market for audiovisual firms, as are spoken word educational videos. All of these products need music to accompany them. For your quick reference, companies working to place music in movies and TV shows (excluding commercials) have an ICON preceding their listing.

Like ad agencies, audiovisual firms look for versatile, well-rounded songwriters. When submitting demos to these firms, you need to demonstrate your versatility in writing specialized background music and themes. Listings for companies will tell what facet(s) of the audiovisual field they are involved in and what types of clients they serve. Your demo tape should also be as professional and fully produced as possible; audiovisual firms often seek demo tapes that can be put on file for future use when the need arises.

COMMERCIAL MUSIC HOUSES & MUSIC LIBRARIES

Commercial music houses are companies contracted (either by an ad agency or the advertiser) to compose custom jingles. Since they are neither an ad agency nor an audiovisual firm, their main concern is music. They use a lot of it, too—some composed by in-house songwriters and some contributed by outside, freelance writers.

Music libraries are different in that their music is not custom composed for a specific client. Their job is to provide a collection of instrumental music in many different styles that, for an annual fee or on a per-use basis, the customer can use however he chooses.

In the following listings, commercial music houses and music libraries, which are usually the most open to works by new composers, are identified as such by **bold** type.

The commercial music market is similar to most other businesses in one aspect: experience is important. Until you develop a list of credits, pay for your work may not be high. Don't pass up opportunities if a job is non- or low-paying. These assignments will add to your list of credits, make you contacts in the field, and improve your marketability.

Money & rights

Many of the companies listed in this section pay by the job, but there may be some situations where the company asks you to sign a contract that will specify royalty payments. If this happens, research the contract thoroughly, and know exactly what is expected of you and how much you'll be paid.

Depending on the particular job and the company, you may be asked to sell one-time rights or all rights. One-time rights involve using your material for one presentation only. All rights means the buyer can use your work any way he chooses, as many times as he likes. Be sure you know exactly what you're giving up, and how the company may use your music in the future.

In the commercial world, many of the big advertising agencies have their own publishing companies where writers assign their compositions. In these situations, writers sign contracts whereby they do receive performance and mechanical royalties when applicable.

ADDITIONAL LISTINGS

For additional names and addresses of ad agencies that may use jingles and/or commercial music, refer to the *Standard Directory of Advertising Agencies* (National Register Publishing). For a list of audiovisual firms, check out the latest edition of *AV Marketplace* (R.R. Bowker). Both of these books may be found at your local library. To contact companies in your area, see the Geographic Index at the back of this book.

THE AD AGENCY

P.O. Box 470572, San Francisco CA 94147. **E-mail:** michaelcarden@msn.com; dgasper@theadagency.com. **Contact:** Michael Carden, creative director. Advertising agency and jingle/commercial music production house. Clients include business, industry and retail. Uses the services of music houses, independent songwriter/composers and lyricists for scoring of commercials, background music for video production, and jingles for commercials. Commissions 20 composers and 15 lyricists/year. Pays by the job or by the hour. Buys all or one-time rights.

HOW TO CONTACT Submit demo tape of previous work. Prefers cassette with 5-8 songs and lyric sheet. Include SASE. Responds in 3 weeks. Uses variety of musical styles for commercials, promotion, TV, video presentations.

TIPS "Our clients and our needs change frequently."

ADVERTEL, INC.

P.O. Box 18053, Pittsburgh PA 15236-0053. (412)714-4431. **E-mail:** info@advertel.com. **Website:** www.advertel.com. Submit demo of previous work. Prefers CD. "Most compositions are 2 minutes strung together in 6-, 12-, 18-minute length productions." Does not return material; prefers to keep on file. Responds "right away if submission fills an immediate need."

TIPS "Go for volume. We have continuous need for all varieties of music in 2-minute lengths. Advertel produces a religious radio program called 'Prayer-in-the-Air.' Feel free to submit songs with lyrics taken from scripture. We also look for catchy, memorable melodies. For those pro bono submissions, no compensation is offered—only national recognition."

CEDAR CREST STUDIO

#17 CR 830, Henderson AR 72544. (870)488-5777. **E-mail:** cedarcrest@springfield.net. **Website:** www.cedarcreststudio.com. **Contact:** Bob Ketchum, owner. **Audiovisual firm and jingle/commercial music production house.** Clients include corporate, industrial, sales, music publishing, training, educational, legal, medical, music and Internet. Sometimes uses the services of independent songwriters/composers for background music for video productions, jingles for TV spots and commercials for radio and TV. Pays by the job or by royalties. Buys all rights or one-time rights. Query with résumé of credits or submit demo tape of previous work. Prefers CD, cassette, or DVD. Does not return material. "We keep it on file for future ref-

erence." Responds in 2 months. Uses **up-tempo pop** (not too "rocky"), **unobtrusive**—no solos for commercials and background music for video presentations.

TIPS "Hang, hang, hang. Be open to suggestions. Improvise, adapt, overcome."

COMMUNICATIONS FOR LEARNING

395 Massachusetts Ave., Arlington MA 02474. (781)641-2350. **E-mail:** comlearn@thecia.net. **Website:** www.communicationsforlearning.com. **Contact:** Jonathan L. Barkan, executive producer/director. Video, multimedia, exhibit and graphic design firm. Clients include multi-nationals, industry, government, institutions, local, national and international nonprofits. Uses services of music houses and independent songwriters/composers as theme and background music for videos and multimedia. Commissions 1-2 composers/year. Pays $2,000-5,000/job and one-time use fees. Rights purchased vary. Submit demo and work available for library use. Prefers CD to Web links. Does not return material; prefers to keep on file. "For each job we consider our entire collection." Responds in 3 months.

TIPS "Please don't call. Just send your best material available for library use on CD. We'll be in touch if a piece works and negotiate a price. Make certain your name and contact information are on the CD itself, not only on the cover letter."

DBF A MEDIA COMPANY

9683 Charles St., LaPlata MD 20646. (301)645-6110. **E-mail:** service@dbfmedia.com. **Website:** www.dbfmedia.com. Video production. Uses the services of music houses for background music for industrial, training, educational, and promo videos, jingles and commercials for radio and TV. Buys all rights. "All genre for MOH, industrial, training, video/photo montages and commercials."

HOW TO CONTACT Submit demo CD of previous work. Prefers CD or DVD with 5-8 songs and lead sheet. Include SASE, but prefers to keep material on file. Responds in 6 months.

○⊛ DISK PRODUCTIONS

1100 Perkins Rd., Baton Rouge LA 70802. **E-mail:** disk_productions@yahoo.com. **Contact:** Joey Decker, director. **Jingle/production house.** Clients include advertising agencies and film companies. Uses the services of music houses, independent songwriters/composers and lyricists for scoring and background music for TV spots, films and jingles for radio and TV.

Commissions 7 songwriters/composers and 7 lyricists/year. Pays by the job. Buys all rights.

HOW TO CONTACT Submit demo of previous work. Prefers DVD, CD, cassette or DAT. Does not return material. Responds in 2 weeks.

MUSIC Needs all types of music for jingles, music beds or background music for TV and radio, etc.

TIPS "Advertising techniques change with time. Don't be locked in a certain style of writing. Give me music that I can't get from pay needle-drop."

HOME, INC.

566 Columbus Ave., Boston MA 02118. (617)427-4663. **Fax:** (617)427-4664. **E-mail:** alanmichel@homeinc.org. **Website:** www.homeinc.org. **Contact:** Alan Michael, director and co-founder. Audiovisual firm and video production company. Clients include cable television, nonprofit organizations, pilot programs, entertainment companies and industrial. Uses the services of music houses and independent songwriters/composers for scoring of music videos, background music and commercials for TV. Commissions 2-5 songwriters/year. Pays up to $200-600/job. Buys all rights and one-time rights.

HOW TO CONTACT Submit demo tape of previous work. Prefers CD or website URL with 6 pieces. Does not return material; prefers to keep on file. Responds as projects require.

MUSIC Mostly synthesizer. Uses all styles of music for educational videos.

TIPS "Have a variety of products available and be willing to match your skills to the project and the budget."

K&R ALL MEDIA PRODUCTIONS LLC

28533 Greenfield Rd., Southfield MI 48076. (248)557-8276. **E-mail:** recordav@knr.net. **Website:** www.knr.net. Scoring service and **jingle/commercial music production house**. Clients include commercial and industrial firms. Services include sound for pictures (Foley, music, dialogue). Uses the services of independent songwriters/composers and lyricists for scoring of film and video, commercials and industrials and jingles and commercials for radio and TV. Commissions 1 composer/month. Pays by the job. Buys all rights.

HOW TO CONTACT Submit demo tape of previous work. Prefers CD or VHS videocassette with 5-7 short pieces. "We rack your tape for client to judge." Does not return material.

TIPS "Keep samples short. Show me what you can do in 5 minutes. Go to knr.net 'free samples' and listen to the sensitivity expressed in emotional music."

KEN-DEL PRODUCTIONS INC.

1500 First State Blvd., First State Industrial Park, Wilmington DE 19804-3596. (302)999-1111. **E-mail:** info@ken-del.com. **Website:** www.ken-del.com. Clients include publishers, industrial firms and advertising agencies, how-to's and radio/TV. Uses services of songwriters for radio/TV commercials, jingles and multimedia. Pays by the job. Buys all rights.

HOW TO CONTACT "Submit all inquiries and demos in any format to the general manager." Does not return material. Will keep on file for 3 years. Generally responds in 1 month or less.

LAPRIORE VIDEOGRAPHY

67 Millbrook St. Ste. 114, Worcester MA 01606. (508)755-9010. **E-mail:** peter@lapriorevideo.com. **Website:** www.lapriorevideo.com. **Contact:** Peter Lapriore, owner/producer. Video production company. Clients include corporations, retail stores, educational and sports. Uses the services of music houses, independent songwriters/composers for background music for marketing, training, educational videos and TV commercials and for scoring video. "We also own several music libraries." Commissions 2 composers/year. Pays $150-1,000/job. Buys all or one-time rights.

HOW TO CONTACT Submit demo of previous work. Prefers CD, or DVD with 5 songs and lyric sheet. Does not return material; prefers to keep on file. Responds in 3 weeks.

MUSIC Uses slow, medium, up-tempo, jazz and classical for marketing, educational films and commercials.

TIPS "Be very creative and willing to work on all size budgets."

◑⊕ NOVUS VISUAL COMMUNICATIONS

59 Page Ave., Suite 300, Tower One, Yonkers NY 10704. (212)473-1377. **Fax:** (212)505-3300. **E-mail:** novuscom@aol.com. **E-mail:** robert@nakinc.com. **Website:** www.novuscommunications.com. **Contact:** Robert Antonik, managing director. Cross media marketing and communications company. Clients include corporations and interactive media. Uses the services of music houses, independent songwriters/composers and lyricists for scoring, background music for documentaries, commercials, multimedia applications, website, film shorts, and commercials

for radio and TV. Commissions 2 composers and 4 lyricists/year. Pay varies per job. Buys one-time rights.
HOW TO CONTACT *Request a submission of demo.* Query with a brief of style and songs. Prefers CD with 2-3 songs or link to website. "We prefer to keep submitted material on file, but will return material if SASE is enclosed. Responds in 6 weeks.

MUSIC Uses all styles for a variety of different assignments.

TIPS "Always present your best and don't add quantity to your demo. Novus is a creative marketing and communications company. We work with special events companies, PR firms, artists' management and media companies."

OMNI COMMUNICATIONS

P.O. Box 302, Carmel IN 46082-0302. (317)846-2345. **Fax:** (317)846-6664. **E-mail:** omni@omniproductions.com. **Website:** www.omniproductions.com. OMNI Productions is an experienced interactive, digital media solutions provider offering the complete infrastructure for production and delivery of digital media services including interactive multipoint Internet training; live event and archived webcasting; video, DVD & CD-ROM production; and encoding, hosting and distribution of streaming video content. OMNI is recognized by Microsoft as a Windows Media Service Provider. This partnership with Microsoft was obtained through vigorous training, testing and experience to ensure that those we serve receive the highest quality service from OMNI's experienced professionals. OMNI's staff includes technology experts certified by Microsoft and other industry vendors.

TIPS "Submit a good demo tape with examples of your range to command the attention of our producers."

UTOPIAN EMPIRE CREATEWORKS

P.O. Box 9, Traverse City MI 49865. (231)943-5050 or (231)943-4000. **E-mail:** creativeservices@utopianempire.com; clientworks@utopianempire.com. **Website:** www.utopianempire.com. **Contact:** Ms. M'Lynn Hartwell, president. Web design, multimedia firm, and motion picture/video production company. Primarily serves commercial, industrial and nonprofit clients. "We provide the following services: advertising, marketing, design/packaging, distribution and booking. Uses services of music houses, independent songwriters/composers for jingles and scoring of and background music for multi-image/multimedia, film and video." Negotiates pay. Buys all or one-time rights.

HOW TO CONTACT Submit CD of previous work, demonstrating composition skills or query with resume of credits. Prefers CD. Does not return material; prefers to keep on file. Responds only if interested.

MUSIC Uses mostly industrial/commercial themes.

⊛ VIDEO I-D, TELEPRODUCTIONS

105 Muller Rd., Washington IL 61571. (309)444-4323. **E-mail:** videoid@videoid.com. **Website:** www.videoid.com. **Contact:** Sam B. Wagner, president. Post production/teleproductions. Clients include law enforcement, industrial and business. Uses the services of music houses and independent songwriters/composers for background music for video productions. Pays per job. Buys one-time rights.

HOW TO CONTACT Submit demo of previous work. Prefers CD with 5 songs and lyric sheet. Does not return material. Responds in 1 month.

PLAY PRODUCERS & PUBLISHERS

//

Finding a theater company willing to invest in a new production can be frustrating for an unknown playwright. But whether you write the plays, compose the music or pen the lyrics, it is important to remember not only where to start but also how to start. Theater in the U.S. is a hierarchy, with Broadway, Off Broadway and Off Off Broadway being pretty much off limits to all but the Stephen Sondheims of the world.

Aspiring theater writers would do best to train their sights on nonprofit regional and community theaters to get started. The encouraging news is that there are a great number of local theater companies throughout the U.S. with experimental artistic directors who are looking for new works to produce, and many are included in this section. This section covers two segments of the industry: theater companies and dinner theaters are listed under Play Producers (beginning on page 201), and publishers of musical theater works are listed under the Play Publishers heading (beginning on page 203). All these markets are actively seeking new works of all types for their stages or publications.

BREAKING IN

Starting locally will allow you to research each company carefully and learn about their past performances, the type of musicals they present, and the kinds of material they're looking for. When you find theaters you think may be interested in your work, attend as many performances as possible, so you know exactly what type of material each theater presents. Or volunteer to work at a theater, whether it be moving sets or selling tickets. This will give you valuable insight into the day-to-day workings of a theater and the creation of a new show. On a national level, you will find prestigious organizations offering workshops and apprenticeships covering every subject from arts administration to directing to costuming. But it could be more helpful to look into professional internships at theaters and attend theater workshops in your area. The more knowledgeable you are about the workings of a particular company or theater, the easier it will be to tailor your work to fit its style and the more responsive they will be to you and your work. (See the Workshops & Conferences section for more information.) As a composer for the stage, you need to know as much as possible about a theater and how it works, its history and the different roles played by the people involved in it. Flexibility is the key to successful productions, and knowing how a theater works will only help you in cooperating and collaborating with the director, producer, technical people and actors.

If you're a playwright looking to have his play published in book form or in theater publications, see the listings under the Play Publishers section (page 203). To find play producers and publishers in your area, consult the Geographic Index at the back of this book.

PLAY PRODUCERS

ARKANSAS REPERTORY THEATRE

601 Main St., P.O. Box 110, Little Rock AR 72201. (501)378-0445. **E-mail:** bhupp@therep.org. **Website:** www.therep.org. Produces 6-10 plays and musicals/year. "We perform in a 354-seat house and also have a 99-seat second stage." Pays 5-10% royalty or $75-150 per performance.

HOW TO CONTACT Query with synopsis, character breakdown and set description. Include SASE. Responds in 6 months.

MUSICAL THEATER "Small casts are preferred, comedy or drama and prefer shows to run 1:45 to 2 hours maximum. Simple is better; small is better, but we do produce complex shows. We aren't interested in children's pieces, puppet shows or mime. We always like to receive a tape of the music with the book."

PRODUCTIONS *Disney's Beauty & the Beast*, by Woolverton/Ashman/Rice/Menken (musical retelling of the myth); *Crowns* by Taylor/Cunningham/Marberry (on the significance of African-American women's hats); and *A Chorus Line*, by Kirkwood/Hamlisch/Kleban (auditions).

TIPS "Include a good CD of your music, sung well, with the script."

WILLIAM CAREY UNIVERSITY DINNER THEATRE

William Carey College, Hattiesburg MS 39401. (601)318-6051. **Website:** www.wmcarey.edu. "Our dinner theater operates only in summer and plays to family audiences." Payment negotiable.

HOW TO CONTACT Query with synopsis, character breakdown and set description. Does not return material. Responds in 1 month.

MUSICAL THEATER "Plays should be simply-staged, have small casts (8-10 maximum), and be suitable for family viewing; two hours maximum length. Score should require piano only, or piano, synthesizer."

PRODUCTIONS *Ring of Fire: The Johnny Cash Musical*; *Smoke on the Mountain*; *Spitfire Grill*; and *Pump Boys and Dinettes*.

CIRCA 21 DINNER PLAYHOUSE

1828 Third Ave., Rock Island IL 61201. (309)786-7733. **Website:** www.circa21.com. Plays produced for a general audience. Three children's works/year, concurrent with major productions. Payment is negotiable.

HOW TO CONTACT Query with synopsis, character breakdown and set description or submit complete manuscript, score and tape of songs. Include SASE. Responds in 3 months.

MUSICAL THEATER "We produce both full length and one act children's musicals. Folk or fairy tale themes. Works that do not condescend to a young audience yet are appropriate for the entire family. We're also seeking full-length, small cast musicals suitable for a broad audience." Would also consider original music for use in a play being developed.

PRODUCTIONS *A Closer Walk with Patsy Cline*, *Swingtime Canteen*, *Forever Plaid* and *Lost Highway*.

TIPS "Small, upbeat, tourable musicals (like *Pump Boys*) and bright musically-sharp children's productions (like those produced by Prince Street Players) work best. Keep an open mind. Stretch to encompass a musical variety—different keys, rhythms, musical ideas and textures."

LA JOLLA PLAYHOUSE

P.O. Box 12039, La Jolla CA 92039. (858)550-1070. **Fax:** (858)550-1075. **E-mail:** information@ljp.org. **Website:** www.lajollaplayhouse.org. Produces 6-show season including 1-2 new musicals/year. Audience is University of California students to senior citizens. Performance spaces include a large proscenium theatre with 492 seats, a 3/4 thrust (384 seats), and a black box with up to 400 seats.

HOW TO CONTACT Query with synopsis, character breakdown, 10-page dialogue sample, demo CD. Include SASE. Responds in 1-2 months.

MUSICAL THEATER "We prefer contemporary music but not necessarily a story set in contemporary times. Retellings of classic stories can enlighten us about the times we live in. For budgetary reasons, we'd prefer a smaller cast size."

PRODUCTIONS *Cry-Baby*, book and lyrics by Thomas Meehan and Mark O'Donnell, music by David Javerbaum and Adam Schlesinger; *Dracula, The Musical*, book and lyrics by Don Black and Christopher Hampton, music by Frank Wildhorn (adaptation of Bram Stoker's novel); *Thoroughly Modern Millie*, book by Richard Morris and Dick Scanlan, new music by Jeanine Tesori, new lyrics by Dick Scanlan (based on the 1967 movie); and *Jane Eyre*, book and additional lyrics by John Cairo, music and lyrics by Paul Gordon (adaptation of Charlotte Bronte's novel).

NORTH SHORE MUSIC THEATRE

62 Dunham Rd., Beverly MA 01915. (978)232-7200. **Fax:** (978)921-9999. **E-mail:** NorthShoreMusicTheatre@nsmt.org. **Website:** www.nsmt.org.

HOW TO CONTACT Submit synopsis and CD of songs. Include SASE. Responds within 6 months.

MUSICAL THEATER Prefers full-length adult pieces not necessarily arena-theatre oriented. Cast sizes from 1-30; orchestras from 1-16.

PRODUCTIONS *Tom Jones* by Paul Leigh, George Stiles; *I Sent A Letter to My Love* by Melissa Manchester and Jeffrey Sweet; *Just So* by Anthony Drewe & George Stiles (musical based on Rudyard Kipling's fables); *Letters from 'Nam* by Paris Barclay (Vietnam War experience as told through letters from GI's); and *Friendship of the Sea* by Michael Wartofsky & Kathleen Cahill (New England maritime adventure musical).

TIPS "Keep at it!"

THE OPEN EYE THEATER

P.O. Box 959, 960 Main St., Margaretville NY 12455. Phone/**Fax:** (845)586-1660. **E-mail:** openeye@catskill.net. **Website:** www.theopeneye.org. **Contact:** Amie Brockway, producing artistic director. Play producer. Estab. 1972. Produces approximately 3 full length or 3 new plays for multi-generational audiences. Pays on a fee basis.

HOW TO CONTACT Query first. "A manuscript will be accepted and read only if it is a play for all ages and is: 1) Submitted by a recognized literary agent; 2) Requested or recommended by a staff or company member; or 3) Recommended by a professional colleague with whose work we are familiar. Playwrights may submit a one-page letter of inquiry including a very brief plot synopsis. Please enclose a self-addressed (but not stamped) envelope. We will reply only if we want you to submit the script (within several months)."

MUSICAL THEATER "The Open Eye Theater is a not-for-profit professional company working in a community context. Through the development, production and performance of plays for all ages, artists and audiences are challenged and given the opportunity to grow in the arts. In residence, on tour, and in the classroom, The Open Eye Theater strives to stimulate, educate, entertain, inspire and serve as a creative resource."

PRODUCTIONS *The Tempest* and *As You Like It* by Shakespeare; John Dilworth Newman's *A Year Down Yonder* based on the novel for young readers by Richard Peck; Willy Russell's *Shirley Valentine*; Sandra Fenichel Asher's *The Princess and the Goblin* and *Keeping Mr. Lincoln*; Robert Harling's *Steel Magnolias*; and Amie Brockway's *The Cricket on the Hearth*, based on the book by Charles Dickens.

PRIMARY STAGES

307 W. 38th St., Suite 1510, New York NY 10018. (212)840-9705. **Fax:** (212)840-9725. **E-mail:** info@primarystages.org. **Website:** www.primarystages.org. "New York theater-going audience representing a broad cross-section, in terms of age, ethnicity, and economic backgrounds. 199-seat, Off-Broadway theater."

HOW TO CONTACT "*No unsolicited scripts accepted. Submissions by agents only.*" Include SASE. Responds in up to 8 months.

MUSICAL THEATER "We are looking for work of heightened theatricality, that challenges realism—musical plays that go beyond film and televisions standard fare. We are looking for small cast shows (under 6 characters total), with limited sets. We are interested in original works that have not been produced in New York."

PRODUCTIONS *I Sent a Letter to My Love* by Melissa Manchester/Jeffrey Sweet; *Nightmare Alley* by Jonathan Brielle; *Call the Children Home* by Mildred Kayden and Thomas Babe; *Adrift in Macao* by Christopher Durang and Peter Melnick.

PRINCE MUSIC THEATER

1412 Chestnut St., Philadelphia PA 19102. (215)569-9700. **E-mail:** msamoff@princemusictheater.org; info@princemusictheater.org. **Website:** www.princemusictheater.org. **Contact:** Marjorie Samoff, producing artistic director. "Professional musical productions. Drawing upon operatic and popular traditions as well as European, African, Asian, and South American forms, new work, and new voices take center stage." Play producer. Produces 4-5 musicals/year. "Our average audience member is in their mid-40s. We perform to ethnically diverse houses."

HOW TO CONTACT Submit 2-page synopsis with tape or CD of 4 songs. Include SASE. "May include complete script, but be aware that response is at least 10 months."

TIPS "Innovative topics and use of media, music, technology a plus. Sees trends of arts in technology (interactive theater, virtual reality, sound design);

works are shorter in length (1 to 1-1/2 hours with no intermissions or 2 hours with intermission)."

THE REPERTORY THEATRE OF ST. LOUIS

130 Edgar Rd., P.O. Box 191730, St. Louis MO 63119. (314)968-7340. **Website:** www.repstl.org. **Contact:** Steven Woolf, artistic director.

HOW TO CONTACT Query with synopsis, character breakdown and set description. Does not return material. Responds in 2 years.

MUSICAL THEATER "We want plays with a small cast and simple setting. No children's shows or foul language. After a letter of inquiry we would prefer script and demo tape."

PRODUCTIONS *Almost September* and *Esmeralda* by David Schechter and Steve Lutvak; *Jack* by Barbara Field and Hiram Titus; and *Young Rube* by John Pielmeier and Nattie Selman, *Ace* by Robert Taylor and Richard Oberacker.

SHAKESPEARE SANTA CRUZ

Theater Arts Center, U.C.S.C., 1156 High Street, Santa Cruz CA 95064. (831)459-2121. **Fax:** (831)459-3316. **E-mail:** mbarrice@ucsc.edu. **Website:** www.shakespearesantacruz.org. **Contact:** Marco Barricelli, artistic director.

HOW TO CONTACT Query first. Include SASE. Responds in 2 months.

MUSICAL THEATER "Shakespeare Santa Cruz produces musicals in its Winter Holiday Season (Oct-Dec). We are also interested in composers' original music for pre-existing plays—including songs, for example, for Shakespeare's plays."

PRODUCTIONS *Cinderella*, by Kate Hawley (book and lyrics) and Gregg Coffin (composer); *Gretel and Hansel* by Kate Hawley (book and lyrics) and composer Craig Bohmler; *The Princess and the Pea* by Kate Hawley (book and lyrics) and composer Adam Wernick; *Sleeping Beauty*, by Kate Hawley (book and lyrics) and composer Adam Wernick.

TIPS "Always contact us before sending material."

THUNDER BAY THEATRE

400 N. Second Ave., Alpena MI 49707. (989)354-2267. **E-mail:** TBT@ThunderBayTheatre.com; ArtisticDirector@ThunderBayTheatre.com. **Website:** www.thunderbaytheatre.com.

HOW TO CONTACT Submit complete ms, score and tape of songs. Include SASE.

MUSICAL THEATER Small cast. Not equipped for large sets. Considers original background music for use in a play being developed or for use in a pre-existing play.

PRODUCTIONS 2009 Musicals *Brigadoon, The Producers, The Rat Pack Lounge, White Christmas, Beauty and the Beast.*

PLAY PUBLISHERS

HEUER PUBLISHING LLC

P.O. Box 248, Cedar Rapids IA 52406. (319)368-8008. **Fax:** (319)368-8011. **E-mail:** editor@hitplays.com. **Website:** www.hitplays.com. Publishes plays, musicals, operas/operettas, and guides (choreography, costume, production/staging) for amateur and professional markets, including junior and senior high schools, college/university and community theatres. Focus includes comedy, drama, fantasy, mystery and holiday. Pays by percentage royalty or outright purchase.

HOW TO CONTACT Query with musical CD/tape or submit complete manuscript and score. Include SASE. Responds in 2 months.

MUSICAL THEATER "We prefer one, two or three act comedies or mystery-comedies with a large number of characters."

PUBLICATIONS *Happily Ever After*, by Allen Koepke (musical fairytale); *Brave Buckaroo*, by Renee J. Clark (musical melodrama); and *Pirate Island*, by Martin Follose (musical comedy).

TIPS "We are willing to review single-song submissions as cornerstone piece for commissioned works. Special interest focus in multicultural, historic, classic literature, teen issues, and biographies."

CLASSICAL PERFORMING ARTS

///

Finding an audience is critical to the composer of orchestral music. Fortunately, baby boomers are swelling the ranks of classical music audiences and bringing with them a taste for fresh, innovative music. So the climate is fair for composers seeking their first performance.

Finding a performance venue is particularly important because once a composer has his work performed for an audience and establishes himself as a talented newcomer, it can lead to more performances and commissions for new works.

BEFORE YOU SUBMIT

Be aware that most classical music organizations are nonprofit groups, and don't have a large budget for acquiring new works. It takes a lot of time and money to put together an orchestral performance of a new composition, therefore these groups are quite selective when choosing new works to perform. Don't be disappointed if the payment offered by these groups is small or even non-existent. What you gain is the chance to have your music performed for an appreciative audience. Also realize that many classical groups are understaffed, so it may take longer than expected to hear back on your submission. It pays to be patient, and employ diplomacy, tact and timing in your follow-up.

In this section you will find listings for classical performing arts organizations throughout the U.S. But if you have no prior performances to your credit, it's a good idea to begin with a small chamber orchestra, for example. Smaller symphony and chamber orchestras are usually more inclined to experiment with new works. A local university or conservatory of music, where you may already have contacts, is a great place to start.

All of the groups listed in this section are interested in hearing new works from contemporary classical composers. Pay close attention to the music needs of each group, and when you find one you feel might be interested in your music, follow submission guidelines carefully. To locate classical performing arts groups in your area, consult the Geographic Index at the back of this book.

ACADIANA SYMPHONY ORCHESTRA

P.O. Box 53632, Lafayette LA 70505. **Website:** www. acadianasymphony.org. 412 Travis St., Lafayette LA 70503. (337)232-4277. **Fax:** (337)237-4712. **Website:** www.acadianasymphony.org. **Contact:** Jenny Krueger, executive director. Estab. 1984. Members are amateurs and professionals. Performs 20 concerts/year, including 1 new work. Commissions 1 new work/year. Performs in 2,230-seat hall with "wonderful acoustics." Pays "according to the type of composition."

HOW TO CONTACT Call first. Does not return material. Responds in 2 months.

MUSIC Full orchestra: 10 minutes at most. Reduced orchestra, educational pieces: short, up to 5 minutes.

PERFORMANCES Quincy Hilliard's *Universal Covenant* (orchestral suite); James Hanna's *In Memoriam* (strings/elegy); and Gregory Danner's *A New Beginning* (full orchestra fanfare).

THE AMERICAN BOYCHOIR

17 Mapleton Rd., Princeton NJ 08540. (609)924-5858. **Fax:** (609)924-5812. **E-mail:** admissions@americanboychoir.org. **Website:** www.americanboychoir.org. General Manager: Christie Starrett. Music director: Fernando Malvar-Ruiz. Professional boychoir. Estab. 1937. Members are musically talented boys in grades 4-8. Performs 150 concerts/year. Commissions 1 new work approximately every 3 years. Actively seeks high quality arrangements. Performs national and international tours, orchestral engagements, church services, workshops, school programs, local concerts, and at corporate and social functions.

HOW TO CONTACT Submit complete score. Include SASE. Responds in 1 year.

MUSIC Choral works in unison, SA, SSA, SSAA or SATB division; unaccompanied and with piano or organ; occasional chamber orchestra or brass ensemble. Works are usually sung by 28-60 boys. Composers must know boychoir sonority.

PERFORMANCES *Four Seasons* by Michael Torke (orchestral-choral); *Garden of Light* by Aaron Kernis (orchestral-choral); *Reasons for Loving the Harmonica* by Libby Larsen (piano); and *Songs Eternity* by Steven Paulus (piano).

ANDERSON SYMPHONY ORCHESTRA

1124 Meridian Plaza, Anderson IN 46016. (765)644-2111. **E-mail:** aso@andersonsymphony.org. **Website:** www.andersonsymphony.org. **Contact:** Dr. Richard Sowers, music director. Symphony orchestra. Estab. 1967. Members are professionals. Performs 7 concerts/year. Performs for typical mid-western audience in a 1,500-seat restored Paramount Theatre. Pay negotiable.

HOW TO CONTACT Query first. Include SASE. Responds in several months.

MUSIC "Shorter lengths better; concerti OK; difficulty level: mod high; limited by typically 3 full service rehearsals."

THE ATLANTA YOUNG SINGERS OF CALLANWOLDE

980 Briarcliff Rd. NE, Atlanta GA 30306 United States. (404)873-3365. **Fax:** (404)873-0756. **E-mail:** info@aysc.org. **Website:** www.aysc.org. **Contact:** Paige F. Mathis, music director. Children's chorus. Estab. 1975. Performs 3 major concerts/year as well as invitational performances and co-productions with other Atlanta arts organizations. Audience consists of community members, families, alumni, and supporters. Performs most often at churches. Pay is negotiable.

HOW TO CONTACT Submit complete score and tape of piece(s). Include SASE. Responds in accordance with request.

MUSIC Subjects and styles appealing to 3rd- to 12th-grade boys and girls. Contemporary concerns of the world of interest. Unusual sacred, folk, classic style. Internationally and ethnically bonding. Medium difficulty preferred, with or without keyboard accompaniment.

TIPS "Our mission is to promote service and growth through singing."

AUGSBURG CHOIR

Augsburg Colleg, 2211 Riverside Ave. S, Minneapolis MN 55454 United States. (612)330-1265. **E-mail:** brauer@augsburg.edu. **Website:** www.augsburg.edu. **Contact:** Tina Brauer, coordinator. Director of Choral Activities: Peter A. Hendrickson. Vocal ensemble (SATB choir). Members are amateurs. Performs 25 concerts/year, including 1-6 new works. Commissions 0-2 composers or new works/year. Audience is all ages, "sophisticated and unsophisticated." Concerts are performed in churches, concert halls and schools. Pays for outright purchase.

HOW TO CONTACT Query first. Include SASE. Responds in 1 month.

MUSIC Seeking "sacred choral pieces, no more than 5-7 minutes long, to be sung a cappella or with obbligato instrument. Can contain vocal solos. We have 50-60 members in our choir."

PERFORMANCES Carol Barnett's *Spiritual Journey*; Steven Heitzeg's *Litanies for the Living* (choral/orchestral); and Morton Lanriclsen's *O Magnum Mysteries* (a cappella choral).

BILLINGS SYMPHONY

2721 Second Ave. N, Suite 350, Billings MT 59101 United States. (406)252-3610. **Fax:** (406)252-3353. **E-mail:** symphony@billingssymphony.org. **Website:** www.billingssymphony.org. **Contact:** Sandra Culhane, executive director. Symphony orchestra, orchestra and chorale. Estab. 1950. Members are professionals and amateurs. Performs 12-15 concerts/year, including 6-7 new works. Traditional audience. Performs at Alberta Bair Theater (capacity 1,416). Pays by outright purchase (or rental).

HOW TO CONTACT Query first. Include SASE. Responds in 2 weeks.

MUSIC Any style. Traditional notation preferred.

PERFORMANCES 2013 Symphony in the Park includes Billings Community Band and Young Conductors' Contest (led by Maestra Anne Harrigan).

TIPS "Write what you feel (be honest) and sharpen your compositional and craftsmanship skills."

BIRMINGHAM-BLOOMFIELD SYMPHONY ORCHESTRA

P.O. Box 1925, Birmingham MI 48012 United States. (248)352-2276. **E-mail:** bbso@bbso.org. **Website:** www.bbso.org. **Contact:** Charles Greenwell, music director and conductor. Conductor Laureate: Felix Resnick. Executive director: Dana Gill. Symphony orchestra. Estab. 1975. Members are professionals. Performs 5 concerts including 1 new work/year. Commissions 1 composer or new work/year "with grants." Performs for middle- to upper-class audience at Temple Beth El's Sanctuary. Pays per performance "depending upon grant received."

HOW TO CONTACT *Query first.* Does not return material. Responds in 6 months.

MUSIC "We are a symphony orchestra but also play pops. Usually 3 works on program (2 hours) Orchestra size 65-75. If pianist is involved, they must rent piano."

PERFORMANCES Brian Belanger's *Tuskegee Airmen Suite* (symphonic full orchestra); Larry Nazer & Friend's *Music from "Warm" CD* (jazz with full orchestra); and Mark Gottlieb's *Violin Concerto for Orchestra*.

THE BOSTON PHILHARMONIC

295 Huntington Ave., Suite 210, Boston MA 02115 United States. (617)236-0999. **E-mail:** info@bostonphil.org. **Website:** www.bostonphil.org. Music Director: Benjamin Zander. Symphony orchestra. Estab. 1979. Members are professionals, amateurs and students. Performs 2 concerts/year. Audience is ages 30-70. Performs at New England Conservatory's Jordan Hall, Boston's Symphony Hall and Sanders Theatre in Cambridge. Both Jordan Hall and Sanders Theatre are small (approximately 1,100 seats) and very intimate.

HOW TO CONTACT *Does not accept new music at this time.*

MUSIC Full orchestra only.

PERFORMANCES Dutilleuxs' *Tout un monde lointain* for cello and orchestra (symphonic); Bernstein's *Fancy Free* (symphonic/jazzy); Copland's *El Salon Mexico* (symphonic); Gershwin's *Rhapsody in Blue*; Shostakovitch's *Symphony No. 10*; Harbison's *Concerto for Oboe*; Holst's *The Planet Suite*; Schwantner's *New Morning for the World*; Berg's *Seven Early Songs*; and Ives' *The Unanswered Question*.

BRAVO! L.A.

CA United States. (818)892-8737. **Fax:** (818)892-1227. **E-mail:** info@bravo-la.com. **Website:** www.bravo-la.com. **Contact:** Cellist Dr. Janice Foy, director. An umbrella organization of recording/touring musicians, formed in 1994. Includes the following musical ensembles: the New American Quartet (string quartet); The Ascending Wave (harp/cello duo); Celllissimo! L.A. (cello ensemble); and Jazz Kats (trio band).

HOW TO CONTACT Submit scores/tape of pieces. Include SASE. Responds in a few months. "We also record DEMOS for those needing entry into various situations and we use a DEMO rate through the Musicians Union Local 47 as our contract for that. If you want to do a Limited Pressing recording, that also goes through the Union with an appropriate contract."

MUSIC "We do all styles from classical to jazz. You can hear examples of most of the above ensembles on the site. You may also read about the latest musical antics of these musicians at the site."

TIPS "Let Bravo! L.A. know about your latest or upcoming performances and if you have a tape/CD of it, please forward or send an audio clip! If you have trouble getting through the spam blocker, let me know!

We do not provide funding but there are many different grants out there for different situations. Good luck!"

♻ CALGARY BOYS CHOIR

4825 Mt. Royal Gate SW, Calgary AB T3E 6K6 Canada. (403)440-6821. **Fax:** (403)440-6594. **E-mail:** cbc.coordinator@gmail.com. **Website:** http://levendis99.wix.com/calgaryboyschoir. **Contact:** Paul Grindlay, artistic director. Boys choir. Estab. 1973. Members are amateurs age 5 and up. Performs 5-10 concerts/year including 1-2 new works. Pay negotiable.

HOW TO CONTACT Query first. Submit complete score and tape of piece(s). Include SASE. Responds in 6 weeks. Does not return material.

MUSIC "Style fitting for boys choir. Lengths depending on project. Orchestration preferable a cappella/for piano/sometimes orchestra."

♻ CANADIAN OPERA COMPANY

227 Front St. E., Toronto ON M5A 1E8 Canada. (416)363-6671. **Fax:** (416)363-5584. **E-mail:** info@coc.ca; music@coc.ca. **Website:** www.coc.ca. **Contact:** Alexander Neef, general director. Opera company. Estab. 1950. Members are professionals. 68-72 performances, including a minimum of 1 new work/year. Pays by contract.

HOW TO CONTACT Submit complete CDs or DVDs of vocal and/or operatic works. "Vocal works please." Include SASE. Responds in 5 weeks.

MUSIC Vocal works, operatic in nature. "Do not submit works which are not for voice. Ask for requirements for the Composers-In-Residence program."

PERFORMANCES Dean Burry's *Brothers Grimm* (children's opera, 50 minutes long); Dean Burry's *Isis and the Seven Scorpions* (45-minute opera for children); James Rolfe's *Swoon*: James Rolfe's *Donna* (work title for forthcoming work); *Nixon in China* by John Adams; *L'Amour Do Loin* by Saariaho.

TIPS "We have a Composers-In-Residence program which is open to Canadian composers or landed immigrants."

CANTATA ACADEMY

P.O. Box 1958, Royal Oak MI 48084 United States. (313)248-7282. **E-mail:** cantata@cantataacademy.org. **Website:** http://cantataacademy.org. **Contact:** Ashley M. Prescott, business manager; Susan Catanese, director. Vocal ensemble. Estab. 1961. Members are professionals. Performs 10-12 concerts/year including 1-3 new works. "We perform in churches and small

auditoriums throughout the Metro Detroit area for audiences of about 500 people." Pays variable rate for outright purchase.

HOW TO CONTACT Submit complete score. Include SASE. Responds in 3 months.

MUSIC Four-part a cappella and keyboard accompanied works, two- and three-part works for men's or women's voices. Some small instrumental ensemble accompaniments acceptable. Work must be suitable for 40 voice choir. No works requiring orchestra or large ensemble accompaniment. No pop.

PERFORMANCES Libby Larsen's *Missa Gaia: Mass for the Earth* (SATB, string quartet, oboe, percussion, 4-hand piano); Dede Duson's *To Those Who See* (SATB, SSA); and Sarah Hopkins' *Past Life Melodies* (SATB with Harmonic Overtone Singing); Eric Whiteacre's *Five Hebrew Love Songs*; and Robert Convery's *Songs of the Children*.

TIPS "Be patient. Would prefer to look at several different samples of work at one time."

CARMEL SYMPHONY ORCHESTRA

P.O. Box 761, Carmel IN 46082 United States. (317)844-9717. **Fax:** (317)844-9916. **E-mail:** info@carmelsymphony.org. **Website:** www.carmelsymphony.org. **Contact:** Alan Davis, president/CEO. Symphony orchestra. Estab. 1976. Members are paid and non-paid professionals. Performs 15 concerts/year, including 1-2 new works. Performs in a 1,600-seat Palladium at the Center for the Performing Arts.

HOW TO CONTACT *Query first.* Include SASE. Responds in 3 months.

MUSIC "Full orchestra works, 5-60 minutes in length. Parents are encouraged to bring a child. 85-piece orchestra, medium difficult to difficult.

PERFORMANCES Brahms' *Concerto in D Major for Violin and Orchestra*, Op. 77; Debussy's *La Mer*; Ravel's Second Suite from *Daphnis and Chloe*; Dvorak's *Carnival Overture*, Op. 92; and Sibelius' *Symphony No. 5 in E-flat Major*, Op. 82. Outstanding guest artists include Michael Feinstein, Sylvia McNair, Cameron Carpenter, Dale Clevenger, and Angela Brown.

CHATTANOOGA GIRLS CHOIR

1831 Hickory Valley Rd., Suite 400, Chattanooga TN 37421 United States. (423)296-1006. **E-mail:** office@chattanoogagirlschoir.com. **Website:** http://chattanoogagirlschoir.com. **Contact:** Emily McKay, interim executive director. Vocal ensemble. Estab. 1986. Members are amateurs. Performs 2 concerts/year including at least 1 new work. Audience consists of cultural and civic organizations and national and international tours. Performance space includes concert halls and churches. Pays for outright purchase or per performance.

HOW TO CONTACT Query first. Include SASE. Responds in 6 weeks.

MUSIC Seeks renaissance, baroque, classical, romantic, twentieth century, folk and musical theatre for young voices of up to 8 minutes. Performers include 5 treble choices: 4th grade (2 pts.); 5th grade (2 pts.) (SA); grades 6-9 (3 pts.) (SSA); grades 10-12 (3-4 pts.) (SSAA); and a combined choir: grades 6-12 (3-4 pts.) (SSAA). Medium level of difficulty. "Avoid extremely high Tessitura Sop I and extremely low Tessitura Alto II."

PERFORMANCES Jan Swafford's *Iphigenia Book: Meagher* (choral drama); Penny Tullock's *How Can I Keep from Singing* (Shaker hymn).

CHEYENNE SYMPHONY ORCHESTRA

1904 Thomes Ave., Cheyenne WY 82001 United States. (307)778-8561. **E-mail:** executivedirector@cheyennesymphony.org. **Website:** www.cheyennesymphony.org. **Contact:** Kim E. Lovett, executive director. Symphony orchestra. Estab. 1955. Members are professionals. Performs 5-6 concerts/year. "Orchestra performs for a conservative, mid-to-upper income audience of 1,200 season members."

HOW TO CONTACT Query first to music director William Intriligator. Does not return material.

CIMARRON CIRCUIT OPERA COMPANY

P.O. Box 1085, Norman OK 73070 United States. (405)364-8962. **Fax:** (405)321-5842. **E-mail:** info@cimarronopera.org. **Website:** www.ccocopera.org. **Contact:** Kevin W. Smith, music director. Opera company. Estab. 1975. Members are semi-professional. Performs 75 concerts/year including 1-2 new works. Commissions 1 or less new work/year. "CCOC performs for children across the state of Oklahoma and for a dedicated audience in central Oklahoma. As a touring company, we adapt to the performance space provided, ranging from a classroom to a full raised stage." Pay is negotiable.

HOW TO CONTACT Query first. Does not return material. Responds in 6 months.

MUSIC "We are seeking operas or operettas in English only. We would like to begin including new, American works in our repertoire. Children's operas should be no longer than 45 minutes and require no more than a synthesizer for accompaniment. Adult operas should be appropriate for families, and may require either full orchestration or synthesizer. CCOC is a professional company whose members have varying degrees of experience, so any difficulty level is appropriate. There should be a small to moderate number of principles. Children's work should have no more than four principles. Our slogan is 'Opera is a family thing to do.' If we cannot market a work to families, we do not want to see it."

PERFORMANCES Menotti's *Amahl & the Night Visitors*; and Barab's *La Pizza Con Funghi*.

TIPS "45-minute fairy tale-type children's operas with possibly a 'moral' work well for our market. Looking for works appealing to K-8 grade students. No more than four principles."

CONNECTICUT CHORAL ARTISTS/CONCORA

City Arts on Pearl, 233 Pearl St., Hartford CT 06103. (860)293-0567. **Fax:** (860)244-0073. **Email:** contact@concora.org. **Website:** www.concora.org. **Contact:** Ann Drinan, executive director. Estab. 1974. Professional concert choir. Members are professionals. Performs 5 concerts per year, including 3-5 new works.

HOW TO CONTACT Query first. "No unsolicited submissions accepted." Include SASE. Responds in 1 year.

MUSIC Seeking "works for mixed chorus of 36 singers; unaccompanied or with keyboard and/or small instrumental ensemble; text sacred or secular/any language; prefers suites or cyclical works, total time not exceeding 15 minutes. Performance spaces and budgets prohibit large instrumental ensembles. Works suited for 750-seat halls are preferable. Substantial organ or piano parts acceptable. Scores should be very legible in every way."

PERFORMANCES Don McCullough's *Holocaust Contata* (choral with narration); Robert Cohen's *Sprig of Lilac: Peter Quince at the Clavier* (choral); Greg Bartholomew's *The 21st Century: A Girl Born in Afghanistan* (choral).

TIPS "Use conventional notation and be sure ms is legible in every way. Recognize and respect the vocal range of each vocal part. Work should have an identifiable rhythmic structure."

🌐 EUROPEAN UNION CHAMBER ORCHESTRA

Hollick, Yarnscombe, Devon EX31 3LQ, United Kingdom. (44)1271 858249. **Fax:** (44)1271 858375. **E-mail:** eucorchl@aol.com. **Website:** www.etd.gb.com. **Contact:** Ambrose Miller, general director. Chamber orchestra. Members are professionals. Performs 70 concerts/year, including 6 new works. Commissions 2 composers or new works/year. Performs regular tours of Europe, Americas and Asia, including major venues. Pays per performance or for outright purchase, depending on work.

HOW TO CONTACT Query first. Does not return material. Responds in 6 weeks.

MUSIC Seeking compositions for strings, 2 oboes and 2 horns with a duration of about 8 minutes.

PERFORMANCES Peeter Vahi "Prayer Wheel"; James MacMillan "Kiss on Wood".

TIPS "Keep the work to less than 15 minutes in duration, it should be sufficiently 'modern' to be interesting but not too difficult as this could take up rehearsal time. It should be possible to perform without a conductor."

FONTANA CONCERT SOCIETY

359 S. Kalamazoo Mall, Suite 200, Kalamazoo MI 49007 United States. (269)382-7774. **Fax:** (269)382-0812. **Website:** www.fontanachamberarts.org. Chamber music ensemble presenter. Estab. 1980. Members are professionals. Fontana Chamber Arts presents over 45 events, including the 6-week Summer Festival of Music and Art, which runs from mid-July to the end of August. Regional and guest artists perform classical, contemporary, jazz and nontraditional music. Commissions and performs new works each year. Fontana Chamber Arts presents 7 classical and 2 jazz concerts during the Fall/Winter season. Audience consists of well-educated individuals who accept challenging new works, but like the traditional as well. Summer—180 seat hall; fall/winter—various venues, 400-1,500 seats.

HOW TO CONTACT Submit complete score, résumé and tapes of piece(s). Include SASE. Responds in approximately 1 month. Music Chamber music—any combination of strings, winds, piano. No "pop" music,

new age type. Special interest in composers attending premiere and speaking to the audience.

TIPS "Provide a résumé and clearly marked tape of a piece played by live performers."

FORT WORTH CHILDREN'S OPERA

1300 Gendy St., Ft. Worth TX 76107 United States. (817)731-0833, ext. 19. **Fax:** (817)731-0835. **E-mail:** info@fwopera.org. **Website:** www.fwopera.org. **Contact:** Hannah Guinn. Opera company. Estab. 1946. Members are professionals. Performs over 180 in-school performances/year." Audience consists of elementary school children; performs in major venues for district-wide groups and individual school auditoriums, cafetoriums and gymnasiums. Pays $40/performance.

HOW TO CONTACT Submit complete score and tape of piece(s). Include SASE. Responds in 6 months.

MUSIC "Familiar fairy tales or stories adapted to music of opera composers, or newly-composed music of suitable quality. Ideal length: 40-45 minutes. Piano or keyboard accompaniment. Should include moral, safety, or school issues. Can be ethnic in subject matter and must speak to pre-K and grade 1-6 children. Prefer pieces with good, memorable melodies. Performed by young, trained professionals on 9-month contract. Requires work for 4 performers, doubled roles OK, SATB plus accompanist/narrator. Special interest in biligual (Spanish/English) works."

GREATER GRAND FORKS SYMPHONY ORCHESTRA

3350 Campus Rd., Mail Stop 7084, Grand Forks ND 58202 United States. (701)732-0579 or (701)777-3359. **E-mail:** symphony@ggfso.org. **Website:** www.ggfso.org. **Contact:** Alexander Platt, music director. Symphony orchestra. Estab. 1908. Members are professionals and/or amateurs. Performs 6 concerts/year. "New works are presented in 2-4 of our programs." Audience is "a mix of ages and musical experience. In 1997-98 we moved into a renovated, 420-seat theater." Pay is negotiable, depending on licensing agreements.

HOW TO CONTACT Submit complete score or complete score and tape of pieces. Include SASE. Responds in 6 months.

MUSIC "Style is open, instrumentation the limiting factor. Music can be scored for an ensemble up to but not exceeding: 3,2,3,2/4,3,3,1/3 perc./strings. Rehearsal time limited to 3 hours for new works."

PERFORMANCES Michael Harwood's *Amusement Park Suite* (orchestra); Randall Davidson's *Mexico Bolivar Tango* (chamber orchestra); and John Corigliano's *Voyage* (flute and orchestra); Linda Tutas Haugen's *Fable of Old Turtle* (saxophone concerto); Michael Wittgraf's *Landmarks*; Joan Tower's *Made in America*.

HEARTLAND MEN'S CHORUS

P.O. Box 32374, Kansas City MO 64171 United States. **Website:** www.hmckc.org. P.O. Box 32374, Kansas City MO 64171-5374. (816)931-3338. **Fax:** (816)531-1367. **E-mail:** hmc@hmckc.org. **Website:** www.hmckc.org. **Contact:** Joseph Nadeau, artistic director. Men's chorus. Estab. 1986. Members are professionals and amateurs. Performs 3 concerts/year; 9-10 are new works. Commissions 1 composer or new works/year. Performs for a diverse audience at the Folly Theater (1,100 seats). Pay is negotiable.
HOW TO CONTACT Query first. Include SASE. Responds in 2 months.
MUSIC "Interested in works for male chorus (ttbb). Must be suitable for performance by a gay male chorus. We will consider any orchestration, or a cappella."
PERFORMANCES Mark Hayes' *Two Flutes Playing* (commissioned song cycle); Alan Shorter's *Country Angel Christmas* (commissioned chidren's musical); Kevin Robinson's *Life is a Cabaret: The Music of Kander and Ebb* (commissioned musical).
TIPS "Find a text that relates to the contemporary gay experience, something that will touch peoples' lives."

HELENA SYMPHONY

48 Hibbard Way, Suite 101, Helena MT 59601 United States. **Website:** www.helenasymphony.org. P.O. Box 1073, Helena MT 59624. (406)442-1860. **E-mail:** llily@helenasymphony.org. **Website:** www.helenasymphony.org. **Contact:** Allan R. Scott, music director and conductor; Leatrice Lily, director of artistic planning. Symphony orchestra. Estab. 1955. Members are professionals and amateurs. Performs 7-10 concerts/year including new works. Performance space is an 1,800 seat concert hall. Payment varies.
HOW TO CONTACT Query first. Include SASE. Responds in 3 months.
MUSIC "Imaginative, collaborative, not too atonal. We want to appeal to an audience of all ages. We don't have a huge string complement. Medium to difficult OK--at frontiers of professional ability we cannot do."

PERFORMANCES Eric Funk's *A Christmas Overture* (orchestra); Donald O. Johnston's *A Christmas Processional* (orchestra/chorale); and Elizabeth Sellers' *Prairie* (orchestra/short ballet piece).
TIPS "Try to balance tension and repose in your works. New instrument combinations are appealing."

HENDERSONVILLE SYMPHONY ORCHESTRA

P.O. Box 1811, Hendersonville NC 28793 United States. (828)697-5884. **Fax:** (828)697-5765. **E-mail:** info@hendersonvillesymphony.org. **Website:** www.hendersonvillesymphony.org. Symphony orchestra. Estab. 1971. Members are professionals and amateurs. Performs 6 concerts/year. "We would welcome a new work per year." Audience is a cross-section of retirees, professionals, and some children. Performance space is a 857-seat high school audiorium.
HOW TO CONTACT Query first. Include SASE. Responds in 1 month.
MUSIC "We use a broad spectrum of music (classical concerts and pops)."
PERFORMANCES Nelson's *Jubilee* (personal expression in a traditional method); Britten's "The Courtly Dances" from *Glorina* (time-tested); and Chip Davis' arrangement for Mannheim Steamroller's *Deck the Halls* (modern adaptation of traditional melody).
TIPS "Submit your work even though we are a community orchestra. We like to be challenged. We have the most heavily patronized fine arts group in the county. Our emphasis is on education."

HERMANN SONS GERMAN BAND

P.O. Box 162, Medina TX 78055 United States. (830)589-2268. **E-mail:** herbert@festmusik.com. **Website:** www.festmusik.com. **Contact:** Herbert Bilhartz, music director. Community band with German instrumentation. Estab. 1990. Members are both professionals and amateurs. Performs 4 concerts/year including 2 new works. Commissions no new composers or new works/year. Performs for "mostly older people who like German polkas, waltzes, and marches. We normally play only published arrangements from Germany."
HOW TO CONTACT Query first; then submit full set of parts and score, condensed or full. Include SASE. Responds in 6 weeks.
MUSIC "We like European-style polkas or waltzes (Viennese or Missouri tempo), either original or arrangements of public domain tunes. Arrangements of

traditional American folk tunes in this genre would be especially welcome. Also, polkas or waltzes featuring one or two solo instruments (from instrumentation below) would be great. OK for solo parts to be technically demanding. Although we have no funds to commission works, we will provide you with a cassette recording of our performance. Also, we would assist composers in submitting works to band music publishers in Germany for possible publication. Polkas and waltzes generally follow this format: Intro; 1st strain repeated; 2nd strain repeated; DS to 1 strain; Trio: Intro; 32 bar strain; 'break-up' strain; Trio DS. Much like military march form. Instrumentation: Fl/Picc, 3 clars in Bb, 2 Fluegelhorns in Bb; 3 Tpts in Bb, 2 or 4 Hns in F or Eb, 2 Baritones (melody/countermelody parts; 1 in Bb TC, 1 in BC), 2 Baritones in Bb TC (rhythm parts), 3 Trombones, 2 Tubas (in octaves, mostly), Drum set, Timpani optional. We don't use saxes, but a German publisher would want 4-5 sax parts. Parts should be medium to medium difficult. All brass parts should be considered one player to the part; woodwinds, two to the part. No concert type pieces; no modern popular or rock styles. However, a 'theme and variations' form with contrasting jazz, rock, country, modern variations would be clever, and our fans might go for such a piece (as might a German publisher)."

PERFORMANCES New music performed in 2005: Stefan Rundel's *Mein Gluecksstern ("My Lucky Star")*.
TIPS "German town bands love to play American tunes. There are many thousands of these bands over there and competition among band music publishers in Germany is keen. Few Americans are aware of this potential market, so few American arrangers get published over there. Simple harmony is best for this style, but good counterpoint helps a lot. Make use of the dark quality of the Fluegelhorns and the bright, fanfare quality of the trumpets. Give the 2 baritones (1 in TC and 1 in BC) plenty of exposed melodic material. Keep them in harmony with each other (3rds and 6ths), unlike American band arrangements, which have only 1 Baritone line. If you want to write a piece in this style, give me a call, and I will send you some sample scores to give you a better idea."

HERSHEY SYMPHONY ORCHESTRA

P.O. Box 93, Hershey PA 17033 United States. (717)533-8449. **Website:** www.hersheysymphony. org. **E-mail:** hsogm@itech.net. **Contact:** Dr. Sandra

Dackow, music director. Symphony orchestra. Estab. 1969. Members are professionals and amateurs. Performs 8 concerts/year, including 1-3 new works. Commissions "possibly 1-2" composers or new works/year. Audience is family and friends of community theater. Performance space is a 1,900 seat grand old movie theater. Pays commission fee.

HOW TO CONTACT Submit complete score and tape of piece(s). Include SASE. Responds in 3 months.
MUSIC "Symphonic works of various lengths and types which can be performed by a non-professional orchestra. We are flexible but like to involve all our players."
PERFORMANCES Paul W. Whear's *Celtic Christmas Carol* (orchestra/bell choir) and Linda Robbins Coleman's *In Good King Charlie's Golden Days* (overture).
TIPS "Please lay out rehearsal numbers/letter and rests according to phrases and other logical musical divisions rather than in groups of ten measures, etc., which is very unmusical and wastes time and causes a surprising number of problems. Also, please do not send a score written in concert pitch; use the usual transpositions so that the conductor sees what the players see; rehearsal is much more effective this way. Cross cue all important solos; this helps in rehearsal where instruments may be missing."

HUDSON VALLEY PHILHARMONIC

35 Market St., Poughkeepise NY 12601 United States. (845)473-5288. **Fax:** (845)473-4259. **Website:** www. bardavon.org. **Contact:** AnnMarie Faust, managing director of development. Symphony orchestra. Estab. 1969. Members are professionals. Performs 20 concerts/year including 1 new work. "Classical subscription concerts for all ages; Pops concerts for all ages; New Wave concerts—crossover projects with a rock 'n' roll artist performing with an orchestra. HVP performs in 3 main theatres which are concert auditoriums with stages and professional lighting and sound." Pay is negotiable.

HOW TO CONTACT Query first. Include SASE. Responds only if interested.
MUSIC "HVP is open to serious classical music, pop music, and rock 'n' roll crossover projects. Desired length of work: 10-20 minutes. Orchestrations can be varied but should always include strings. There is no limit to difficulty since our musicians are professional. The ideal number of musicians to write for would in-

clude up to a Brahms-size orchestra 2222, 4231, T, 2P, piano, harp, strings."

PERFORMANCES Joan Tower's *Island Rhythms* (serious classical work); Bill Vanaver's *P'nai El* (symphony work with dance); and Joseph Bertolozzi's *Serenade* (light classical, pop work).

TIPS "Don't get locked into doing very traditional orchestrations or styles. Our music director is interested in fresh, creative formats. He is an orchestrator as well and can offer good advice on what works well. Songwriters who are into crossover projects should definitely submit works. Over the past four years, HVP has done concerts featuring the works of Natalie Merchant, John Cale, Sterling Morrison, Richie Havens, and R. Carlos Naka (Native American flute player), all reorchestrated by our music director for small orchestra with the artist."

INDIANA UNIVERSITY NEW MUSIC ENSEMBLE

Indiana University Bloomington, School of Music, Bloomington IN 47405 United States. **E-mail:** ddzubay@indiana.edu. **Website:** www.indiana.edu/~nme. **Contact:** David Dzubay, director. Performs solo, chamber and large ensemble works. Estab.1974. Members are students. Presents 4 concerts/year.

PERFORMANCES Peter Lieberson's *Free and Easy Wanderer*; Sven-David Sandstrom's *Wind Pieces*; Atar Arad's *Sonata*; and David Dzubay's *Dancesing in a Green Bay*.

KENTUCKY OPERA

323 W. Broadway, Suite 601, Louisville KY 40202 United States. (502)584-4500. **Fax:** (502)584-7484. **E-mail:** alise_oliver@kyopera.org. **Website:** www.kyopera.org. **Contact:** Alise Oliver, artistic administration. Opera. Estab. 1952. Members are professionals. Performs 3 main stage/year. Performs at Brown Theatre, 1,400. Pays by royalty, outright purchase or per performance.

HOW TO CONTACT *Write or call first before submitting. No unsolicited submissions.* Submit complete score. Include SASE. Responds in 6 months.

MUSIC Seeks opera—1 to 3 acts with orchestrations. No limitations.

PERFORMANCES *Cavalleria Rusticana, The Elixir of Love, Madame Butterfly.*

LAMARCA AMERICAN VARIETY SINGERS

2655 W. 230th Place, Torrance CA 90505 United States. 2655 W. 230th Place, Torrance CA 90505. (310)325-8708. **Contact:** Priscilla LaMarca-Kandel,

director. Composer of children's songs for home and school use, educational and entertaining. Also, vocal, ear training, and sight-singing exercises to help other songwriters improve their singing demo techniques.

HOW TO CONTACT Query first. Include SASE. Responds in 2 weeks.

MUSIC "Seeks 3-10 or 15-minute medleys; a variety of musical styles from Broadway--pop styles to humorous specialty songs. Top 40 dance music, light rock, and patriotic themes. No rap or anything not suitable for family audiences."

PERFORMANCES *Disney Movie Music* (uplifting); *Children's Music* (educational/positive); and *Beatles Medley* (love songs).

LEXINGTON PHILHARMONIC SOCIETY

161 N. Mill St., Lexington KY 40507 United States. (859)233-4226. **E-mail:** sterrell@lexphil.org. **Website:** www.lexphil.org. **Contact:** Scott Terrell, music director. Symphony orchestra. Estab. 1961. Members are professionals. Series includes "8 serious, classical subscription concerts (hall seats 1,500); 3 concerts called Pops the Series; 3 Family Concerts; 10 outdoor pops concerts (from 1,500 to 5,000 tickets sold); 5-10 runout concerts (1/2 serious/1/2 pops); and 10 children's concerts." Pays via ASCAP and BMI, rental purchase and private arrangements.

HOW TO CONTACT Submit complete score and tape of piece(s). Include SASE.

MUSIC Seeking "good current pops material and good serious classical works. No specific restrictions, but overly large orchestra requirements, unusual instruments and extra rentals help limit our interest."

PERFORMANCES "Visit our website for complete concert season listing."

TIPS "When working on large-format arrangement, use cross-cues so orchestra can be cut back if required. Submit good quality copy, scores and parts. Tape is helpful."

LIMA SYMPHONY ORCHESTRA

133 N. Elizabeth St., Lima OH 45801 United States. (419)222-5701. **Fax:** (419)222-6587. **Website:** www.limasymphony.com. **Contact:** Crafton Beck, music conductor. Symphony orchestra. Estab. 1953. Members are professionals. Performs 17-18 concerts including at least 1 new work/year. Commissions at least 1 composer or new work/year. Middle to older audience; also Young People's Series. Mixture for stage and summer productions. Performs in Veter-

ans' Memorial Civic & Convention Center, a beautiful hall seating 1,670; various temporary shells for summer outdoors events; churches; museums and libraries. Pays $2,500 for outright purchase (Anniversary commission) or grants $1,500-5,000.

HOW TO CONTACT Submit complete score if not performed; otherwise submit complete score and tape of piece(s). Include SASE. Responds in 3 months.

MUSIC "Good balance of incisive rhythm, lyricism, dynamic contrast and pacing. Chamber orchestra to full (85-member) symphony orchestra." Does not wish to see "excessive odd meter changes."

PERFORMANCES Frank Proto's *American Overture* (some original music and fantasy); Werner Tharichen's *Concerto for Timpani and Orchestra*; and James Oliverio's *Pilgrimage--Concerto for Brass* (interesting, dynamic writing for brass and the orchestra).

TIPS "Know your instruments, be willing to experiment with unconventional textures, be available for in depth analysis with conductor, be at more than 1 rehearsal. Be sure that individual parts are correctly matching the score and done in good, neat calligraphy."

LYRIC OPERA OF CHICAGO

20 N. Wacker Dr., Chicago IL 60606 United States. (312)332-2244. **Fax:** (312)419-8345. **Website:** www. lyricopera.org. **Email:** orchaud@lyricopera.org. Opera company. Estab. 1953. Members are professionals. Performs 80 operas/year including 1 new work in some years. Commissions 1 new work every 4 or 5 years. "Performances are held in a 3,563 seat house for a sophisticated opera audience, predominantly 30+ years old." Payment varies.

HOW TO CONTACT Query first. Does not return material. Responds in 6 months.

MUSIC "Full-length opera suitable for a large house with full orchestra. No musical comedy or Broadway musical style. We rarely perform one-act operas. We are only interested in works by composers and librettists with extensive theatrical experience. We have few openings for new works, so candidates must be of the highest quality. Do not send score or other materials without a prior contact."

PERFORMANCES William Bolcom's *View from the Bridge*; John Corigliano's *Ghosts of Versailles*; and Leonard Bernstein's *Candide*.

TIPS "Have extensive credentials and an international reputation."

MILWAUKEE YOUTH SYMPHONY ORCHESTRA

325 W. Walnut St., Milwaukee WI 53212 United States. (414)267-2950. **Fax:** (414)267-2960. **E-mail:** general@ myso.org. **Website:** www.myso.org. **Contact:** Linda Edelstein, executive director. Multiple youth orchestras and other instrumental ensembles. Estab. 1956. Members are students. Performs 12-15 concerts/year including 1-2 new works. "Our groups perform in Uihlein Hall at the Marcus Center for the Performing Arts in Milwaukee plus area sites. The audiences usually consist of parents, music teachers and other interested community members, with periodic reviews in the *Milwaukee Journal Sentinel*." Payment varies.

HOW TO CONTACT Query first. Include SASE. Does not return material. Responds in 1 month.

PERFORMANCES James Woodward's *Tuba Concerto*.

TIPS "Be sure you realize you are working with *students* (albeit many of the best in southeastern Wisconsin) and not professional musicians. The music needs to be on a technical level students can handle. Our students are 8-18 years of age, in 2 full symphony orchestras, a wind ensemble and 2 string orchestras, plus two flute choirs, advanced chamber orchestra and 15-20 small chamber ensembles."

MOORES OPERA CENTER

Moores School of Music, University of Houston, 120 School of Music Building, Houston TX 77204 United States. (713)743-3009. **Fax:** (713)743-3166. **E-mail:** bross@uh.edu. **Website:** www.uh.edu/music/Mooresopera. Director of Opera: Buck Ross. Opera/music theater program. Members are professionals, amateurs, and students. Performs 12-14 concerts/year including 1 new work. Performs in a proscenium theater which seats 800. Pit seats approximately up to 75 players. Audience covers wide spectrum, from first time opera-goers to very sophisticated. Pays per performance.

HOW TO CONTACT Submit complete score and tapes of piece(s). Include SASE. Responds in 6 months.

MUSIC "We seek music that is feasible for high graduate level student singers. Chamber orchestras are very useful. No more than 2 1/2 hours. No children's operas."

PERFORMANCES *The Grapes of Wrath*, *Florencia en el Amazonas*, *Elmer Gantry*, *A Wedding*.

OPERA MEMPHIS

6745 Wolf River Pkwy., Memphis TN 38120 United States. (901)257-3100. **Fax:** (901)257-3109. **E-mail:** info@operamemphis.org. **Website:** www.operamemphis.org. **Contact:** Ned Canty, director of artistic administration. Opera company. Estab. 1955. Members are professionals. Performs 8-12 concerts/year including new works. Occasionally commissions composers. Audience consists of older, wealthier patrons, along with many students and young professionals. Pay is negotiable.

HOW TO CONTACT Query first. Include SASE. Responds in 1 year or less.

MUSIC "Accessible practical pieces for educational or second stage programs. Educational pieces should not exceed 90 minutes or 4-6 performers. We encourage songwriters to contact us with proposals or work samples for theatrical works. We are very interested in crossover work."

PERFORMANCES Mike Reid's *Different Fields* (one act opera); David Olney's *Light in August* (folk opera); and Sid Selvidge's *Riversongs* (one act blues opera).

TIPS "Spend many hours thinking about the synopsis (plot outline)."

ORCHESTRA SEATTLE/SEATTLE CHAMBER SINGERS

P.O. Box 15825, Seattle WA 98115 United States. (206)682-5208. **E-mail:** osscs@osscs.org. **Website:** www.osscs.org. **Contact:** Rob Harahill, managing director. Symphony orchestra, chamber music ensemble, and community chorus. Estab. 1969. Members are amateurs and professionals. Performs 8 concerts/year including 2-3 new works. Commissions 1-2 composers or new works/year. "Our audience is made up of both experienced and novice classical music patrons. The median age is 45 with an equal number of males and females in the upper income range. Most concerts now held in Benaroya Hall."

HOW TO CONTACT Query first. Include SASE. Responds in 1 year.

PERFORMANCES Beyer's *The Turns of a Girl*; Bernstein's Choruses from *The Lark*; Edstrom's *Concerto for Jazz Piano and Orchestra*.

PALMETTO MASTERSINGERS

P.O. Box 7441, Columbia SC 29202 United States. (803)765-0777. **E-mail:** info@palmettomastersing-ers.org. **Website:** www.palmettomastersingers.org. **Contact:** Walter Cuttino, music director. 80 voice male chorus. Estab. 1981 by the late Dr. Arpad Darasz. Members are professionals and amateurs. Performs 8-10 concerts/year. Commissions 1 composer of new works every other year (on average). Audience is generally older adults, "but it's a wide mix." Performance space for the season series is the Koger Center (approximately 2,000 seats) in Columbia, SC. More intimate venues also available. Fee is negotiable for outright purchase.

HOW TO CONTACT Query first. Include SASE. Or e-mail.

MUSIC Seeking music of 10-15 minutes in length, "not too far out tonally. Orchestration is negotiable, but chamber size (10-15 players) is normal. We rehearse once a week and probably will not have more than 8-10 rehearsals. These rehearsals (2 hours each) are spent learning a 1-1/2-hour program. Only 1-2 rehearsals (max) are with the orchestra. Piano accompaniments need not be simplified, as our accompanist is exceptional."

PERFORMANCES Randal Alan Bass' *Te Deum* (12-minutes, brass and percussion); Dick Goodwin's *Mark Twain Remarks* (40 minutes, full symphony); and Randol Alan Bass' *A Simple Prayer* (a capella 6 minutes).

TIPS "Contact us as early as possible, given that programs are planned by July. Although this is an amateur chorus, we have performed concert tours of Europe, performed at Carnegie Hall, The National Cathedral and the White House in Washington, DC. We are skilled amateurs."

PICCOLO OPERA COMPANY INC.

24 Del Rio Blvd., Boca Raton FL 33432-4734 United States. (800)282-3161. **Fax:** (561)394-0520. **E-mail:** leejon51@msn.com. **Contact:** Marjorie Gordon, executive director. Traveling opera company. Estab. 1962. Members are professionals. Performs 1-50 concerts/year including 1-2 new works. Commissions 0-1 composer or new work/year. Operas are performed for a mixed audience of children and adults. Pays by performance or outright purchase. Operas in English.

HOW TO CONTACT *Query first.* Include SASE.

MUSIC "Productions for either children or adults. Musical theater pieces, lasting about one hour, for adults to perform for adults and/or youngsters. Performers are mature singers with experience. The cast should have few performers (up to 10), no chorus or ballet, accompanied by piano or local orchestra. Skeletal scenery. All in English."

PERFORMANCES Menotti's *The Telephone*; Mozart's *Cosi Fan Tutte*; and Puccini's *La Boheme* (repertoire of more than 22 productions).

PRINCETON SYMPHONY ORCHESTRA

P.O. Box 250, Princeton NJ 08542 United States. (609)497-0020. **Fax:** (609)497-0904. **E-mail:** info@ princetonsymphony.org. **Website:** www.princetonsymphony.org. **Contact:** Rossen Milanov, music director. Symphony orchestra. Estab. 1980. Members are professionals. Performs 6-10 concerts/year including some new works. Commissions 1 composer or new work/year. Performs in a "beautiful, intimate 800-seat hall with amazing sound." Pays by arrangement.

MUSIC "Orchestra usually numbers 40-60 individuals."

PRISM SAXOPHONE QUARTET

30 Seaman Ave., #4M, New York NY 10034; or, 257 Harvey St., Philadelphia PA 19144. (215)438-5282. **E-mail:** info@prismquartet.com. **Website:** www. prismquartet.com. **Contact:** Matthew Levy. Chamber music ensemble. Estab. 1984. Members are professionals. Performs 80 concerts/year including 10-15 new works. Commissions 4 composers or new works/year. "Ours are primarily traditional chamber music audiences." Pays royalty per performance from BMI or ASCAP or commission range from $100 to $15,000.

HOW TO CONTACT Submit complete score (with parts) and tape of piece(s). Does not return material. Responds in 3 months.

MUSIC "Orchestration—sax quartet, SATB. Lengths—5-25 minutes. Styles—contemporary, classical, jazz, crossover, ethnic, gospel, avant-garde. No limitations on level of difficulty. No more than 4 performers (SATB sax quartet). No transcriptions. The Prism Quartet places special emphasis on crossover works which integrate a variety of musical styles."

PERFORMANCES David Liebman's *The Gray Convoy* (jazz); Bradford Ellis's *Tooka-Ood Zasch* (ethnic-world music); and William Albright's *Fantasy Etudes* (contemporary classical).

SACRAMENTO MASTER SINGERS

P.O. Box 417997, Sacramento CA 95841 United States. (916)788-7464. **E-mail:** smsbusiness@surewest.net. **Website:** www.mastersingers.org. **Contact:**

Dr. Ralph Edward Hughes, conductor/artistic director. Vocal ensemble. Estab. 1984. Members are professionals and amateurs. Performs 9 concerts/year including 5-6 new works. Commissions 2 new works/year. Audience is made up of mainly college age and older patrons. Performs mostly in churches with 500-900 seating capacity. Pays $200 for outright purchase.

HOW TO CONTACT Submit complete score and tape of piece(s). Include SASE. Responds in 5 weeks.

MUSIC "A cappella works; works with small orchestras or few instruments; works based on classical styles with a 'modern' twist; multi-cultural music; shorter works probably preferable, but this is not a requirement. We usually have 38-45 singers capable of a high level of difficulty, but find that often simple works are very pleasing."

PERFORMANCES Joe Jennings' *An Old Black Woman, Homeless and Indistinct* (SATB, oboe, strings, dramatic).

TIPS "Keep in mind we are a chamber ensemble, not a 100-voice choir."

⊙ SAN FRANCISCO GIRLS CHORUS

44 Page St., Suite 200, San Francisco CA 94102 United States. (415)863-1752. **E-mail:** info@sfgirlschorus.org. **Website:** www.sfgirlschorus.org. **Contact:** Susan McMane, artistic director. Choral ensemble. Estab. 1978. Advanced choral ensemble of young women's voices. Performs 8-10 concerts/year including 3-4 new works. Commissions 2 composers or new works/year. Concerts are performed for "choral/classical music lovers, plus family audiences and audiences interested in international repertoire. Season concerts are performed in a 800-seat church with excellent acoustics and in San Francisco's Davies Symphony Hall, a 2,800-seat state-of-the-art auditorium." Pay negotiable for outright purchase. **Editorial Comment:** The San Francisco Girls Chorus has won 5 Grammy Awards as guest performers on the San Francisco Symphony's recordings.

HOW TO CONTACT Submit complete score and CD recording, if possible. Does not return material. Responds in 6 months.

MUSIC "Music for treble voices (SSAA); a cappella, piano accompaniment, or small orchestration; 3-10 minutes in length. Wide variety of styles; 45 singers; challenging music is encouraged."

PERFORMANCES See website under "Music/Commissions" for a listing of SFGC commissions. Examples: Jake Heggie's *Patterns* (piano, mezzo-soprano soloist, chorus); and Chen Yi's *Chinese Poems* (a cappella).

TIPS "Choose excellent texts and write challenging music. The San Francisco Girls Chorus has pioneered in establishing girls choral music as an art form in the U.S. The Girls Chorus is praised for its 'stunning musical standard' (*San Francisco Chronicle*) in performances in the San Francisco Bay Area and on tour. SFGC's annual concert season showcases the organization's concert/touring ensemble, Chorissima, in performances of choral masterworks from around the world, commissioned works by contemporary composers, and 18th-century music from the Venetian Ospedali and Mexican Baroque which SFGC has brought out of the archives and onto the concert stage. Chorissima tours through California with partial support provided by the California Arts Council Touring Program and have represented the U.S. and the City of San Francisco nationally and abroad. The chorus provides ensemble and solo singers for performances and recordings with the San Francisco Symphony and San Francisco Opera, Women's Philharmonic, and many other music ensembles. The Chorus has produced many solo CD recordings including: *Voices of Hope and Peace,* a recording that includes 'Anne Frank: A Living Voice' by an American composer Linda Tutas Haugen; *Christmas*, featuring diverse holiday selections; *Crossroads*, a collection of world folk music; and *Music from the Venetian Ospedali*, a disc of Italian Baroque music of which the *New Yorker* described the Chorus as 'tremendously accomplished.'"

SINGING BOYS OF PENNSYLVANIA

P.O. Box 206, Wind Gap PA 18091 United States. (610)759-6002. **Fax:** (610)759-6042. **Website:** www.singingboysofpennsylvania.org. **Contact:** K. Bernard Schade, conductor. Vocal ensemble. Estab. 1970. Members are professional children. Performs 100 concerts/year including 3-5 new works. "We attract general audiences: family, senior citizens, churches, concert associations, university concert series, and schools." Pays $300-3,000 for outright purchase.

HOW TO CONTACT *Query first.* Does not return material. Responds in 3 weeks.

MUSIC "We want music for commercials, voices in the SSA or SSAA ranges, sacred works or arrangements of American folk music with accompaniment. Our range of voices are from G below middle C to

A (13th above middle C). Reading ability of choir is good but works that require a lot of work with little possibility of more than one performance are of little value. We sing very few popular songs except for special events. We perform music by composers who are well-known and works by living composers who are writing in traditional choral forms. Works which have a full orchestral score are of interest. The orchestration should be fairly light, so as not to cover the voices. Works for Christmas have more value than some others, since we perform with orchestras on an annual basis."

PERFORMANCES Don Locklair's *The Columbus Madrigals* (opera).

TIPS "It must be appropriate music and words for children. We do not deal in pop music. Folk music, classics and sacred are acceptable."

SOLI DEO GLORIA CANTORUM

3402 Woolworth Ave., Omaha NE 68105 United States. (402)341-4111. **Fax:** (402)341-9381. **E-mail:** cantorum@berkey.com. **Website:** www.berkey.com. **Contact:** Almeda Berkey, music director. Professional choir. Estab. 1988. Members are professionals. Performs 5-7 concerts/year; several are new works. Commissions 1-2 new works/year. Performance space: "cathedral, symphony hall, smaller intimate recital halls as well." Payment is "dependent upon composition and composer."

HOW TO CONTACT Submit complete score and tape of piece(s). Include SASE. Responds in 2 months.

MUSIC "Chamber music mixed with topical programming (e.g., all Celtic or all Hispanic programs, etc.). Generally a cappella compositions from very short to extended range (6-18 minutes) or multi-movements. Concerts are of a formal length (approximately 75 minutes) with 5 rehearsals. Difficulty must be balanced within program in order to adequately prepare in a limited rehearsal time. 28 singers. Not seeking orchestral pieces, due to limited budget."

PERFORMANCES Jackson Berkey's *Native Am Ambience* (eclectic/classical); John Rutter's *Hymn to the Creator of Light* (classical); and Arvo Part's *Te Deum* (multi-choir/chant-based classical).

ST. LOUIS CHAMBER CHORUS

P.O. Box 11558, Clayton MO 63105 United States. (636)458-4343. **E-mail:** stlchamberchorus@gmail.com. **Website:** www.chamberchorus.org. **Contact:** Philip Barnes, artistic director. Vocal ensemble, chamber music ensemble. Estab. 1956. Members are professionals and amateurs. Performs 6 concerts/year including 5-10 new works. Commissions 3-4 new works/year. Audience is "diverse and interested in unaccompanied choral work and outstanding architectural/acoustic venues." Performances take place at various auditoria noted for their excellent acoustics--churches, synagogues, schools, and university halls. Pays by arrangement.

HOW TO CONTACT Query first. Does not return material. "Panel of 'readers' submit report to artistic director. Responds in 3 months. 'General Advice' leaflet available on request."

MUSIC *"Only a cappella writing!* No contemporary 'popular' works; historical editions welcomed. No improvisatory works. Our programs are tailored for specific acoustics—composers should indicate their preference."

PERFORMANCES Sir Richard Rodney Bennett's *A Contemplation Upon Flowers* (a cappella madrigal); Ned Rorem's *Ode to Man* (a cappella chorus for mixed voices); and Sasha Johnson Manning's *Requiem* (a cappella oratorio).

TIPS "We only consider a cappella works which can be produced in five rehearsals. Therefore pieces of great complexity or duration are discouraged. Our seasons are planned 2-3 years ahead, so much lead time is required for programming a new work. We will accept hand-written manuscript, but we prefer typeset music."

SUSQUEHANNA SYMPHONY ORCHESTRA

P.O. Box 963, Abingdon MD 21009 United States. **Fax:** (410)306-6069. **E-mail:** sheldon.bair@ssorchestra.org. **Website:** www.ssorchestra.org. **Contact:** Sheldon Bair, founder/music director. Symphony orchestra. Estab. 1978. Members are amateurs. Performs 6 concerts/year including 1-2 new works. Composers paid depending on the circumstances. "We perform in 1 hall, 600 seats with fine acoustics. Our audience encompasses all ages."

HOW TO CONTACT Query first. Include SASE. Responds in 3 or more months.

MUSIC "We desire works for large orchestra, any length, in a 'conservative 20th and 21st century' style. Seek fine music for large orchestra. We are a community orchestra, so the music must be within our grasp. Violin I to 7th position by step only; Violin II—stay within 5th position; English horn and harp are OK. Full orchestra pieces preferred."

PERFORMANCES *Stabat Mater* by Stanislaw Moryto; *Elegy*, Amanda Harberg; *I Choose the Mountain* by Stacey Zyriek; *Little Gift* by Benny Russell.

☺ TORONTO MENDELSSOHN CHOIR

720 Bathurst St., Suite 404, Toronto ON M5S 2R4, Canada. (416)598-0422. **Fax:** (416)598-2992. **E-mail:** manager@tmchoir.org. **Website:** www.tmchoir.org. **Contact:** Cynthia Hawkins, executive director. Vocal ensemble. Members are professionals and amateurs. Performs 25 concerts/year including 1-3 new works. "Most performances take place in Roy Thomson Hall. The audience is reasonably sophisticated, musically knowledgeable but with moderately conservative tastes." Pays by commission and ASCAP/SOCAN.

HOW TO CONTACT Query first or submit complete score and tapes of pieces. Include SASE. Responds in 6 months.

MUSIC All works must suit a large choir (180 voices) and standard orchestral forces or with some other not-too-exotic accompaniment. Length should be restricted to no longer than 1/2 of a nocturnal concert. The choir sings at a very professional level and can sight-read almost anything. "Works should fit naturally with the repertoire of a large choir which performs the standard choral orchestral repertoire."

PERFORMANCES Holman's *Jezebel*; Orff's *Catulli Carmina*; and Lambert's *Rio Grande*.

☺ VANCOUVER CHAMBER CHOIR

1254 W. 7th Ave., Vancouver BC V6H 1B6 Canada. **E-mail:** info@vancouverchamberchoir.com. **Website:** www.vancouverchamberchoir.com. **Contact:** Jon Washburn, artistic director. Vocal ensemble. Members are professionals. Performs 40 concerts/year including 5-8 new works. Commissions 2-4 composers or new works/year. Pays SOCAN royalty or negotiated fee for commissions.

HOW TO CONTACT Submit complete score and tape of piece(s). Does not return material. Responds in 6 months if possible.

MUSIC Seeks "choral works of all types for small chorus, with or without accompaniment and/or soloists. Concert music only. Choir made up of 20 singers. Large or unusual instrumental accompaniments are less likely to be appropriate. No pop music."

PERFORMANCES The VCC has commissioned and premiered over 200 new works by Canadian and international composers, including Alice Parker's *That Sturdy Vine* (cantata for chorus, soloists and orchestra); R. Murray Schafer's *Magic Songs* (SATB a cappella); and Jon Washburn's *A Stephen Foster Medley* (SSAATTBB/piano).

TIPS "We are looking for choral music that is performable yet innovative, and that has the potential to become 'standard repertoire.' Although we perform much new music, only a small portion of the many scores which are submitted can be utilized."

VANCOUVER YOUTH SYMPHONY ORCHESTRA SOCIETY

3214 W. 10th Ave., Vancouver BC V6K 2L2 Canada. (604)737-0714. **Fax:** (604)737-0739. **E-mail:** vyso@telus.net. **Website:** www.vyso.com. Music directors: Roger Cole, artistic director and senior orchestra conductor; Jin Zhang, intermediate orchestra conductor; Margitta Krebs, debut and junior orchestra conductor. Youth orchestra. Four divisions consisting of musicians ranging in ages 8-22. Estab. 1930. Members are amateurs. Performs 10-15 concerts/year in various lower mainland venues. Concert admission by donation.

MUSIC "Extensive and varied orchestral repertoire is performed by all divisions. Please contact the VYSO for more information."

VIRGINIA OPERA

P.O. Box 2580, Norfolk VA 23501 United States. (757)627-9545. **E-mail:** info@vaopera.com. **Website:** www.vaopera.org. **Contact:** Andrew Chugg, artistic administration director. Opera company. Estab. 1974. Members are professionals. Performs more than 560 concerts/year. Commissions vary on number of composers or new works/year. Concerts are performed for school children throughout Virginia, grades K-5, 6-8, and 9-12 at the Harrison Opera House in Norfolk and at the Carpenter Theatre in Richmond. Pays on commission.

HOW TO CONTACT Query first. Include SASE. Response time varies.

MUSIC "Audience accessible style approximately 45 minutes in length. Limit cast list to 3 vocal artists of any combination. Accompanied by piano and/or keyboard. Works are performed before school children of all ages. Pieces must be age appropriate both aurally and dramatically. Musical styles are encouraged to be diverse, contemporary as well as traditional. Works are produced and presented with sets, costumes, etc."

Limitations: "Three vocal performers (any combination). One keyboardist. Medium to difficult acceptable, but prefer easy to medium. Seeking only pieces that are suitable for presentation as part of an opera education program for Virginia Opera's education and outreach department. Subject matter must meet strict guidelines relative to Learning Objectives, etc. Musical idiom must be representative of current trends in opera, musical theater. Extreme dissonance, row systems not applicable to this environment."

PERFORMANCES Seymour Barab's *Cinderella*; John David Earnest's *The Legend of Sleepy Hollow*; and Seymour Barab's *The Pied Piper of Hamelin*.

TIPS "Theatricality is very important. New works should stimulate interest in musical theater as a legitimate art form for school children with no prior exposure to live theatrical entertainment. Composer should be willing to create a product that will find success within the educational system."

WHEATON SYMPHONY ORCHESTRA

344 Spring Ave., Glen Ellyn IL 60137 United States. (630)790-1430. **Fax:** (630)790-9703. **E-mail:** info@wheatonsymphony.org. **Website:** www.wheatonsymphony.org. **Contact:** Don Mattison, manager. Symphony orchestra. Estab. 1959. Members are professionals and amateurs. Performs 6 concerts/year including a varying number of new works. "No pay for performance but can probably record your piece."

HOW TO CONTACT Query first. Include SASE. Responds in 1 month.

MUSIC "This is a good amateur orchestra that wants pieces to be performed in the mode of John Williams or Samuel Barber, Corliango, etc. Large scale works for orchestra only. No avant garde, 12-tone or atonal material. Pieces should be 20 minutes or less and must be prepared in 3 rehearsals. Instrumentation needed for woodwinds in 3s, full brass 4-3-3-1, 4 percussion and strings--full-instrumentation only. Selections for full orchestra only. No pay for reading your piece, but we will record it at our expense. We will rehearse and give a world premiere of your piece if it is in the stated orchestration, probably with keyboard added."

PERFORMANCES Richard Williams's *Symphony in G Minor* (4 movement symphony); Dennis Johnson's *Must Jesus Bear the Cross Alone, Azon* (traditional); and Michael Diemer's *Skating* (traditional style).

CONTESTS & AWARDS

//

Participating in contests is a great way to gain exposure for your music. Prizes vary from contest to contest, from cash to musical merchandise to studio time, and even publishing and recording deals. For musical theater and classical composers, the prize may be a performance of your work. Even if you don't win, valuable contacts can be made through contests. Many times, contests are judged by music publishers and other industry professionals, so your music may find its way into the hands of key industry people who can help further your career.

HOW TO SELECT A CONTEST

It's important to remember when entering any contest to do proper research before signing anything or sending any money. We have confidence in the contests listed in *Songwriter's Market*, but it pays to read the fine print. First, be sure you understand the contest rules and stipulations once you receive the entry forms and guidelines. Then you need to weigh what you will gain against what they're asking you to give up. If a publishing or recording contract is the only prize a contest is offering, you may want to think twice before entering. Basically, the company sponsoring the contest is asking you to pay a fee for them to listen to your song under the guise of a contest, something a legitimate publisher or record company would not do. For those contests offering studio time, musical equipment or cash prizes, you need to decide if the entry fee you're paying is worth the chance to win such prizes.

Be wary of exorbitant entry fees, and if you have any doubts whatsoever as to the legitimacy of a contest, it's best to stay away. Songwriters need to approach a contest, award or grant in the same manner as they would a record or publishing company. Make your submission as professional as possible; follow directions and submit material exactly as stated on the entry form.

Contests in this section encompass all types of music and levels of competition. Read each listing carefully and contact them if the contest interests you. Many contests now have websites that offer additional information and even entry forms you can print. Be sure to read the rules carefully and be sure you understand exactly what a contest is offering before entering.

AGO/ECS PUBLISHING AWARD IN CHORAL COMPOSITION

American Guild of Organists, 475 Riverside Dr., Suite 1260, New York NY 10115. (212)870-2310. **Fax:** (212)870-2163. **E-mail:** info@agohq.org. **Website:** www.agohq.org. **Contact:** Harold Calhoun, manager of competitions. Biannual award.

REQUIREMENTS Composers are invited to submit a work for SATB choir and organ in which the organ plays a significant and independent role. Works submitted must be unpublished and are usually no longer than 8 minutes in length. There is no age restriction. Deadline: usually late fall in even numbered years. Application information on the website.

AWARDS $2,000 cash prize, publication by ECS Publishing, and premier performance at the AGO National Convention. Further details are published in *The American Organist*.

AGO/MARILYN MASON AWARD IN ORGAN COMPOSITION

American Guild of Organists, 475 Riverside Dr., Suite 1260, New York NY 10115. (212)870-2310. **Fax:** (212)870-2163. **E-mail:** info@agohq.org. **Website:** www.agohq.org. **Contact:** Harold Calhoun, manager of competitions. For composers and performing artists. Biennial award.

REQUIREMENTS Organ solo, not less than 4 minutes and not more than 6 minutes in duration. Specifics vary from year to year. Deadline: TBA, but usually early spring of odd numbered years. Visit website for application.

AWARDS $2,000; publication by Hinshaw Music Inc.; performance at the biennial National Convention of the American Guild of Organists.

ALEA III INTERNATIONAL COMPOSITION PRIZE

855 Commonwealth Ave., Boston MA 02215. (617)353-3340. **E-mail:** aleaiii@bu.edu. **Website:** www.aleaiii.com. Annual award.

PURPOSE To promote and encourage young composers in the composition of new music.

REQUIREMENTS Composers born after January 1, 1972 may participate; 1 composition per composer. Works may be for solo voice or instrument or for chamber ensemble up to 15 members lasting between 6 and 15 minutes. Available instruments are: 1 flute (doubling piccolo or alto), 1 oboe (doubling English horn), 1 clarinet (doubling bass clarinet), 1 bassoon, 1 saxophone, 1 horn, 1 trumpet, 1 trombone, 1 tuba, 2 percussion players, 1 harp, 1 keyboard player, 1 guitar, 2 violins, 1 viola, 1 cello, 1 bass, tape, and 1 voice. "One of the 15 performers could play an unusual, exotic or rare instrument, or be a specialized vocalist. For more info and guidelines, please refer to our website." All works must be unpublished and must not have been publicly performed or broadcast, in whole or in part or in any other version before the announcement of the prize in late September or early October of 2013. Works that have won other awards are not eligible. Deadline: March 15, 2014. Application on website. Submitted work required with application. "Real name should not appear on score; a *nom de plume* should be signed instead. Sealed envelope with entry form should be attached to each score."

AWARDS $2,500; awarded once annually. Between 6-8 finalists are chosen and their works are performed in a competition concert by the ALEA III contemporary music ensemble. At the end of the concert, one piece will be selected to receive the prize. One grand prize winner is selected by a panel of judges.

TIPS "Emphasis placed on works written in 20th and 21st century compositional idioms."

AMERICAN SONGWRITER LYRIC CONTEST

113 19th Ave. S., Nashville TN 37203. (615)321-6096. **Fax:** (615)321-6097. **E-mail:** info@americansongwriter.com. **Website:** www.americansongwriter.com. For songwriters and composers. Award for each bimonthly issue of *American Songwriter* magazine, plus grand prize winner at year-end.

PURPOSE To promote and encourage the craft of lyric writing.

REQUIREMENTS Contest is open to any amateur songwriter. AS defines an amateur as one who has not earned more than $5,000 from songwriting related to royalties, advances, or works for hire. Lyrics must be typed and a check for $15 (per entry) must be enclosed. Deadlines: January, March, May, July, September, November. See website for exact dates. Submit online through AmericanSongspace.com. Lyrics only. "If you enter 2 or more lyrics, you automatically receive a 1-year subscription to *American Songwriter* magazine (Canada: 3 or more; other countries: 4 or more)."

AWARDS The annual winner will be chosen from the 6 bimonthly contest winners. First place winners also receive 1 legendary Shure SM58 microphone and a Songwriter Deluxe Standard. Grand Prize: The annual winner, chosen from the 6 contest winners, will receive round trip airfare to Nashville and a dream co-writing session.

TIPS "You do not have to be a subscriber to enter or win. You may submit as many entries as you like. All genres of music accepted."

ANNUAL NSAI SONG CONTEST

1710 Roy Acuff Place, Nashville TN 37203. (615)256-3354. **Fax:** (615)256-0034. **E-mail:** songcontest@nashvillesongwriters.com. **Website:** www.nashvillesongwriters.com; www.nsai.cmt.com. **Contact:** David Petrelli, NSAI event director.

PURPOSE "A chance for aspiring songwriters to be heard by music industry decision makers."

REQUIREMENTS Entry fee: $35 per song (NSAI member); $45 per song (nonmember). Submissions accepted from August 1-October 31. In order to be eligible contestants must not be receiving income from any work submitted—original material only. Mail-in submissions must be in CD form and include entry form, lyrics and melody. Online submissions available through nsai.cmt.com. Visit website for complete list of rules and regulations. Deadline is different each year; check website or send for application. Samples are required with application in the format of cassette or CD.

AWARDS Grand Prize winner receives a one-on-one mentoring session with music superstar, Darius Rucker. CMT Listener's Choice award gives fans a chance to vote for their favorite song entry. Visit website for complete list of rules and prizes.

ARTISTS' FELLOWSHIPS

New York Foundation for the Arts, 20 Jay St., 7th Floor, Brooklyn NY 11201. (212)366-6900. **Fax:** (212)366-1778. **E-mail:** fellowships@nyfa.org. **Website:** www.nyfa.org. For songwriters, composers, and musical playwrights. Annual award, but each category funded biennially.

PURPOSE "Artists' Fellowships are $7,000 grants awarded by the New York Foundation for the Arts to individual originating artists living in New York State. The Foundation is committed to supporting artists from all over New York State at all stages of their professional careers. Fellows may use the grant according to their own needs; it should not be confused with project support."

REQUIREMENTS Must be 18 years of age or older; resident of New York State for 2 years prior to application; and cannot be enrolled in any graduate or undergraduate degree program. Applications will be available in July. Deadline: October. Samples of work are required with application. One or 2 original compositions on separate audiotapes or audio CDs and at least 2 copies of corresponding scores or fully harmonized lead sheets.

AWARDS All Artists' Fellowships awards are for $7,000. Payment of $6,300 upon verification of NY State residency, and remainder upon completion of a mutually agreed upon public service activity. Nonrenewable. "Fellowships are awarded on the basis of the quality of work submitted. Applications are reviewed by a panel of 5 composers representing the aesthetic, ethnic, sexual and geographic diversity within New York State. The panelists change each year and review all allowable material submitted."

TIPS "Please note that musical playwrights may submit only if they write the music for their plays—librettists must submit in our playwriting category."

ARTIST TRUST FELLOWSHIP AWARD

1835 12th Ave., Seattle WA 98122. (209)467-8734 ext. 9. **Fax:** (866)218-7878. **E-mail:** miguel@artisttrust.org. **Website:** artisttrust.org. **Contact:** Miguel Guillen, Program Manager. "The fellowship is a merit-based award of $7,500 to practicing professional Washington State artists of exceptional talent and demonstrated ability. Literature fellowships are offered every other year. The award is made on the basis of work of the past 5 years. Applicants must be individual artists; Washington State residents; not matriculated students; and generative artists. Offered every 2 years in even years. Guidelines and application online."

THE ART OF MUSIC BIENNIAL WRITING CONTEST

P.O. Box 85, Del Mar CA 92014. (619)884-1401. **Fax:** (858)755-1104. **E-mail:** info@theartofmusicinc.org. **E-mail:** eaxford@aol.com. **Website:** www.theartofmusicinc.org; www.pianopress.com. **Contact:** Elizabeth C. Axford. Offered biannually. Categories are: Essay, short story, poetry, song lyrics, and illustrations for cover art. Acquires one-time rights. All entries must be accompanied by an entry form indicating category and age; parent signature is required of all writers under age 18. Poems may be of any length and in any style; essays and short stories should not exceed 5 double-spaced, typewritten pages. All entries shall be previously unpublished (except poems and song lyrics) and the original work of the author. Inquiries accepted by e-mail, phone. Short stories should be no longer than 5 pages typed and double spaced. Open to any writer. "Make sure all work is fresh and original. Music-related topics only." Results announced October 31. Winners notified by mail. For contest results, send SASE or visit website.

PURPOSE "The purpose of the contest is to promote the art of music through writing."

THE ASCAP DEEMS TAYLOR AWARDS

American Society of Composers, Authors & Publishers, One Lincoln Plaza, New York NY 10023. (212)621-6318. **E-mail:** jsteinblatt@ascap.com. **Website:** www.ascap. com. **Contact:** Jim Steinblatt.

PURPOSE "The ASCAP Deems Taylor Awards program recognizes books, articles, broadcasts, and websites on the subject of music selected for their excellence."

THE BLANK THEATRE COMPANY YOUNG PLAYWRIGHTS FESTIVAL

P.O. Box 38756, Hollywood CA 90038. (323)662-7734. **Fax:** (323)661-3903. **E-mail:** info@theblank.com. **E-mail:** submissions@youngplaywrights.com. **Website:** www.youngplaywrights.com. For both musical and non-musical playwrights. Annual award.

PURPOSE "To give young playwrights an opportunity to learn more about playwriting and to give them a chance to have their work mentored, developed, and presented by professional artists."

REQUIREMENTS Playwrights must be 19 years old or younger on March 15, 2014. Send legible, original plays of any length and on any subject (co-written plays are acceptable provided all co-writers meet eligibility requirements). Submissions must be postmarked by March 15 and must include a cover sheet with the playwright's name, date of birth, school (if any), home address, home phone number, e-mail address and production history. Pages must be numbered and submitted unbound (unstapled). For musicals, a tape or CD of a selection from the score should be submitted with the script. Mss will not be returned; do not send originals. Semifinalists and winners will be contacted in May.

AWARDS Winning playwrights receive a workshop presentation of their work.

CRS COMPETITION FOR COMPOSERS' RECORDINGS

724 Winchester Rd., Broomall PA 19008. (610)544-5920. **Fax:** (610)544-5920. **E-mail:** crsnews@verizon.

net. **Website:** www.crsnews.org. **Contact:** Caroline Hunt, administrative assistant; Jack Shusterman, senior representative. For songwriters, composers, and performing artists. College faculty and gifted artists. Each annual competition is limited to the first 300 applicants—all fees beyond this limit will be returned.

REQUIREMENTS "Each category requires a separate application fee. The work submitted must be non-published (prior to acceptance) and not commercially recorded on any label. The work submitted must not exceed 9 performers. Each composer/performer may submit 1 work for each application submitted. (Taped performances by composers are additionally encouraged.) Composition must not exceed 16 minutes in length. CRS reserves the right not to accept a First Prize Winner. Write with SASE for application or visit website. Add $5 for postage and handling. Must send a detailed résumé with application form available on our Web page under 'Events' category. Samples of work required with application. Send score and parts with optional CD or DAT. Application fee: $50."

AWARDS First prize will consist of a commercially distributed new compact disc recording grant featuring 1 composition along with other distinguished composers and performing artists. Second and Third Prizes will be awarded Honorable Mention toward future recordings with CRS and Honorary Life Membership to the Society. Applications are judged by panel of judges determined each year.

DELTA OMICRON INTERNATIONAL COMPOSITION COMPETITION

910 Church St., P.O. Box 752, Jefferson City TN 37760. (865)471-6155. **Fax:** (865)475-9716. **E-mail:** ninabdurr@bellsouth.net. **Website:** www.delta-omicron. org. Composition Competition Chair: Nina Belle Durr. For composers. Triennial award. Next contest: 2015.

PURPOSE "To encourage composers worldwide to continually add to our wonderful heritage of musical creativity instrumentally and/or vocally."

REQUIREMENTS People from college age on (or someone younger who is enrolled in college). Work must be unpublished and unperformed in public. "View our website for specific submission guidelines such as instrument selection and deadline. Click on 'Composition Competition' on homepage." Mss should be legibly written in ink or processed, signed with *nom de plume*, and free from any marks that would identify the composer to the judges. Entry fee:

$25 per composition. Send for application. Composition is required with application. A total of 3 copies of composition are required, one for each judge. Music copies should *not* be spiral bound.

AWARDS 1st Place: $1,000 and world premiere at Delta Omicron Triennial Conference. Judged by 2-3 judges (performers, conductors, and/or composers).

EUROPEAN INTERNATIONAL COMPETITION FOR COMPOSERS/IBLA FOUNDATION

226 East 2nd St., Suite 1B, New York NY 10009. (212)387-0111. **E-mail:** iblanewyork@gmail.com. **Website:** www.ibla.org. **Contact:** Michael Yasenak, executive director; Dr. Salvatore Moltisanti, chairman. For songwriters and composers. Annual award.

PURPOSE "To promote the winners' career through exposure, publicity, recordings with Athena Records, and nationwide distribution with the Empire Group."

REQUIREMENTS Deadline: April 30. Send for application. Music score and/or recording of one work are required with application. Application fee is refunded if not admitted into the program.

AWARDS Winners are presented in concerts in Europe-Japan, USA.

FULBRIGHT SCHOLAR PROGRAM, COUNCIL FOR INTERNATIONAL EXCHANGE OF SCHOLARS

1400 K St. NW, Suite 5L, Washington DC 20005. (202)686-4000. **Fax:** (202)686-4029. **E-mail:** scholars@iie.org. **Website:** www.cies.org.

PURPOSE "Annual awards for university lecturing and advanced research abroad are offered annually in virtually all academic disciplines including musical composition."

REQUIREMENTS "U.S. citizenship at time of application; M.F.A., Ph.D. or equivalent professional qualifications; for lecturing awards, university teaching experience (some awards are for professionals non-academic)." Applications become available in March each year, for grants to be taken up 1-1/2 years later. See website for application deadlines. Write or call for application. Samples of work are required with application.

AWARDS "Benefits vary by country, but generally include round-trip travel for the grantee and for most full academic-year awards, one dependent; stipend in U.S. dollars and/or local currency; in many countries, tuition allowance for school age children; and book and baggage allowance. Grant duration ranges from 3 months to 1 academic year."

GRASSY HILL KERRVILLE NEW FOLK COMPETITION

P.O. Box 291466, Kerrville TX 78029. (830)257-3600. **Fax:** (830)257-8680. **E-mail:** info@kerrville-music. com. **Website:** http://kerrville-music.com/newfolk. htm. **Contact:** Dalis Allen, producer. For songwriters. Annual award.

○ Also see the listing for Kerrville Folk Festival in the Workshops section of this book.

PURPOSE "To provide an opportunity for emerging songwriters to be heard and rewarded for excellence."

REQUIREMENTS Songwriter enters 2 original songs burned to CD (cassettes no longer accepted), or uploaded to Sonicbids, with entry fee; no more than one submission may be entered; 6-8 minutes total for 2 songs. Application online, no lyric sheets or press material needed. Submissions accepted between December 1 and March 15 or first 800 entries received prior to that date. Call or e-mail to request rules. Entry fee: $25.

AWARDS New Folk Award Winner. Thirty-two finalists invited to sing the 2 songs entered during The Kerrville Folk Festival in May. Six writers are chosen as award winners. Each of the 6 receives a cash award of $450 or more and performs at a winner's concert during the Kerrville Folk Festival in June. Initial round of entries judged by the Festival Producer and a panel of online listeners from the music industry. Thirty-two finalists judged by panel of 3 performer/songwriters.

TIPS "Do not allow instrumental accompaniment to drown out lyric content. Don't enter without complete copy of the rules. Former winners and finalists include Lyle Lovett, Nanci Griffith, Hal Ketchum, John Gorka, David Wilcox, Lucinda Williams and Robert Earl Keen, Tish Hinojosa, Carrie Newcomer, and Jimmy Lafave."

GREAT AMERICAN SONG CONTEST

PMB 135, 6327-C SW Capitol Hill Hwy., Portland OR 97239-1937. **E-mail:** info@greatamericansong.com. **Website:** www.greatamericansong.com. For songwriters, composers and lyricists. Annual award.

○ Also see the listing for Songwriters Resource Network in the Organizations section of this book.

PURPOSE To help songwriters get their songs heard by music-industry professionals; to generate educational and networking opportunities for participating songwriters; to help songwriters open doors in the music business.

REQUIREMENTS Entry fee: $30 for first 2 entries; $25 after first 2. "Annual deadline. Check our website for details or send SASE along with your mailed request for information."

AWARDS Winners receive a mix of cash awards and prizes. The focus of the contest is on networking and educational opportunities. (All participants receive detailed evaluations of their songs by industry professionals.) Songs are judged by knowledgeable music-industry professionals, including prominent hit songwriters, producers and publishers.

TIPS "Focus should be on the song. The quality of the demo isn't important. Judges will be looking for good songwriting talent. They will base their evaluations on the song—not the quality of the recording or the voice performance."

HARVEY GAUL COMPOSITION CONTEST

The Pittsburgh New Music Ensemble, Inc., 527 Coyne Terrace, Pittsburgh PA 15207. (412)889-7231. **E-mail:** contactpnme@gmail.com. **Website:** www.pnme.org. **Contact:** Kevin Noe, artistic director. For composers. Biennial.

PURPOSE Objective is to encourage composition of new music.

REQUIREMENTS "Must be citizen of the U.S. Please submit score and recording, if available (CDs only) of a representative instrumental score." Send SASE for application or download from www.pnme.org. Samples of work are required with application. Entry fee: $20. Deadline: January 1, 2015 (postmark).

AWARDS $6,000. Winner also receives commission for new work to be premiered by the PNME.

IAMA (INTERNATIONAL ACOUSTIC MUSIC AWARDS)

2881 E. Oakland Park Blvd., Suite 414, Fort Lauderdale FL 33306. **E-mail:** info@inacoustic.com. **Website:** www.inacoustic.com. For singer-songwriters, musicians, performing musicians in the acoustic genre.

PURPOSE "The purpose is to promote the excellence in acoustic music performance and songwriting." Genres include: Folk, Alternative, Bluegrass, etc.

REQUIREMENTS Visit website for entry form and details. "All songs submitted must be original. There must be at least an acoustic instrument (voice) in any song. Electric and electronic instruments, along with loops, are allowed, but acoustic instruments (or voice) must be clearly heard in all songs submitted. Contestants may enter as many songs in as many categories as desired but each entry requires a separate CD, entry form, lyric sheet, and entry fee. CDs and lyrics will not be returned. Winners will be chosen by a Blue Ribbon Judging Committee comprised of music industry professionals including A&R managers from record labels, publishers and producers. Entries are judged equally on music performance, production, originality, lyrics, melody and composition. Songs may be in any language. Winners will be notified by e-mail and must sign and return an affidavit confirming that winner's song is original and he/she holds rights to the song. Entry fee: $35/entry.

AWARDS Overall Grand Prize receives $11,000 worth of merchandise. First prizes in all categories win $900 worth of merchandise and services. Runner-up prizes in all categories receive $600 worth of merchandise and services. All first prizes and runner-up winners will receive a track on IAMA compilation CD which goes out to radio stations.

TIPS "Judging is based on music performance, music production, songwriting, and originality/artistry."

KATE NEAL KINLEY MEMORIAL FELLOWSHIP

University of Illinois, College of Fine and Applied Arts, 100 Architecture Bldg., 608 E. Lorado Taft Dr., Champaign IL 61820. (217)333-1661. **E-mail:** faa@illinois.edu. **Website:** http://faa.illinois.edu/kate_neal_kinley_memorial_fellowship. For students of architecture, art or music. Annual award.

PURPOSE The advancement of study in the fine arts.

REQUIREMENTS "The Fellowship will be awarded upon the basis of unusual promise in the fine arts. Open to college graduates whose principal or major studies have been in the fields of architecture, art or music." Deadline for 2014-2015 fellowship: December 1, 2013. Call or visit website for application. Samples of work are required with application.

AWARDS "One major fellowship which yields the sum of $20,000 is to be used by the recipients toward defraying the expenses of advanced study of the fine arts in America or abroad." Two or 3 smaller fellowships may also be awarded upon committee recommendations. Good for 1 year. Grant is nonrenewable.

THE JOHN LENNON SONGWRITING CONTEST

180 Brighton Rd., Suite 801, Clifton NJ 07012. (888)884-5572. **E-mail:** info@jlsc.com; tiana@jlsc.com. **Website:** www.jlsc.com. **Contact:** Tiana Lewis, assistant director. Open year-round.

PURPOSE "The purpose of the John Lennon Songwriting Contest is to promote the art of songwriting by assisting in the discovery of new talent as well as providing more established songwriters with an opportunity to advance their careers."

REQUIREMENTS "Each entry must consist of the following: completed and signed application; audio cassette, CD or MP3 containing 1 song only, 5 minutes or less in length; lyric sheet typed or printed legibly (English translation is required when applicable); $30 entry fee. Deadline: December 15, 2013. Applications can be found in various music-oriented magazines and on our website. Prospective entrants can also send for an application by e-mailing Tiana Lewis at tiana@jlsc.com."

AWARDS Entries are accepted in the following 12 categories: rock, country, jazz, pop, world, gospel/inspirational, R&B, hip-hop, Latin, electronic, folk and children's music. Winners will receive EMI Publishing Contracts, Studio Equipment from Brian Moore Guitars, Roland, Edirol and Audio Technica, 1,000 CDs in full color with premium 6-panel Digipaks courtesy of Discmakers, and gift certificates from Musiciansfriend.com. One entrant will be chosen to TOUR and PERFORM for 1 week on Warped Tour 2014. One Lennon Award winning song will be named "Song of the Year" and take home an additional $20,000 in cash.

MAXIM MAZUMDAR NEW PLAY COMPETITION

1 Curtain Up Alley, Buffalo NY 14202-1911. (716)852-2600. **Fax:** (716)852-2266. **E-mail:** newplays@alleyway.com. **Website:** http://alleyway.com/playwrights.html. For musical playwrights. Annual award.

PURPOSE Alleyway Theatre is dedicated to the development and production of new works. Winners of the competition will receive production and royalties.

REQUIREMENTS Unproduced full-length work not less than 90 minutes long with cast limit of 10 and unit or simple set, or unproduced one-act work less than 15 minutes long with cast limit of 6 and simple set; prefers work with unconventional setting that explores the boundaries of theatricality; limit of 1 submission in each category; guidelines available online, no entry form. $25 playwright entry fee. Script, résumé, SASE optional. CD or cassette mandatory. Deadline: July 1.

AWARDS Production for full-length play or musical with royalty and production for one-act play or musical.

TIPS "Entries may be of any style, but preference will be given to those scripts tht take place in unconventional settings and explore the boundaries of theatricality. No more than ten performers is a definite, unchangeable requirement."

MID-ATLANTIC SONG CONTEST

4200 Wisconsin Ave., NW, PMB 106-137, Washington DC 20016. **E-mail:** contact@saw.org. **Website:** www.saw.org. For songwriters and composers. Annual award.

◑ Also see the listing for Songwriters Association of Washington in the Organizations section.

PURPOSE "This is one of the longest-running contests in the nation; SAW has organized 27 contests since 1982. The competition is designed to afford rising songwriters in a wide variety of genres the opportunity to receive awards and exposure in an environment of peer competition."

REQUIREMENTS Amateur status is important. Applicants should request a brochure/application using the contact information above. Rules and procedures are clearly explained in the brochure and also online. CD and 3 copies of the lyrics are to be submitted with an application form and fee for each entry, or submit MP3 entries by applying online or through Sonicbids. Reduced entry fees are offered to members of Songwriters' Association of Washington; membership can be arranged simultaneously with entering. Multiple song discounts are also offered. Applications are mailed out and posted on their website around June 1; the submission deadline is September 15; awards are typically announced late in the fall.

AWARDS The 2 best songs in each of 10 categories win prize packages donated by the contest's corporate sponsors: BMI, Oasis CD Manufacturing, Omega Recording Studios, Mary Cliff, and Sonic Bids. Winning songwriters are invited to perform in Washington, DC at the Awards Ceremony Gala, and the winning songs are included on a compila-

tion CD. The best song in each category is eligible for three grand cash prizes. Certificates are awarded to other entries meriting finalist and honorable mention. **TIPS** "Enter the song in the most appropriate category. Make the sound recording the best it can be (even though judges are asked to focus on melody and lyric and not on production.) Avoid clichés, extended introductions, and long instrumental solos."

THELONIOUS MONK INTERNATIONAL JAZZ COMPOSERS COMPETITION

5225 Wisconsin Ave. NW, Suite 605, Washington DC 20015. (202)364-7272. **Fax:** (202)364-0176. **E-mail:** lebrown@monkinstitute.org; info@monkinstitute.org. **Website:** www.monkinstitute.org. **Contact:** Leonard Brown, program director. For songwriters and composers. Annual award sponsored by BMI.
PURPOSE The award is given to an aspiring jazz composer who best demonstrates originality, creativity, and excellence in jazz composition.
REQUIREMENTS Deadline: See website. Send for application. Submission must include application form, résumé of musical experience, CD or MP3, entry, 4 copies of the full score, and a photo. The composition features a different instrument each year. Entry fee: $50.
AWARDS $10,000. Applications are judged by panel of jazz musicians. "The Institute will provide piano, bass, guitar, drum set, tenor saxophone, and trumpet for the final performance. The winner will be responsible for the costs of any different instrumentation included in the composition."

NACUSA YOUNG COMPOSERS' COMPETITION

Box 49256 Barrington Station, Los Angeles CA 90049. (541)765-2406. **E-mail:** nacusa@music-usa.org. **Website:** www.music-usa.org/nacusa. **Contact:** Greg Steinke. **Contact:** Greg Steinke, president, NACUSA. Estab. 1978. For composers. Annual award.
○ Also see the National Association of Composers/USA (NACUSA) listing in the Organization section.
PURPOSE Encourages the composition of new American concert hall music.
REQUIREMENTS Entry fee: $20 (membership fee). Deadline: October 30. Send for application. Samples are not required.
AWARDS 1st Prize: $400; 2nd Prize: $100; and possible Los Angeles performances. Applications are

judged by a committee of experienced NACUSA composer members.

SAMMY NESTICO AWARD/USAF BAND AIRMEN OF NOTE

201 McChord St., Joint Base Anacostia-Bolling, Washington DC 20032-0202. (202)767-1756. **Fax:** (202)767-0686. **E-mail:** alan.baylock@bolling.af.mil. **Website:** www.usafband.af.mil/nesticoaward. **Contact:** Alan Baylock. For composers. Annual award.
PURPOSE Purpose: To carry on the tradition of excellence of Sammy Nestico's writing through jazz composition. The winner will have their composition performed by the USAF Airmen of Note, have it professionally recorded and receive an opportunity for a $2,000 follow-up commission.
REQUIREMENTS Unpublished work for jazz ensemble instrumentation (5,4,4,4) style, form and length are unrestricted. Deadline: November 1. Send for application. Samples of work are required with full score and set of parts (or CD recording).
AWARDS Performance by the USAF Band Airmen of Note; expense paid travel to Washington, DC, for the performance; professionally produced recording of the winning composition; and an opportunity for a $2,000 follow-up commission. Applications are judged by panel of musicians.

PULITZER PRIZE IN MUSIC

Columbia University, 709 Pulitzer Hall, 2950 Broaday, New York NY 10027. (212)854-3841. **Fax:** (212)854-3342. **E-mail:** pulitzer@pulitzer.org. **Website:** www.pulitzer.org. **Contact:** Music Secretary. For composers and musical playwrights. Annual award.
REQUIREMENTS "For distinguished musical composition by an American that has had its first perfomance or recording in the United States during the year." Entries should reflect current creative activity. Works that receive their American premiere between January 1, 2013 and December 31, 2013 are eligible. A public performance or the public release of a recording shall constitute a premiere. Deadline: December 31. Samples of work are required with application, biography and photograph of composer, date and place of performance, score or manuscript and recording of the work, entry form, and $50 entry fee.
AWARDS One award: $10,000. Applications are judged first by a nominating jury, then by the Pulitzer Prize Board.

RICHARD RODGERS AWARDS FOR MUSICAL THEATER

American Academy of Arts and Letters, 633 W. 155 St., New York NY 10032. (212)368-5900. **Fax:** (212)491-4615. **E-mail:** academy@artsandletters.org. **Website:** www.artsandletters.org. **Contact:** Jane Bolster, coordinator. Deadline: November 1. "The Richard Rodgers Awards subsidize staged reading, studio productions, and full productions by nonprofit theaters in New York City of works by composers and writers who are not already established in the field of musical theater. The awards are only for musicals—songs by themselves are not eligible. The authors must be citizens or permanent residents of the United States." Guidelines for this award may be obtained by sending an SASE to above address or download from www.artsandletters.org.

ROCKY MOUNTAIN FOLKS FESTIVAL SONGWRITER SHOWCASE

ATTN: Folks Showcase Contest, P.O. Box 769, Lyons CO 80540. (800)624-2422; (303)823-0848. **Fax:** (303)823-0849. **E-mail:** planet@bluegrass.com. **Website:** www.bluegrass.com. **Contact:** Steve Szymanski, director. For songwriters, composers, and performers. Annual award.

PURPOSE Award based on having the best song and performance.

REQUIREMENTS Deadline: June. Finalists notified by July. Rules available on website. Samples of work are required with application. Send CD with $10/song entry fee. Can now submit online at www.sonicbids.com. "Contestants cannot be signed to a major label or publishing deal. No backup musicians allowed. Awards: 1st Place is a 2014 Festival Main Stage set, custom Hayes Guitar, $100, and a free 1 song drumoverdubs (www.drumoverdubs.com) certificate (valued at $300); 2nd Place is $500 and a Baby Taylor Guitar; 3rd Place is $400 and a Baby Taylor Guitar; 4th Place is $300; 5th Place is $200; 6th to 10th Place is $100 each. Each finalist will also receive a complimentary 3-day Folks Festival pass that includes onsite camping, and a Songwriter In The Round slot during the Festival on our workshop stage."

ROME PRIZE COMPETITION FELLOWSHIP

American Academy in Rome, 7 E. 60th St., New York NY 10022-1001. (212)751-7200. **Fax:** (212)751-7220. **E-mail:** info@aarome.org. **Website:** www.aarome.org. For composers. Annual award.

PURPOSE "Through its annual Rome Prize Competition, the academy awards up to 30 fellowships in 11 disciplines, including musical composition. Winners of the Rome Prize pursue independent projects while residing at the Academy's 11 acre center in Rome."

REQUIREMENTS "Applicants for 11-month fellowships must be U.S. citizens and hold a bachelor's degree in music, musical composition, or its equivalent." Deadline: November 1. Entry fee: $30. Application guidelines are available through the Academy's website.

AWARDS "Up to 2 fellowships are awarded annually in musical composition. Fellowship consists of room, board, and a studio at the Academy facilities in Rome as well as a stipend of $26,000. In all cases, excellence is the primary criterion for selection, based on the quality of the materials submitted. Winners are announced in mid-April and fellowships generally begin in early September."

TELLURIDE TROUBADOUR CONTEST

ATTN: Troubadour Competition, P.O. Box 769, Lyons CO 80540. (303)823-0848; (800)624-2422. **Fax:** (303)823-0849. **E-mail:** planet@bluegrass.com. **Website:** www.bluegrass.com. **Contact:** Steve Szymanski, director. For songwriters, composers, and performers. Annual award.

PURPOSE Award based on having best song and performance.

REQUIREMENTS Deadline: must be postmarked by April 13; notified May 6, if selected. Rules available on website. Send CD and $10/song entry fee (limit of 2 songs). Can now submit music online at www.sonicbids.com. Contestants cannot be signed to a major label or publishing deal. No backup musicians allowed.

AWARDS 1st Prize: custom Shanti Guitar, $300, and Festival Main Stage Set; 2nd Prize: $500; 3rd Prize: $400; 4th Prize: $300; 5th Prize: $200. Applications judged by panel of judges.

TIGER'S EYE POETRY CHAPBOOK CONTEST

Tiger's Eye Press, P.O. Box 9723, Denver CO 80209. (541)285-8355. **E-mail:** tigerseyepoet@yahoo.com. **Website:** www.tigerseyejournal.com.

USA SONGWRITING COMPETITION

2881 E. Oakland Park Blvd., Suite 414, Ft. Lauderdale FL 33306. (954)537-3127. **Fax:** (954)537-9690. **E-mail:** info@songwriting.net. **Website:** www.songwriting.net. **Contact:** Contest Manager. For songwriters, composers, performing artists, and lyricists. Annual award.

PURPOSE "To honor good songwriters/composers all over the world, especially the unknown ones."

REQUIREMENTS Open to professional and beginner songwriters. No limit on entries. Each entry must include an entry fee, a CD, MP3, or audio cassette tape of song(s) and lyric sheet(s). Judged by music industry representatives. Past judges have included record label representatives and publishers from Arista Records, EMI and Warner/Chappell. Deadline: See website. Entry fee: $35 per song. See website or e-mail for entry forms at any time. Samples of work are not required.

AWARDS Prizes include cash and merchandise in 15 different categories: pop, rock, country, Latin, R&B, gospel, folk, jazz, "lyrics only" category, instrumental, and many others.

TIPS "Judging is based on lyrics, originality, melody, and overall composition. CD-quality production is great but not a consideration in judging."

U.S.-JAPAN CREATIVE ARTISTS EXCHANGE FELLOWSHIP PROGRAM

Japan-U.S. Friendship Commission, 1201 15th St. NW, Suite 330, Washington DC 20005. (202)418-9800. **Fax:** (202)418-9802. **E-mail:** mmihori@jusfc.gov; jusfc@jusfc.gov. **Website:** www.jusfc.gov. **Contact:** Margaret Mihori, associate executive director. For all creative artists. Annual award.

PURPOSE "For artists to go as seekers, as cultural visionaries, and as living liaisons to the traditional and contemporary life of Japan."

REQUIREMENTS "Artists' works must exemplify the best in U.S. arts." Deadline: See website. Send for application and guidelines. Applications available on website. Samples of work are required with application. Requires 2 pieces on CD or DVD.

AWARDS Five artists are awarded a 3-month residency anywhere in Japan. Awards monthly stipend for living expenses, housing, and professional support services; up to $2,000 for round-trip transportation will be provided for the artist.

TIPS "Applicants should anticipate a highly rigorous review of their artistry and should have compelling reasons for wanting to work in Japan."

WESTERN WRITERS OF AMERICA

271CR 219, Encampment WY 82325. (307)329-8942. **Fax:** (307)327-5465 (call first). **E-mail:** wwa.moulton@gmail.com. **Website:** www.westernwriters.org. **Contact:** Candy Moulton, executive director. "17 Spur Award categories in various aspects of the American West."

PURPOSE "The nonprofit Western Writers of America has promoted and honored the best in Western literature with the annual Spur Awards, selected by panels of judges. Awards, for material published last year, are given for works whose inspirations, image and literary excellence best represent the reality and spirit of the American West."

TIPS "Accepts multiple submissions, each with its own entry form."

Y.E.S. FESTIVAL OF NEW PLAYS

Northern Kentucky University, Department of Theatre and Dance, Nunn Dr., Highland Heights KY 41099-1007. (859)572-6303. **Fax:** (859)572-6057. **E-mail:** forman@nku.edu. **Contact:** Sandra Forman, project director. For musical playwrights. Biennial award (odd numbered years).

PURPOSE "The festival seeks to encourage new playwrights and develop new plays and musicals. Three plays or musicals are given full productions."

REQUIREMENTS "No entry fee. Submit a script with a completed entry form. Musicals should be submitted with a piano/conductor's score and/or a vocal parts score. Scripts may be submitted May 1 through Sept. 30, 2014, for the New Play Festival occuring April 2015. Send SASE for application."

AWARDS Three awards of $500. "The winners are brought to NKU at our expense to view late rehearsals and opening night." Submissions are judged by a panel of readers.

TIPS "Plays/musicals that have heavy demands for mature actors are not as likely to be selected as an equally good script with roles for 18-30 year olds."

ORGANIZATIONS

One of the first places a beginning songwriter should look for guidance and support is a songwriting organization. Offering encouragement, instruction, contacts and feedback, these groups of professional and amateur songwriters can help an aspiring songwriter hone the skills needed to compete in the ever-changing music industry.

The type of organization you choose to join depends on what you want to get out of it. Local groups can offer a friendly, supportive environment where you can work on your songs and have them critiqued in a constructive way by other songwriters. They're also great places to meet collaborators. Larger, national organizations can give you access to music business professionals and other songwriters across the country.

Most of the organizations listed in this book are non-profit groups with membership open to specific groups of people—songwriters, musicians, classical composers, etc. They can be local groups with a membership of less than 100 people, or large national organizations with thousands of members from all over the country. In addition to regular meetings, most organizations occasionally sponsor events such as seminars and workshops to which music industry personnel are invited to talk about the business, and perhaps listen to and critique demo tapes.

Check the following listings, bulletin boards at local music stores and your local newspapers for area organizations. If you are unable to locate an organization within an easy distance of your home, you may want to consider joining one of the national groups. These groups, based in New York, Los Angeles and Nashville, keep their members involved and informed through newsletters, regional workshops and large yearly conferences. They can help a writer who feels isolated in his hometown get his music heard by professionals in the major music centers.

In the following listings, organizations describe their purpose and activities, as well as how much it costs to join. Before joining any organization, consider what they have to offer and how becoming a member will benefit you. To locate organizations close to home, see the Geographic Index at the back of this book.

ACADEMY OF COUNTRY MUSIC

5500 Balboa Blvd., Encino CA 91316. (818)788-8000. **Fax:** (818)788-0999. **E-mail:** info@acmcountry.com. **Website:** www.acmcountry.com. Serves country music industry professionals. Eligibility for professional members is limited to those individuals who derive some portion of their income directly from country music. Each member is classified by one of the following categories: artist/entertainer, club/venue operator, musician, on-air personality, manager, talent agent, composer, music publisher, public relations, publications, radio, TV/motion picture, record company, talent buyer or affiliated (general). The purpose of ACM is to promote and enhance the image of country music. The Academy is involved year-round in activities important to the country music community. Some of these activities include charity fund-raisers, participation in country music seminars, talent contests, artist showcases, assistance to producers in placing country music on television and in motion pictures and backing legislation that benefits the interests of the country music community. The ACM is governed by directors and run by officers elected annually. Applications are accepted throughout the year. Membership: $75/year.

AMERICAN MUSIC CENTER, INC.

part of New Music USA, 90 John St., Suite 312, New York NY 10038. (212)645-6949. **Fax:** (212)490-0998. **E-mail:** info@newmusicusa.org. **Website:** www.amc. net. **Contact:** Membership Department. The American Music Center, founded by a consortium led by Aaron Copland in 1939, is the first-ever national service and information center for new classical music and jazz by American composers. The Center has a variety of innovative new programs and services, including a monthly Internet magazine (www.newmusicbox.org) for new American music, online databases of contemporary ensembles and ongoing opportunities for composers, an online catalog of new music for educators specifically targeted to young audiences, a series of professional development workshops, and an online listening library. Each month, AMC provides its over 2,500 members with a listing of opportunities including calls for scores, competitions, and other new music performance information. Each year, AMC's Information Services Department fields thousands of requests concerning composers, performers, data, funding, and support programs. The AMC Collection at the New York Public Library for the Performing Arts presently includes over 60,000 scores and recordings, many unavailable elsewhere. "AMC also continues to administer several grant programs: the Aaron Copland Fund for Music; the Henry Cowell Performance Incentive Fund; and its own programs Live Music for Dance and the Composer Assistance Program." Members also receive a link to their websites on www.amc.net. The American Music Center is not-for-profit and has an annual membership fee.

AMERICAN SOCIETY OF COMPOSERS, AUTHORS AND PUBLISHERS (ASCAP)

One Lincoln Plaza, New York NY 10023. (212)621-6000 (administration). **Fax:** (212)621-8453. **Website:** www.ascap.com. **Contact:** Member Services at (800)95-ASCAP. **Regional offices—West Coast:** 7920 W. Sunset Blvd., 3rd Floor, Los Angeles CA 90046, (323)883-1000; **Nashville:** Two Music Square W., Nashville TN 37203, (615)742-5000; **Atlanta:** 950 Joseph E. Lowery Blvd. NW, Suite 23, Atlanta GA 30318, (404)685-8699; **Miami:** 420 Lincoln Rd., Suite 385, Miami Beach FL 33139, (305)673-3446; **London:** 8 Cork St., London W1S 3LJ England, 011-44-207-439-0909; **Puerto Rico:** Ave. Martinez Nadal, c/ Hill Side 623, San Juan, Puerto Rico 00920, (787)707-0782. ASCAP is a membership association of over 240,000 composers, lyricists, songwriters, and music publishers, whose function is to protect the rights of its members by licensing and collecting royalties for the nondramatic public performance of their copyrighted works. ASCAP licensees include radio, television, cable, live concert promoters, bars, restaurants, symphony orchestras, new media, and other users of music. ASCAP is the leading performing rights society in the world. All revenues, less operating expenses, are distributed to members (about 86 cents of each dollar). ASCAP was the first U.S. performing rights organization to distribute royalties from the Internet. Founded in 1914, ASCAP is the only society created and owned by writers and publishers. The ASCAP Board of Directors consists of 12 writers and 12 publishers, elected by the membership. ASCAP's Member Card provides exclusive benefits geared towards working music professionals. Among the benefits are health, musical instrument and equipment, tour and studio liability, term life and long-term care insurance, discounts on musical instruments, equipment and supplies, access to a credit union, and much more. ASCAP hosts a wide array of showcases and workshops throughout the year, and offers grants, special awards, and networking opportunities in a variety of genres. Visit their website listed above for more information.

ARIZONA SONGWRITERS ASSOCIATION

428 E. Thunderbird Rd. #737, Phoenix AZ 85022. E-mail: azsongwriters@cox.net. Website: www.azsongwriters.com. Contact: John Iger, president. Members are all ages; all styles of music, novice to pro; many make money placing their songs in film and TV. Most members are residents of Arizona. Purpose is to educate about the craft and business of songwriting and to facilitate networking with business professionals and other songwriters, musicians, singers and studios. Offers instruction, e-newsletter, workshops, performance, and song pitching opportunities. Applications accepted year-round. Membership fee: $25/year.

☾ ASSOCIATION DES PROFESSIONEL. LE.S DE LA CHANSON ET DE LA MUSIQUE

450 Rideau St., Suite 401, Ottawa ON K1N 5Z4 Canada. (613)745-5642. Fax: (613)745-9715. E-mail: communications@apcm.ca. Website: www.apcm.ca. Contact: Mathilde Hountchegnon, head of communications and promotion. Members are French Canadian singers and musicians. Members must be French singing and may have a CD to be distributed. Purpose is to gather French speaking artists (outside of Quebec, mainly in Ontario) to distribute their material, other workshops, instructions, lectures, etc. Offers instruction, newsletter, lectures, workshops, and distribution. Applications accepted year-round. Membership fee: $60 (Canadian).

ASSOCIATION OF INDEPENDENT MUSIC PUBLISHERS

P.O. Box 69473, Los Angeles CA 90069. (818)771-7301. E-mail: LAinfo@aimp.org; NYinfo@aimp.org; NAinfo@aimp.org. Website: www.aimp.org. Purpose is to educate members on new developments in the music publishing industry and to provide networking opportunities. Offers monthly panels and networking events. Applications accepted year-round. Membership fee: $75/year.

AUSTIN SONGWRITERS GROUP

P.O. Box 2578, Austin TX 78768. (512)698-4237. E-mail: info@austinsongwritersgroup.com. Website: www.austinsongwritersgroup.com. Contact: Lee Duffy, executive director. Serves all ages and all levels, from just beginning to advanced. "Prospective members should have an interest in the field of songwriting, whether it be for profit or hobby. The main purpose of this organization is to educate members in the craft and business of songwriting; to provide resources for growth and advancement in the area of songwriting; and to provide opportunities for performance and contact with the music industry." The primary benefit of membership to a songwriter is exposure to music industry professionals, which increases contacts and furthers the songwriter's education in both craft and business aspects. Offers competitions, instruction, lectures, library, newsletter, performance opportunities, evaluation services, workshops and contact with music industry professionals through special guest speakers at meetings, plus our yearly Austin Songwriters Symposium, which includes instruction, song evaluations, and song pitching direct to those pros currently seeking material for their artists, publishing companies, etc." Applications accepted year-round. Membership fee: $50/year.

TIPS "Our newsletter is top-quality-packed with helpful information on all aspects of songwriting-craft, business, recording and producing tips, and industry networking opportunities. Go to our website and sign up for emails to keep you informed about ongoing and upcoming events!"

BALTIMORE SONGWRITERS ASSOCIATION

P.O. Box 22496, Baltimore MD 21203. (443)813-4039. E-mail: info@baltimoresongwriters.org. Website: www.baltimoresongwriters.org. "The BSA is an inclusive organization with all ages, skill levels and genres of music welcome. We are trying to build a musical community that is more supportive and less competitive. We are dedicated to helping songwriters grow and become better in their craft." Offers instruction, newsletter, lectures, workshops, performance opportunities. Applications accepted year-round; membership not limited to location or musical status. Membership fee: $25.

THE BLACK ROCK COALITION

P.O. Box 1054, Cooper Station, New York NY 10276. E-mail: brcmembersinfo@gmail.com. Website: www.blackrockcoalition.org. Contact: Darrell M. McNeil, director of operations. Serves musicians, songwriters--male and female ages 18-40 (average). Also engineers, entertainment attorneys and producers. Looking for members who are "mature and serious about music as an artist or activist willing to help fellow musicians. The BRC independently produces, promotes and distributes black alternative music acts as a collective and supportive voice for such musicians within the music and record business. The main purpose of this organization is to produce, promote, and distribute the full spectrum of black music along with educating the public on what black music is. The BRC is now soliciting recorded music by bands and individuals for Black Rock Coalition Records. Please send copyrighted and original material only." Offers instruction, newsletter, lectures, free seminars and workshops, monthly membership meeting, quarterly magazine, performing opportunities, evaluation services, business advice, and full roster of all members. Applications accepted year-round. Bands must submit a tape, bio with picture and a self-addressed, stamped envelope before sending their membership fee. Membership fee: $25.

BROADCAST MUSIC, INC. (BMI)

7 World Trade Center, 250 Greenwich St., New York NY 10007. (212)220-3000. **E-mail:** newyork@bmi.com. **Website:** www.bmi.com. **Los Angeles:** 8730 Sunset Blvd., 3rd Floor West, Los Angeles CA 90069. (310)659-9109. **E-mail:** losangeles@bmi.com. **Nashville:** 10 Music Square East, Nashville TN 37203. (615)401-2000. **E-mail:** nashville@bmi.com. **Miami:** 1691 Michigan Ave., Miami FL 33139. (305)673-5148. **E-mail:** miami@bmi.com. **Atlanta:** 3340 Peachtree Rd., NE, Suite 570, Atlanta GA 30326. (404)261-5151. **E-mail:** atlanta@bmi.com. **Puerto Rico:** 1250 Ave. Ponce de Leon, San Jose Building Santurce PR 00907. (787)754-6490. **United Kingdom:** 84 Harley House, Marylebone Rd., London NW1 5HN United Kingdom. 011-44-207-486-2036. **E-mail:** london@bmi.com. President and CEO: Del R. Bryant. Senior vice presidents: Phillip Graham, New York, writer/publisher relations; Alison Smith, rerforming rights. Vice presidents: Charlie Feldman, New York; Barbara Cane and Doreen Ringer Ross, Los Angeles; Paul Corbin, Nashville; Diane J. Almodovar, Miami; Catherine Brewton, Atlanta. Senior executive, London: Brandon Bakshi. BMI is a performing rights organization representing approximately 300,000 songwriters, composers and music publishers in all genres of music, including pop, rock, country, R&B, rap, jazz, Latin, gospel and contemporary classical. "Applicants must have written a musical composition, alone or in collaboration with other writers, which is commercially published, recorded or otherwise likely to be performed." Purpose: BMI acts on behalf of its songwriters, composers and music publishers by insuring payment for performance of their works through the collection of licensing fees from radio stations, Internet outlets, broadcast and cable TV stations, hotels, nightclubs, aerobics centers and other users of music. This income is distributed to the writers and publishers in the form of royalty payments, based on how the music is used. BMI also undertakes intensive lobbying efforts in Washington D.C. on behalf of its affiliates, seeking to protect their performing rights through the enactment of new legislation and enforcement of current copyright law. In addition, BMI helps aspiring songwriters develop their skills through various workshops, seminars and competitions it sponsors throughout the country. Applications accepted year-round. There is no membership fee for songwriters; a one-time fee of $150 is required to affiliate an individually-owned publishing company; $250 for partnerships, corporations and limited-liability companies. "Visit our website for specific contacts, e-mail addresses and additional membership information."

CALIFORNIA LAWYERS FOR THE ARTS

Fort Mason Center, C-255, San Francisco CA 94123. (415)775-7200. **Fax:** (415)775-1143. **E-mail:** support@calawyersforthearts.org; sanfrancisco@calawyersforthearts.org. **Website:** www.calawyersforthearts.org. "For artists of all disciplines, skill levels, and ages, supporting individuals and organizations, and arts organizations. Artists of all disciplines are welcome, whether professionals or amateurs. We also welcome groups and individuals who support the arts. We work most closely with the California arts community. Our mission is to establish a bridge between the legal and arts communities so that artists and art groups may handle their creative activities with greater business and legal competence; the legal profession will be more aware of issues affecting the arts community; and the law will become more responsive to the arts community." Offers newsletter, lectures, library, workshops, mediation service, attorney referral service, housing referrals, publications and advocacy. Membership fees: $20 for senior citizens and full-time students, $30 for working artists, $45 for general individual, $70 for non-panel attorney, $75 for panel attorney, $100 for patrons; organizations: $50 for small organizations (budget under $100,000), $90 for large organizations (budget of $100,000 or more), $100 for corporate sponsors.

☯ CANADA COUNCIL FOR THE ARTS/ CONSEIL DES ARTS DU CANADA

350 Albert St., P.O. Box 1047, Ottawa ON K1P 5V8 Canada. (613)566-4414. **Fax:** (613)566-4390. **Website:** www.canadacouncil.ca. **Contact:** Melisa Kamibayashi, program officer. An independent agency that fosters and promotes the arts in Canada by providing grants and services to professional artists including songwriters and musicians. "Individual artists must be Canadian citizens or permanent residents of Canada, and must have completed basic training and/or have the recognition as professionals within their fields. The Canada Council offers grants to professional musicians to pursue their individual artistic development and creation. There are specific deadline dates for the various programs of assistance. Visit our website for more details."

☯ CANADIAN ACADEMY OF RECORDING ARTS AND SCIENCES (CARAS)

345 Adelaide St. W, 2nd Floor, Toronto ON M5V 1R5 Canada. (416)485-3135. **Fax:** (416)485-4978. **E-mail:** info@carasonline.ca; meghan@junoawards.ca. **Website:** www.carasonline.ca. **Contact:** Meghan McCabe, manager, communications. Membership is open to all employees (including support staff) in broadcasting and record companies, as well as producers, personal managers, recording artists, recording engineers, arrangers, composers, music publishers, album designers, promoters, talent and booking agents, record retailers, rack jobbers, distributors, recording studios and other music industry related professions (on approval). Applicants must be affiliated with the Canadian recording industry. Offers newsletter, nomination and voting privileges for Juno Awards and discount tickets to Juno Awards show. "CARAS strives to foster the development of the Canadian music and recording industries and to contribute toward higher artistic standards." Applications accepted year-round. Membership fee: $50/year (Canadian) + HST ($56.50 total). Applications accepted from individuals only, not from companies or organizations.

☯ CANADIAN COUNTRY MUSIC ASSOCIATION

120 Adelaide St. E., Suite 200, Toronto ON M5C 1K9 Canada. (416)947-1331. **Fax:** (416)947-5924. **E-mail:** country@ccma.org. **Website:** www.ccma.org. Members are artists, songwriters, musicians, producers, radio station personnel, managers, booking agents and others. Offers newsletter, workshops, performance opportunities and the CCMA awards every September. "Through our newsletters and conventions we offer a means of meeting and associating with artists and others in the industry. The CCMA is a federally chartered, nonprofit organization, dedicated to the promotion and development of Canadian country music throughout Canada and the world and to providing a unity of purpose for the Canadian country music industry." See website for membership information and benefits.

☯ CANADIAN MUSICAL REPRODUCTION RIGHTS AGENCY LTD.

56 Wellesley St. W, #320, Toronto ON M5S 2S3 Canada. (416)926-1966. **Fax:** (416)926-7521. **E-mail:** inquiries@cmrra.ca. **Website:** www.cmrra.ca. **Contact:** Michael Mackie, membership services and copyright. Members are music copyright owners, music publishers, sub-publishers and administrators. Representation by CMRRA is open to any person, firm or corporation anywhere in the world, that owns and/or administers one or more copyrighted musical works. CMRRA is a music licensing agency—Canada's largest—which represents music copyright owners, publishers and administrators for the purpose of mechanical and synchronization licensing in Canada. Offers mechanical and synchronization licensing. Applications accepted year-round.

CENTRAL CAROLINA SONGWRITERS ASSOCIATION (CCSA)

131 Henry Baker Rd., Zebulon NC 27597. (919)727-6647. **Website:** www.ccsa-raleigh.com. "CCSA welcomes songwriters of all experience levels from beginner to professional within the local RDU/Triad/Eastern area of North Carolina to join our group. Our members' musical background varies, covering a wide array of musical genres. CCSA meets monthly in Raleigh, NC. We are unable to accept applications from incarcerated persons or those who do not reside in the local area as our group's primary focus is on songwriters who are able to attend the monthly meetings — to ensure members get the best value for their yearly dues." CCSA strives to provide each songwriter and musician a resourceful organization where members grow musically by networking and sharing with one

another. Offers annual songwriters forum, periodic workshops, critiques at the monthly meetings, opportunities to perform and network with fellow members. Applications are accepted year round. Dues are $24/year (pro-rated for new members at $2/month by date of application) with annual renewal each January.

CENTRAL OREGON SONGWRITERS ASSOCIATION

1900 NE Third St., Suite 106-132, Bend OR 97701. **E-mail:** laurencorinne333@yahoo.com. **Website:** http://oregonsongwriters.org. **Contact:** Lauren Kershner, president. "Our members range in age from their 20s into their 80s. Membership includes aspiring beginners, accomplished singer/songwriter performing artists and all in between. Anyone with an interest in songwriting (any style) is invited to and welcome at COSA. COSA is a nonprofit organization to promote, educate and motivate members in the skills of writing, marketing and improving their craft." Offers competitions, instruction, newsletter, lectures, library, workshops, performance opportunities, songwriters round, awards, evaluation services, and collaboration. Applications accepted year-round. Membership fee: $25.

THE COLLEGE MUSIC SOCIETY

312 E. Pine St., Missoula MT 59802. (406)721-9616. **Fax:** (406)721-9419. **E-mail:** cms@music.org. **Website:** www.music.org. **Contact:** Shannon Devlin, member services. Serves college, university and conservatory professors, as well as independent musicians. "The College Music Society promotes music teaching and learning, musical creativity and expression, research and dialogue, and diversity and interdisciplinary interaction. A consortium of college, conservatory, university, and independent musicians and scholars interested in all disciplines of music, the Society provides leadership and serves as an agent of change by addressing concerns facing music in higher education." Offers journal, newsletter, lectures, workshops, performance opportunities, job listing service, databases of organizations and institutions, music faculty, and mailing lists. Applications accepted year-round. Membership fees: $70 (regular dues), $35 (student dues), $35 (retiree dues).

CONNECTICUT SONGWRITERS ASSOCIATION

P.O. Box 511, Mystic CT 06355. **E-mail:** info@ctsongs.com. **Website:** www.ctsongs.com. **Contact:** Bill Pere, president and executive director. "We are an educa-

tional, nonprofit organization dedicated to improving the art and craft of original music. Founded in 1979, CSA has had almost 2,000 active members and has become one of the best known and respected songwriters' associations in the country. Membership in the CSA admits you to 12-18 seminars/workshops/song critique sessions per year throughout Connecticut and the surrounding region. Out-of-state members may mail in songs for free critiques at our meetings. Noted professionals deal with all aspects of the craft and business of music including lyric writing, music theory, music technology, arrangement and production, legal and business aspects, performance techniques, song analysis and recording techniques." CSA offers song screening sessions for members and songs that become eligible for inclusion on the CSA sampler anthology through various retail and online outlets and are brought to national music conferences. CSA is well connected in both the independent music scene and the traditional music industry. CSA also offers showcases and concerts which are open to the public and designed to give artists a venue for performing their original material for an attentive, listening audience. CSA benefits help local soup kitchens, group homes, hospice, world hunger, libraries, nature centers, community centers and more. CSA encompasses ballads to bluegrass and Bach to rock. Membership fee: $45/year.

DALLAS SONGWRITERS ASSOCIATION

Sammons Center for the Arts, 3630 Harry Hines Blvd. #20, Dallas TX 75219. (214)750-0916. **E-mail:** info@dallassongwriters.org. **Website:** www.dallassongwriters.org. Serves songwriters and lyricists of Dallas/Ft. Worth metroplex. Members are adults ages 18-75, Dallas/Ft. Worth area songwriters/lyricists who are or aspire to be professionals. Purpose is to provide songwriters an opportunity to meet other songwriters, share information, find co-writers and support each other through group discussions at monthly meetings; to provide songwriters an opportunity to have their songs heard and critiqued by peers and professionals by playing cassettes and providing an open mic at monthly meetings and open mics, showcases, and festival stages, and by offering contests judged by publishers; to provide songwriters opportunities to meet other music business professionals by inviting guest speakers to monthly meetings and workshops; and to provide songwriters opportunities to learn more about the craft of songwriting and the business of music by presenting mini-workshops at each monthly meeting. "We offer a chance for the songwriter to learn from peers and industry professionals and an opportunity to belong to a supportive group environment to encourage the individual to continue his/her songwriting endeavors." Offers competitions (including the Annual Song Contest with over $5,000 in prizes, and the Quarterly Lyric Contest), field trips, instruction, lectures, newsletter, performance opportunities, social outings, workshops and seminars. "Our members are eligible for discounts at several local music stores and seminars." Applications accepted year-round. Membership fee: $50. "When inquiring by phone, please leave complete mailing address and phone number or e-mail address where you can be reached day and night."

THE DRAMATISTS GUILD OF AMERICA, INC.

1501 Broadway, Suite 701, New York NY 10036. (212)398-9366. **Fax:** (212)944-0420. **E-mail:** rtec@ dramatistsguild.com. **Website:** www.dramatistsguild.com. **Contact:** Roland Tec, director of membership. For over three-quarters of a century, The Dramatists Guild has been the professional association of playwrights, composers and lyricists, with more than 6,000 members across the country. All theater writers, whether produced or not, are eligible for Associate membership ($90/year); students enrolled in writing degree programs at colleges or universities are eligible for Student membership ($45/year); writers who have been produced on Broadway, Off-Broadway or on the main stage of a LORT theater are eligible for Active membership ($130/year). The Guild offers its members the following activities and services: use of the Guild's contracts (including the Approved Production Contract for Broadway, the Off-Broadway contract, the LORT contract, the collaboration agreements for both musicals and drama, the 99 Seat Theatre Plan contract, the Small Theatre contract, commissioning agreements, and the Underlying Rights Agreements contract; advice on all theatrical contracts including Broadway, Off-Broadway, regional, showcase, Equity-waiver, dinner theater and collaboration contracts); a nationwide toll-free number for all members with business or contract questions or problems; advice and information on a wide spectrum of issues affecting writers; free and/or discounted ticket service; symposia led by experienced professionals

in major cities nationwide; access to health insurance programs; and a spacious meeting room that can accommodate up to 50 people for readings and auditions on a rental basis. The Guild's publications are: *The Dramatist*, a bimonthly journal containing articles on all aspects of the theater (which includes The Dramatists Guild Newsletter, with announcements of all Guild activities and current information of interest to dramatists); and an annual resource directory with up-to-date information on agents, publishers, grants, producers, playwriting contests, conferences and workshops, and an interactive website that brings our community of writers together to exchange ideas and share information.

THE FIELD

75 Maiden Lane, Suite 906, New York NY 10038. (212)691-6969. **E-mail:** jennifer@thefield.org. **Website:** www.thefield.org. **Contact:** Jennifer Wright Cook, executive director. "Founded by artists for artists, The Field has been dedicated to providing impactful services to thousands of performing artists in New York City and beyond since 1986. From fostering creative exploration to stewarding innovative fundraising strategies, we are delighted to help artists reach their fullest potential. More than 1,900 performing artists come to The Field annually to build their businesses, 2,000+ new art works are developed under our stewardship each year, and our services are replicated in 11 cities across the US and in Europe. At the same time, we remain true to our grassroots origin and artist-centered mission: to strategically and comprehensively serve the myriad artistic and administrative needs of independent performing artists and companies who work in the fields of dance, theater, music, text, and performance art. Our core values of affordability, accessibility and rigorous delivery infuse all of our interactions. Field services include career-building workshops (grant writing, touring, internet strategies, etc.), fiscal sponsorship, creative residences in New York City and out of town, an 'Artists' Kinkos' Resource Center, and Membership benefits." Offers fiscal sponsorship, arts management and creative workshops, residencies, and performance opportunities. Applications accepted year-round. Membership fee: $100/year.

TIPS "The Field offers the most affordable and accessible fiscal sponsorship program in New York City. The Sponsored Artist Program offered by The Field enables performing artists and groups to accumulate the funds they need to make their artistic and career goals a reality. Fiscal sponsorship provides independent performing artists and groups with: eligibility to apply for most government, foundation, and corporate grants which require a 501(c)(3), not-for-profit status; eligibility to receive tax-deductible donations of both money and goods from individuals; and other services where 501(c)(3) status is necessary."

FILM MUSIC NETWORK

13101 Washington Blvd. Suite 466, Los Angeles CA 90066. **Website:** www.filmmusic.net. "The Film Music Network, established in 1997, is a leading worldwide professional association of composers, songwriters, bands, recording artists, and more who are seeking to place their music or compose custom music for film or television projects. One of the Film Music Network's most popular member benefits is providing leads for projects seeking music or composers, including film projects, television projects, corporate videos, music libraries and more. Additional member benefits include a free introductory legal consultation, discounted movie theater and event tickets, resources including a directory of film music agents and managers, our Film Music Salary and Rate survey, and more." Membership fee: $11.95/month.

FORT WORTH SONGWRITERS' ASSOCIATION

P.O. Box 330233, Fort Worth TX 76163. (817)654-5400. **E-mail:** fwsanewsletter@gmail.com. **Website:** www.fwsa.com. Members are ages 18-83, beginners up to and including published writers. Interests cover gospel, country, western swing, rock, pop, bluegrass, and blues. Purpose is to allow songwriters to become more proficient at songwriting; to provide an opportunity for their efforts to be performed before a live audience; and to provide songwriters an opportunity to meet co-writers. "We provide our members free critiques of their efforts. We provide a monthly newsletter outlining current happenings in the business of songwriting. We offer competitions and mini workshops with guest speakers from the music industry. We promote a weekly open mic for singers of original material, and hold invitational songwriter showcase events at various times throughout the year. Each year, we hold a Christmas Song Contest, judged by independent music industry professionals. We also offer free web pages for members or links to member websites." Applications accepted year-round. Membership fee: $35.

GOSPEL MUSIC ASSOCIATION

P.O. Box 22697, Nashville TN 37202. (615)242-0303. **Fax:** (615)254-9755. **E-mail:** info@gospelmusic.org. **Website:** www.gospelmusic.org. Serves songwriters, musicians and anyone directly involved in or who supports gospel music. Professional members include advertising agencies, musicians, songwriters, agents/managers, composers, retailers, music publishers, print and broadcast media, and other members of the recording industry. Associate members include supporters of gospel music and those whose involvement in the industry does not provide them with income. The primary purpose of the GMA is to expose, promote, and celebrate the Gospel through music. A GMA membership offers newsletters, performance experiences and workshops, as well as networking opportunities. Applications accepted year-round. Membership fees: $95/year for professionals; $25/year for iMembers (supporters of gosepl music and those whose involvement in the industry does not provide them a source of income).

⦿ THE GUILD OF INTERNATIONAL SONGWRITERS & COMPOSERS

Sovereign House, 12 Trewartha Rd., Praa Sands, Penzance, Cornwall TR20 9ST United Kingdom. (01)(736)762826. **Fax:** (01)(736)763328. **E-mail:** songmag@aol.com. **Website:** www.songwriters-guild.co.uk. The Guild of International Songwriters & Composers is an international music industry organisation based in England in the United Kingdom. Guild members are songwriters, composers, lyricists, poets, performing songwriters, musicians, music publishers, studio owners, managers, independent record companies, music industry personnel, etc., from many countries throughout the world. The Guild of International Songwriters & Composers has been publishing *Songwriting and Composing Magazine* since 1986, which is issued free to all Guild members throughout their membership. The Guild of International Songwriters and Composers offers advice, guidance, assistance, copyright protection service, information, encouragement, contact information, intellectual property/copyright protection of members works through the Guild's Copyright Registration Centre along with other free services and more to Guild members with regard to helping members achieve their aims, ambitions, progression and advancement in respect to the many different aspects of the music industry. Information, advice and services available to Guild members throughout their membership includes assistance, advice and help on many matters and issues relating to the music industry in general. Annual membership fees: are £55.

INTERNATIONAL BLUEGRASS MUSIC ASSOCIATION (IBMA)

608 W. Iris Dr., Nashville TN 37204. (615)256-3222. **Fax:** (615)256-0450. **E-mail:** info@ibma.org. **Website:** www.ibma.org. Serves songwriters, musicians and professionals in bluegrass music. "IBMA is a trade association composed of people and organizations involved professionally and semi-professionally in the bluegrass music industry, including performers, agents, songwriters, music publishers, promoters, print and broadcast media, local associations, recording manufacturers and distributors. Voting members must be currently or formerly involved in the bluegrass industry as full- or part-time professionals. A songwriter attempting to become professionally involved in our field would be eligible. Our mission statement reads: *IBMA: Working together for high standards of professionalism, a greater appreciation for our music, and the success of the worldwide bluegrass music community.* IBMA publishes a bimonthly *International Bluegrass*, holds an annual trade show/convention with a songwriters showcase in the fall, represents our field outside the bluegrass music community, and compiles and disseminates databases of bluegrass related resources and organizations. Market research on the bluegrass consumer is available and we offer Bluegrass in the Schools information and matching grants. The primary value in this organization for a songwriter is having current information about the bluegrass music field and contacts with other songwriters, publishers, musicians and record companies." Offers workshops, liability insurance, rental car discounts, consultation and databases of record companies, radio stations, press, organizations and gigs. Applications accepted year-round. Membership fee: for a non-voting patron, $40/year; for an individual voting professional, $75/year; for an organizational voting professional, $205/year.

☻ INTERNATIONAL SONGWRITERS ASSOCIATION LTD.

P.O. Box 46, Limerick City, Ireland United Kingdom. (01)(71)486-5353. **E-mail:** jliddane@songwriter.iol.ie.

Website: www.songwriter.co.uk. **Contact:** Anna M. Sinden, membership department. Serves songwriters and music publishers. "The ISA headquarters is in Limerick City, Ireland, and from there it provides its members with assessment services, copyright services, legal and other advisory services and an investigations service, plus a magazine for one yearly fee. Our members are songwriters in more than 50 countries worldwide, of all ages. There are no qualifications, but applicants under 18 are not accepted. We provide information and assistance to professional or semi-professional songwriters. Our publication, *Songwriter*, which was founded in 1967, features detailed exclusive interviews with songwriters and music publishers, as well as directory information of value to writers." Offers competitions, instruction, library, newsletter and a weekly e-mail newsletter *Songwriter Newswire*. Applications accepted year-round. Membership fee for European writers is £19.95; for non-European writers, U.S. $30.

JUST PLAIN FOLKS MUSIC ORGANIZATION

5327 Kit Dr., Indianapolis IN 46237. **E-mail:** JPFolksPro@aol.com. **Website:** www.jpfolks.com. "Just Plain Folks is among the world's largest Music Organizations. Our members cover nearly every musical style and professional field, from songwriters, artists, publishers, producers, record labels, entertainment attorneys, publicists and PR experts, performing rights organization staffers, live and recording engineers, educators, music students, musical instrument manufacturers, TV, Radio and Print Media, and almost every major Internet music entity. Representing all 50 U.S. states and over 160 countries worldwide, we have members of all ages, musical styles and levels of success, including winners and nominees of every major music industry award, as well as those just starting out. A complete demographics listing of our group is available on our website. Whether you are a #1 hit songwriter or artist, or the newest kid on the block, you are welcome to join. Membership does require an active e-mail account." The purpose of this organization is "to share wisdom, ideas and experiences with others who have been there, and to help educate those who have yet to make the journey. Just Plain Folks provides its members with a friendly networking and support community that uses the power of the Internet and combines it with good old-fashioned human interaction. We help promote our members ready for success and educate those still learning."

TIPS *Just Plain Notes Newsletter:* "Members receive our frequent e-mail newsletters full of expert info on how to succeed in the music business, profiles of members successes and advice, opportunities to develop your career and tons of first-person networking contacts to help you along the way. (Note: we send this out 2-3 times/month via e-mail only.) "Our motto is 'We're All In This Together!'"

KNOXVILLE SONGWRITERS ASSOCIATION

P.O. Box 603, Knoxville TN 37901. **E-mail:** edna1riddick@yahoo.com. **Website:** www.knoxvillesongwritersassociation.com. **Contact:** Edna Riddick, president. Serves songwriters of all ages. "Some have been members since 1982, others are beginners. Members must be interested in learning the craft of songwriting. Not only a learning organization but a support group of songwriters who wants to learn what to do with their song after it has been written. We open doors for aspiring writers. The primary benefit of membership is to supply information to the writer on how to write a song. Many members have received major cuts." Offers showcases, instruction, lectures, library, newsletter, performance opportunities, evaluation services and workshops. Applications accepted year-round. Membership fee: $30/year.

THE LAS VEGAS SONGWRITERS ASSOCIATION

P.O. Box 42683, Las Vegas NV 89116-0683. (702)223-7255. **E-mail:** lasvegassongwriters@yahoo.com. "We are an educational, nonprofit organization dedicated to improving the art and craft of the songwriter. We want members who are serious about their craft. We want our members to respect their craft and to treat it as a business. Members must be at least 18 years of age. We offer quarterly newsletters, monthly information meetings, workshops three times a month and quarterly seminars with professionals in the music business. We provide support and encouragement to both new and more experienced songwriters. We critique each song or lyric that's presented during workshops, we make suggestions on changes—if needed. We help turn amateur writers into professionals. Several of our songwriters have had their songs recorded on both independent and major labels." Membership fee: $30/year.

LOS ANGELES MUSIC NETWORK

P.O. Box 2446, Toluca Lake CA 91610. (818)769-6095. **E-mail:** info@lamn.com. **Website:** www.lamn.com. "Connections. Performance opportunities. Facts. Career advancement. All that is available with your membership in the Los Angeles Music Network (LAMN). Our emphasis is on sharing knowledge and information, giving you access to top professionals and promoting career development. LAMN is an association of music industry professionals, i.e., artists, singers, songwriters, and people who work in various aspects of the music industry with an emphasis on the creative. Members are ambitious and interested in advancing their careers. LAMN promotes career advancement, communication and education among artists and creatives. LAMN sponsors industry events and educational panels held at venues in the Los Angeles area and now in other major music hubs around the country (New York, Las Vegas, Phoenix, and San Francisco). LAMN Jams are popular among our members. Experience LAMN Jams in L.A. or N.Y. by performing your original music in front of industry experts who can advance your career by getting your music in the hands of hard-to-reach music supervisors. The singer-songwriter contest gives artists an opportunity to perform in front of industry experts and receive instant feedback to their music, lyrics and performance. As a result of the exposure, Tim Fagan won the John Mayer Songwriting Contest and was invited to tour with the Goo Goo Dolls, Lifehouse, and platinum recording artist Colbie Caillat. This paired him with multi-platinum songwriter and recording artist John Mayer, with whom Fagan co-wrote 'Deeper.' Publisher Robert Walls has pitched music from LAMN Jam performers to hit TV shows like *The O.C.* and *Grey's Anatomy*, and the flick *The Devil Wears Prada*. Other performers have received offers including publishing and production deals and studio gigs. Offers performance opportunities, instruction, newsletter, lectures, seminars, music industry job listings, career counseling, resume publishing, mentor network, and many professional networking opportunities. See our website for current job listings and a calendar of upcoming events." Applications accepted year-round. Annual membership fee: $15.

LOUISIANA SONGWRITERS ASSOCIATION

P.O. Box 82009, Baton Rouge LA 70884. **E-mail:** info@louisianamusichalloffame.org. **Website:** http://louisianamusichalloffame.org. Serves songwriters. Membership fee: $25/year.

☺ MANITOBA MUSIC

1-376 Donald St., Winnipeg MB R3B 2J2 Canada. (204)942-8650. **Fax:** (204)942-6083. **E-mail:** info@manitobamusic.com. **Website:** www.manitobamusic.com. **Contact:** Sara Stasiuk, executive director. Organization consists of "songwriters, producers, agents, musicians, managers, retailers, publicists, radio, talent buyers, media, record labels, etc. (no age limit, no skill level minimum). Must have interest in the future of Manitoba's music industry." The main purpose of Manitoba Music is to foster growth in all areas of the Manitoba music industry primarily through education, promotion and lobbying. Offers newsletter, extensive website, directory of Manitoba's music industry, workshops and performance opportunities. Manitoba Music is also involved with the Western Canadian Music Awards festival, conference and awards show. Applications accepted year-round. Membership fee: $50 (Canadian).

MEMPHIS SONGWRITERS' ASSOCIATION

P.O. Box 343106, Memphis TN 38184. (901)577-0906. **E-mail:** membership@memphissongwriters.org; songkindler@memphissongwriters.org. **Website:** www.memphissongwriters.org. "MSA is a nonprofit songwriters organization serving songwriters nationally. Our mission is to dedicate our services to promote, advance, and help songwriters in the composition of music, lyrics and songs; to work for better conditions in our profession; and to secure and protect the rights of MSA songwriters. The Memphis Songwriters Association are organizational members of the Folk Alliance (FA.org). We also supply copyright forms. We offer critique sessions for writers at our monthly meetings. We also have monthly open mic songwriters night to encourage creativity, networking and co-writing. We host an annual songwriter's seminar and an annual songwriter's showcase, as well as a bi-monthly guest speaker series, which provide education, competition and entertainment for the songwriter. In addition, our members receive a bimonthly newsletter to keep them informed of MSA activities, demo services, and opportunities in the songwriting field." Membership fees: $50/year; $35/year for students and seniors.

MINNESOTA ASSOCIATION OF SONGWRITERS

P.O. Box 4262, St. Paul MN 55104. **E-mail:** info@mnsongwriters.org. **Website:** www.mnsongwriters.org. "Includes a wide variety of members, ranging in age from 18 to 80; type of music is very diverse, ranging from alternative rock to contemporary Christian; skill levels range from beginning songwriters to writers with recorded and published material. Main requirement is an interest in songwriting. Although most members come from the Minneapolis-St. Paul area, others come in from surrounding cities, nearby Wisconsin, and other parts of the country. Some members are full-time musicians, but most represent a wide variety of occupations. MAS is a nonprofit community of songwriters which informs, educates, inspires, and assists its members in the art and business of songwriting." Offers instruction, newsletter, lectures, workshops, performance opportunities, and evaluation services. Applications accepted year-round. Membership fee: $35.

TIPS "Members are kept current on resources and opportunities. Original works are played at meetings and are critiqued by involved members. Through this process, writers hone their skills and gain experience and confidence in submitting their works to others."

☺ MUSIC BC INDUSTRY ASSOCIATION

#100-938 Howe St., Vancouver BC V6Z 1N9 Canada. (604)873-1914. **Fax:** (604)873-9686. **E-mail:** info@musicbc.org; musicbcinfo@gmail.com. **Website:** www.musicbc.org. Music BC (formerly PMIA) is a nonprofit society that supports and promotes the spirit, development, and growth of the BC music community provincially, nationally, and internationally. Music BC provides education, resources, advocacy, opportunities for funding, and a forum for communication. Visit the website for membership benefits.

MUSICIANS CONTACT

P.O. Box 788, Woodland Hills CA 91365. (818)888-7879. **E-mail:** information@musicianscontact.com. **Website:** www.musicianscontact.com. "The primary source of paying jobs for musicians and vocalists nationwide. Job opportunities are posted daily on the Internet. Also offers exposure to the music industry for solo artists and complete acts seeking representation."

NASHVILLE SONGWRITERS ASSOCIATION INTERNATIONAL (NSAI)

1710 Roy Acuff Place, Nashville TN 37203. (615)256-3354. **E-mail:** nsai@nashvillesongwriters.com. **Website:** www.nashvillesongwriters.com. Purpose: a not-for-profit service organization for both aspiring and professional songwriters in all fields of music. Membership: Spans the U.S. and several foreign countries. Songwriters may apply in 1 of 4 annual categories: Active ($200 U.S currency for songwriters who are actively working to improve in the craft of writing and/or actively pursing a career within the songwriting industry); Professional ($100 U.S. currency for songwriters who are staff writers for a publishing company or earn 51% of their annual income from songwriting, whether from advances, royalties, or performances, or are generally regarded as a professional songwriter within the music industry); Lifetime (please contact NSAI for details). Membership benefits: music industry information and advice, song evaluations, eNews, access to industry professionals through weekly Nashville workshops and several annual events, regional workshops, use of office facilities, and discounts on books and NSAI's 3 annual events. There are also "branch" workshops of NSAI. Workshops must meet certain standards and are accountable to NSAI.

TIPS Also see the listing for NSAI Songwriters Song-Posium (formerly NSAI Spring Symposium) in the Workshops section of this book.

THE NATIONAL ASSOCIATION OF COMPOSERS/USA (NACUSA)

P.O. Box 49256, Barrington Station, Los Angeles CA 90049. **E-mail:** nacusa@music-usa.org; tdmmusic8@gmail.com. **Website:** www.music-usa.org/nacusa. **Contact:** Greg A. Steinke, Ph.D, membership coordinator. "We are of most value to the concert hall composer. Members are serious music composers of all ages and from all parts of the country, who have a real interest in composing, performing, and listening to modern concert hall music. The main purpose of our organization is to perform, publish, broadcast and write news about composers of serious concert hall music—mostly chamber and solo pieces. Composers may achieve national notice of their work through our newsletter and concerts, and the fairly rare feeling of supporting a non-commercial music enterprise dedicated to raising the musical and social position of the serious composer. 99% of the money earned in music is earned, or so it seems, by popular songwriters who might feel they owe the art of music something, and this is one way they might help support that art. It's a chance to foster fraternal solidarity with their less prosperous, but wonderfully interesting classical colleagues at a time when the very existence of serious art seems to be questioned by the general populace." Offers competitions, lectures, performance opportunities, library and newsletter. Applications accepted year-round. Membership fee: National (regular): $30; National (students/seniors): $15.

TIPS Also see the listing for NACUSA Young Composers' Competition in the Contests & Awards section of this book.

NEW MUSIC USA

90 John St., Suite 312, New York NY 10038. (212)645-6949. **Fax:** (646)490-0998. **E-mail:** info@newmusicusa.org. **Website:** www.newmusicusa.org. **Contact:** Lorna Krier, program manager. "New Music USA was formed by the merger of the American Music Center and Meet the Composer. We provide over $1 million each year in grant support for the creation and performance of new work and community building throughout the country. We amplify the voice of the new music community through NewMusicBox, profiling the people and ideas that energize and challenge music makers today. We stream a wide-ranging catalogue of new music around the clock on Counterstream Radio and provide an online home for composers to feature their own music. This is not a membership organization; all musicians are eligible for support." Offers grant programs and information services. Deadlines vary for each grant program.

OPERA AMERICA

330 Seventh Ave., New York NY 10001. (212)796-8620. **Fax:** (212)796-8631. **E-mail:** info@operaamerica.org; SSnook@operaamerica.org. **Website:** www.operaamerica.org. **Contact:** Sam Snook, membership manager. Members are composers, librettists, musicians, singers, and opera/music theater producers. Offers conferences, workshops, and seminars for artists. Publishes online database of opera/music theater companies in the U.S. and Canada, database of opportunities for performing and creative artists, online directory of opera and musical performances world-wide and in the U.S., and an online directory of new works created and being developed by current-day composers and librettists, to encourage the performance of new works. Applications accepted year-

round. Publishes a quarterly magazine and a variety of electronic newsletters. Membership fees are on a sliding scale by membership level.

OUTMUSIC

1206 Pacific St., Suite 3D, New York NY 11216. **E-mail:** info@outmusicfoundation.org. **Website:** www.outmusicfoundation.org; http://thelara.org. "OUTMUSIC—The LGBT Academy of Recording Artists (LARA) is a 501c3 nonprofit, charitable foundation that serves as an advocacy and awareness platform, and offers programming to support its mission to promote the advancement and appreciation of LGBT music culture and heritage, create opportunities to support the development of young aspiring artists, increase the viability and visibility of the LGBT music and entertainment platform and honor, document and archive the contributions and achievements of out and proud LGBT music artists." Offers newsletter, lectures, workshops, performance opportunities, networking, industry leads. Sponsors OUTMUSIC Awards. Applications accepted year-round. Membership: $100 for individual artist; $150 for duo or group; $100 for individual patrons; $150 for business patrons.

PORTLAND SONGWRITERS ASSOCIATION

P.O. Box 28355, Portland OR 97228. **E-mail:** info@portlandsongwriters.org. **Website:** http://portlandsongwriters.org. "The PSA is a nonprofit organization providing education and opportunities that will assist writers in creating and marketing their songs. The PSA offers an annual National Songwriting Contest, monthly workshops, songwriter showcases, special performance venues, quarterly newsletter, mail-in critique service, and discounted seminars by music industry pros." Membership fee: $25 (no eligibility requirements).

TIPS "Although most of our members are from the Pacific Northwest, we offer services that can assist songwriters anywhere. Our goal is to provide information and contacts to help songwriters grow artistically and gain access to publishing, recording and related music markets. For more information, please call, write, or e-mail."

RHODE ISLAND SONGWRITERS' ASSOCIATION

P.O. Box 9246, Warwick RI 02889. **E-mail:** generalinfo@risongwriters.com; memberships@risongwriters.com. **Website:** www.risongwriters.com. "Member-

ship consists of novice and professional songwriters. RISA provides opportunities to the aspiring writer or performer as well as the established regional artists who have recordings, are published and perform regularly. The only eligibility requirement is an interest in the group and the group's goals. Non-writers are welcome as well." The main purpose is to "encourage, foster and conduct the art and craft of original musical and/or lyrical composition through education, information, collaboration and performance." Offers instruction, newsletter, lectures, workshops, performance opportunities and evaluation services. Applications accepted year-round. Membership fees: $25/year (individual); $35/year (family/band). "The group holds twice monthly critique sessions; twice monthly performer showcases (one performer featured) at a local coffeehouse; songwriter showcases (usually 6-8 performers); a weekly open mic; and a yearly songwriter festival called 'Hear In Rhode Island,' featuring approximately 50 Rhode Island acts, over two days."

SAN DIEGO SONGWRITERS GUILD

4809 Clairemont Dr. #413, San Diego CA 92117. (858)376-7374. **Website:** http://sdsongwriters.org. "Members range from their early 20s to senior citizens with a variety of skill levels. Several members perform and work full time in music. Many are published and have songs recorded. Some are getting major artist record cuts. Most members are from San Diego county. New writers are encouraged to participate and meet others. All musical styles are represented." The purpose of this organization is to "serve the needs of songwriters and artists, especially helping them in the business and craft of songwriting through industry guest appearances." Offers competitions, newsletter, workshops, performance opportunities, discounts on services offered by fellow members, in-person song pitches and evaluations by publishers, producers and A&R executives. Applications accepted year-round. Membership dues: $50/year.

SESAC INC.

55 Music Square East, Nashville TN 37203. (615)320-0055. **Fax:** (615)963-3527. **Website:** www.sesac.com. "SESAC is a selective organization taking pride in having a repertory based on quality rather than quantity. Serves writers and publishers in all types of music who have their works performed by radio, television, nightclubs, cable TV, etc. Purpose of the organization is to collect and distribute performance royalties to all

active affiliates. As a SESAC affiliate, the individual may obtain equipment insurance at competitive rates. Music is reviewed upon invitation by the Writer/Publisher Relations department."

⊙ SOCAN

41 Valleybrook Dr., Toronto ON M3B 2S6 Canada. (866)307-6226. **E-mail:** info@socan.ca; members@socan.ca. **Website:** www.socan.ca. "SOCAN is the Canadian copyright collective for the communication and performance of musical works. We administer these rights on behalf of our members (composers, lyricists, songwriters, and their publishers) and those of affiliated international organizations by licensing the use of their music in Canada. The fees collected are distributed as royalties to our members and to affiliated organizations throughout the world. We also distribute royalties received from those organizations to our members for the use of their music worldwide. SOCAN has offices in Toronto, Montreal, Vancouver, and Dartmouth."

SOCIETY OF COMPOSERS & LYRICISTS

8447 Wilshire Blvd., Suite 401, Beverly Hills CA 90211. (310)281-2812. **Fax:** (310)284-4861. **E-mail:** execdir@thescl.com. **Website:** www.thescl.com. The professional nonprofit trade organization for members actively engaged in writing music/lyrics for films, TV, and/or video games, or who are students of film composition or songwriting for film. Primary mission is to advance the interests of the film and TV music community. Offers an award-winning quarterly publication, educational seminars, screenings, special member-only events, and other member benefits. Applications accepted year-round. Membership fees: $135 Full Membership (composers, lyricists, songwriters—film/TV music credits must be submitted); $85 Associate/Student Membership for composers, lyricists, songwriters without credits only; $135 Sponsor/Special Friend Membership (music editors, music supervisors, music attorneys, agents, etc.).

⊙O SODRAC INC.

Tower B, Suite 1010, 1470 Peel, Montreal QC H3A 1T1 Canada. (514)845-3268. **Fax:** (514)845-3401. **E-mail:** sodrac@sodrac.ca; members@sodrac.ca. **Website:** www.sodrac.ca. **Contact:** Alain Lauzon, general manager. "SODRAC is a reproduction rights collective society facilitating the clearing of rights on musical and artistic works based on the Copyright Board of Canada tariffs or through collective agreements concluded

with any users and is responsible for the distribution of royalties to its national and international members. The Society counts over 6,000 Canadian members and represents musical repertoire originating from nearly 100 foreign countries and manages the rights of over 25,000 Canadian and foreign visual artists. SODRAC is the only reproduction rights society in Canada where both songwriters and music publishers are represented, equally and directly." Serves those with an interest in songwriting and music publishing no matter what their age or skill level is. "Members must have written or published at least one musical work that has been reproduced on an audio (CD, cassette, or LP) or audio-visual support (TV, DVD, video), or published 5 musical works that have been recorded and used for commercial purposes. The new member will benefit from a society working to secure his reproduction rights (mechanicals) and broadcast mechanicals." Applications accepted year-round.

SONGWRITERS & POETS CRITIQUE

P.O. Box 21065, Columbus OH 43221. **Website:** www.timothysklugh.com/spc. **Contact:** Jane Harmon, activities director; Lee Ann Pretzman, secretary. "Benefits: A group of songwriters interested in improving your musical works; regular meetings to discuss songs and poetry; organized scheduling of music seminar trips and other music-related trips; annual Song of the Year competitions; group song critiques; access to website to catalogue and make available your music to the public; access to other musicians for nominal fees; access to other vocalists for nominal fees; access to demo recording studios for nominal fees; advice on the songs or poetry you are working on; sharing of opportunities and resources to improve your musical work; friendly support group of seasoned artists who share a passion for music, and poetry and are serious in their musical pursuits." Membership: $30/year.

SONGWRITERS ASSOCIATION OF WASHINGTON

4200 Wisconsin Ave. NW, PMB 106-137, Washington DC 20016. **E-mail:** contact@SAW.org. **Website:** www.saw.org. The Songwriters' Association of Washington (SAW) is a nonprofit organization established in 1979 to benefit aspiring and professional songwriters. "Our mission: Strengthen the craft of songwriting; foster the talents of our members; provide an active forum for songwriters and their work; celebrate the power of music." Membership: $35/year, $20/year for students.

THE SONGWRITERS GUILD OF AMERICA

5120 Virginia Way, Suite C22, Brentwood TN 37027. (615)742-9945. **Fax:** (615)630-7501. **E-mail:** membership@songwritersguild.com. **Website:** www.songwritersguild.com. "The Songwriters Guild of America Foundation offers a series of workshops with discounts for some to SGA members, including online classes and song critique opportunities. There is a charge for some songwriting classes and seminars; however, online classes and some monthly events may be included with an SGA membership. Charges vary depending on the class or event. Current class offerings and workshops vary. Visit the website to sign up for the newsletter and e-events, and for more information on current events and workshops. Some current events in Nashville are the Ask-a-Pro and ProCritique sessions that give SGA members the opportunity to present their songs and receive constructive feedback from industry professionals. Various performance opportunities are also available to members, including an SGA Showcase at the Bluebird. The New York office hosts a weekly Pro-Shop, which is coordinated by producer/musician/award-winning singer Ann Johns Ruckert. For each of 6 sessions an active publisher, producer or A&R person is invited to personally screen material from SGA writers. Participation is limited to 10 writers and an audit of 1 session. Audition of material is required. Various performance opportunities and critique sessions are also available from time to time. SGAF Week is held periodically and is a week of scheduled events and seminars of interest to songwriters that includes workshops, seminars and showcases."

SONGWRITERS HALL OF FAME (SONGHALL)

330 W. 58th St., Suite 411, New York NY 10019. (212)957-9230. **Fax:** (212)957-9227. **E-mail:** info@songhall.org. **Website:** www.songhall.org. **Contact:** Jimmy Webb, chairman. "SongHall membership consists of songwriters of all levels, music publishers, producers, record company executives, music attorneys, and lovers of popular music of all ages. There are different levels of membership, all able to vote in the election for inductees, except supporters and Associates, who pay only $15 and $25 in dues (respectively), but are unable to vote. SongHall's mission is to honor the popular songwriters who write the soundtrack for the world, as well as providing educational and net-working opportunities to our members through our workshop and showcase programs." Offers: newsletter, workshops, performance opportunities, networking meetings with industry pros and scholarships for excellence in songwriting. Applications accepted year-round. Membership fees: $15 and up.

SONGWRITERS OF WISCONSIN INTERNATIONAL

P.O. Box 1027, Neenah WI 54957. **E-mail:** sowi2012@gmail.com. **Website:** www.SongwritersOfWisconsin.org. Serves songwriters. "Membership is open to songwriters writing all styles of music. Residency in Wisconsin is recommended but not required. Members are encouraged to bring tapes and lyric sheets of their songs to the meetings, but it is not required. We are striving to improve the craft of songwriting in Wisconsin. Living in Wisconsin, a songwriter would be close to any of the workshops and showcases offered each month at different towns. The primary value of membership for a songwriter is in sharing ideas with other songwriters, being critiqued and helping other songwriters." Offers competitions (contest entry deadline: June 15), field trips, instruction, lectures, newsletter, performance opportunities, social outings, workshops and critique sessions. Applications accepted year-round. Membership dues: $30/year.

SONGWRITERS RESOURCE NETWORK

Portland OR **E-mail:** info@songwritersresourcenetwork.com. **Website:** www.SongwritersResourceNetwork.com. "For songwriters and lyricists of every kind, from beginners to advanced." No eligibility requirements. "Purpose is to provide free information to help songwriters develop their craft, market their songs, and learn about songwriting opportunities." Sponsors the annual Great American Song Contest, offers marketing tips and website access to music industry contacts. "We provide leads to publishers, producers and other music industry professionals." Visit website or send SASE for more information.

TIPS Also see the listing for Great American Song Contest in the Contests and Awards section of this book.

SOUTHWEST VIRGINIA SONGWRITERS ASSOCIATION

P.O. Box 698, Salem VA 24153. **E-mail:** svsasongwriters@gmail.com. **Website:** www.svsasongs.com. Accepts members of all ages and all skill levels, mainly country, folk, gospel, contemporary, and rock but other musical interests too. "The purpose of SVSA is to increase, broaden and expand the knowledge of each member and to support, better and further the progress and success of each member in songwriting and related fields of endeavor." Offers performance opportunities, evaluation services, instruction, workshops, monthly meetings and monthly newsletter. Applications accepted year-round. Membership fee: $20/year.

TEXAS ACCOUNTANTS & LAWYERS FOR THE ARTS

1540 Sul Ross, Houston TX 77006. (713)526-4876. **Fax:** (713)526-1299. **E-mail:** info@talarts.org; office@talarts.org. **Website:** www.talarts.org. TALA's members include accountants, attorneys, museums, theatre groups, dance groups, actors, artists, musicians and filmmakers. Our members are of all age groups and represent all facets of their respective fields. TALA is a nonprofit organization that provides pro bono legal and accounting services to income-eligible artists from all disciplines and to nonprofit arts organizations. TALA also provides mediation services for resolving disputes as a low-cost nonadversarial alternative to litigation. Offers newsletter, lectures, library and workshops. Applications accepted year-round. Annual membership fees: students, $30; artists, $50; bands, $100; nonprofit organizations, $200. **TIPS** TALA's speakers program presents low-cost seminars on topics such as The Music Business, Copyright and Trademark, and The Business of Writing. These seminars are held annually at a location in Houston. TALA's speakers program also provides speakers for seminars by other organizations.

TEXAS MUSIC OFFICE

P.O. Box 13246, Austin TX 78711. (512)463-6666. **Fax:** (512)463-4114. **E-mail:** music@governor.state.tx.us. **Website:** http://governor.state.tx.us/music. **Contact:** Casey J. Monahan, director. "The Texas Music Office (TMO) is a state-funded business promotion office and information clearinghouse for the Texas music industry. The TMO assists more than 14,000 individual clients each year, ranging from a new band trying to make statewide business contacts to BBC journalists seeking information on Down South Hip hop. The TMO is the sister office to the Texas Film Commission, both of which are within the Office of the Governor. The TMO serves the Texas music industry by using its Business Referral Network: Texas Music Industry (7,880 Texas music businesses in 96 music

business categories); Texas Music Events (625 Texas music events); Texas Talent Register (8,036 Texas recording artists); Texas Radio Stations (942 Texas stations); U.S. Music Contacts; Classical Texas (detailed information for all classical music organizations in Texas); and International (1,425 foreign businesses interested in Texas music). Provides referrals to Texas music businesses, talent and events in order to attract new business to Texas and/or to encourage Texas businesses and individuals to keep music business in-state. Serves as a liaison between music businesses and other government offices and agencies. Publicizes significant developments within the Texas music industry."

⊙ TORONTO MUSICIANS' ASSOCIATION

15 Gervais Dr., Suite 500, Toronto ON M3C 1Y8 Canada. (416)421-1020. **Fax:** (416)421-7011. **E-mail:** info@tma149.ca. **Website:** www.tma149.ca. "Local 149 of the American Federation of Musicians of the United States and Canada is the Professional Association for musicians in the greater Toronto Area. A member driven association of 3,500 members, the TMA represents professional musicians in all facets of music in the greater Toronto area. Dedicated to the development of musical talent and skills the Toronto Musicians' Association has for the past 100 years fostered the opportunity through the collective efforts of our members for professional musicians to live and work in dignity while receiving fair compensation." Joining fee: $225; thereafter, members pay $61.25 per quarter.

VOLUNTEER LAWYERS FOR THE ARTS

1 E. 53rd St., 6th Floor, New York NY 10022. (212)319-2787, ext. 1. **Fax:** (212)752-6575. **E-mail:** vlany@vlany.org. **Website:** www.vlany.org. Purpose of organization: Volunteer Lawyers for the Arts is dedicated to providing free arts-related legal assistance to low-income artists and not-for-profit arts organizations in all creative fields. Over 1,000 attorneys in the New York area donate their time through VLA to artists and arts organizations unable to afford legal counsel. Everyone is welcome to use VLA's Art Law Line, a legal hotline for any artist or arts organization needing quick answers to arts-related questions. VLA also provides clinics, seminars and publications designed to educate artists on legal issues that affect their careers. Members receive discounts on publications and seminars as well as other benefits. Some of the many publications we carry are *All You Need to Know About the Music Business*; *Business and Legal Forms for Fine*

Artists, Photographers & Authors & Self-Publishers; *Contracts for the Film & TV Industry*, plus many more.

WASHINGTON AREA MUSIC ASSOCIATION

6263 Occoquan Forest Dr., Manassas VA 20112. (703)368-3300. **Fax:** (703)393-1028. **E-mail:** dcmusic@wamadc.com. **Website:** www.wamadc.com. Serves songwriters, musicians and performers, managers, club owners and entertainment lawyers; "all those with an interest in the Washington music scene." The organization is designed to promote the Washington, D.C., music scene and increase its visibility. Its primary value to members is its seminars and networking opportunities. Offers lectures, newsletter, performance opportunities and workshops. WAMA sponsors the annual Washington Music Awards (The Wammies) and The Crosstown Jam or annual showcase of artists in the DC area. Applications accepted year-round. Membership fee: $35/year.

WEST COAST SONGWRITERS

1724 Laurel St., Suite 120, San Carlos CA 94070. (650)654-3966. **E-mail:** info@westcoastsongwriters.org; ian@westcoastsongwriters.org. **Website:** www.westcoastsongwriters.org. "Our 1,200 members are lyricists and composers from ages 16-80, from beginners to professional songwriters. No eligibility requirements. Our purpose is to provide the education and opportunities that will support our writers in creating and marketing outstanding songs. WCS provides support and direction through local networking and input from Los Angeles and Nashville music industry leaders, as well as valuable marketing opportunities. Most songwriters need some form of collaboration, and by being a member they are exposed to other writers, ideas, critiquing, etc." Offers annual West Coast Songwriters Conference, "the largest event of its kind in northern California. This 2-day event held the second weekend in September features 16 seminars, 50 screening sessions (over 1,200 songs listened to by industry professionals) and a sunset concert with hit songwriters performing their songs." Also offers monthly visits from major publishers, songwriting classes, competitions, seminars conducted by hit songwriters ("we sell audio tapes of our seminars--list of tapes available on request"), mail-in song-screening service for members who cannot attend due to time or location, a monthly e-newsletter, monthly performance opportunities and workshops. Applications accepted year-round. Membership fees: $40/year for students; $90/year, regular individual; $119, bands; $150+, contributing members.

TIPS "WCS's functions draw local talent and nationally recognized names together. This is of a tremendous value to writers outside a major music center. We are developing a strong songwriting community in Northern and Southern California. We serve the San Jose, Monterey Bay, East Bay, San Francisco, Los Angeles, Sacramento and Portland, WA areas and we have the support of some outstanding writers and publishers from both Los Angeles and Nashville. They provide us with invaluable direction and inspiration."

RETREATS & COLONIES

//

This section provides information on retreats and artists' colonies. These are places for creatives, including songwriters, to find solitude and spend concentrated time focusing on their work. While a residency at a colony may offer participation in seminars, critiques or performances, the atmosphere of a colony or retreat is much more relaxed than that of a conference or workshop. Also, a songwriter's stay at a colony is typically anywhere from one to twelve weeks (sometimes longer), while time spent at a conference may only run from one to fourteen days.

Like conferences and workshops, however, artists' colonies and retreats span a wide range. Yaddo, perhaps the most well-known colony, limits its residencies to artists "working at a professional level in their field, as determined by a judging panel of professionals in the field." The Brevard Music Center offers residencies only to those involved in classical music. Despite different focuses, all artists' colonies and retreats have one thing in common: They are places where you may work undisturbed, usually in nature-oriented, secluded settings.

SELECTING A COLONY OR RETREAT

When selecting a colony or retreat, the primary consideration for many songwriters is cost, and you'll discover that arrangements vary greatly. Some colonies provide residencies as well as stipends for personal expenses. Some suggest donations of a certain amount. Still others offer residencies for substantial sums but have financial assistance available.

When investigating the various options, consider meal and housing arrangements and your family obligations. Some colonies provide meals for residents, while others require residents to pay for meals. Some colonies house artists in one main building; others provide separate cottages. A few have provisions for spouses and families. Others prohibit families altogether.

Overall, residencies at colonies and retreats are competitive. Since only a handful of spots are available at each place, you often must apply months in advance for the time period you desire. A number of locations are open year-round, and you may find that planning to go during the "off-season" lessens your competition. Other colonies, however, are only available during certain months. In any case, be prepared to include a sample of your best work with your application. Also, know what project you'll work on while in residence and have alternative projects in mind in case the first one doesn't work out once you're there.

Each listing in this section details fee requirements, meal and housing arrangements, and space and time availability, as well as the retreat's surroundings, facilities and special activities. Of course, before making a final decision, send an SASE to the colonies or retreats that interest you to receive their most up-to-date details. Costs, application requirements and deadlines are particularly subject to change.

MUSICIAN'S RESOURCE

For other listings of songwriter-friendly colonies, see *Musician's Resource* (available from Watson-Guptill—www.watsonguptill.com), which not only provides information about conferences, workshops and academic programs but also residencies and retreats. Also check the Publications of Interest section in this book for newsletters and other periodicals providing this information.

BREVARD MUSIC CENTER

P.O. Box 312, Brevard NC 28712. (828)862-2140. **Fax:** (828)884-2036. **Website:** www.brevardmusic.org. **Contact:** Frank McConnell, director of operations. The Brevard Music Center is a community of student and professional musicians who aspire to ever-higher levels of artistry. Since all members of the community reside on campus, learning occurs constantly and is manifest through intensive practice and rehearsal and a challenging concert schedule. A consistently high level of public performance is a hallmark of the Brevard Music Center.

● THE TYRONE GUTHRIE CENTRE

Annaghmakerrig, Newbliss, County Monaghan Ireland. (353)(047)54003. **Fax:** (353)(047)54380. **E-mail:** info@tyroneguthrie.ie. **Website:** www.tyroneguthrie.ie. Offers year-round residencies. Artists may stay for anything from 1 week to 3 months in the Big House, or for up to 6 months at a time in one of the 5 self-catering houses in the old farmyard. Open to artists of all disciplines. Accommodates 13 in the big house and up to 7 in the farmyard cottages. Personal living quarters include bedroom with bathroom en suite. Offers a variety of workspaces. There is a music room for composers and musicians with a Yamaha C3M-PE conservative grand piano, a performance studio with a Yamaha upright, a photographic darkroom and a number of studios for visual artists, one of which is wheelchair accessible. At certain times of the year it is possible, by special arrangement, to accommodate groups of artists, symposiums, master classes, workshops and other collaborations.
COSTS Irish and European artists: €300/week for the big house; €150 for self-catering cottages; others pay €600 per week, all found, for a residency in the Big House and €300 per week (plus gas and electricity costs) for one of the self-catering farmyard houses. To qualify for a residency, it is necessary to show evidence of a significant level of achievement in the relevant field.

THE HAMBIDGE CENTER

105 Hambidge Court, Rabun Gap GA 30568. (706)746-5718. **Fax:** (706)746-9933. **E-mail:** center@hambidge.org; director@hambidge.org. **Website:** www.hambidge.org. **Contact:** Debra Sanders, office manager; Jamie Badoud, executive director. Hambidge provides a residency program that empowers talented artists to explore, develop, and express their creative voices. Situated on 600 acres in the mountains of north Georgia, Hambidge is a sanctuary of time and space that inspires artists working in a broad range of disciplines to create works of the highest caliber. Hambidge's Residency Program opens the first week of February and closes mid-to late-December through the month of January. Application deadlines are: January 15 for May-August; April 15 for September-December; September 15 for March-April of the following year.
COSTS Resident fellows pay $200/week.

ISLE ROYALE NATIONAL PARK ARTIST-IN-RESIDENCE PROGRAM

800 E. Lakeshore Dr., Houghton MI 49931. (906)482-0984. **Fax:** (906)482-8753. **E-mail:** Greg_Blust@nps.gov. **Website:** www.nps.gov/getinvolved/artist-in-residence.htm. Offers 2-3 week residencies from mid-June to mid-September. Open to all art forms. Accommodates 1 artist with 1 companion at 1 time. Personal living quarters include cabin with shared outhouse. A canoe is provided for transportation. Offers a guest house at the site that can be used as a studio. The artist is asked to contribute a piece of work representative of their stay at Isle Royale, to be used by the park in an appropriate manner. During their residency, artists will be asked to share their experience (1 presentation per week of residency, about 1 hour/week) with the public by demonstration, talk, or other means.
REQUIREMENTS Deadline: postmarked February 16, 2014. Send for application forms and guidelines. Accepts inquiries via fax or e-mail. A panel of professionals from various disciplines, and park representatives will choose the finalists. The selection is based on artistic integrity, ability to reside in a wilderness environment, a willingness to donate a finished piece of work inspired on the island, and the artist's ability to relate and interpret the park through their work.

KALANI OCEANSIDE RETREAT

RR2, Box 4500, Pahoa HI 96778. (808)965-7828. **Fax:** (808)965-0527. **Website:** www.kalani.com. **Contact:** Richard Koob, founder and director.

> "Kalani Honua means harmony of heaven and earth, and this is what we aspire to. We welcome all in the spirit of aloha and are guided by the Hawai'ian tradition of 'ohana (extended family), respecting our diversity yet sharing in unity. We invite you to open your heart to the

Big Island of Hawaii at Kalani Oceanside Retreat."

COSTS $76-235/night, lodging only. Full meal plan (3 chef-prepared meals/day) available for $42/day. Prices subject to change. Airport transportation by Kalani service $65/trip, or taxi $90/trip.

SITKA CENTER FOR ART & ECOLOGY

56605 Sitka Dr., Otis OR 97368. (541)994-5485. **Fax:** (541)994-8024. **E-mail:** info@sitkacenter.org. **Website:** www.sitkacenter.org.

COSTS Residency and housing provided. The resident is asked to provide some form of community service on behalf of Sitka.

VIRGINIA CENTER FOR THE CREATIVE ARTS

154 San Angelo Dr., Amherst VA 24521. (434)946-7236. **Fax:** (434)946-7239. **E-mail:** vcca@vcca.com. **Website:** www.vcca.com. Offers residencies year-round, typical residency lasts 2 weeks to 2 months. Open to originating artists: composers, writers, and visual artists. Accommodates 25 at one time. Personal living quarters include 22 single rooms, 2 double rooms, bathrooms shared with one other person. All meals are served. Kitchens for fellows' use available at studios and residence. The VCCA van goes into town twice a week. Fellows share their work regularly. Four studios have pianos. No transportation costs are covered. "Artists are accepted into the VCCA without regard for their ability to contribute financially to their residency. Daily cost is $180 per fellow. We ask fellows to contribute according to their ability."

COSTS Application fee: $30. Deadline: May 15 for October-January residency; September 15 for February-May residency; January 15 for June-September residency. Send SASE for application form or download from website. Applications are reviewed by panelists.

WORKSHOPS & CONFERENCES

///

For a songwriter just starting out, conferences and workshops can provide valuable learning opportunities. At conferences, songwriters can have their songs evaluated, hear suggestions for further improvement and receive feedback from music business experts. They are also excellent places to make valuable industry contacts. Workshops can help a songwriter improve his craft and learn more about the business of songwriting. They may involve classes on songwriting and the business, as well as lectures and seminars by industry professionals.

Each year, hundreds of workshops and conferences take place all over the country. Songwriters can choose from small regional workshops held in someone's living room to large national conferences such as South by Southwest in Austin, Texas, which hosts more than 6,000 industry people, songwriters and performers. Many songwriting organizations—national and local—host workshops that offer instruction on just about every songwriting topic imaginable, from lyric writing and marketing strategy to contract negotiation. Conferences provide songwriters the chance to meet one-on-one with publishing and record company professionals and give performers the chance to showcase their work for a live audience (usually consisting of industry people) during the conference. There are conferences and workshops that address almost every type of music, offering programs for songwriters, performers, musical playwrights and much more.

This section includes national and local workshops and conferences with a brief description of what they offer, when they are held and how much they cost to attend. Write or call any that interest you for further information. To find out what workshops or conferences take place in specific parts of the country, see the Geographic Index at the end of this book.

APPEL FARM ARTS AND MUSIC FESTIVAL

P.O. Box 888, Elmer NJ 08318. (856)358-2472. **Fax:** (856)358-6513. **E-mail:** jdunaway@appelfarm.org; stimmons@appelfarm.org. **Website:** www.appel-farm.org. **Contact:** Sean Timmons, artistic director. Appel Farm's mission is "to provide people of all ages, cultures and economic backgrounds with a supportive, cooperative environment in which to explore the fine and performing arts." We believe that the arts are an exciting and essential part of the learning process and that artistic talent is innate and waiting to be developed in every person.

ASCAP I CREATE MUSIC EXPO

1 Lincoln Plaza, New York NY 10023. **E-mail:** expo@ascap.com. **Website:** www.ascap.com. "The ASCAP I Create Music EXPO puts you face-to-face with some of the world's most successful songwriters, composers, producers and music business leaders, all who willingly share their knowledge and expertise and give you the know-how to take your music to the next level." For more info and to register, visit the website.

ASCAP MUSICAL THEATRE WORKSHOP

1 Lincoln Plaza, New York NY 10023. **Website:** www.ascap.com. Workshop is for musical theatre composers and lyricists only. Its purpose is to nurture and develop new musicals for the theatre. Offers programs for songwriters. Offers programs annually, usually April through May. Events take place in New York City. Four musical works are selected. Others are invited to audit the workshop. Participants are amateur and professional songwriters, composers and musical playwrights. Participants are selected by demo CD submission. Deadline: see website. Also available: the annual ASCAP/Disney Musical Theatre Workshop in Los Angeles. It takes place in January and February. Deadline is late November. Details similar to New York workshop as above.

ASCAP WEST COAST/LESTER SILL SONGWRITERS WORKSHOP

7920 Sunset Blvd., 3rd Floor, Los Angeles CA 90046. **Website:** www.ascap.com. Annual workshop for advanced songwriters sponsored by the ASCAP Foundation. Re-named in 1995 to honor ASCAP's late Board member and industry pioneer Lester Sill, the workshop takes place over a four-week period and features prominent guest speakers from various facets of the music business. Workshop dates and deadlines vary from year to year; refer to the website for updated info. Applicants must submit 2 songs on a CD (cassette tapes not accepted), lyric sheets, brief bio and short explanation as to why they would like to participate, e-mail address, and telephone number. Limited number of participants are selected each year.

BILLBOARD & THE HOLLYWOOD REPORTER FILM & TV MUSIC CONFERENCE

Sofitel LA, 8555 Beverly Blvd., Los Angeles CA 90048. (212)493-4026. **E-mail:** conferences@billboard.com. **Website:** www.billboardevents.com. **Contact:** Nicole Carbone. Promotes all music for film and television. Offers programs for songwriters and composers. Held at the Directors Guild of America in October. More than 350 songwriters/musicians participate in each event. Participants are professional songwriters, composers, producers, directors, etc. Conference panelists are selected by invitation. For registration information, including fees, call Nicole Carbone at (212)493-4263.

THE BMI LEHMAN ENGEL MUSICAL THEATRE WORKSHOP

7 World Trade Center, 250 Greenwich St., New York NY 10007. (212)230-3000. **Fax:** (212)262-2824. **E-mail:** theater@bmi.com. **Website:** www.bmi.com. **Contact:** Patricia Cook, director. "BMI is a music licensing company which collects royalties for affiliated writers and publishers. We offer programs to musical theatre composers, lyricists and librettists. The BMI-Lehman Engel Musical Theatre Workshops were formed if an effort to refresh and stimulate professional writers, as well as to encourage and develop new creative talent for the musical theatre. Each workshop meets 1 afternoon a week for 2 hours at BMI, New York. Participants are professional songwriters, composers and playwrights. The BMI Lehman Musical Theatre Workshop Showcase presents the best of the workshop to producers, agents, record and publishing company execs, press and directors for possible option and production. Visit www.bmi.com/genres/entry/musical_theatre_workshop_application for application. Tape and lyrics of 3 compositions required with applications."

TIPS BMI also sponsors a jazz composers workshop. For more information, contact Raette Johnson at rjohnson@bmi.com.

BROADWAY TOMORROW PREVIEWS

Science of Light, Inc., 191 Claremont Ave., New York NY 10027. **E-mail:** solministry@earthlink.net. **Website:** www.solministry.com/bway_tom.html. **Contact:** Elyse Curtis, artistic director. Purpose is the enrichment of American theater by nurturing new musicals. Offers series in which composers living in New York city area present self-contained scores of their new musicals in concert. Submission is by CD of music or video, synopsis, cast breakdown, résumé, reviews, if any, acknowledgement postcard and SASE. Participants selected by screening of submissions. Programs are presented in fall and spring with possibility of full production of works presented in concert.

CMJ MUSIC MARATHON & FILM FESTIVAL

1201 Broadway, Suite 706, New York NY 10001. (212)277-7120. **Fax:** (212)719-9396. **E-mail:** marketing@cmj.com. **Website:** www.cmj.com/marathon. "Premier annual alternative music gathering of more than 9,000 music business and film professionals. Fall, NYC; October 15-19, 2013. Features 5 days and nights of more than 75 panels and workshops focusing on every facet of the industry; exclusive film screenings; keynote speeches by the world's most intriguing and controversial voices; exhibition area featuring live performance stage; over 1,000 of music's brightest and most visionary talents (from the unsigned to the legendary) performing over 5 evenings at more than 80 of NYC's most important music venues." Participants are selected by submitting demonstration tape. Visit website for application (through Sonicbids.com).

CUTTING EDGE C.E.

(Formerly the Cutting Edge Music Business Conference), New Orleans LA 70116. (504)945-1800. **E-mail:** eric@cuttingedgenola.com. **Website:** www.cuttingedgenola.com. The conference is a 5-day international conference that covers the business and educational aspects of the music industry. As part of the conference, the New Works showcase features over 200 bands and artists from around the country and Canada in showcases of original music. All music genres are represented. Offers programs for songwriters and performers. "Bands and artists should submit material for consideration of entry into the New Works showcase." Event takes place during August in New Orleans. 1,000 songwriters/musicians participate in each event. Participants are songwriters, vocalists and bands. Send for application. Deadline: July 1.

FOLK ALLIANCE ANNUAL CONFERENCE

509 Delaware St. #101, Kansas City MO 64105. (816)221-3655. **Fax:** (816)221-3658. **E-mail:** fa@folk.org. **Website:** www.folk.org. **Contact:** Louis Meyes, executive director. Conference/workshop topics change each year. Conference takes place late-February and lasts 4 days at a different location each year. 2,000-plus attendees include artists, agents, arts administrators, print/broadcast media, folklorists, folk societies, merchandisers, presenters, festivals, recording companies, etc. Artists wishing to showcase should contact the office for a showcase application form. Closing date for official showcase application is in November.

INDEPENDENT MUSIC CONFERENCE

304 Main Ave., PMB 287, Norwalk CT 06851. (203)606-4649. **E-mail:** IMC@intermixx.com. **Website:** www.indiemusicon.com. "The purpose of the IMC is to bring together rock, hip hop and acoustic music for panels and showcases. Offers programs for songwriters, composers and performers. 250 showcases at 20 clubs around the city. Also offers a DJ cutting contest." Held annually in the fall. 3,000 amateur and professional songwriters, composers, individual vocalists, bands, individual instrumentalists, attorneys, managers, agents, publishers, A&R, promotions, club owners, etc., participate each year. Send for application.
◖ Formerly the Philadelphia Music Conference.

KERRVILLE FOLK FESTIVAL

Kerrville Festivals, Inc., P.O. Box 291466, Kerrville TX 78029. **E-mail:** info@kerrville-music.com. **Website:** www.kerrvillefolkfestival.com. **Contact:** Dalis Allen, producer. Hosts 3-day songwriters' school, a 4-day music business school and New Folk concert competition. Festival produced in late spring and late summer. Spring festival lasts 18 days and is held outdoors at Quiet Valley Ranch. 110 or more songwriters participate. Performers are professional songwriters and bands. Participants selected by submitting demo, by invitation only. Send cassette, or CD, promotional material and list of upcoming appearances. "Songwriter and music schools include lunch, experienced professional instructors, camping on ranch and concerts. Rustic facilities. Food available at reasonable cost. Audition materials accepted at above address. These three-day and four-day seminars include noon meals, handouts and camping on the ranch. Usually held during Kerrville Folk Festival, first and second week in June. Write or check the website for contest rules, schools and seminars information, and festival schedules. Also establishing a Phoenix Fund to provide assistance to ill or injured singer/songwriters who find themselves in distress."

LAMB'S RETREAT FOR SONGWRITERS

presented by Springfed Arts, a nonprofit organization, P.O. Box 304, Royal Oak MI 48068-0304. (248)589-3913. **E-mail:** johndlamb@ameritech.net. **Website:** www.springfed.org. **Contact:** John D. Lamb, director. Offers programs for songwriters on annual basis; November 7-10, 2013, and November 14-17, 2013, at The Birchwood Inn, Harbor Springs, MI. Sixty songwriters/musicians participate in each event. Participants are amateur and professional songwriters. Anyone can participate. Send for registration or e-mail. Deadline: 2 weeks before event begins. Fee: $275-525; includes all meals. Facilities are single/double occupancy lodging with private baths; 2 conference rooms and hospitality lodge. Offers song assignments, songwriting workshops, song swaps, open mic, and one-on-one mentoring. Faculty are noted songwriters, such as Doug and Telisha Williams, Dana Cooper, Michael Camp, Seth Glier and Carrie Elkin. Partial scholarships may be available by writing: Blissfest Music Organization, Jim Gillespie, P.O. Box 441, Harbor Springs, MI 49740. Deadline: 2 weeks before event.

MANCHESTER MUSIC FESTIVAL

P.O. Box 33, 42 Dillingham Ave., Manchester VT 05254. (802)362-1956. **Fax:** (802)362-0711. **E-mail:** info@mmfvt.org. **Website:** www.mmfvt.org. **Contact:** Joana Genova, education director. Offers classical music education and performances. Summer program for young professional musicians offered in tandem with a professional concert series in the mountains of Manchester, Vermont. Up to 23 young professionals, age 19 and up, are selected by audition for the Young Artists Program, which provides instruction, performance and teaching opportunities, with full scholarship for all participants. Commissioning opportunities for new music, and performance opportunities for professional chamber ensembles and soloists for both summer and fall/winter concert series.

THE NEW HARMONY PROJECT

P.O. Box 441062, Indianapolis IN 46244-1062. (317)464-1103. **E-mail:** mhunter@newharmonyproject.org; jgrynheim@newharmonyproject.org. **Web-**site: www.newharmonyproject.org. **Contact:** Mead Hunter, artistic director; Joel Grynheim, project director.

○ "The purpose of The New Harmony Project shall be to create, nurture, and promote new works for stage, television and film that sensitively and truthfully explore the positive aspects of life. Our goal is to bring the writers who seek to produce uplifting, high-quality entertainment alternatives to our conference, surround them with professional resources, provide them with the opportunity to develop these works in a supportive and life-affirming environment that further enables their writing creativity and help each writer to tell their story well."

NEWPORT FOLK FESTIVAL

New Festival Productions, LLC, PO Box 3865, Newport RI 02840. **E-mail:** info@newportfolkfest.net. **Website:** www.newportfolkfest.net. Held annually in mid-summer at the International Tennis Hall of Fame and Fort Adams State Park.

NEWPORT JAZZ FESTIVAL

New Festival Productions, LLC, Newport RI **E-mail:** jazz@newportjazzfest.net. **Website:** www.newportjazzfest.net. "Hailed by *The New York Times* as "the festival that put jazz festivals on the map," the Newport Jazz Festival, now the CareFusion Newport Jazz Festival, was founded by Jazz pianist George Wein in 1954 as the first outdoor music festival of its kind devoted entirely to Jazz, and is now universally acknowledged as the grandfather of all Jazz festivals. During the last half-century, the name Newport has become synonymous with the best in Jazz music. In its long illustrious history, the Newport Jazz Festival has presented a virtual pantheon of Jazz immortals alongside an array of rising young artists: Duke Ellington's 1956 rebirth framing Paul Gonzalves' epic solo; subject of the classic 1958 documentary *Jazz on a Summer's Day*; origin of famous recordings by Thelonious Monk, John Coltrane and Miles Davis; showcase for emerging young masters including Wynton Marsalis, Diana Krall, Joshua Redman and Esperanza Spalding. Referred to as a Mecca of Jazz, the event draws thousands of people from all over the world to its uniquely picturesque outdoor stages at the International Tennis Hall of Fame and Fort Adams State Park."

NORFOLK CHAMBER MUSIC FESTIVAL

P.O. Box 208246, New Haven CT 06520. **E-mail:** norfolk@yale.edu. **Website:** www.yale.edu/norfolk. Festival season of chamber music. Offers programs for composers and performers. Offers programs summer only. Approximately 45 fellows participate. Participants are up-and-coming composers and instrumentalists. Participants are selected by following a screening round. Auditions are held in New Haven, CT. Send for application. Deadline: mid-January. Fee: $50. "Held at the Ellen Battell Stoeckel Estate, the Festival offers a magnificent Music Shed with seating for 1,000, practice facilities, music library, dining hall, laundry and art gallery. Nearby are hiking, bicycling and swimming."

◯ NORTH BY NORTHEAST MUSIC FESTIVAL AND CONFERENCE

189 Church St., Lower Level, Toronto ON M5B 1Y7 Canada. (416)863-6963. **Fax:** (416)863-0828. **E-mail:** info@nxne.com; michaelh@nowtoronto.com. **Website:** www.nxne.com. **Contact:** Michael Hollett, managing director. "Our festival takes place mid-June at over 30 venues across downtown Toronto, drawing over 2,000 conference delegates, 500 bands and 50,000 music fans. Musical genres include everything from folk to funk, roots to rock, polka to punk and all points in between, bringing exceptional new talent, media front-runners, music business heavies and music fans from all over the world to Toronto." Participants include emerging and established songwriters, vocalists, composers, bands and instrumentalists. Festival performers are selected by submitting a CD and accompanying press kit or applying through sonicbids.com. Application forms are available by website or by calling the office. Submission period each year is from November 1 to the third weekend in January.

NSAI SONG CAMPS

1710 Roy Acuff Place, Nashville TN 37023. (800)321-6008; (615)256-335. **Fax:** (615)256-0034. **E-mail:** events@nashvillesongwriters.com. **Website:** www.nashvillesongwriters.com. Offers programs strictly for songwriters. Events held in mid-July in Nashville. "We provide most meals and lodging is available. We also present an amazing evening of music presented by the faculty." Camps are 3-4 days long, with 36-112 participants, depending on the camp. "There are different levels of camps, some having preferred prerequisites. Each camp varies. Please call, e-mail or refer

to the website. It really isn't about the genre of music, but the quality of the song itself. Song Camp strives to strengthen the writer's vision and skills, therefore producing the better song. Song Camp is known as 'boot camp' for songwriters. It is guaranteed to catapult you forward in your writing! Participants are all aspiring songwriters led by a pro faculty. We do accept lyricists only and composers only with the hopes of expanding their scope." Participants are selected through submission of 2 songs with lyric sheet. Song Camp is open to NSAI members, although anyone can apply and upon acceptance join the organization. There is no formal application form. See website for membership and event information. •Also see the listing for Nashville Songwriters Association International (NSAI) in the Organizations section of this book.

NSAI SONGWRITERS SONGPOSIUM

1710 Roy Acuff Place, Nashville TN 37203. (615)256-3354; (800)321-6008. **E-mail:** songposium@nashvillesongwriters.com; events@nashvillesongwriters.com. **Website:** www.nashvillesongwriters.com. Covers "all types of music. Participants take part in publisher evaluations, as well as large group sessions with different guest speakers." Offers annual programs for songwriters. Event takes place annually in downtown Nashville. Three-hundred amateur songwriters/musicians participate in each event. Send for application.

◯ ORFORD FESTIVAL

Orford Arts Centre, 3165 chemin du Parc, Orford QC J1X 7A2 Canada. (819)843-9871; (800)567-6155. **Fax:** (819)843-7274. **E-mail:** info@arts-orford.org. **Website:** www.arts-orford.org. The Orford Arts Centre plays host to a world-class Academy of Music, which offers advanced training to particularly gifted young musicians who are at the beginning of a professional career in classical music. Together with internationally renowned professors and artists who are devoted to training the next generation, we are committed to providing our students with pedagogical activities that are as unique as they are enriching. In pursuit of its mission, the Centre abides by the following values: excellence, discipline, dedication, open-mindedness, respect and the will to surpass individual expectations.

◯ REGGAE SUMFEST

Shops 9 & 10 Parkway Plaza, Rose Hall, Montego Bay Jamaica. **Website:** http://reggaesumfest.com. **Con-**

tact: Tina Mae Davis, festival coordinator. "Reggae Sumfest is a musical event to which we welcome 30,000+ patrons each year. The festival showcases the best of Dancehall and Reggae music, as well as top R&B/hip hop performers. The festival also offers delicious Jamaican cuisine as well as arts and crafts from all over the island. The main events of the festival is held at Catherine Hall, Montego Bay, Jamaica over a three-day period which usually falls in the third week of July." Reggae Sumfest is presented by Summerfest Productions and accepts press kit submissions for persons wishing to perform at the festival between November and January each year. Send to address above.

THE SONGWRITERS GUILD OF AMERICA FOUNDATION

5120 Virginia Way, Suite C22, Brentwood TN 37027. (800)524-6742; (615)742-9945. **E-mail:** ny@songwritersguild.com; nash@songwritersguild.com; la@songwritersguild.com. **Website:** www.songwritersguild.com. **Contact:** Mark Saxon, director of operations. The Foundation is in charge of many events, including workshops in the NY, Nashville, and L.A. areas.

SOUTH BY SOUTHWEST MUSIC CONFERENCE

SXSW Headquarters, P.O. Box 685289, Austin TX 78768. **E-mail:** sxsw@sxsw.com. **Website:** www.sxsw.com. South by Southwest (SXSW) is a private company based in Austin, Texas, with a year-round staff of professionals dedicated to building and delivering conference and festival events for entertainment and related media industry professionals. Since 1987, SXSW has produced the internationally-recognized music and media conference and festival (SXSW). As the entertainment business adjusted to issues of future growth and development, in 1994, SXSW added conferences and festivals for the film industry (SXSW Film) as well as for the blossoming interactive media (SXSW Interactive Festival). Now three industry events converge in Austin during a Texas-sized week, mirroring the ever increasing convergence of entertainment/media outlets. The next SXSW Music Conference and Festival will be held in March. Offers panel discussions, "Crash Course" educational seminars and nighttime showcases. SXSW Music seeks out speakers who have developed unique ways to create and sell music. From Thursday through Saturday, the conference includes over fifty sessions including a panel of label heads discussing strategy, interviews

with notable artists, topical discussions, demo listening sessions and the mentor program. And when the sun goes down, a multitude of performances by musicians and songwriters from across the country and around the world populate the SXSW Music Festival, held in venues in central Austin." Write, e-mail or visit website for dates and registration instructions.

TIPS "Visit the website in August to apply for showcase consideraton. SXSW is also involved in North by Northeast (NXNE), held in Toronto, Canada in late Spring."

THE SWANNANOA GATHERING— CONTEMPORARY FOLK WEEK

Warren Wilson College, P.O. Box 9000, Asheville NC 28815-9000. (828)298-3434. **Fax:** (828)298-3434. **E-mail:** gathering@warren-wilson.edu. **Website:** www.swangathering.com. **Contact:** Jim Magill, director. "For anyone who ever wanted to make music for an audience, we offer a comprehensive week in artist development, including classes in songwriting, performance, and vocal coaching; 2012 staff included Cheryl Wheeler, Buddy Mondlock, Ellis Paul, LJ Booth, Cliff Eberhardt, Jon Vezner, Sally Barris, Cosy Sheridan, David Roth, Danny Ellis, Siobhán Quinn, and Ray Chesna." For a brochure or other info, contact The Swannanoa Gathering at the phone number/address above. Takes place last week in July. Tuition: See website. Housing (including all meals): $385. Annual program of The Swannanoa Gathering Folk Arts Workshops.

UNDERCURRENTS

P.O. Box 94040, Cleveland OH 44101-6040. **E-mail:** music@undercurrents.com. **Website:** www.undercurrents.com. **Contact:** John Latimer, executive director. A music, event and art marketing and promotion network with online and offline exposure featuring music showcases, seminars, trade shows, networking forums. Ongoing programs and performances for songwriters, composers, and performers. Participants are selected by EPK, demo, biography, and photo. Register on the website.

WEST COAST SONGWRITERS CONFERENCE

(formerly Northern California Songwriters Association), 1724 Laurel St., Suite 120, San Carlos CA 94070. (650)654-3966. **E-mail:** info@westcoastsongwriters.org. **Website:** www.westcoastsongwriters.org. "Conference offers opportunity and education; 16 seminars,

50 song screening sessions (1,500 songs reviewed), performance showcases, one on one sessions and concerts." Offers programs for lyricists, songwriters, composers and performers. "During the year we have competitive live Songwriter competitions. Winners go into the playoffs. Winners of the playoffs perform at the sunset concert at the conference." Event takes place second weekend in September at Foothill College, Los Altos Hills, CA. Over 500 songwriters/musicians participate in this event. Participants are songwriters, composers, musical playwrights, vocalists, bands, instrumentalists and those interested in a career in the music business. Send for application. Deadline: September 1. Fee: $150-280. "See our listing in the Organizations section of this book."

WESTERN WIND WORKSHOP IN ENSEMBLE SINGING

263 W. 86th St., New York NY 10024. (212)873-2848. **E-mail:** workshops@westernwind.org; info@westernwind.org. **Website:** www.westernwind.org. **Contact:** William Zukoff, executive producer. Participants learn the art of ensemble singing—no conductor, one on-a-part. Workshops focus on blend, diction, phrasing, and production. Offers programs for performers. Limited talent-based scholarship available. Offers programs annually. Takes place June and August in the music department at Smith College, Northampton, MA. 70-80 songwriters and/or musicians participate in each event. Participants are amateur and professional vocalists. Anyone can participate. Send for application or register at their website. Arrangers' works are frequently studied and performed. Also offers additional workshops President's Day weekend in Brattleboro, VT and Columbus Day weekend in Woodstock, VT.

WINTER MUSIC CONFERENCE INC.

3450 NE 12 Terrace, Ft. Lauderdale FL 33334. (954)563-4444. **Fax:** (954)563-1599. **E-mail:** info@wintermusicconference.com. **Website:** www.wintermusicconference.com. Features educational seminars and showcases for dance, hip hop, alternative, and rap. Offers programs for songwriters and performers. Offers programs annually. Event takes place March of each year in Miami, Florida. 3,000 songwriters/musicians participate in each event. Participants are amateur and professional songwriters, composers, musical playwrights, vocalists, bands and instrumentalists. Participants are selected by submitting demo tape. Send SASE, visit website or call for application. Deadline: February. Event held at either nightclubs or hotel with complete staging, lights and sound.

VENUES

//

VENUES

THE 4TH AVENUE TAVERN

210 E. Fourth Ave., Olympia WA 98501. (360)951-7887. **E-mail:** the4thave@gmail.com. **Website:** www.the4t-have.com. Music: indie, alternative, funk, rock, punk.

40 WATT CLUB

285 W. Washington St., Athens GA 30601. (706)549-7871. **E-mail:** fortywatt@athens.net. **Website:** www.40watt.com. Music: indie, rock, alternative.

123 PLEASANT STREET

123 Pleasant St., Morgantown WV 26505. (304)292-0800. **E-mail:** 123pleasantstreet@gmail.com. **Website:** www.123pleasantstreet.com. "An eclectic crowd can be expected any given night and is as diverse as the bands that grace our stage whether it be rock, bluegrass, punk, jazz, reggae, salsa, country, DJs, indie, hardcore, old time, or some mixture of some or all or the above."

ABG'S BAR

190 W. Center St., Provo UT 84106. (801)373-1200. **E-mail:** booking@abgsbar.com. **Website:** http://abgsbar.com. Music: rock, alt-country, alternative, folk, blues, jazz.

ARMADILLO'S BAR & GRILL

132 Dock St., Annapolis MD 21401. (401)280-0028. **E-mail:** armadillosannapolis@gmail.com. **Website:** www.armadillosannapolis.com. "Armadillo's is the top choice for nightlife in downtown Annapolis. We are the only venue in town to provide two levels of live entertainment. Upstairs, Armadillo's brings you the hottest local and national bands, in a casual, intimate setting, while DJ's keep the crowd moving downstairs." Music: rock, acoustic, reggae, soul, pop, indie, alternative.

ART BAR

1211 Park St., Columbia SC 29201. (803)929-0198. **E-mail:** booking@artbarsc.com. **Website:** www.artbarsc.com. Music: rock, alternative, indie, punk, hard rock, hip-hop.

ASHLAND COFFEE & TEA

100 N. Railroad Ave., Ashland VA 23005. (804)798-1702. **Website:** http://ashlandcoffeeandtea.com. "Join us most Thursdays, Fridays and Saturdays in our intimate 'Listening Room' for an evening of Americana, bluegrass, folk, blues, jazz, pop —you never know what we'll have on tap with our wide range of performers. Don't miss 'Homegrown Wednesday' featuring local Virginia talent, or the 'Songwriter's Showdown', a songwriting and vocal performance competition every Tuesday."

BACKBOOTH

37 W. Pine St., Orlando FL 32801. (407)999-2570. **E-mail:** bookings@backbooth.com. **Website:** www.backbooth.com. "BackBooth's reputation as a music venue has grown to being named one of the best live music venues in the city, according to Orlando Weekly,

and still boasts the most impressive draft selection in downtown. With a capacity of 350, a large stage, a powerful sound / lighting system, balcony, and back bar area; the club still maintains a very comfortable and inviting, almost pub-like atmosphere with an Old English decor including wood work and dark curtains throughout. As a venue, Back Booth continues to play host to many popular national and regional acts, while remaining a favorite among locals. The club is also known for its dance parties; which are among the most popular and recognized in town. Whether it be for an intimate live performance, a rousing rock show, or a night of dancing and drinks, Back Booth is established in the heart of the central Florida community as a favorite destination." Music: reggae, acoustic, alternative, indie, pop, hip-hop, jam, roots, soul, gospel, funk, dubstep, country, rock, metal.

BACK EAST BAR & GRILL

9475 Briar Village Point, Colorado Springs CO 80920. (719)264-6161. **Website:** www.backeastbarandgrill. com. "We have created the perfect place for you to watch your favorite game and enjoy the incredible food and flavors that we have brought from home. We know you will enjoy every minute that you share with us. So sit back and have a drink, eat some great food, and enjoy your favorite team on one of our many TVs." Music: rock, alternative, R&B, blues, country, pop.

THE BARLEY STREET TAVERN

2735 N. 62nd St., Omaha NE 68104. (402)408-0028. **E-mail:** bookings@barleystreet.com. **Website:** www. barleystreet.com. "We have live music performances on scheduled nights, featuring some great local and regional performers, as well as, national touring acts. This is the music venue to find the best in all music styles." Music: rock, alternative, folk, indie, country, pop, Americana.

BERKELEY CAFE

217 W. Martin St., Raleigh NC 27601. (919)821-0777. **E-mail:** lakeboonee@bellsouth.net. **Website:** www. berkeleycafe.net. **Contact:** Jim Shires. Music: rock, bluegrass, alternative, blues, punk, folk.

BILLY'S LOUNGE

1437 Wealthy SE, Grand Rapids MI 49506. (616)459-5757. **E-mail:** billysbooking@gmail.com. **Website:** www.billyslounge.com. "In keeping the long standing tradition of service and entertainment, Billy's offers live music. Although deeply rooted in the Blues,

acts from all genres, ranging in size from local to international, can be heard blazing from Billy's premier sound system on any given night." Music: blues, country, rock, R&B, Americana, hip-hop, jazz.

BLUE

650A Congress St., Portland ME 04101. (207)774-4111. **E-mail:** booking@portcityblue.com. **Website:** http://portcityblue.com. "Located in the heart of Portland's Arts District, Blue is Portland's most intimate live music venue. We present an array of music such as Celtic, Middle Eastern, Blues, Old Time, Jazz, Folk, and more."

THE BLUE DOOR

2805 N. McKinley Ave., Oklahoma City OK 73106. (405)524-0738. **E-mail:** bluedoormusic@yahoo.com. **Website:** www.bluedoorokc.com. **Contact:** Greg Johnson. "We have grown to become Oklahoma's premiere venue for performing songwriters, hosting such legends as Jimmy Webb, Joe Ely, Ramblin' Jack Elliott, David Lindley and Tom Rush. We love working with new songwriters who are developing their audience and always welcome the best in bluegrass, folk, rock, country and blues."

BO'S BAR

2310 University Blvd., Tuscaloosa AL 35401. (205)259-1331. **E-mail:** bosbar2310@gmail.com. **Website:** www. bos-bar.com. **Contact:** Bo Hines, owner. Music: rock, alternative, country, alt-country, bluesgrass. "The most freedom loving bar in the world!"

THE BOTTLENECK

737 New Hampshire, Lawrence KS 66044. (785)841-5483. **E-mail:** booking@pipelineproductions.com. **Website:** www.thebottlenecklive.com. "The Bottleneck is considered by many to be a Rock & Roll historical landmark. The Bottleneck cemented its status as a scheduled stop on many major-city, national tours, giving nearby University of Kansas students access to some of the best names in modern music." Music: indie, rock, alternative, folk, jazz, blues, funk, dance, ska, psychedelic.

THE BOTTLETREE

3719 Third Ave. S, Birmingham AL 35222. (205)533-6288. **E-mail:** info@thebottletree.com. **E-mail:** merrilee@thebottletree.com; booking@thebottletree.com. **Website:** www.thebottletree.com. **Contact:** Merrilee Challiss. Music: punk, indie, folk, rock, country, soul, alternative.

BOTTOM OF THE HILL

1233 17th St., San Francisco CA 94107. (415)621-4455. **E-mail:** booking@bottomofthehill.com. **Website:** http://bottomofthehill.com. **Contact:** Ramona Downey; Ursula Rodriguez, bookers. Music: alternative, rock, rockabilly, punk, hard rock.

THE BRASS RAIL

1121 Broadway, Ft. Wayne IN 46802. (260)422-0881. **E-mail:** corey@brassrailfw.com. **Website:** www.brassrailfw.com. **Contact:** Corey Rader. Music: rock, punk, metal, alternative.

THE BREWERY

3009 Hillsborough St., Raleigh NC 27607. (919)838-6789. **E-mail:** tom@brewerync.com. **Website:** www.brewerync.com. "The Brewery has been a staple of the NC music scene since 1983. Having hosted some of the biggest names in the music industry, The Brewery is the perfect spot to see the best local musicians as well as the stars of tomorrow." Music: rock, pop, alternative, hip-hop.

THE BRICKYARD

129 N. Rock Island, Wichita KS 67202. (316)263-4044. **E-mail:** booking@brickyardoldtown.com. **Website:** www.brickyardoldtown.com. Music: rock, indie, alternative, punk, classic rock, country.

BROOKLYN BOWL

61 Wythe Ave., Brooklyn NY 11211. (718)963-3369. **E-mail:** rock.androll@brooklynbowl.com; booking@brooklynbowl.com. **Website:** www.brooklynbowl.com. "Brooklyn Bowl redefines the entertainment experience for the 21st century. Centered around a 16-lane bowling alley, 600-capacity performance venue with live music 7 nights a week, and food by Blue Ribbon, Brooklyn Bowl stakes out expansive new territory, literally and conceptually, in the 23,000-square foot former Hecla Iron Works (1882), one block from the burgeoning waterfront." Music: rock, indie, hip-hop, R&B, alternative, punk, funk, folk, reggae, soul.

THE BROTHERHOOD LOUNGE

119 Capital Way N, Olympia WA 98501. (360)352-4153. **Website:** www.thebrotherhoodlounge.com. Music: soul, funk, rock, pop, hip-hop, R&B.

THE BUNKHOUSE SALOON

124 S. 11th St., Las Vegas NV 89101. (702)384-4536. **E-mail:** booking@bunkhouselv.com. **Website:** www.bunkhouselv.com. **Contact:** Keith Fox, general manager. Music: indie, rock, punk, alternative, pop.

THE CACTUS CLUB

2496 S. Wentworth Ave., Milwaukee WI 53207. (414)897-0663. **E-mail:** cactuscl@execpc.com. **Website:** www.cactusclubmilwaukee.com. Music: punk, rock, alternative, indie, funk, pyschedelic.

CAFE 939

939 Boylston St., Boston MA 02215. (617)747-6040 or (617)747-6143. **E-mail:** 939booking@beklee.edu. **Website:** www.cafe939.com. "Cafe 939 showcases Berklee's emerging student performers and local Boston artists, as well as national acts seeking a more intimate, personal space in which to connect with their fans. The venue is open to the general public and aims to attract musicians and music fans from all walks of life." Music: rock, jazz, folk, Americana, bluegrass, hip-hop, electronica, pop, indie.

CAFE NINE

250 State St., New Haven CT 06511. (203)789-8281. **E-mail:** bookcafenine@gmail.com. **Website:** www.cafenine.com. **Contact:** Paul Mayer, booker. "Cafe Nine features live music from national, regional and local acts seven nights a week. Catch some of your favorites getting back to their roots in our intimate setting or see tomorrows stars on their way to the stadiums." Music: indie, rock, alternative, jazz, punk, garage, alt-country.

CALEDONIA LOUNGE

365 W. Clayton St., Athens GA 30601. (706)549-5577. **E-mail:** booking@caledonialounge.com. **Website:** http://caledonialounge.com. Music: indie, rock, alternative, folk.

THE CANOPY CLUB

708 S. Goodwin Ave., Champaign-Urbana IL 61801. (217)344-2263. **E-mail:** seth@jaytv.com; mikea@jaytv.com. **Website:** www.canopyclub.com. **Contact:** Seth Fein; Mike Armintrout. "In striving to achieve the highest level of entertainment, the Canopy Club prides itself on being able to offer entertainment for all walks of life. Whether you like rock, country, hip hop, jazz, funk, indie or anything in between, the Canopy Club has something to offer you. If you're a fan of live music and entertainment, the Canopy Club is your home in central Illinois!"

CASSELMAN'S BAR & VENUE

2620 Walnut St., Denver CO 80205. (720)242-8923. **E-mail:** booking@casselmans.com. **Website:** www.casselmans.com. "Casselman's is a multi-use live music and special events venue located in NoDo (North-Downtown) Denver. Casselman's opened in 2009 and started to brand "NoDo" as the new entertainment and arts district of Denver. The name Casselman is the maiden name of our great grandmother and was carried as the middle name down to three members of the family business. Casselman's is a proud recipient of the Westword's 2010 Best New Club award!" Music: pop, rock, R&B, hip-hop, alternative.

THE CAVE

452 1/2 W. Franklin St., Chapel Hill NC 27516. (919)968-9308. **E-mail:** info@caverntavern.com. **Website:** http://caverntavern.com. Music: pop, rock, country, twang, folk, acoustic, funk, indie, punk, blues, bluegrass.

TIPS Use online booking form.

CHELSEA'S CAFE

2857 Perkins Rd., Baton Rouge LA 70808. (225)387-3679. **E-mail:** dave@chelseascafe.com. **Website:** www.chelseascafe.com. "Chelsea's Cafe is Baton Rouge's favorite place to relax, offering good food, drinks and live music in an intimate, casual atmosphere." Music: rock, indie, alternative, soul.

CHILKOOT CHARLIE'S

2435 Spenard Rd., Anchorage AK 99503. (907)272-1010. **E-mail:** promo@koots.com. **Website:** www.koots.com. "Chilkoot Charlie's features a rustic Alaska atmosphere with sawdust-covered floors, 3 stages, 3 dance floors and 10 bars (11 in the summertime!) with padded tree stumps and beer kegs for seating. Literally filled to the rafters with such things as famous band photos and autographs, huge beer can collections, hilarious gags, and tons of Alaska memorabilia, a person could wander around Chilkoot Charlie's for days and still not see everything." Music: rock, punk, metal, ska.

CHROME HORSE SALOON

1202 Third St. SE, Cedar Rapids IA 52401. (319)365-1234. **E-mail:** chromehorsesaloon@mchsi.com. **Website:** www.chromehorsesaloon.net. "In addition to weekly shows inside on Friday and Saturday nights, a series of Friday night outdoor concerts are held in the parking lot during the summer months. The bar also has hosted a variety of national acts, including The Jeff Healey Band, L.A. Guns, Saliva, Hank Williams III, Black Oak Arkansas, The Buckinghams, The Grass Roots, American Idol finalist Amanda Over-

myer and Blues Traveler." Music: rock, funk, punk, indie, alternative.

CHURCHILL'S

5501 NE Second Ave., Miami FL 33137. (305)757-1807. **E-mail:** bookings@churchillspub.com. **Website:** www.churchillspub.com. Music: rock, alternative, indie, pop, jazz, hip-hop, electronica, acoustic.

CITY TAVERN

1402 Main St., Dallas TX 75201. (214)745-1402. **E-mail:** info@citytaverndowntown.com. **E-mail:** booking@citytaverndowntown.com. **Website:** www.citytaverndowntown.com. Music: country, rock, jam, pop, alternative.

CLUB 209

209 N. Boulder Ave., Tulsa OK 74103. (918)584-9944. **E-mail:** thegang@club209tulsa.com. **Website:** www.club209tulsa.com. Music: indie, Americana, alt-country, folk.

CLUB CONGRESS

311 E. Congress St., Tucson AZ 85701. (520)622-8848. **E-mail:** clubcongressbooking@gmail.com. **Website:** www.hotelcongress.com. **Contact:** David Slutes, entertainment and booking director. Music: rock, alternative, indie, folk, Americana.

THE CLUBHOUSE

1320 E. Broadway Rd., Tempe AZ 85282. (460)968-3238. **E-mail:** clubhousegigs@hotmail.com. **Website:** www.clubhousemusicvenue.com. "A club that features the best in local, touring, and regional acts. Voted Best Local Music Venue by *The New Times Magazine*, We have been in the valley of the sun for 6 years hosting shows for all age groups on a nightly basis." Music: rock, punk, metal, alternative.

CONGRESS THEATER

2135 North Milwaukee Ave., Chicago IL 60647. 773-252-4000. **E-mail:** alberto@congresschicago.com. **Website:** www.congresschicago.com. "The Congress Theater is always looking for local/regional talent. Please send us your information through our online form and we'll take a look."

MUSIC Alternative, Classic Rock, Electronic/Dance/DJ, Hip-Hop/Rap, Metal, Punk, Rock, and Urban/R&B.

🎧 "The theater dates back to the '20s when it was a movie palace in the style of Italian Renaissance and Classical Revival styles."

TIPS "Bands: if you're interested in getting on a current bill, or being considered for a future bill, pursue those opportunities through promoters in the entertainment community. Draw well at smaller venues in the city, and you won't have to call them. They'll call your agent."

D.B.A.

618 Frenchmen St., New Orleans LA 70116. (504)942-3731. **E-mail:** dbaneworleans@yahoo.com. **Website:** http://dbabars.com/dbano. "We are proud to present some of New Orleans and the region's greatest musicians, and are privileged to have had appearances on our stage by greats such as Clarence "Gatemouth" Brown, David "Honeyboy" Edwards, Jimmy Buffet and Stevie Wonder. When in New Orleans, get away from the tourist traps of Bourbon Street and head down to the "Marigny," just downriver from the French Quarter, voted w/ Williamsburg, Brooklyn and the Inner Mission in San Francisco as one of the hippest neighborhoods in the country." Music: blues, jazz, R&B, Cajun.

THE DOGFISH BAR & GRILLE

128 Free St., Portland ME 04101. (207)772-5483. **E-mail:** michele@thedogfishcompany.com. **Website:** www.thedogfishbarandgrille.com. "Great food, drink and service in a casual and unpretentious atmosphere and a great place to hear live local artists. The Dogfish Bar and Grille is an intimate, informal restaurant with a great dinner menu and daily specials. We have two very comfortable decks for those who enjoy eating outside, a dining room upstairs, and a friendly tavern on the ground floor. The Dogfish Bar and Grille books local, regional,and national talent most evenings of the week. The music is mostly acoustic, blues, and jazz. There is never a cover charge" Music: jazz, be-bop, blues, soul, jam, acoustic.

THE DOUBLE DOOR INN

1218 Charlottetowne Ave., Charlotte NC 28204. (704)376-1446. **E-mail:** info@doubledoorinn.com. **E-mail:** maxxmusic2@gmail.com. **Website:** www.doubledoorinn.com. **Contact:** Gregg McGraw, main talent buyer/promoter. "Established in 1973 and recognized as the "Oldest Live Music Venue East of the Mississippi," the Double Door Inn oozes musical tradition. Looking at our walls, packed with 35 years of autographed photos, has been described as being like "viewing a timeline for live music in the Queen City." Also holding the title "Oldest Blues Club In The U.S. Under Original Ownership," the Double Door Inn strives to bring the best in local, regional, and national touring and recording artists to the discriminating music lover. Legendary performers like Eric Clapton, Stevie Ray Vaughn, Dave Alvin, Leon Russell, Buddy Guy, Junior Brown, Bob Margolin, and others, have graced the stage of our historic and intimate venue." Music: blues, rock, soul, pop, funk, jazz, bluegrass, acoustic, folk, alt-country, R&B, Americana, reggae.

DOUG FIR LOUNGE

830 E. Burnside, Portland OR 97214. (503)231-9663. **E-mail:** booking@dougfirlounge.com. **Website:** www.dougfirlounge.com. Music: rock, alternative, indie, funk, garage, pop, dance, folk, bluegrass, soul, Americana.

DUFFY'S TAVERN

1412 O St., Lincoln NE 68508. (402)474-3543. **E-mail:** management@duffyslincoln.com. **E-mail:** booking@duffyslincoln.com. **Website:** www.duffyslincoln.com. **Contact:** Jeremy "Dub" Wardlaw, booking and promotions. "We're known for a lot of things, but if you ask any of us, we will tell you that we're a music venue. Many national acts have graced our stage, including Nirvana, 311, Bright Eyes, the Boss Martians, Slobberbone, Wesley Willis, and many others. A lot of us think some of the local acts are even better, and on any Sunday or Wednesday night, you can be assured Duffy's stage will be jumping with some of the best original music around." Music: rock, folk, Americana, indie, psychedelic, pop, hard rock.

THE ECHO

1822 Sunset Blvd., Los Angeles CA 90026. (213)413-8200. **Website:** www.attheecho.com. Music: funk, punk, rock, indie, folk, hip-hop, electronica, Mexicana, pop.

EL BAIT SHOP

200 SW Second St., Des Moines IA 50309. (515)284-1970. **E-mail:** music@elbaitshop.com. **Website:** http://elbaitshop.com. Music: rock, alternative, pop, indie, folk, country, Americana, blues, jam, bluegrass, psychedelic.

ELBOW ROOM

E-mail: paffer17@yahoo.com. **Website:** www.elbowroombar.com. **Contact:** Josh Paffhausen, owner and general manager. "With entertainment at least five nights a week, ranging from karaoke and red hot DJs to favorite local bands, and major headliners." Music: rock, alternative, country.

THE EMPTY BOTTLE

1035 N. Western Ave., Chicago IL 60622. (773)276-3600. **E-mail:** pete@emptybottle.com; christen@emptybottle.com; bookingasst@emptybottle.com. **Website:** www.emptybottle.com. **Contact:** Peter Toalson, booking agent/talent buyer. Music: rock, indie, psychedelic, anti-pop, garage, metal, country, dance, electronica, soul, blues, folk.

THE EMPTY GLASS

410 Elizabeth St., Charleston WV 25311. (304)345-3914. **E-mail:** booking@emptyglass.com. **Website:** www.emptyglass.com. Music: blues, jazz, rock, folk, bluegrass, indie.

EXIT/IN

2208 Elliston Place, Nashville TN 37203. (615)321-3340. **Website:** www.exitin.com. "The Exit/In began it's role as a Nashville music venue back in 1971. Since then countless shows and great memories have happened within these walls." Music: rock, country, alt-country, folk, punk, pop, psychedelic.

FAT CATZ MUSIC CLUB

440 Bourbon St., New Orleans LA 70130. (504)525-0303. **E-mail:** info@fatcatzmusicclub.com. **Website:** www.fatcatzmusicclub.com. "When you are looking for a great place to hang out in New Orleans, look no further! Stop by for a great time any day of the week. We have awesome music all the time, and our staff is second to none. Kick back, relax, and enjoy quality music with us! We have live bands EVERY night of the week that feature a large variety of music styles." Music: R&B, rock, alternative, jazz, hip-hop, pop, blues.

THE FINELINE MUSIC CAFE

318 First Ave., Minneapolis MN 55401. (612)338-8100. **E-mail:** finelinemusiccafe@gmail.com. **E-mail:** jeneen.flbooking@gmail.com; brad.flbooking@gmail.com; finelinebooking@gmail.com. **Website:** www.finelinemusic.com. **Contact:** Janeen Andersen; Brad Danielson; Kim King. Music: rock, acoustic, indie, folk, alternative.

FIVE SPOT

1123 Euclid Ave., Atlanta GA 30307. (404)223-1100. **E-mail:** booking@fivespot-atl.com. **Website:** http://fivespot-atl.com. **Contact:** Bryan Aust, general manager/owner. "On any given night, the Five Spot features live music of all genres, from bluegrass to indie

rock, jam bands to acid jazz, and form funk to hip-hop. We also feature live art, short films and animations. The Five Spot is Atlanta's most inclusive music and arts venue and features acoustic acts every Monday, a diverse Musician's Jam on Tuesdays, monthly Bluegrass Jams and many touring and national acts Wednesday through Sunday."

FLIPNOTICS

1601 Barton Springs Rd., Austin TX 78704. (512)658-7633. **E-mail:** flip@flipnotics.com. **E-mail:** flipsbooking@gmail.com. **Website:** http://flipnotics.com. "Flipnotics has been a local live music icon since it opened in 1992. We keep the South Austin tradition alive by serving up great coffee, local food and live music every night of the week." Music: indie, rock, alternative, pop, folk, country, Americana.

FREAKIN' FROG

4700 S. Maryland Pkwy., Las Vegas NV 89119. **E-mail:** music@freakinfrog.com. **Website:** www.freakinfrog.com. **Contact:** Tommy Marth, director of marketing. Music: pop, rock, punk, blues, alternative.

FREIGHT HOUSE DISTRICT

250 Evans Ave., Reno NV 89501. (775)334-7094. **E-mail:** info@freighthouse.com. **Website:** www.freighthouse.com. Includes: Duffy's Ale House, 205 Lounge, Bugsy's Sports Bar and Grill, Arroyo Mexican Grill. Music: funk, rock, Latin, pop, dance, alternative, soul, reggae, blues.

THE FREQUENCY

121 W. Main St., Madison WI 53703. (608)819-8777. **E-mail:** contact@madisonfrequency.com. **E-mail:** booking@madisonfrequency.com. **Website:** www.madisonfrequency.com. "The Frequency is serving up a wide variety of live music in downtown Madison seven nights a week featuring a smattering of local, regional, national and international acts playing bluegrass, punk, metal, jazz, electronic, indie, hip hop."

GEORGE'S MAJESTIC LOUNGE

519 W. Dickson St., Fayetteville AR 72701. (479)527-6618. **E-mail:** saxsafe@aol.com. **Website:** www.georgesmajesticlounge.com. **Contact:** Brian Crowne, owner/operator/booking; Harold Weities, general manager. "George's is perhaps best known for the incredible musicians that have graced our stages, bringing the best in local, regional, and national acts through our doors. Some artists of note that have performed at Georges through the years include Robert

Cray, Leon Russell, Little River Band, Delbert Mc-Clinton, Eddie Money, Pat Green, Derek Trucks, Sam Bush, Tower of Power, Leftover Salmon, Bob Margolin, Chubby Carrier, Tommy Castro, Coco Montoya, Anthony Gomes, Bernard Allison, Michael Burks, Charlie Robison, Cross Canadian Ragweed, Jason Boland, Dark Star Orchestra, Steve Kimock, Martin Fierro, North Mississippi Allstars, Robert Randolph, David Lindley, Big Smith, Cate Brothers, Oteil Burbridge, and so many more. Music: rock, folk, alternative, country, bluegrass, punk.

THE GOLDEN FLEECE TAVERN

132 W. Loockerman St., Dover DE 19904. (302)674-1776. **E-mail:** goldenfleecetavern@gmail.com. **Website:** www.thegoldenfleecetavern.com. Music: rock, indie, classic rock, pop, alternative.

THE GRAMOPHONE

4243 Manchester Ave., St. Louis MO 63110. (314)531-5700. **E-mail:** info@thegramophonelive.com. **Website:** http://thegramophonelive.com. "The Gramophone features an eclectic schedule of live music and DJs in an intimate concert setting." Music: hip-hop, funk, soul, indie, rock, Americana.

GREAT AMERICAN MUSIC HALL

859 O'Farrell St., San Francisco CA 94109. (415)885-0750. **E-mail:** dana@slims-sf.com. **Website:** www.gamh.com. **Contact:** Dana Smith, booking. "The past three decades at the Great American Music Hall have been full of music, with artists ranging from Duke Ellington, Sarah Vaughan and Count Basie to Van Morrison, the Grateful Dead and Bobby McFerrin." Music: contemporary pop, indie, jazz, folk, rock, alternative, Americana.

THE GREAT NORTHERN BAR & GRILL

27 Central Ave., Whitefish MT 59937. (406)862-2816. **E-mail:** info@greatnorthernbar.com. **Website:** www.greatnorthernbar.com. "The Great Northern Bar & Grill is the premiere destination in the Flathead Valley for good food, good music, and good times." Music: rock, alternative.

GREAT SCOTT

1222 Commonwealth Ave., Allston MA 02134. (617)566-9014. **E-mail:** submissions@greatscottboston.com. **Website:** www.greatscottboston.com. **Contact:** Carl Lavin. Music: rock, metal, alternative, indie.

THE GREEN LANTERN

497 W. Third St., Lexington KY 40508. (859)252-9539. **Website:** www.myspace.com/greenlanternbar. "Making the best neighborhood bar in Lex a reality." Music: rock, alternative, indie, folk, punk, metal.

GUNPOWDER LODGE

10092 Bel Air Rd., Kingsville MD 21087. (410)256-2626. **Website:** www.thegunpowderlodge.com. Music: rock, indie, acoustic, classic rock.

HAL & MAL'S

200 S. Commerce St., Jackson MS 39204. (601)948-0888. **E-mail:** april@halandmals.com. **Website:** www.halandmals.com. "The most talked about, upscale honky tonk in all of Mississippi. Here, art is made, music is played and locals gather to share community and celebrate the very best of Mississippi's creative spirit." Music: honky-tonk, country, rock, blues, classic rock, alternative.

HANK'S CAFE

1038 Nuuanu Ave., Honolulu HI 96817. (808)526-1411. **Website:** www.hankscafehonolulu.com. Music: rock, doo-wop, dance, country, pop.

THE HAVEN

6700 Aloma Ave., Winter Park FL 32792. (407)673-2712. **E-mail:** thehavenbooking@gmail.com. **Website:** www.thehavenrocks.com. **Contact:** Dave Himes. The Haven is a 350-plus capacity venue with a full-liquor bar located in the Aloma Square Shopping Center in Winter Park, FL. Music: Alternative, Classic Rock, Cover Band, Funk, Jam Band, Metal, Punk, Reggae, Rock, and Singer/Songwriter--all types of live music with local, regional and national bands, and most shows are age 18 and up.

TIPS See House P.A., Stage and Lighting Specs, Mains, Monitors, Microphones, Stage Dimensions, and Lighting Specs at: www.thehavenrocks.com/specs/.

HEADLINERS MUSIC HALL

1386 Lexington Rd., Louisville KY 40206. (502)584-8088. **E-mail:** booking@headlinerslouisville.com. **Website:** http://headlinerslouisville.com. "Locally owned and operated, Headliners Music Hall is the premiere live entertainment venue of Louisville, Kentucky. We bring the best local and national acts to our stage, with fantastic sound and a fun atmosphere. We've had the privilege of hosting some amazing rock, metal, acoustic, hip-hop, and alternative bands such as My Morning Jacket, Jimmy Eat World, Neko Case,

Clutch, Sharon Jones & The Dap Kings, Umphrey's McGee, Old Crow Medicine Show, Kings of Leon, Talib Kweli, Girl Talk and more." Music: rock, indie, punk, folk, reggae, soul, R&B, psychedelic.

THE HIDEOUT

1354 W. Wabansia, Chicago IL 60642. (773)227-4433. **Website:** www.hideoutchicago.com. "The Hideout is music, art, performance, plays, poetry, rock and rebellion." Music: indie, folk, rock, alternative, country.

HIGHLANDS TAP ROOM

1279 Bardstown Rd., Louisville KY 40204. (502)459-2337. **E-mail:** booking@highlandstaproom.com. **Website:** www.highlandstaproom.com. "Fun, friendly neightborhood bar in the heart of the Highlands, Louisville, KY. Live entertainment seven days a week." Music: rock, acoustic, hip-hop, folk, blues, bluegrass, alt-country.

HIGH-NOON SALOON

701A E. Washington Ave., Madison WI 53703. (608)268-1122. **E-mail:** info@high-noon.com. **E-mail:** booking@high-noon.com. **Website:** www.high-noon.com. **Contact:** Cathy Dethmers, owner/manager. "Founded in 2004 in downtown Madison, Wisconsin, High Noon Saloon is a live music venue that features many different styles of music, including rock, alternative, metal, indie, alt-country, pop, punk, bluegrass, folk, jam, world music, and more. We host large national acts, smaller touring bands from around the world, and lots of local music."

HI-TONE CAFE

1913 Poplar Ave., Memphis TN 38104. (901)278-8663. **E-mail:** thehitonecafe@gmail.com. **Website:** www.hitonememphis.com. **Contact:** Jonathan Kiersky, general manager/talent buyer. Music: rock, alternative, indie, pop, alt-country, Americana.

HOT TUNA

2817 Shore Dr., Virginia Beach VA 23451. (757)481-2888. **E-mail:** rstreet@hottunavb.com. **Website:** www.hottunavb.com. Music: rock, acoustic, alternative, dance, pop.

HOWLER'S COYOTE CAFE

4509 Liberty Ave., Pittsburgh PA 15224. (412)682-0320. **E-mail:** booking@howlerscoyotecafe.com. **Website:** www.howlerscoyotecafe.com. "Howler's Coyote Cafe is an independent mid-level music venue and bar in Pittsburgh's east end hosting local and national acts of all genres 5 days a week." Music: rock,

alternative, pop, dance, blues, alt-country, punk, jam, psychedelic, folk, indie.

HUMPY'S

610 W. Sixth Ave., Anchorage AK 99501. (907)276-2337. **Website:** www.humpys.com. Music: folk, rock, metal, blues, Americana.

JEREMIAH BULLFROGS LIVE

4115 SW Huntoon St., Topeka KS 66604. (785)273-0606. **E-mail:** bullfrogslive@gmail.com. **Website:** www.bullfrogslive.com. **Contact:** Rob Fateley. Music: blues, soul, rock, alternative, dance.

THE JEWISH MOTHER

600 Nevan Rd., Virginia Beach VA 23451. (757)428-1515. **E-mail:** quivaproductions@cox.net; jmomsmusic@aol.com. **Website:** www.jewishmother.com. Music: rock, Americana, indie, alternative, funk, soul.

JUANITA'S PARTY ROOM

614 President Clinton Ave., Little Rock AR 72201. (501)372-1228. **E-mail:** jsnyder@juanitas.com. **Website:** www.juanitas.com. **Contact:** James Snyder, general manager. Music: rock, reggae, alternative, country, alt-country, indie.

KILBY COURT

741 S. Kilby Ct., Salt Lake City UT 84101. (801)364-3538. **E-mail:** will@sartainandsaunders.com. **Website:** www.kilbycourt.com. **Contact:** Will Sartain. Music: rock, alternative, Americana, indie, pop, ska, punk.

KNICKERBOCKERS

901 O St., Lincoln NE 68508. (402)476-6865. **E-mail:** mail@knickerbockers.net. **Website:** www.knickerbockers.net. Music: alternative, rock, metal, punk, indie, folk, electronica, Americana.

LARIMER LOUNGE

2721 Larimer St., Denver CO 80205. (303)296-1003. **Website:** www.larimerlounge.com; www.booklarimer.com. **Contact:** James Irvine, booking manager. Music: rock, pop, electronica, indie, garage, alternative.

LAUNCHPAD

618 Central Ave. SW, Albuquerque NM 87102. (505)764-8887. **Website:** www.launchpadrocks.com. Music: rock, punk, reggae, alternative.

LEADBETTERS TAVERN

1639 Thames St., Baltimore MD 21231. (410)675-4794. **E-mail:** leadbetterstavern@gmail.com. **Web-**

site: www.leadbetterstavern.com. Music: blues, rock, soul, jazz, punk, alternative, funk, pop, indie.

LIQUID LOUNGE

405 S. 8th St. #110, Boise ID 83702. (208)287-5379. E-mail: liquidbooking@gmail.com. **Website:** www.liquidboise.com. Music: rock, reggae, funk, ska, bluegrass, dance, soul, folk, punk.

THE LOFT

2502 W. Colorado Ave., #301, Colorado Springs CO 80904. (719)445-9278. **Website:** http://theloftmusic.wordpress.com. "We are here to bring you the best musical experience in Colorado Springs with an intimate atmosphere, amazing sound and GREAT music. We hope you come often and tell your friends about our place." Music: rock, pop, country, acoustic, indie, blues, jazz, bluegrass, folk.

THE LOST LEAF BAR & GALLERY

914 N. Fifth St., Phoenix AZ 85004. (602)481-4004. **E-mail:** solnotes@hotmail.com. **Website:** www.thelostleaf.org. **Contact:** Tato Caraveo. Music: Latin, blues, salsa, hip-hop, R&B, funk, outlaw country, Americana.

THE LOUNGE AT HOTEL DONALDSON

101 Broadway, Fargo ND 58102. (701)478-1000 or (888)478-8768. **E-mail:** info@hoteldonaldson.com. **Website:** www.hoteldonaldson.com. **Contact:** Karen Stoker, founder/owner. Music: Americana, folk, indie, country, bluegrass.

LOW SPIRITS

2823 2nd St. NW, Albuquerque NM 87107. (505)433-9555. **Website:** www.lowspiritslive.com. Music: rock, indie, blues, alternative, folk.

LUCKEY'S CLUB CIGAR STORE

933 Olive St., Eugene OR 97401. (541)687-4643. **Website:** www.luckeysclub.com. **Contact:** Sam Hahn. "Today, Luckey's combines art nouveau decor, saloon sensibilities, serious pool players, cutting edge music, and a chair for everyone in the community. It still has echoes of the sounds, smells, pool games, and conversations from the past 100 years. It's like a time capsule with a hip twist." Music: folk, acoustic, blues, indie, Americana, rock.

MAD ANTHONY BREWING COMPANY

2002 Broadway, Ft. Wayne IN 46802. (260)426-2537. **E-mail:** madbrew@msn.com. **Website:** www.madbrew.com. "A cool, laid back atmosphere, full food menu and weekly live music." Music: rock, jam, jazz, blues, funk, soul, pop.

THE MAJESTIC/MAGIC STICK

4140 Woodward Ave., Detroit MI 48201. (313)833-9700. **E-mail:** dave@majesticdetroit.com; traci@majesticdetroit.com. **E-mail:** booking@majesticdetroit.com. **Website:** www.majesticdetroit.com. **Contact:** Dave Zainea, owner/general manager; Traci Zainea, talent buyer. Music: funk, Americana, rock, indie, alternative, hip-hop, punk, hard rock, soul, electronica.

MAJESTIC THEATRE

115 King St., Madison WI 53703. (608)255-0901. **E-mail:** info@majesticmadison.com. **Website:** www.majesticmadison.com. Estab. 1906. The Majestic Theatre is a world-class venue located in Madison, WI, that hosts major national touring acts. Seeks established local and regional acts to open for high-profile headlining acts. Music: Acoustic, Alternative, Americana, Classic Rock, Country, Electronic/Dance/DJ, Folk, Funk, Hip-Hop/Rap, Jam Band, Metal, Pop, Punk, Reggae, Rock, Singer/Songwriter, Spoken Word, and Urban/R&B.

TIPS Contact/submit online at website.

THE MANGY MOOSE RESTAURANT & SALOON

3285 McCollister Dr., Teton Village WY 83025. (307)733-4913. **E-mail:** management@mangymoose.net. **E-mail:** booking@mangymoose.net. **Website:** www.mangymoose.net. Music: funk, punk, electronica, indie, folk, rock, bluegrass.

MARTIN'S DOWNTOWN BAR & GRILL

413 First St. SW, Roanoke VA 24015. (540)985-6278. **E-mail:** jmart1175@aol.com. **Website:** www.martinsdowntown.com. Estab. 2005. Music: rock, jam band, reggae, grass, funk, ska.

MAXWELL'S

1039 Washington St., Hoboken NJ 07030. (201)653-1703. **E-mail:** TelstarRec@aol.com. **Website:** www.maxwellsnj.com. Music: rock, alternative, blues, punk, indie.

TIPS Please mail all booking information via postal mail.

MELODY INN

3826 N. Illinois St., Indianapolis IN 46208. (317)923-4707. **E-mail:** melodyinn2001@gmail.com. **Website:** www.melodyindy.com. Music: punk, rock, metal, indie, pop, rockabilly, bluegrass.

MEMPHIS ON MAIN

55 E. Main St., Champaign IL 61820. (217)398-1097. **E-mail:** info@memphisonmain.com. **Website:** http://memphisonmain.com. Music: rock, classic rock, R&B, blues, soul, funk, folk, country, metal, rockabilly, punk, reggae.

MERCURY LOUNGE

1747 S. Boston Ave., Tulsa OK 74119. (918)382-0012. **E-mail:** reggiemerc@gmail.com. **Website:** www.mercurylounge918.com. **Contact:** Reggie Dobson. Music: country, alt-country, Americana, blues, jazz, rock, reggae, rockabilly, pop.

MERCY LOUNGE/CANNERY BALLROOM

One Cannery Row, Nashville TN 37203. (615)251-3020. **E-mail:** info@mercylounge.com. **Website:** www.mercylounge.com. **Contact:** Drew Mischke and Todd Ohlhauser, managers. "Since the doors to the Mercy Lounge first opened back in January of 2003, the cozy little club on Cannery Row has been both locally-favored and nationally-renowned. Building a reputation for showcasing the best in burgeoning buzz-bands and renowned national talents, the club has maintained its relevance by consistently offering reliable atmosphere and entertainment." Music: pop, country, rock, folk, Americana, indie, funk, soul, psychedelic.

THE MET

1005 Main St., Pawtucket RI 02860. (401)729-1005. **E-mail:** info@themetri.com. **Website:** www.themetri.com. Music: rock, funk, folk, blues, soul, punk, alternative.

THE MIDDLE EAST NIGHTCLUB

472 Massachusetts Ave., Cambridge MA 02139. (617)864-3278. **E-mail:** booking@mideastclub.com. **Website:** www.mideastclub.com. Downstairs room capacity is 575. Upstairs is 195. Parking garage is attached to the Meridian Hotel. Music: funk, rock, alternative, dance, pop, hip-hop, punk, Americana.

MILLCREEK TAVERN

4200 Chester Ave., University City, Philadelphia PA 19104. (215)222-9194. **Website:** www.millcreektavernphilly.com.

MILLER THEATRE

Columbia University School of the Arts, 2960 Broadway, MC 1801, New York NY 10027. (212)854-6205. **Website:** www.millertheatre.com. **Contact:** Melissa Smey, director. "Miller Theatre's mission is to devel-op the next generation of cultural consumers, to re-invigorate public enthusiasm in the arts nationwide by pioneering new approaches to programming, to educate the public by presenting specialized, informative programs inviting to a broad audience, to discover new and diverse repertoire and commission new works, and to share Columbia University's intellectual riches with the public." Music: dance, contemporary and early music, jazz, opera, and performance.

MILLY'S TAVERN

500 Commercial St., Manchester NH 03101. (603)625-4444. **E-mail:** info@millystavern.com. **Website:** www.millystavern.com. "There is always something happening in our lounge. Whether it's from 4-7 pm, or all night, you are bound to have a good time. We offer live music every Tuesday, Thursday, Friday and Saturday." Music: blues, rock, retro, funk, dance.

MISSISSIPPI STUDIOS

3939 N. Mississippi, Portland OR 97227. (503)288-3895. **E-mail:** info@mississippistudios.com; matt@mississippistudios.com; katherine@mississippistudios.com. **E-mail:** booking@mississippistudios.com. **Website:** www.mississippistudios.com. **Contact:** Matt King, talent buyer; Katherine Paul, booking assistant. "Portland's premier concert venue, offering guests the best sound and an intimate concert experience." Music: indie, folk, rock, Americana, alternative, pop, blues.

THE MOHAWK PLACE

47 E. Mohawk Place, Buffalo NY 14203. (716)465-2368. **E-mail:** buffalomohawk@gmail.com. **E-mail:** erikspicoli@gmail.com. **Website:** www.themohawkplace.com. **Contact:** Erik Roesser, in-house booking agent. Music: indie, rock, alternative, punk.

◖ "We book shows predominantly through email. Contact Erik Roesser or Nicholas Heim to book a show. Please understand we get a high volume of emails daily. In most cases, local bands get priority. If we are interested we will get back to you."

MOJO 13

1706 Philadelphia Ave., Wilmington DE 19809. (302)798-5798. **E-mail:** mojo13booking@gmail.com. **Website:** www.mojothirteen.com. "We play host to local and touring music acts as well as a whole host of other forms of entertainment that cater to the rock and roll lifestyle. We're looking to become the home away from home for the alternative minded music community here in Delaware and beyond...so if you've got a band, are a musician, entertainer or just a fan... please join us." Music: punk, rock, alternative, indie.

THE MONKEY HOUSE

30 Main St., Winooski VT 05404. (802)655-4563. E-mail: info@monkeyhousevt.com. Website: http://monkeyhousemusic.com. Music: folk, indie, hard rock, punk, rock, alternative, Americana, funk, blues.

MOTR PUB

1345 Main St., Cincinnati OH 45202. (513)381-6687. Website: www.motrpub.com. Music: rock, alternative, folk, indie, Americana.

THE M ROOM

15 W. Girard Ave., Philadelphia PA 19123. (215)739-5577. E-mail: info@mroomphilly.com. E-mail: booking@mroomphilly.com. Website: http://mroomphilly.com. Music: blues, folk, soul, bluegrass, classic rock, rock, alt-country, pop, jazz, electronica, dance.

MUSE MUSIC CAFE

115 N. University Ave., Provo UT 84106. (801)377-6873. Website: http://musemusiccafe.com. Contact: Justin Hyatt; Colin Hatch, general managers. "The hub of Music, Art and Culture in Utah Valley." Music: rock, hard rock, hip-hop, electronica, indie, alternative, pop, Americana.

THE MUSIC HALL AT CAPITAL ALE HOUSE

619 E. Main St., Richmond VA 23219. (804)780-2537. E-mail: booking@capitalalehouse.com. Website: www.capitalalehouse.com. Contact: Kyle Johnson, booking. Music: indie, rock, jazz, blues, pop.

NATASHA'S BISTRO & BAR

112 Esplanade Alley, Lexington KY 40507. (859)259-2754. Website: www.beetnik.com. Contact: Kamilla Olsen. "Natasha's has hosted a wide variety of acts, including jazz, rock, world, comedy, pop, country, Americana, folk, singer/songwriter, indie and blues. Over The Rhine, Punch Brothers, Vienna Teng, Sara Watkins, Michelle Shocked, Richard Shindell, Patty Larkin,and Nellie McKay have all played recently on our stage."

THE NATIONAL UNDERGROUND NYC

159 E. Houston Street, New York NY 10002. (212)475-0611. E-mail: newyorkbooking@thenationalunderground.com. Website: www.thenationalunderground.com. Contact: Neeka DeGraw. "Musican brothers Joey & Gavin DeGraw opened The National Underground to provide a home for New York City and the nation's best independent musicians to showcase their talents to an appreciative audience. Featuring live music seven days and nights a week on two floors, The National Underground has more live bands performing per week then any club in New York City. We are a throwback NYC Rock/Americana/Country venue. Celebrity appearances have included Joss Stone, Norah Jones, Moby, John Popper of Blues Traveler, Robert Randolph, Billy Joe Armstrong of Green Day, Ryan Reynolds, Scarlett Johannson and NASCAR driver Jimmie Johnson. "

NECTAR'S

188 Main St., Burlington VT 05401. (802)658-4771. E-mail: info@liveatnectars.com. E-mail: alex@liveatnectars.com; assistant@liveatnectars.com. Website: www.liveatnectars.com. Contact: Alex Budney, talent buyer; Ryan Clausen, assistant talent buyer. "A long-standing landmark on Main Street in Burlington, Nectar's restaurant and bar has been the headquarters for thousands of local (and not-so local) music acts. From Phish to Led Loco, from reggae to rock, Nectar's Bar and Lounge is THE place to see live music in downtown Burlington." Music: blues, Americana, folk, rock, alternative, punk, indie, jazz, pop, dance, funk, psychedelic.

NEUMOS

925 E. Pike St., Seattle WA 98122. (206)709-9442. E-mail: steven@neumos.com; jason@neumos.com; eli@neumos.com. Website: http://neumos.com. "The Concert Hall side of the business has always been our priority, and the lifeline to all other things that surround it. We pride ourselves on our always relevant and carefully curated music calendar, light production and state of the art sound system. The Concert Hall has 3 full service bars, and a second floor with a nicely seated mezzanine and balcony overlooking the showroom. The showroom is fitted with an ample size stage, merch area, and superior unobstructed sight lines. We play host to several musical genres, by national and local artists alike including but not excluded to indie rock, hip-hop, punk rock, DJs, metal, singer/songwriters, country and much more."

NEUROLUX

111 N. 11th St., Boise ID 83702. (208)343-0886. Website: www.neurolux.com. Music: funk, indie, rock, reggae, folk, country, bluegrass.

THE NICK ROCKS

2514 10th Ave. S, Birmingham AL 35205. (205)252-3831. **E-mail:** nolenreevesmusic@mindspring.com. **Website:** www.thenickrocks.com. **Contact:** Dan Nolen, talent buyer. "The music heard almost every night of the week includes local, regional and national acts. The diverse range of acts add to the appeal of an evening at the Nick. One can hear blues, rock, punk, emo, pop, country, metal, bluegrass, rock-a-billy, roots rock or whatever your genre of choice. The Nick has had it all. It is an upclose and personal room voted three times in a row as Birmingham's best live music venue by *Birmingham Weekly*."

NIETZSCHE'S

248 Allen St., Buffalo NY 14201. (716)886-8539. **Website:** www.nietzsches.com. Call for information regarding booking. Music: blues, jazz, rock, alternative, funk, soul.

NORTH STAR BAR & RESTAURANT

2639 Poplar St., Philadelphia PA 19130. (215)787-0488. **E-mail:** booking@sunnydaymusic.com. **Website:** www.northstarbar.com. Music: rock, indie, psychedelic, pop, funk, jam, ska, punk, alternative.

THE OLD ROCK HOUSE

1200 S. Seventh St., St. Louis MO 63104. (314)588-0505. **E-mail:** info@oldrockhouse.com. **Website:** http://oldrockhouse.com. **Contact:** Tim Weber, co-owner. Music: rock, indie, alternative, punk, folk, pop.

ONE TRICK PONY GRILL & TAPROOM

136 E. Fulton, Grand Rapids MI 49503. (616)235-7669. **E-mail:** thepony@onetrick.biz. **Website:** www.onetrick.biz. **Contact:** Dan Verhil, owner. Music: acoustic, rock, country, blues.

ON STAGE DRINKS & GRINDS

802 Kapahulu Ave., Honolulu HI 96816. (808)738-0004. **Website:** www.onstagedrinksandgrinds.com. "Onstage is our ultimate living room. A cool, "off the beaten path," fun & comfortable spot to hang and chill. Equipped with a stage area complete with sound system, guitars, congas, and drums. We feature live music, and at times, surprise jams by well-known local artists that pop in. A kind of neat, underground music scene." Music: blues, rock, Hawaiian, acoustic.

PARADISE ROCK CLUB

967 Commonwealth Ave., Boston MA 02115. (617)547-0620. **E-mail:** paradiserockclub@gmail.com. **Website:** www.thedise.com. **Contact:** Lee Zazofsky, general manager. Music: pop, reggae, alternative, rock, indie, punk, hip-hop, Americana.
TIPS "Booking is handled by Crossroads Presents."

PEARL AT COMMERCE

2038 Commerce St., Dallas TX 75201. (214)655-8824. **E-mail:** info@pearlatcommerce.com. **Website:** www.pearlatcommerce.com. "Pearl is a neighborhood bar and live music venue located in a 108 year old building in downtown Dallas, TX. We present primarily jazz and blues—local, regional and national acts. We also occasionally have zydeco, singer-songwriters, Americana, reggae, latin, tribute bands and world music."

PJ'S LAGER HOUSE

1254 Michigan Ave., Detroit MI 48226. (313)961-4668. **E-mail:** info@pjslagerhouse.com. **E-mail:** lagerhousebooking@yahoo.com. **Website:** www.pjslagerhouse.com. "PJ's features the best of Detroit's original rock'n'roll. Up and coming and established acts along with a variety of touring bands occupy PJ's stage most nights." Music: rock, alternative, hard rock, pop, folk, indie, punk.

PLOUGH AND STARS

912 Massachusetts Ave., Cambridge MA 02139. (617)576-0032. **Website:** www.ploughandstars.com. "The Plough and Stars Irish pub and restaurant in Cambridge has become a favorite of locals and visitors alike. With its warm cozy atmosphere and great music scene, The Plough has become a staple of the Cambridge community. There is live music nearly every night." Music: alternative, pop, rock, indie, psychedelic, acoustic, folk.

PLUSH

340 E. Sixth St., Tucson AZ 85705. (502)798-1298. **E-mail:** plushtucson@gmail.com. **Website:** www.plushtucson.com. **Contact:** Kris Kerry. "Dynamic and comfy! Plush, yet affordable! Come hither and partake. PLUSH is dedicated to Tucson's live music scene. YES, we book 'em live! Talented local, regional, and national touring acts 5-7 nights a week. AND our rooms and sound system were designed to sound good and look good so you feeeeel good!" Music: rock, indie, garage, electronica, alt-country, rockabilly.

POSITIVE PIE

22 State St., Montpelier VT 05602. (802)229-0453. **E-mail:** info@positivepie.com. **E-mail:** music@positivepie.com. **Website:** www.positivepie.com. Music: hip-hop, pop, R&B.

THE POUR HOUSE

1977 Maybank Hwy., Charleston SC 29412. (843)571-4343. **E-mail:** alex@charlestonpourhouse.com. **Website:** www.charlestonpourhouse.com. **Contact:** Alex Harris, owner/booking. Music: bluegrass, classic rock, indie, rock, funk, folk, country.

THE QUARTER

2504 13th St., Gulfport MS 39501. (228)863-2650. **E-mail:** info@thequarterbar.com. **E-mail:** manager@thequarterbar.com. **Website:** www.thequarterbar.com. "Our goal is to provide the coast with live music up to 5 nights a week or more in a relaxing French Quarter-like atmosphere." Music: metal, pop, rock, country, blues, classic rock.

THE RAVE/EAGLES CLUB

2401 W. Wisconsin Ave., Milwaukee WI 53233. (414)342-7283. **E-mail:** info@therave.com. **Website:** www.theravelive.com. "The Rave/Eagles Club is a multi-room entertainment complex. Bands like Pearl Jam, Dave Matthews Band, and Creed all played their first gig at The Rave on The Rave Bar stage. Music: rock, alternative, pop, indie, hip-hop, funk, metal.

RECORD BAR

1020 Westport Rd., Kansas City MO 64111. (816)753-5207. **E-mail:** booking@therecordbar.com. **Website:** www.therecordbar.com. "We strive to provide our guests with diverse live entertainment, special events and gourmet food in a comfortable atmosphere. You'll see the best of the Kansas City music scene, as well as nationally known touring artists." Music: rock, punk, indie, jazz, swing, folk, pop, alternative.

RED SQUARE

136 Church St., Burlington VT 05401. (802)859-8909. **E-mail:** info@redsquarevt.com; booking@redsquarevt.com. **Website:** www.redsquarevt.com. Music: jazz, blues, rock, reggae.

RHYTHM & BREWS

2308 4th St., Tuscaloosa AL 35401. (205)750-2992. **Website:** www.rhythmnbrews.com. "Rhythm & Brews first opened in Tuscaloosa, AL. The club has the reputation of being the premiere location for the best live bands in the region. From dance music to performances by Nashville recording artists, the music you find at Rhythm & Brews will please all. We are committed to bringing you a fun and friendly atmosphere by offering a wide variety of drinks, great service, and great entertainment." Music: pop, rock, country, blues.

RICK'S BAR

2721 Main Ave., Fargo ND 58103. (701)232-8356. **E-mail:** meghanc@ricks-bar.com. **Website:** www.ricks-bar.com. **Contact:** Meghan Carik. Music: rock, metal, alternative.

ROCK ISLAND LIVE

101 N. Rock Island, Wichita KS 67202. (316)303-9800. **Website:** www.rockislandlive.com. Use online contact form. Music: rock, alternative, pop, indie, dance.

SAM BONDS GARAGE

407 Blair, Eugene OR 97405. (541)431-6603. **E-mail:** info@sambonds.com. **E-mail:** bondsbooking@hotmail.com. **Website:** www.sambonds.com. "Opened in 1995, we've strived to represent the uniqueness of the neighborhood with a warm, laid back atmosphere, always changing local and regional microbrew selection, a full bar, quality vittles and of course, one of the West Coast's best places to see diverse local, regional and worldly entertainment on a nightly basis." Music: bluegrass, rock, Irish jam, funk, alternative, folk, Americana.

SANTA FE SOL

37 Fire Place, Santa Fe NM 87508. (505)474-7322. **Website:** www.solsantafelive.com. Music: rock, Mexicana, Latin, alternative.

SCHUBAS TAVERN

3159 N. Southport, Chicago IL 60657. (773)525-2508. **E-mail:** rucins@schubas.com. **Website:** www.schubas.com. Paul Massaro, production manager. **Contact:** Matt Rucins, talent buyer. Schubas presents a diverse line-up of live music seven nights a week. From Honky-Tonk to Indie Rock, from Americana to Jazz, from Pop to Country.

◯ Building is a brick and masonry neo-Gothic neighborhood landmark built in 1903.

TIPS "Have a confirmed show? Use the Media and Retail link on the website to help better promote your show. Advance your show with our Production Manager, Paul Massaro. Send any promotional materials (posters, CDs, bios, photos) to Rob Jensen."

SHANK HALL

1434 N. Farewell Ave., Milwaukee WI 53202. (414)276-7288. **E-mail:** shank@wi.rr.com. **Website:** www.shankhall.com. Music: indie, rock, alternative, Americana, pop, folk, bluegrass.

THE SHED

15094 Mills Rd., Gulfport MS 39503. (228)832-7240. **E-mail:** contact@theshedbbq.com. **E-mail:** booking@theshedbbq.com. **Website:** http://theshedbbq.com. **Contact:** Brett Orrison, entertainment director. Music: blues, folk, country, bluegrass, rock, alternative.

SILVER DOLLAR

478 King St., Charleston SC 29403. (843)722-7223. **E-mail:** daveb@Charlestoncocktail.com. **Website:** www.charlestoncocktail.com/silverdollar.html. **Contact:** David Beiderman. Music: rock, pop, dance, hip-hop, R&B, funk.

THE SLOWDOWN

729 N. 14th St., Omaha NE 68102. (402)345-7569. **E-mail:** info@theslowdown.com. **Website:** www.theslowdown.com. Music: rock, indie, alternative, psychedelic, punk, folk, pop.

THE SMILING MOOSE

1306 E. Carson St., Pittsburgh PA 15203. (412)431-4668. **Website:** www.smiling-moose.com. Music: rock, alt-country, indie, country, acoustic, pop, garbage, funk, hip-hop, metal.

SMITH'S OLDE BAR

1578 Piedmont Ave., Atlanta GA 30307. (404)876-8436. **E-mail:** nolenreevesbooking@gmail.com. **Website:** www.smithsoldebar.com. **Contact:** Dan Nolen, talent buyer. "Smith's Olde Bar is an Atlanta institution, offering some of the best music to be found anywhere in the city. Our atmosphere is very relaxed, and you can find something good to eat and something fun to do almost every night." Music: rock, indie, punk, hip-hop, alternative, garage, bluegrass, reggae, jazz, funk.

THE SOUND FACTORY

812 Kanawha Blvd. E, Charleston WV 25301. (304)342-8001. **E-mail:** soundfactorybooking@yahoo.com. **Website:** www.soundfactorywv.com. **Contact:** John Sanese, agent/owner. Music: dance, rock, pop, reggae, country, Americana, psychedelic, funk, punk.

THE SPACE

295 Treadwell St., New Haven CT 06514. (203)288-6400. **E-mail:** spacebooking@gmail.com. **Website:** www.thespace.tk. **Contact:** Steve Rodgers; Susannah Frew. "The Space (since 2003) exists to build a safe, positive community for people of all ages through music and the arts. Physically, we are a listening room venue located in an unlikely industrial park in a sleepy suburb of New Haven." Music: alternative, rock, blues, Latin, folk, pop, indie, dance, hip-hop, Americana.

THE SPANISH MOON

1109 Highland Rd., Baton Rouge LA 70802. (225)383-6666. **E-mail:** moonbooking@hotmail.com. **Website:** http://thespanishmoon.com. **Contact:** Aaron Scruggs. Music: rock, pop, dubstep, indie, alternative, Americana.

THE SPOT UNDERGROUND

15 Elbow St., Providence RI 02903. (401)383-7133. **E-mail:** 725@TheSpotOnThayer.com. **E-mail:** 725@TheSpotProvidence.com. **Website:** www.thespotprovidence.com. **Contact:** Kevin Blanchette, director of operations. Music: rock, indie, world, hip-hop, R&B, funk, dance, jam, pop.

STATION 4

201 E. Fourth St., St. Paul MN 55101. (651)224-6372. **E-mail:** info@station-4.com. **E-mail:** dawn@station-4.com. **Website:** www.station-4.com. "Station 4 is a fully independent live music venue seven nights a week in St. Paul, MN. We support all genres of local and national talent." Music: rock, alternative, punk, metal, indie.

STRANGE BREW TAVERN

88 Market St., Manchester NH 03101. (603)666-4292. **E-mail:** info@strangebrewtavern.net. **Website:** www.strangebrewtavern.net. Music: blues, acoustic, rock, alternative.

SULLY'S PUB

2701 Park St., Hartford CT 06106. (860)231-8881. **E-mail:** sully@sullyspub.com. **Website:** www.sullyspub.com. **Contact:** Darrell "Sully" Sullivan, owner; Rob Salter, manager. "This mantra is an important one in any community. Original Music must be supported on every level of society. Sully's is proud to stand on the front lines of musical evolution. Blazing a trail with the very musicians composing and performing." Music: pop, rock, alternative, indie.

TOAD

1912 Massachusetts Ave., Cambridge MA 02140. (617)499-6992. **E-mail:** info@toadcambridge.com. **E-mail:** bookagig@toadcambridge.com. **Website:** www.toadcambridge.com. **Contact:** Billy Beard. "Toad is a small neighborhood bar and music club featuring live music seven nights a week." Music: folk, alternative, rock, acoustic, Americana, indie.

TRACTOR TAVERN

5213 Ballard Ave. NW, Seattle WA 98107. (206)789-3599. **E-mail:** schedule@tractortavern.com. **E-mail:** booking@tractortavern.com. **Website:** www.tractortavern.com. "The Tractor hosts live shows 5-7 nights a week featuring a wide range of local and national acts. Check out all of your favorite rock, alternative country, rockabilly, groove and psychedelia, celtic, cajun and zydeco, folk, blues, jazz, and bluegrass acts to name a few."

THE TREE BAR

887 Chambers Rd., Columbus OH 43212. (614)725-0955. **Website:** http://treebarcolumbus.com. Music: rock, classic rock, alternative, indie, Americana, folk, pop.

TRIPLE CROWN

206 N. Edward Gary St., San Marcos TX 78666. (512)396-2236. **E-mail:** booking@triplecrownlive.com. **Website:** www.triplecrownlive.com. **Contact:** Eric Shaw. Music: rock, country, Americana, jazz, blues, bluegrass, punk, hip-hop, folk.

TRIPLE ROCK SOCIAL CLUB

629 Cedar Ave., Minneapolis MN 55454. (612)333-7399. **E-mail:** info@triplerocksocialclub.com. **E-mail:** booking@triplerocksocialclub.com. **Website:** www.triplerocksocialclub.com. Estab. 2003. The Triple Rock has become one of the big destination punk, indie rock and underground hip hop clubs in the Twin Cities—a good-sized music venue with a capacity of 400. The Triple Rock is owned and operated by the members of punk rock band Dillinger Four. Music: Acoustic, Alternative, Blues, Classic Rock, Country, Cover Band, Electronic/Dance/DJ, Folk, Funk, Goth, Hip-Hop/Rap, Jam Band, Metal, Pop, Punk, Reggae, Rock, Singer/Songwriter, Soul, and Urban/R&B.

TIPS To advance shows that have been confirmed, please e-mail: zartan@triplerocksocialclub.com.

TROCADERO

1003 Arch St., Philadelphia PA 19107. (215)922-6888. **E-mail:** trocadero@thetroc.com. **Website:** www.thetroc.com. Music: pop, indie, Americana, alternative, rock, hip-hop, rap, folk, bluegrass.

TROUBADOUR

9081 Santa Monica Blvd., West Hollywood CA 90069. (310)276-1158. **Website:** www.troubadour.com. Estab. 1958. "The Troubadour is rich with musical history. Elton John, Billy Joel, James Taylor and Joni Mitchell have all made debuts at the Troubadour. The legendary musical lineups at the Troubadour continue til today. The Troubadour schedule features a wide arrangement of musical performances. Nada Surf, Bob Schneider, The Morning Benders and Manchester Orchestra were some of the performances featured on the Troubadour schedule for 2010." Music: pop, indie, alternative, rock, hip-hop, Americana, jazz, blues.

◯ To contact use the form online at http://www.troubadour.com/contact-booking/. See also the lighting plot, stage layout, and technical rider links at same site.

TURF CLUB

1601 University Ave. W, St. Paul MN 55104. (651)647-0486. **E-mail:** booking@turfclub.net. **Website:** www.turfclub.net. "Turf Club is a perfect setting for rock. The long, prominent bar scales one side of the narrow interior; the stage is at the back and the entire space is enveloped in dark woods. The music is loud, the crowd is devoted." Music: rock, indie, alternative, punk, classic rock.

THE UNDERGROUND

555 E. Fourth St., Reno NV 89512. (775)786-2582. **E-mail:** contact@renounderground.com. **Website:** http://renounderground.com. Use online booking forms. "The Underground is one of Reno's largest music venues and cannot be classified easily. Shows here range from all-ages top 40 parties, national, regional and local artist concerts. The music style varies wildly depending on the night, with shows ranging from hardcore to world beat, just about any other genre you can think of." Music: rock, alternative, pop, funk, hip-hop, Latin, World, acoustic, jazz, electronica, reggae, dubstep.

UNDERGROUND 119

119 S. President St., Jackson MS 39201. (601)352-2322. **E-mail:** booking@underground119.com. **Website:** www.underground119.com. **Contact:** Bill Ellison, entertainment director. Music: blues, jazz, bluegrass, country, funk, rock, alternative.

UNION POOL

484 Union Ave., Brooklyn NY 11211. (718)609-0484. **E-mail:** booking@union-pool.com. **Website:** www.union-pool.com. Music: rock, indie, alternative, Americana.

URBAN LOUNGE

241 S. 500 E, Salt Lake City UT 84102. (801)824-1000. **E-mail:** will@sartainandsaunders.com. **Website:** www.theurbanloungeslc.com. **Contact:** Will Sartain. "The Urban Lounge has been a staple in the Salt Lake City, Utah music community for more than a decade. What started off as a local live music bar has flourished into a regular stop for headlining national acts-hosting a variety of music from independent artists of all genres including rock, hip-hop, folk, electronic, reggae, and experimental. Nearly every night of the week you can find a fresh take on a familiar scene."

THE VAGABOND

30 NE 14th St., Miami FL 33132. (305)379-0508. **E-mail:** info@thevagabondmiami.com. **E-mail:** bookings@thevagabondmiami.com. **Website:** http://thevagabondmiami.com. Music: rock, punk, soul, jam, dance.

VAUDEVILLE MEWS

212 Fourth St., Des Moines IA 50309. (515)243-3270. **E-mail:** booking@vaudevillemews.com. **Website:** www.vaudevillemews.com. Music: folk, pop, blues, rock, alternative, Americana, hip-hop, soul, rap, country, hard rock, electronica.

THE VISULITE THEATRE

1615 Elizabeth Ave., Charlotte NC 28204. (704)358-9200. **E-mail:** info@visulite.com. **E-mail:** booking@visulite.com. **Website:** www.visulite.com. Music: rock, pop, funk, Americana, indie, blues, folk.

THE WEBSTER UNDERGROUND

21 Webster St., Hartford CT 06114. (860)246-8001. **E-mail:** booking@webstertheater.com. **Website:** www.webstertheater.com. "The Main Theater is a great room for sizeable events or concerts. Book now and share the same stage that launched careers such as Staind, Marilyn Manson, Sevendust, Incubus, 311, Jay Z, Method Man, Godsmack, Fall Out Boy, and many more. The Underground is our intimate room equipped for shows and more—perfect for national, or regional acts and locals who are looking to create their own show in a historic room." Music: rock, reggae, punk, alternative, pop, soul, indie, funk, hard rock.

WHISKEY BAR

125 Washington St. #G, Hoboken NJ 07030. (201)963-3400. **E-mail:** scott@107productions.net; whiskeybar.nj@gmail.com. **Website:** www.whiskey-bar.com. Music: rock, alternative, punk, pop.

WHISKY A GO-GO

8901 W. Sunset Blvd., West Hollywood CA 90069. (310)360-1110. **E-mail:** mproductionsrocks@gmail.com; booking@whiskyagogo.com. **Website:** www.whiskyagogo.com. **Contact:** Luke Iblings; Jake Perry; Cynthia Lempitsky. "As long as there has been a Los Angeles rock scene, there has been the Whisky A Go-Go. An anchor on the Sunset Strip since its opening in 1964, the Whisky A Go-Go has played host to rock 'n' roll's most important bands, from the Doors, Janis Joplin, and Led Zeppelin to today's up and coming new artists." Music: hip-hop, rock, punk, metal, alternative, reggae, pop, classic rock, indie, Americana.

THE WHITE MULE

1530 Main St., Columbia SC 29201. (803)661-8199. **E-mail:** management@thewhitemule.com. **E-mail:** tmayn.ent@hotmail.com; davebritt@sc.rr.com. **Website:** www.thewhitemule.com. **Contact:** Travis Maynard; Dave Britt, booking. "The White Mule, simply put, is an establishment with great food and great music brought to you by people who love great food and great music. We want you to have a memorable experience from the minute you walk in the door." Music: rock, alternative, pop.

WHITE ROOM MIAMI

1306 N. Miami Ave., Miami FL 33136. (786)444-8647. **E-mail:** heynastie@gmail.com. **Website:** www.whiteroomshows.com. "White Room is a cutting edge nightclub and premier live music venue located in downtown Miami's entertainment district. We offer 3 distinct areas of sound from up and coming local bands to national acts to Djs and producers. White Room hosts live performances of different genres such as rock, alternative, electronica, funk, fusion, D&B, and more. Artists may be compensated by merchandise sales and ticket sales depending on the draw. The age restriction is 18 and over." Capacity is 500-1,000. Music: Alternative, House, Pop/Top 40, Techno.

WHITE WATER TAVERN

2500 W. Seventh St., Little Rock AR 72205. (501)375-8400. **E-mail:** whitewaterbooking@gmail.com. **Website:** www.whitewatertavern.com. Music: rock, country, alternative, Americana, punk.

WILD WILLY'S ROCK HOUSE & SPORTS SALOON

2072 Somerville Rd., Annapolis MD 21401. (410)841-5599. **E-mail:** wild@wildwillyssaloon.com. **Website:**

www.wildwillyssaloon.com. "Wild Willy's Rock House & Sports Saloon features live entertainment with a rock and roll edge. The venue features weekly live music, ongoing special events, optimum sports viewing, classic food & signature drinks." Music: rock, pop, alternative.

THE WINCHESTER

12112 Madison Ave., Cleveland OH 44107. (216)226-5681. **E-mail:** jams@thewinchester.net. **Website:** http://thewinchester.net. Estab. 2002. Music: blues, jazz, prog, fusion, rock, classic rock, alternative, rockabilly, alt-country, bluegrass and swing/big band. The Winchester Music Hall is well known for featuring the best musicians both nationally and locally.

WOODLANDS TAVERN

1200 W. Third Ave., Columbus OH 43212. (614)299-4987 or (614)406-4799. **E-mail:** booking@woodlandstavern.com; promotions@woodlandstavern.com. **Website:** www.woodlandstavern.com. **Contact:** Paul Painter, booking. Music: bluegrass, acoustic, psychedelic, reggae, jam, funk, rock, classic rock, jazz, blues.

WORMY DOG SALOON

311 E. Sheridan Ave., Oklahoma City OK 73104. (405)601-6276. **E-mail:** booking@wormydog.com. **Website:** www.wormydog.com. Music: country, bluegrass, rock, Americana, rockabilly, folk.

YOUNG AVENUE DELI

2119 Young Ave., Memphis TN 38104. (901)278-0034. **E-mail:** phillip@youngavenuedeli.com. **Website:** www.youngavenuedeli.com. **Contact:** Phillip Stroud. Music: rock, country, pop, folk.

STATE & PROVINCIAL GRANTS

//

Arts councils in the United States and Canada provide assistance to artists (including poets) in the form of fellowships or grants. These grants can be substantial and confer prestige upon recipients; however, **only state or province residents are eligible**. Because deadlines and available support vary annually, query first (with a SASE) or check websites for guidelines.

UNITED STATES ARTS AGENCIES

ALABAMA STATE COUNCIL ON THE ARTS, 201 Monroe St., Montgomery AL 36130-1800. (334)242-4076. E-mail: staff@arts.alabama.gov. Website: www.arts.state.al.us.

ALASKA STATE COUNCIL ON THE ARTS, 411 W. Fourth Ave., Suite 1-E, Anchorage AK 99501-2343. (907)269-6610 or (888)278-7424. E-mail: aksca.info@alaska.gov. Website: www.eed.state.ak.us/aksca.

ARIZONA COMMISSION ON THE ARTS, 417 W. Roosevelt St., Phoenix AZ 85003-1326. (602)771-6501. E-mail: info@azarts.gov. Website: www.azarts.gov.

ARKANSAS ARTS COUNCIL, 1500 Tower Bldg., 323 Center St., Little Rock AR 72201. (501)324-9766. E-mail: info@arkansasarts.com. Website: www.arkansasarts.com.

CALIFORNIA ARTS COUNCIL, 1300 I St., Suite 930, Sacramento CA 95814. (916)322-6555. E-mail: info@cac.ca.gov. Website: www.cac.ca.gov.

COLORADO COUNCIL ON THE ARTS, 1625 Broadway, Suite 2700, Denver CO 80202. (303)892-3802. E-mail: online form. Website: www.cooradocreativeindustries.org.

CONNECTICUT COMMISSION ON CULTURE & TOURISM, Arts Division, One Constitution Plaza, 755 Main St., Hartford CT 06103. (860)256-2800. Website: www.cultureandtourism.org.

DELAWARE DIVISION OF THE ARTS, Carvel State Office Bldg., 4th Floor, 820 N. French St., Wilmington DE 19801. (302)577-8278 (New Castle Co.) or (302)739-5304 (Kent or Sussex Counties). E-mail: delarts@state.de.us. Website: www.artsdel.org.

DISTRICT OF COLUMBIA COMMISSION ON THE ARTS & HUMANITIES, 410 Eighth St. NW, 5th Floor, Washington DC 20004. (202)724-5613. E-mail: cah@dc.gov. Website: http://dcarts.dc.gov.

FLORIDA ARTS COUNCIL, Division of Cultural Affairs, R.A. Gray Building, Third Floor, 500 S. Bronough St., Tallahassee FL 32399-0250. (850)245-6470. E-mail: info@florida-arts.org. Website: http://dcarts.dc.gov.

GEORGIA COUNCIL FOR THE ARTS, 75 Fifth Street, NW, Suite 1200, Atlanta GA 30308. (404)685-2787. E-mail: gaarts@gaarts.org. Website: www.gaarts.org.

GUAM COUNCIL ON THE ARTS & HUMANITIES AGENCY, P.O. Box 2950, Hagatna GU 96932. (671)646-2781. Website: www.guamcaha.net.

HAWAII STATE FOUNDATION ON CULTURE & THE ARTS, 2500 S. Hotel St., 2nd Floor, Honolulu HI 96813. (808)586-0300. E-mail: ken.hamilton@hawaii.gov. Website: http.hawaii.gov/sfca.

IDAHO COMMISSION ON THE ARTS, 2410 N. Old Penitentiary Rd., Boise ID 83712. (208)334-2119 or (800)278-3863. E-mail: info@arts.idaho.gov. Website: www.arts.idaho.gov.

ILLINOIS ARTS COUNCIL, James R. Thompson Center, 100 W. Randolph, Suite 10-500, Chicago IL 60601. (312)814-6750. E-mail: iac.info@illinois.gov. Website: www.arts.illinois.gov.

INDIANA ARTS COMMISSION, 100 North Senate Avenue, Room N505, Indianapolis IN 46204. (317)232-1268. E-mail: IndianaArtsCommission@iac.in.gov. Website: www.in.gov/arts.

IOWA ARTS COUNCIL, 600 E. Locust, Des Moines IA 50319-0290. (515)242-6194. Website: www.iowaartscouncil.org.

KANSAS ARTS COMMISSION, 1000 Jackson Street , Suite 1000, Topeka KS 66612. (785)296-3335. E-mail: KAC@arts.state.ks.us. Website: http://arts.ks.gov.

KENTUCKY ARTS COUNCIL, 21st Floor, Capital Plaza Tower, 500 Mero St., Frankfort KY 40601-1987. (502)564-3757 or (888)833-2787. E-mail: kyarts@ky.gov. Website: http://artscouncil. ky.gov.

LOUISIANA DIVISION OF THE ARTS, Capitol Annex Bldg., 1051 N. 3rd St., 4th Floor, Room #420, Baton Rouge LA 70804. (225)342-8180. Email: ltgov@crt.la.gov. Website: www.crt. state.la.us/arts.

MAINE ARTS COMMISSION, 193 State St., 25 State House Station, Augusta ME 04333-0025. (207)287-2724. E-mail: MaineArts.info@maine.gov. Website: http://mainearts.maine.gov.

MARYLAND STATE ARTS COUNCIL, 175 W. Ostend St., Suite E, Baltimore MD 21230. (410)767-6555. E-mail: msac@msac.org. Website: www.msac.org.

MASSACHUSETTS CULTURAL COUNCIL, 10 St. James Ave., 3rd Floor, Boston MA 02116-3803. (617)727-3668. E-mail: mcc@art.state.ma.us. Website: www.massculturalcouncil.org.

MICHIGAN COUNCIL FOR ARTS AND CULTURAL AFFAIRS, 300 N. Washington Square, Lansing MI, 48913. (888)522-0103. E-mail: Online form. Website: www.michiganadvantage.org/Arts.

MINNESOTA STATE ARTS BOARD, Park Square Court, 400 Sibley St., Suite 200, St. Paul MN 55101-1928. (651)215-1600 or (800)866-2787. E-mail: msab@arts.state.mn.us. Website: www. arts.state.mn.us.

MISSISSIPPI ARTS COMMISSION, 501 N. West St., Suite 701B, Woolfolk Bldg., Jackson MS 39201. (601)359-6030. Website: www.arts.state.ms.us.

MISSOURI ARTS COUNCIL, 815 Olive St., Suite 16, St. Louis MO 63101-1503. (314)340-6845 or (866)407-4752. E-mail: moarts@ded.mo.gov. Website: www.missouriartscouncil.org.

MONTANA ARTS COUNCIL, PO Box 202201, Helena MT 59620-2201. (406)444-6430. E-mail: mac@mt.gov. Website: http://art.mt.gov.

NATIONAL ASSEMBLY OF STATE ARTS AGENCIES, 1029 Vermont Ave. NW, 2nd Floor, Washington DC 20005. (202)347-6352. E-mail: nasaa@nasaa-arts.org. Website: www.nasaa-arts.org.

NEBRASKA ARTS COUNCIL, 1004 Farnam St., Plaza Level, Omaha NE 68102. (402)595-2122 or (800)341-4067. Website: www.nebraskaartscouncil.org.

NEVADA ARTS COUNCIL, 716 N. Carson St., Suite A, Carson City NV 89701. (775)687-6680. E-mail: infonvartscouncil@nevadaculture.org. Website: www.nac.nevadaculture.org.

NEW HAMPSHIRE STATE COUNCIL ON THE ARTS, 19 Pillsbury Street - 1st Floor, Concord, NH 03301. (603)271-2789. Website: www.nh.gov/nharts.

NEW JERSEY STATE COUNCIL ON THE ARTS, 225 W. State St., P.O. Box 306, Trenton NJ 08625. (609)292-6130. Website: www.artscouncil.nj.gov.

NEW MEXICO ARTS, Dept. of Cultural Affairs, P.O. Box 1450, Santa Fe NM 87504-1450. (505)827-6490 or (800)879-4278. Website: www.nmarts.org.

NEW YORK STATE COUNCIL ON THE ARTS, 300 Park Ave. South, 10th Floor, New York NY 10010. (212)459-8800. Website: www.nysca.org.

NORTH CAROLINA ARTS COUNCIL, 109 East Jones St., Cultural Resources Building, Raleigh NC 27601. (919)807-6500. E-mail: ncarts@ncdcr.gov. Website: www.ncarts.org.

NORTH DAKOTA COUNCIL ON THE ARTS, 1600 E. Century Ave., Suite 6, Bismarck ND 58503. (701)328-7590. Website: www.nd.gov/arts.

COMMONWEALTH COUNCIL FOR ARTS AND CULTURE (NORTHERN MARIANA ISLANDS), P.O. Box 5553, CHRB, Saipan MP 96950. (670)322-9982 or (670)322-9983. E-mail: galaidi@vzpacifica.net. Website: www.geocities.com/ccacarts/ccacwebsite.html.

OHIO ARTS COUNCIL, 30 E broad Street, 33rd Floor, Columbus OH 43215-3414. (614)466-2613. Website: www.oac.state.oh.us.

OKLAHOMA ARTS COUNCIL, Jim Thorpe Building, 2101 N. Lincoln Blvd., Suite 640, Oklahoma City OK 73105. (405)521-2931. E-mail: okarts@arts.ok.gov. Website: www.arts.ok.gov.

OREGON ARTS COMMISSION, 775 Summer St. NE, Suite 200, Salem OR 97301-1280. (503)986-0082. E-mail: oregon.artscomm@state.or.us. Website: www.oregonartscommission.org.

PENNSYLVANIA COUNCIL ON THE ARTS, 216 Finance Bldg., Harrisburg PA 17120. (717)787-6883. Website: www.pacouncilonthearts.org.

INSTITUTE OF PUERTO RICAN CULTURE, P.O. Box 9024184, San Juan PR 00902-4184. (787)724-0700. E-mail: info@IPRAC.org. Website: www.iprac.org.

RHODE ISLAND STATE COUNCIL ON THE ARTS, One Capitol Hill, Third Floor, Providence RI 02908. (401)222-3880. E-mail: info@arts.ri.gov. Website: www.arts.ri.gov.

SOUTH CAROLINA ARTS COMMISSION, 1800 Gervais St., Columbia SC 29201. (803)734-8696. E-mail: info@arts.sc.gov. Website: www.southcarolinaarts.com.

SOUTH DAKOTA ARTS COUNCIL, 711 E. Wells Ave., Pierre SD 57501-3369. (605)773-3301. E-mail: sdac@state.sd.us. Website: www.artscouncil.sd.gov.

TENNESSEE ARTS COMMISSION, 401 Charlotte Ave., Nashville TN 37243-0780. (615)741-1701. Website: www.tn.gov/arts.

TEXAS COMMISSION ON THE ARTS, E.O. Thompson Office Building, 920 Colorado, Suite 501, Austin TX 78701. (512)463-5535. E-mail: front.desk@arts.state.tx.us. Website: www.arts.texas.gov.

UTAH ARTS COUNCIL, 617 E. South Temple, Salt Lake City UT 84102-1177. (801)236-7555. Website: www.artsandmuseums.utah.gov.

VERMONT ARTS COUNCIL, 136 State St., Drawer 33, Montpelier VT 05633-6001. (802)828-3291. E-mail: online form. Website: www.vermontartscouncil.org.

VIRGIN ISLANDS COUNCIL ON THE ARTS, 5070 Norre Gade, St. Thomas VI 00802-6872. (340)774-5984. Website: http://vicouncilonarts.org.

VIRGINIA COMMISSION FOR THE ARTS, 1001 East Broad Street, Suite 330, Richmond VA 23219. (804)225-3132. E-mail: arts@arts.virginia.gov. Website: www.arts.virginia.gov.

WASHINGTON STATE ARTS COMMISSION, 711 Capitol Way S., Suite 600, P.O. Box 42675, Olympia WA 98504-2675. (360)753-3860. E-mail: online form Website: www.arts.wa.gov.

WEST VIRGINIA COMMISSION ON THE ARTS, The Cultural Center, Capitol Complex, 1900 Kanawha Blvd. E., Charleston WV 25305-0300. (304)558-0220. Website: www.wvculture. org/arts.

WISCONSIN ARTS BOARD, 101 E. Wilson St., 1st Floor, Madison WI 53702. (608)266-0190. E-mail: artsboard@wisconsin.gov. Website: www.artsboard.wisconsin.gov.

WYOMING ARTS COUNCIL, 2320 Capitol Ave., Cheyenne WY 82002. (307)777-7742. E-mail: online form. Website: http://wyoarts.state.wy.us.

CANADIAN PROVINCIAL ARTS AGENCIES

ALBERTA FOUNDATION FOR THE ARTS, 10708-105 Ave., Edmonton AB T5H 0A1. (780)427-9968. Email: online form. Website: www.affta.ab.ca.

BRITISH COLUMBIA ARTS COUNCIL, P.O. Box 9819, Stn. Prov. Govt., Victoria BC V8W 9W3. (250)356-1718. E-mail: BCArtsCouncil@gov.bc.ca. Website: www.bcartscouncil.ca.

THE CANADA COUNCIL FOR THE ARTS, 350 Albert St., P.O. Box 1047, Ottawa ON K1P 5V8. (613)566-4414 or (800)263-5588 (within Canada). Email: info@canadacouncil.ca. Website: www.canadacouncil.ca.

MANITOBA ARTS COUNCIL, 525-93 Lombard Ave., Winnipeg MB R3B 3B1. (204)945-2237 or (866)994-2787 (in Manitoba). E-mail: info@artscouncil.mb.ca. Website: www.artscouncil. mb.ca.

NEW BRUNSWICK ARTS BOARD (NBAB), 634 Queen St., Suite 300, Fredericton NB E3B 1C2. (506)444-4444 or (866)460-2787. Website: www.artsnb.ca.

NEWFOUNDLAND & LABRADOR ARTS COUNCIL, P.O. Box 98, St. John's NL A1C 5H5. (709)726-2212 or (866)726-2212. E-mail: nlacmail@nlac.ca. Website: www.nlac.ca.

NOVA SCOTIA DEPARTMENT OF TOURISM, CULTURE, AND HERITAGE, P. O. Box 456, STN Central, Halifax NS B3J 2R5. (902)424-5000. Website: http://novascotia.ca/cch/.

ONTARIO ARTS COUNCIL, 151 Bloor St. W., 5th Floor, Toronto ON M5S 1T6. (416)961-1660 or (800)387-0058 (in Ontario). E-mail: info@arts.on.ca. Website: www.arts.on.ca.

PRINCE EDWARD ISLAND COUNCIL OF THE ARTS, 115 Richmond St., Charlottetown PE C1A 1H7. (902)368-4410 or (888)734-2784. E-mail: info@peiartscouncil.com. Website: www.peiartscouncil.com.

QUÉBEC COUNCIL FOR ARTS & LITERATURE, 79 boul. René-Lévesque Est, 3e étage, Québec QC G1R 5N5. (418)643-1707 or (800)897-1707. E-mail: info@calq.gouv.qc.ca. Website: www.calq. gouv.qc.ca.

THE SASKATCHEWAN ARTS BOARD, 2135 Broad St., Regina SK S4P 1Y6. (306)787-4056 or (800)667-7526 (Saskatchewan only). E-mail: sab@artsboard.sk.ca. Website: www.artsboard.sk.ca.

YUKON ARTS FUNDING PROGRAM, Cultural Services Branch, Dept. of Tourism & Culture, Government of Yukon, Box 2703 (L-3), Whitehorse YT Y1A 2C6. (867)667-8589 or (800)661-0408 (in Yukon). E-mail: arts@gov.yk.ca. Website: www.tc.gov.yk.ca/216.html.

PUBLICATIONS OF INTEREST

Knowledge about the music industry is essential for both creative and business success. Staying informed requires keeping up with constantly changing information. Updates on the evolving trends in the music business are available to you in the form of music magazines, music trade papers, and books. There is a publication aimed at almost every type of musician, songwriter, and music fan, from the most technical knowledge of amplification systems to gossip about your favorite singer. These publications can enlighten and inspire you, and provide information vital in helping you become a more well-rounded, educated, and, ultimately, successful musical artist.

This section lists all types of magazines and books you may find interesting. From songwriters' newsletters and glossy music magazines to tip sheets and how-to books, there should be something listed here that you'll enjoy and benefit from.

PERIODICALS

ALLEGHENY MUSIC WORKS, 1611 Menoher Blvd., Johnstown PA 15905. (814)255-4007. Website: www.alleghenymusicworks.com. *Monthly tip sheet.*

ALTERNATIVE PRESS, 1305 West 80th Street, Suite 214, Cleveland OH 44102-3045. (216)631-1510. Email: subscriptions@altpress.com. Website: http://altpress.com. *Reviews, news, and features for alternative and indie music fans.*

AMERICAN SONGWRITER MAGAZINE, 113 19th Avenue South Nashville, TN 37203. (615)321-6096. E-mail: info@americansongwriter.com. Website: www.americansongwriter.com. *Bimonthly publication for and about songwriters.*

BACK STAGE (NYC), 770 Broadway, 15th floor, New York, NY 10003 (212)493-4420.

BACK STAGE (LA), 5055 Wilshire Blvd., Los Angeles CA 90036. (323)525-2358 or (800)745-8922. Website: www.backstage.com. *Weekly East and West Coast performing artist trade papers.*

BASS PLAYER, 28 E. 28 St., 12th floor, New York, NY 10016. (800)234-1831. E-mail: bassplayer@ neodata.com. Website: www.bassplayer.com. *Monthly magazine for bass players with lessons, interviews, articles, and transcriptions.*

BILLBOARD, 770 Broadway, 7th floor, New York, NY 10003. (800)684-1873. E-mail: subscriptions@billboard.biz. Website: www.billboard.com. *Weekly industry trade magazine.*

CANADIAN MUSICIAN, 23 Hannover Dr., Suite 7, St. Catharines ON L2W 1A3 Canada. (877)746-4692. Website: www.canadianmusician.com. *Bimonthly publication for amateur and professional Canadian musicians.*

CHART ATTACK, 200-41 Britain St., Toronto ON M5A 1R7 Canada. (416)363-3101. E-mail: hello@chartattack.com. Website: www.chartattack.com. *Monthly magazine covering the Canadian and international music scenes.*

CMJ NEW MUSIC REPORT/CMJ NEW MUSIC MONTHLY, 151 W. 25th St., 12 Floor, New York NY 10001. (917)606-1908. Website: www.cmj.com. *Weekly college radio and alternative music tip sheet.*

COUNTRY LINE MAGAZINE,16150 S. IH-35, Buda TX 78610. (512)295-8400. E-mail: editor@ countrylinemagazine.com. Website: www.countrylinemagazine.com. *Monthly Texas-only country music cowboy and lifestyle magazine.*

ENTERTAINMENT LAW & FINANCE, Website: www.lawjournalnewsletters.com/ljn_entertainment *Monthly newsletter covering music industry contracts, lawsuit filings, court rulings, and legislation.*

EXCLAIM!, 7849A Bloor St. W., Toronto ON M6G 1M3 Canada. (416)535-9735. E-mail: exclaim@exclaim.ca. Website: www.exclaim.ca. *Canadian music monthly covering all genres of non-mainstream music.*

FAST FORWARD, Disc Makers, 7905 N. Rt. 130, Pennsauken NJ 08110-1402. (800)468-9353. Website: www.discmakers.com/music/ffwd. *Quarterly newsletter featuring companies and products for performing and recording artists in the independent music industry. Provides custom CD and DVD packaging and promotional materials.*

GUITAR PLAYER, P.O Box 469073 Escondido, CA 92046. (800)289-9839. Website: www.guitarplayer.com. *Monthly guitar magazine with transcriptions, columns, and interviews, including occasional articles on songwriting.*

JAZZTIMES, 8737 10801 Margate Road, Silver Spring MD 20910-3921. (301)588-4114. Website: www.jazztimes.com. *10 issues/year magazine covering the American jazz scene.*

MUSIC CONNECTION MAGAZINE, Website: www.musicconnection.com. *Biweekly music industry trade publication.*

MUSIC ROW MAGAZINE, 1231 17th Ave. S, Nashville TN 37212. (615)349-2171. E-mail: info@ musicrow.com. Website: www.musicrow.com. *Biweekly Nashville industry publication.*

OFFBEAT MAGAZINE, OffBeat Publications, 421 Frenchman St., Suite 200, New Orleans LA 70116. (504)944-4300. E-mail: offbeat@offbeat.com. Website: www.offbeat.com. *Monthly magazine covering Louisiana music and artists.*

THE PERFORMING SONGWRITER, Performing Songwriter Enterprises, LLC P.O. Box 158989, Nashville TN 37215. (800)883-7664. E-mail: order@performingsongwriter.com. Website: www.performingsongwriter.com. *Bimonthly songwriters' magazine.*

RADIR, Radio Mall, 2412 Unity Ave. N., Dept. WEB, Minneapolis MN 55422-3450. (800)759-4561. E-mail: info@radio-mall.com. Website: www.bbhsoftware.com. *Quarterly radio station database on disk.*

SING OUT!, P.O. Box 5460, Bethlehem PA 18015. (888)SING-OUT. Fax: (215)895-3052. E-mail: info@singout.org. Website: www.singout.org. *Quarterly folk music magazine.*

SONG CAST, Song Cast Distribution, 2926 State Rd., Suite 111, Cuyahoga Falls, OH 44223. Email: info@songcastmusic.com. Offers assistance selling music through online retail sites like iTunes or Amazon.

SONGLINK INTERNATIONAL, 23 Belsize Crescent, London NW3 5QY England. +44 (0) 207-794-2540 Fax: +44(0)207-794-7393. Website: www.songlink.com. *10 issues/year newsletter including details of recording artists looking for songs; contact details for industry sources; also news and features on the music business.*

VARIETY, 5700 Wilshire Blvd., Suite 120, Los Angeles CA 90036. (323)857-6600. Fax: (323)857-0494. Website: www.variety.com. *Weekly entertainment trade newspaper.*

WORDS AND MUSIC, 41 Valleybrook Dr., Toronto ON M3B 2S6 Canada. (416)445-8700. Website: www.socan.ca. *Monthly songwriters' magazine.*

BOOKS & DIRECTORIES

101 SONGWRITING WRONGS & HOW TO RIGHT THEM, by Pat & Pete Luboff, Writer's Digest Books, 10151 Carver Rd., Suite. 200, Blue Ash OH 45242. (800)448-0915. Website: www.writersdigest.com.

THE A&R REGISTRY, by Ritch Esra, SRS Publishing, 7510 Sunset Blvd. #1041, Los Angeles CA 90046-3418. (800)377-7411 or (800)552-7411. E-mail: musicregistry@compuserve.com.

THE BILLBOARD GUIDE TO MUSIC PUBLICITY, rev. ed., by Jim Pettigrew, Jr., Billboard Books, 1745 Broadway. New York, NY 10019. (212)782-9000.

BREAKIN' INTO NASHVILLE, by Jennifer Ember Pierce, Madison Books, University Press of America, 4501 Forbes Rd., Suite 200, Lanham MD 20706. (800)462-6420.

CMJ DIRECTORY, 1201 Broadway, Ste. 706, New York NY 10001. (917)591-4661. Website: www.cmj.com.

THE CRAFT AND BUSINESS OF SONGWRITING, by John Braheny, Writer's Digest Books, 10151 Carver Rd., Suite. 200, Blue Ash OH 45242 (800)448-0915. Website: www.writersdigest.com.

THE CRAFT OF LYRIC WRITING, by Sheila Davis, Writer's Digest Books, 10151 Carver Rd., Suite. 200, Blue Ash OH 45242 (800)448-0915. Website: www.writersdigest.com.

DISC MAKERS, by Jason Ojalvo, Disc Makers, 7905 N. Rt. 130, Pennsauken NJ 08110. (800)468-9353. E-mail: discman@discmakers.com. Website: www.discmakers.com.

HOLLYWOOD CREATIVE DIRECTORY, 3000 W. Olympic Blvd. #2525, Santa Monica CA 90404. (800)815-0503. Website: www.hcdonline.com. *Lists producers in film and TV.*

THE HOLLYWOOD REPORTER, The Writers Store, 3510 West Magnolia Blvd., Burbank, CA, 91505. (800)272-8927. Website: www.hollywoodreporter.com.

HOW TO GET SOMEWHERE IN THE MUSIC BUSINESS FROM NOWHERE WITH NOTHING, by Mary Dawson, CQK Books, CQK Music Group, 2221 Justin Rd., Suite 119-142, Flower Mound TX 75028. (972)317-2720. Fax: (972)317-4737. Website: www.FromNowhereWithNothing.com.

HOW TO PROMOTE YOUR MUSIC SUCCESSFULLY ON THE INTERNET, by David Nevue, Midnight Rain Productions, 228 Stags Leap Ct., Eugene OR 97402. (541741-3262. Website: www.rainmusic.com.

HOW TO MAKE IT IN THE NEW MUSIC BUSINESS: LESSONS, TIPS, AND INSPIRATIONS FROM MUSIC'S BIGGEST AND BEST, by Robert Wolff, Billboard Books. , 1745 Broadway. New York, NY 10019. (212)782-9000.. Website: www.billboard.com.

HOW YOU CAN BREAK INTO THE MUSIC BUSINESS: BUSINESS: WITHOUT BREAKING YOUR HEART, YOUR DREAM, OR YOUR BANK ACCOUNT, by Marty Garrett, Lonesome Wind Corporation, (800)210-4416.

LOUISIANA MUSIC DIRECTORY, OffBeat, Inc., 421 Frenchmen St., Suite 200, New Orleans LA 70116. (504)944-4300. Website: www.offbeat.com.

LYDIAN CHROMATIC CONCEPT OF TONAL ORGANIZATION, VOLUME ONE: THE ART AND SCI-ENCE OF TONAL GRAVITY, by George Russell, Concept Publishing Company, 258 Harvard St., #296, Brookline MA 02446-2904. E-mail: lydconcept@aol.com. Website: www.lydian chromaticconcept.com.

MELODY IN SONGWRITING, by Jack Perricone, Berklee Press, 1140 Boylston St., Boston MA 02215. (617)747-2146. E-mail: info@berkleepress.com. Website: www.berkleepress.com.

MUSIC ATTORNEY LEGAL & BUSINESS AFFAIRS REGISTRY, by Ritch Esra and Steve Trumbull, SRS Publishing, 7510 Sunset Blvd. #1041, Los Angeles CA 90046-3418. (800)552-7411. E-mail: musicregistry@compuserve.com or srspubl@aol.com.

THE MUSIC BUSINESS REGISTRY, by Ritch Esra, SRS Publishing, 7510 Sunset Blvd. #1041, Los Angeles CA 90046-3418. (800)552-7411. E-mail: musicregistry@compuserve.com or srspu bl@ aol.com. Website: www.musicregistry.com.

MUSIC DIRECTORY CANADA, 7th ed., Norris-Whitney Communications Inc., 23 Hannover Dr., Suite 7, St. Catherines ON L2W 1A3 Canada. (877)RING-NWC. E-mail: mail@nor.com. Website: http://nor.com. www.musicdirectorycanada.com

MUSIC LAW: HOW TO RUN YOUR BAND'S BUSINESS, by Richard Stin, Nolo Press, 950 Parker St., Berkeley CA 94710-9867. (510)549-1976. Website: www.nolo.com.

MUSIC, MONEY AND SUCCESS: THE INSIDER'S GUIDE TO THE MUSIC INDUSTRY, by Jeffrey Brabec and Todd Brabec, Schirmer Books, 180 Madison Avenue, 24th Floor New York, NY 10016. (212) 254-2100.

THE MUSIC PUBLISHER REGISTRY, by Ritch Esra, SRS Publishing, 7510 Sunset Blvd. #1041, Los Angeles CA 90046-3418. (800)552-7411. E-mail: musicregistry@compuserve.com or srspubl@ aol.com.

MUSIC PUBLISHING: A SONGWRITER'S GUIDE, rev. ed., by Randy Poe, Writer's Digest Books, 10151 Carver Rd., Suite. 200, Blue Ash OH 45242. (800)448-0915. Website: www.writersdigest.com.

THE MUSICIAN'S GUIDE TO MAKING & SELLING YOUR OWN CDS & CASSETTES, by Jana Stanfield, Writer's Digest Books, 10151 Carver Rd., Suite. 200, Blue Ash OH 45242. (800)448-0915. Website: www.writersdigest.com.

MUSICIANS' PHONE BOOK, THE LOS ANGELES MUSIC INDUSTRY DIRECTORY, Get Yourself Some Publishing, 28336 Simsalido Ave., Canyon Country CA 91351. (805)299-2405. E-mail: mpb@ earthlink.net. Website: www.musiciansphonebook.com.

NASHVILLE MUSIC BUSINESS DIRECTORY, by Mark Dreyer, NMBD Publishing, 9 Music Square S., Suite 210, Nashville TN 37203. (615)826-4141. E-mail: nmbd@nashvilleconnection.com. Website: www.nashvilleconnection.com.

NASHVILLE'S UNWRITTEN RULES: INSIDE THE BUSINESS OF THE COUNTRY MUSIC MACHINE, by Dan Daley, Overlook Press, 141 Wooster Street New York, NY 10012. (212) 673-2210. E-mail: sales@overlookny.com.

THE REAL DEAL—HOW TO GET SIGNED TO A RECORD LABEL FROM A TO Z, by Daylle Deanna Schwartz, Billboard Books, 1745 Broadway. New York, NY 10019. (212)782-9000.

RECORDING INDUSTRY SOURCEBOOK, Music Books Plus, 4600 Witmer Industrial Estates, Suite 6, Niagra Falls, NY 14305. (800)265-8481. Website: www.musicbooksplus.com.

REHARMONIZATION TECHNIQUES, by Randy Felts, Berklee Press, 1140 Boylston St., Boston MA 02215. (617)747-2146. E-mail: info@berkleepress.com. Website: www.berkleepress.com.

THE SONGWRITERS IDEA BOOK, by Sheila Davis, Writer's Digest Books, 10151 Carver Rd., Suite. 200, Blue Ash OH 45242. (800)448-0915. Website: www.writersdigest.com.

SONGWRITER'S MARKET GUIDE TO SONG & DEMO SUBMISSION FORMATS, Writer's Digest Books, 10151 Carver Rd., Suite. 200, Blue Ash OH 45242. (800)448-0915. Website: www.writersdigest.com.

SONGWRITER'S PLAYGROUND—INNOVATIVE EXERCISES IN CREATIVE SONGWRITING, by Barbara L. Jordan, Creative Music Marketing, 1085 Commonwealth Ave., Suite 323, Boston MA 02215. (617)926-8766. www.songwritersplayground.com

THE SONGWRITER'S WORKSHOP: HARMONY, by Jimmy Kachulis, Berklee Press, 1140 Boylston St., Boston MA 02215. (617)747-2146. E-mail: info@berkleepress.com. Website: www.berkleepress.com.

THE SONGWRITER'S WORKSHOP: MELODY, by Jimmy Kachulis, Berklee Press, 1140 Boylston St., Boston MA 02215. (617)747-2146. E-mail: info@berkleepress.com. Website: www.berkleepress.com.

SONGWRITING AND THE CREATIVE PROCESS, by Steve Gillette, Sing Out! Publications, P.O. Box 5640, Bethlehem PA 18015-0253. (888)SING-OUT. E-mail: singout@libertynet.org. Website: www.singout.org/sopubs.html.

SONGWRITING: ESSENTIAL GUIDE TO LYRIC FORM AND STRUCTURE, by Pat Pattison, Berklee Press, 1140 Boylston St., Boston MA 02215. (617)747-2146. E-mail: info@berkleepress.com. Website: www.www.berkleepress.com.

SONGWRITING: ESSENTIAL GUIDE TO RHYMING, by Pat Pattison, Berklee Press, 1140 Boylston St., Boston MA 02215. (617)747-2146. E-mail: info@berkleepress.com. Website: www.berkleepress.com.

THE SONGWRITING SOURCEBOOK: HOW TO TURN CHORDS INTO GREAT SONGS, by Rikky Rooksby, Hal Leonard Corporation, P.O. Box 13819, Milwaukee, WI 53213. (415)947-6615. E-mail: books@musicplayer.com. Website: www.halleonardbooks.com.

SONGWRITING WITHOUT BOUNDARIES, by Pat Pattison, 10151 Carver Rd., Suite. 200, Blue Ash OH 45242. (800)448-0915. Website: www.writersdigest.com.

THE SOUL OF THE WRITER, by Susan Tucker with Linda Lee Strother, Journey Publishing, P.O. Box 92411, Nashville TN 37209. (615)952-4894. Website: www.journeypublishing.com.

SUCCESSFUL LYRIC WRITING, by Sheila Davis, Writer's Digest Books, 10151 Carver Rd., Suite. 200, Blue Ash OH 45242. (800)448-0915. Website: www.writersdigest.com.

THIS BUSINESS OF MUSIC MARKETING AND PROMOTION, by Tad Lathrop and Jim Pettigrew, Jr., Billboard Books, Watson-Guptill Publications, 1745 Broadway. New York, NY 10019. (212)782-9000. E-mail: info@watsonguptill.com.

TIM SWEENEY'S GUIDE TO RELEASING INDEPENDENT RECORDS, by Tim Sweeney, TSA Books, 31805 Highway 79 S., Temecula CA 92592. (909)303-9506. E-mail: info@tsamusic.com. Website: www.tsamusic.com.

TIM SWEENEY'S GUIDE TO SUCCEEDING AT MUSIC CONVENTIONS, by Tim Sweeney, TSA Books, 31805 Highway 79 S., Temecula CA 92592. (909)303-9506. Website: www.tsamusic.com.

TEXAS MUSIC INDUSTRY DIRECTORY, Texas Music Office, Office of the Governor, P.O. Box 13246, Austin TX 78711. (512)463-6666. E-mail: music@governor.state.tx.us. Website: www.enjoytexasmusic.com.

TUNESMITH: INSIDE THE ART OF SONGWRITING, by Jimmy Webb, Hyperion, 1500 Broadway, 3rd floor, New York NY 10036. (800)759-0190.

VOLUNTEER LAWYERS FOR THE ARTS GUIDE TO COPYRIGHT FOR MUSICIANS AND COMPOSERS, One E. 53rd St., 6th Floor, New York NY 10022. (212)319-2787.

WRITING BETTER LYRICS, by Pat Pattison, Writer's Digest Books, 10151 Carver Rd., Suite. 200, Blue Ash OH 45242. (800)448-0915. Website: www.writersdigest.com.

WRITING MUSIC FOR HIT SONGS, by Jai Josefs, Schirmer Trade Books, Music Sales Corporation, 257 Park Ave. S., New York NY 10010. (212)254-2100.

THE YELLOW PAGES OF ROCK, The Album Network, 120 N. Victory Blvd., Burbank CA 91502. (800)222-4382. Fax: (818)955-9048. E-mail: ypinfo@yprock.com.

WEBSITES OF INTEREST

The Internet provides a wealth of information for songwriters and performers, and the number of sites devoted to music grows each day. Below is a list of websites that can offer you information, links to other music sites, contact with other songwriters, and places to showcase your songs. Due to the dynamic nature of the online world, this is certainly not a comprehensive list, but it gives you a place to start on your Internet journey to search for opportunities to get your music heard.

ABOUT.COM MUSICIANS' EXCHANGE http://musicians.about.com/
Site features headlines and articles of interest to independent musicians and songwriters, as well as links and label profiles.

ABSOLUTE PUNK www.absolutepunk.net
Searchable online community focusing on punk and rock music, including news, reviews, articles, and interviews; forums to discuss music and pop culture.

AMERICAN MUSIC CENTER www.amc.net
Classical and jazz archives. Includes a list of organizations and contacts for composers.

AMERICAN SOCIETY OF COMPOSERS, AUTHORS AND PUBLISHERS (ASCAP) www.ascap.com
Database of works in ASCAP's repertoire. Includes performer, songwriter, and publisher information as well as membership information and industry news.

AMERICAN SONGWRITER MAGAZINE HOMEPAGE www.americansongwriter.com
This is the official homepage for *American Songwriter* Magazine. Features an online article archive, e-mail newsletter, and links.

BANDCAMP www.bandcamp.com

An online music store and platform for artist promotion that caters mainly to independent artists

BEAIRD MUSIC GROUP DEMOS www.beairdmusicgroup.com

Nashville demo service which offers a variety of demo packages.

BILLBOARD.COM www.billboard.com

Industry news and searchable online database of music companies by subscription.

THE BLUES FOUNDATION www.blues.org

Nonprofit organization located in Memphis, TN; website contains information on the foundation, membership, and events.

BROADCAST MUSIC, INC. (BMI) www.bmi.com

Offers lists of song titles, writers, and publishers of the BMI repertoire. Includes membership information and general information on songwriting and licensing.

THE BUZZ FACTOR www.thebuzzfactor.com

Website offers free tips on the music marketing and self-promotion ideas.

BUZZNET www.buzznet.com

Searchable networking and news site featuring music and pop culture; photos, videos, concert reviews, more.

CDBABY www.cdbaby.com

An online CD store dedicated to the sales of independent music.

CADENZA www.cadenza.org

Online resource for contemporary and classical music and musicians, including methods of contacting other musicians.

CHORUS AMERICA www.chorusamerica.org

The website for Chorus America, a national organization for professional and volunteer choruses. Includes job listings and professional development information.

FINETUNE www.finetune.com

Internet radio/streaming audio. User can create personalized channels and playlists online.

FILM MUSIC NETWORK www.filmmusicworld.com or www.filmmusic.net

Network of links, news, and job listings within the film music world.

GET SIGNED www.getsigned.com

Interviews with musicians, songwriters, and industry veterands, how-to business information, and more.

GOVERNMENT LIAISON SERVICES www.trademarkinfo.com
An intellectual property research firm. Offers a variety of trademark searches.

GUITAR NINE RECORDS www.guitar9.com
Offers articles on songwriting, music theory, guitar techniques, etc.

GOOGLE www.google.com
Online search engine can be used to look up music, information, lyrics.

HARMONY CENTRAL www.harmony-central.com
Online community for musicians with in-depth reviews and discussions.

HARRY FOX AGENCY www.harryfox.com
Offers a comprehensive FAQ about licensing songs for use in recording, performance, and film.

ILIKE www.ilike.com
Music networking site. Signed and unsigned artists can sign up for free artists' page and upload songs and events. Works with other social networks such as www.face book.com.

INDEPENDENT DISTRIBUTION NETWORK www.idnmusic.com
Website of independent bands distributing their music with advice on everything from starting a band to finding labels.

INDEPENDENT SONGWRITER WEB MAGAZINE www.independentsongwriter.com/
Independent music reviews, classifieds, message board, and chat sessions.

INDIE-MUSIC.COM www.indie-music.com/
Website of how-to articles, record label directory, links to musicians and venue listings.

JAZZ CORNER www.jazzcorner.com
Portal for the websites of jazz musicians and organizations. Includes the jazz video share, jukebox, and the "Speakeasy" bulletin board.

JUST PLAIN FOLKS www.jpfolks.com or www.justplainfolks.org
Website for songwriting organization featuring message boards, lyric feedback forums, member profiles and music, contact listings, chapter homepages, and more.

LAST.FM www.last.fm/
Music tracking and social networking site.

LI'L HANK'S GUIDE FOR SONGWRITERS IN L.A. www.halsguide.com
Website for songwriters with information on clubs, publishers, books, etc. Links to other songwriting sites.

LIVE365 www.live365.com/index.live
Internet radio/audio stream search engine.

LIVEJOURNAL www.livejournal.com
Social networking community using open source technology; music communities provide news, interviews, and reviews.

LOS ANGELES GOES UNDERGROUND http://lagu.somaweb.org
Website dedicated to underground rock bands from Los Angeles and Hollywood.

LYRIC IDEAS www.lyricideas.com
Offers songwriting prompts, themes, and creative techniques for songwriting.

LYRICIST www.lyricist.com/
Site offers advice, tips, and events in the music industry.

MI2N (THE MUSIC INDUSTRY NEWS NETWORK) www.mi2n.com
Offers news on happenings in the music industry and career postings.

THE MUSE'S MUSE www.musesmuse.com
Classifieds, catalog of music samples, songwriting articles, newsletter, and chat room.

MOG http://mog.com
Internet radio/streaming audio. Contains music news and concert reviews, personalized recommendations.

MUSIC BOOKS PLUS www.musicbooksplus.com
Online bookstore dedicated to music books on every music-related topic, plus a free newsletter.

MUSIC PUBLISHERS ASSOCIATION www.mpa.org
Ofers directories for music publishers and imprints, copyright resource center, and information on the organization.

MUSIC YELLOW PAGES www.musicyellowpages.com
Listings of music-related businesses.

MYSPACE www.myspace.com
Social networking site featuring music Web pages for musicians and songwriters.

NASHVILLE SONGWRITERS ASSOCIATION INTERNATIONAL (NSAI) www.nashvillesongwriters.com

Official NSAI homepage. Offers news, links, online registration, and message board for members.

NATIONAL ASSOCIATION OF COMPOSERS USA (NACUSA) www.music-usa.org/nacusa
A nonprofit organization devoted to the promotion and performance of American concert hall music.

NATIONAL MUSIC PUBLISHERS ASSOCIATION www.nmpa.org
Organization's online site filled with information about copyright, legislation, and other concerns of the music publishing world.

ONLINE ROCK www.onlinerock.com
Range of membership options including a free option, offers webpage services, articles, chat rooms, links, and more.

OPERA AMERICA www.operaamerica.org
Website of Opera America features information on advocacy and awareness programs, publications, conference schedules, and more.

PANDORA www.pandora.com
A site created by the founders of the Music Genome Project; a searchable music radio/streaming audio site.

PERFORMER MAG www.performermag.com
Offers articles, music industry news, classifieds and reviews.

PERFORMING SONGWRITER MAGAZINE HOMEPAGE www.performingsongwriter.com
Official homepage for the magazine features articles and links.

PITCHFORK www.pitchforkmedia.com
Offers Indie news, reviews, media, and features.

PUBLIC DOMAIN MUSIC www.pdinfo.com
Articles on public domain works and copyright including public domain song lists, research sources, tips and FAQs.

PUMP AUDIO www.pumpaudio.com/
License music for film and television on a non-exclusive basis. No submission fees, rights retained by songwriter.

PUREVOLUME www.purevolume.com
Music hosting site with searchable database of songs by signed and unsigned artists. Musicians and songwriters can upload songs and events.

THE RECORDING PROJECT www.recordingproject.com/
  Online community for musicians and recording artists, every level welcome.

RECORD PRODUCER.COM www.record-producer.com
  Extensive site dedicated to audio engineering and record production. Offers a free newsletter, online instruction, and e-books on various aspects of record production and audio engineering.

ROCK AND ROLL HALL OF FAME + MUSEUM www.rockhall.com/
  Website for the Rock and Roll Hall of Fame and Museum, including events listings, visitor info, and more.

SESAC INC. www.sesac.com
  Website for performing rights organization with songwriter profiles, industry news updates, licensing information, and links to other sites.

SINGERSONGWRITER www.singersongwriter.ws
  Resources for singer-songwriters, including an extensive list, featured resources, and lists of radio stations organized geographically.

SLACKER www.slacker.com
  Internet radio/streaming audio. User can create personalized channels and playlists online.

SOMA FM www.somafm.com
  Internet underground/alternative radio with commercial-free broadcasting from San Francisco.

SONG CATALOG www.songcatalog.com
  Online song catalog database for licensing.

SONGLINK www.songlink.com
  Offers opportunities to pitch songs to music publishers for specific recording projects and industry news.

SONGRAMP www.songramp.com
  Online songwriting organization with message boards, blogs, news, and streaming music channels. Offers variety of membership packages.

SONGSALIVE! www.songsalive.org
  Online songwriters organization and community.

SONGWRITER 101 www.songwriter101.com
  Offers articles, industry news, and message boards.

SONGWRITER'S GUILD OF AMERICA (SGA) www.songwritersguild.com
  Industry news, member services information, newsletters, contract reviews, and more.

SONGWRITER'S RESOURCE NETWORK www.songwritersresourcenetwork.com
  News and education resource for songwriters, lyricists, and composers.

SONGWRITERUNIVERSE www.songwriteruniverse.com
  In-depth articles, business information, education, and recommended reading.

THE SONGWRITING EDUCATION RESOURCE www.craftofsongwriting.com
  An educational website for songwriters. Offers discussion boards, articles, and links.

SONIC BIDS www.sonicbids.com
  Features an online press kit with photos, bio, music samples, date calendar. Free trial period first month for artists/bands to sign up, newsletter.

SOUNDCLOUD http://soundcloud.com
  An online audio distribution platform which allows collaboration, promotion and distribution of audio recordings.

SOUNDPEDIA http://soundpedia.com
  Internet Radio/streaming audio. User can create personalized channels and playlists online.

STARPOLISH www.starpolish.com
  Features articles and interviews on the music industry.

SUMMERSONGS SONGWRITING CAMPS www.summersongs.com
  Information about songwriting camps, staff, and online registration.

TAXI www.taxi.com
  Independent A&R vehicle that shops demos to A&R professionals.

TUNECORE www.tunecore.com
  Service that allows musicans to sell their music digitally via online retailers such as iTunes, Amazon, Spotify, and more.

UNITED STATES COPYRIGHT OFFICE www.copyright.gov
  Homepage for the US Copyright office. Offers information on registering songs.

THE VELVET ROPE www.velvetrope.com
  Famous/infamous online music industry message board.

WEIRDO MUSIC www.weirdomusic.com

Online music magazine with articles, reviews, downloads, and links to Internet radio shows.

YAHOO! http://new.music.yahoo.com/
Search engine with radio station guide, music industry news, and listings.

YOUTUBE www.youtube.com
Social networking site which hosts audiovisual content. Searchable database provides links to music videos, interviews, and more.

GLOSSARY

A CAPPELLA. Choral singing without accompaniment.

AAA FORM. A song form in which every verse has the same melody; often used for songs that tell a story.

AABA, ABAB. A commonly used song pattern consisting of two verses, a bridge, and a verse, or a repeated pattern of verse and bridge, where the verses are musically the same.

A&R DIRECTOR. Record company executive in charge of the Artists and Repertoire Department who is responsible for finding and developing new artists and matching songs with artists.

A/C. Adult contemporary music.

ADVANCE. Money paid to the songwriter or recording artist, which is then recouped before regular royalty payment begins. Sometimes called "up front" money, advances are deducted from royalties.

AFIM. Association for Independent Music (formerly NAIRD). Organization for independent record companies, distributors, retailers, manufacturers, etc.

AFM. American Federation of Musicians. A union for musicians and arrangers.

AFTRA. American Federation of Television and Radio Artists. A union for performers.

AIMP. Association of Independent Music Publishers.

AIRPLAY. The radio broadcast of a recording.

AOR. Album-Oriented Rock. A radio format that primarily plays selections from rock albums as opposed to hit singles.

ARRANGEMENT. An adaptation of a composition for a recording or performance, with consideration for the melody, harmony, instrumentation, tempo, style, etc.

ASCAP. American Society of Composers, Authors and Publishers. A performing rights society. (See the "Organizations" section.)

ASSIGNMENT. Transfer of rights of a song from writer to publisher.

AUDIO VISUAL INDEX (AVI). A database containing title and production information for cue sheets which are available from a performing rights organization. Currently, BMI, ASCAP, SOCAN, PRS, APRA and SACEM contribute their cue sheet listings to the AVI.

AUDIOVISUAL. Refers to presentations that use audio backup for visual material.

BACKGROUND MUSIC. Music used that creates mood and supports the spoken dialogue of a radio program or visual action of an audiovisual work. Not feature or theme music.

B&W. Black-and-white.

BED. Prerecorded music used as background material in commercials. In rap music, often refers to the sampled and looped drums and music over which the rapper performs.

BLACK BOX. Theater without fixed stage or seating arrangements, capable of a variety of formations. Usually a small space, often attached to a major theater complex, used for workshops or experimental works calling for small casts and limited sets.

BMI. Broadcast Music, Inc. A performing rights society. (See the "Organizations" section.)

BOOKING AGENT. Person who schedules performances for entertainers.

BOOTLEGGING. Unauthorized recording and selling of a song.

BUSINESS MANAGER. Person who handles the financial aspects of artistic careers.

BUZZ. Attention an act generates through the media and word of mouth.

B/W. Backed with. Usually refers to the B-side of a single.

C&W. Country and western.

CATALOG. The collected songs of one writer, or all songs handled by one publisher.

CD. Compact-disc (*see* below).

CD-R. A recordable CD.

CD-ROM. Compact Disc-Read Only Memory. A computer information storage medium capable of holding enormous amounts of data. Information on a CD-ROM cannot be deleted. A computer user must have a CD-ROM drive to access a CD-ROM.

CHAMBER MUSIC. Any music suitable for performance in a small audience area or chamber.

CHAMBER ORCHESTRA. A miniature orchestra usually containing one instrument per part.

CHART. The written arrangement of a song.

CHARTS. The trade magazines' lists of the bestselling records.

CHR. Comtemporary Hit Radio. Top 40 pop music.

COLLABORATION. Two or more artists, writers, etc., working together on a single project; for instance, a playwright and a songwriter creating a musical together.

COMPACT DISC. A small disc (about 4.7 inches in diameter) holding digitally encoded music that is read by a laser beam in a CD player.

COMPOSERS. The men and women who create musical compositions for motion pictures and other audio visual works, or the creators of classical music composition.

COPUBLISH. Two or more parties own publishing rights to the same song.

COPYRIGHT. The exclusive legal right giving the creator of a work the power to control the publishing, reproduction, and selling of the work. Although a song is technically copyrighted at the time it is written, the best legal protection of that copyright comes through registering the copyright with the Library of Congress.

COPYRIGHT INFRINGEMENT. Unauthorized use of a copyrighted song or portions thereof.

COVER RECORDING. A new version of a previously recorded song.

CROSSOVER. A song that becomes popular in two or more musical categories (e.g., country and pop).

CUT. Any finished recording; a selection from a LP. Also to record.

DAT. Digital Audio Tape. A professional and consumer audiocassette format for recording and playing back digitally encoded material. DAT cassettes are approximately one-third smaller than conventional audiocassettes.

DCC. Digital Compact Cassette. A consumer audio cassette format for recording and playing back digitally encoded tape. DCC tapes are the same size as analog cassettes.

DEMO. A recording of a song submitted as a demonstration of a writer's or artist's skills.

DERIVATIVE WORK. A work derived from another work, such as a translation, musical arrangement, sound recording, or motion picture version.

DISTRIBUTOR. Wholesale marketing agent responsible for getting records from manufacturers to retailers.

DONUT. A jingle with singing at the beginning and end and instrumental background in the middle. Ad copy is recorded over the middle section.

E-MAIL. Electronic mail. Computer address where a company or individual can be reached via modem.

ENGINEER. A specially trained individual who operates recording studio equipment.

ENHANCED CD. General term for an audio CD that also contains multimedia computer information. It is playable in both standard CD players and CD-ROM drives.

EP. Extended play record or cassette containing more selections than a standard single, but fewer than a standard album.

EPK. Electronic press kit. Usually contains photos, sound files, bio information, reviews, tour dates, etc., posted online. Sonicbids.com is a popular EPK hosting website.

FINAL MIX. The art of combining all the various sounds that take place during the recording session into a two-track stereo or mono tape. Reflects the total product and all of the energies and talents the artist, producer, and engineer have put into the project.

FLY SPACE. The area above a stage from which set pieces are lowered and raised during a performance.

FOLIO. A softcover collection of printed music prepared for sale.

FOLLOWING. A fan base committed to going to gigs and buying albums.

FOREIGN RIGHTS SOCIETIES. Performing rights societies other than domestic which have reciprocal agreements with ASCAP and BMI for the collection of royalties accrued by foreign radio and television airplay and other public performance of the writer members of the above groups.

HARRY FOX AGENCY. Organization that collects mechanical royalties.

GRAMMY. Music industry awards presented by the National Academy of Recording Arts and Sciences.

HIP-HOP. A dance-oriented musical style derived from a combination of disco, rap, and R&B.

HIT. A song or record that achieves top 40 status.

HOOK. A memorable "catch" phrase or melody line that is repeated in a song.

HOUSE. Dance music created by remixing samples from other songs.

HYPERTEXT. Words or groups of words in an electronic document that are linked to other text, such as a definition or a related document. Hypertext can also be linked to illustrations.

INDIE. An independent record label, music publisher, or producer.

INFRINGEMENT. A violation of the exclusive rights granted by the copyright law to a copyright owner.

INTERNET. A worldwide network of computers that offers access to a wide variety of electronic resources.

IPS. Inches per second; a speed designation for tape recording.

IRC. International reply coupon, necessary for the return of materials sent out of the country. Available at most post offices.

JINGLE. Usually a short verse set to music designed as a commercial message.

LEAD SHEET. Written version (melody, chord symbols, and lyric) of a song.

LEADER. Plastic (non-recordable) tape at the beginning and between songs for ease in selection.

LIBRETTO. The text of an opera or any long choral work. The booklet containing such text.

LISTING. Block of information in this book about a specific company.

LP. Designation for long-playing record played at 33⅓rpm.

LYRIC SHEET. A typed or written copy of a song's lyrics.

MARKET. A potential song or music buyer; also a demographic division of the record-buying public.

MASTER. Edited and mixed tape used in the production of records; the best or original copy of a recording from which copies are made.

MD. MiniDisc. A 2.5-inch disk for recording and playing back digitally encoded music.

MECHANICAL RIGHT. The right to profit from the physical reproduction of a song.

MECHANICAL ROYALTY. Money earned from record, tape and CD sales.

MIDI. Musical instrument digital interface. Universal standard interface that allows musical instruments to communicate with each other and computers.

MINI DISC. (*see* MD above.)

MIX. To blend a multi-track recording into the desired balance of sound, usually to a 2-track stereo master.

MODEM. MOdulator/DEModulator. A computer device used to send data from one computer to another via telephone line.

MOR. Middle of the road. Easy-listening popular music.

MP3. File format of a relatively small size that stores audio files on a computer. Music saved in a MP3 format can be played only with a MP3 player (which can be downloaded onto a computer).

MS. Manuscript.

MULTIMEDIA. Computers and software capable of integrating text, sound, photographic-quality images, animation, and video.

MUSIC BED. (*see* Bed above.)

MUSIC JOBBER. A wholesale distributor of printed music.

MUSIC LIBRARY. A business that purchases canned music, which can then be bought by producers of radio and TV commercials, films, videos, and audiovisual productions to use however they wish.

MUSIC PUBLISHER. A company that evaluates songs for commercial potential, finds artists to record them, finds other uses (such as TV or film) for the songs, collects income generated by the songs, and protects copyrights from infringement.

MUSIC ROW. An area of Nashville, TN, encompassing Sixteenth, Seventeeth and Eighteenth avenues where most of the major publishing houses, recording studios, mastering labs, songwriters, singers, promoters, etc., practice their trade.

NARAS. National Academy of Recording Arts and Sciences.

THE NATIONAL ACADEMY OF SONGWRITERS (NAS). The largest U.S. songwriters' association. (See the "Organizations" section.)

NEEDLE-DROP. Refers to a type of music library. A needle-drop music library is a licensed library that allows producers to borrow music on a rate schedule. The price depends on how the music will be used.

NETWORK. A group of computers electronically linked to share information and resources.

NMPA. National Music Publishers Association.

ONE-OFF. A deal between songwriter and publisher that includes only one song or project at a time. No future involvement is implicated. Many times a single song contract accompanies a one-off deal.

ONE-STOP. A wholesale distributor of who sells small quantities of records to "mom and pop" record stores, retailers and jukebox operators.

OPERETTA. Light, humorous, satiric plot or poem, set to cheerful, light music with occasional spoken dialogue.

OVERDUB. To record an additional part (vocal or instrumental) onto a basic multi-track recording.

PARODY. A satirical imitation of a literary or musical work. Permission from the owner of the copyright is generally required before commercial exploitation of a parody.

PAYOLA. Dishonest payment to broadcasters in exchange for airplay.

PERFORMING RIGHTS. A specific right granted by U.S. copyright law protecting a composition from being publicly performed without the owner's permission.

PERFORMING RIGHTS ORGANIZATION. An organization that collects income from the public performance of songs written by its members and then proportionally distributes this income to the individual copyright holder based on the number of performances of each song.

PERSONAL MANAGER. A person who represents artists to develop and enhance their careers. Personal managers may negotiate contracts, hire and dismiss other agencies and personnel relating to the artist's career, review material, help with artist promotions, and perform many services.

PIRACY. The unauthorized reproduction and selling of printed or recorded music.

PITCH. To attempt to solicit interest for a song by audition.

PLAYLIST. List of songs a radio station will play.

POINTS. A negotiable percentage paid to producers and artists for records sold.

PRODUCER. Person who supervises every aspect of a recording project.

PRODUCTION COMPANY. Company specializing in producing jingle packages for advertising agencies. May also refer to companies specializing in audiovisual programs.

PROFESSIONAL MANAGER. Member of a music publisher's staff who screens submitted material and tries to get the company's catalog of songs recorded.

PROSCENIUM. Permanent architectural arch in a theater that separates the stage from the audience.

PUBLIC DOMAIN. Any composition with an expired, lapsed, or invalid copyright, and therefore belonging to everyone.

PURCHASE LICENSE. Fee paid for music used from a stock music library.

QUERY. A letter of inquiry to an industry professional soliciting his interest.

R&B. Rhythm and blues.

RACK JOBBER. Distributors who lease floor space from department stores and put in racks of albums.

RATE. The percentage of royalty as specified by contract.

RELEASE. Any record issued by a record company.

RESIDUALS. In advertising or television, payments to singers and musicians for use of a performance.

RIAA. Recording Industry Association of America.

ROYALTY. Percentage of money earned from the sale of records or use of a song.

RPM. Revolutions per minute. Refers to phonograph turntable speed.

SAE. Self-addressed envelope (with no postage attached).

SASE. Self-addressed stamped envelope.

SATB. The abbreviation for parts in choral music, meaning Soprano, Alto, Tenor, and Bass.

SCORE. A complete arrangement of all the notes and parts of a composition (vocal or instrumental) written out on staves. A full score, or orchestral score, depicts every orchestral part on a separate staff and is used by a conductor.

SELF-CONTAINED. A band or recording act that writes all their own material.

SESAC. A performing rights organization, originally the Society of European Stage Authors and Composers. (*see* the "Organizations" section.)

SFX. Sound effects.

SHOP. To pitch songs to a number of companies or publishers.

SINGLE. 45rpm record with only one song per side. A 12£ single refers to a long version of one song on a 12£ disc, usually used for dance music.

SKA. Fast-tempo dance music influenced primarily by reggae and punk, usually featuring horns, saxophone, and bass.

SOCAN. Society of Composers, Authors and Music Publishers of Canada. A Canadian performing rights organization. (*see* the "Organizations" section.)

SOLICITED. Songs or materials that have been requested.

SONG PLUGGER. A songwriter representative whose main responsibility is promoting uncut songs to music publishers, record companies, artists, and producers.

SONG SHARK. Person who deals with songwriters deceptively for his own profit.

SOUNDSCAN. A company that collates the register tapes of reporting stores to track the actual number of albums sold at the retail level.

SOUNDTRACK. The audio, including music and narration, of a film, videotape, or audiovisual program.

SPACE STAGE. Open stage that features lighting and, perhaps, projected scenery.

SPLIT PUBLISHING. To divide publishing rights between two or more publishers.

STAFF SONGWRITER. A songwriter who has an exclusive agreement with a publisher.

STATUTORY ROYALTY RATE. The maximum payment for mechanical rights guaranteed by law that a record company may pay the songwriter and his publisher for each record or tape sold.

SUBPUBLISHING. Certain rights granted by a U.S. publisher to a foreign publisher in exchange for promoting the U.S. catalog in his territory.

SYNCHRONIZATION. Technique of timing a musical soundtrack to action on film or video.

TAKE. Either an attempt to record a vocal or instrument part, or an acceptable recording of a performance.

TEJANO. A musical form begun in the late 1970s by regional bands in south Texas, its style reflects a blended Mexican-American culture. Incorporates elements of rock, country, R&B, and jazz, and often features accordion and 12-string guitar.

THRUST STAGE. Stage with audience on three sides and a stagehouse or wall on the fourth side.

TOP 40. The first 40 songs on the pop music charts at any given time. Also refers to a style of music which emulates that heard on the current top 40.

TRACK. Divisions of a recording tape (e.g., 24-track tape) that can be individually recorded in the studio, then mixed into a finished master.

TRADES. Publications covering the music industry.

12-SINGLE. A 12-inch record containing one or more remixes of a song, originally intended for dance club play.

UNSOLICITED. Songs or materials that were not requested and are not expected.

VOCAL SCORE. An arrangement of vocal music detailing all vocal parts, and condensing all accompanying instrumental music into one piano part.

WEBSITE. An address on the World Wide Web that can be accessed by computer modem. It may contain text, graphics, and sound.

WING SPACE. The offstage area surrounding the playing stage in a theater, unseen by the audience, where sets and props are hidden, actors wait for cues, and stagehands prepare to chance sets.

WORLD MUSIC. A general music category that includes most musical forms originating outside the U.S. and Europe, including reggae and calypso. World music finds its roots primarily in the Caribbean, Latin America, Africa, and the South Pacific.

WORLD WIDE WEB (WWW). An Internet resource that utilizes hypertext to access information. It also supports formatted text, illustrations, and sounds, depending on the user's computer capabilities.

CATEGORY INDEX

MANAGERS & BOOKING AGENTS

ALL GENRES / ALL STYLES

ALTERNATIVE

BLUES

CLASSICAL

CONTEMPORARY

COUNTRY

DANCE

FOLK

GOSPEL

GENERAL INDEX

GEOGRAPHICAL
INDEX

GEOGRAPHICAL
INDEX

CANADA